# Ordinary after Pentecost Sermons

# Ordinary after Pentecost Sermons

From the Untrained Mind

Robert Tippett

Copyright © 2020

All rights reserved. Produced in the United States of America. No part of this publication may be reproduced, or transmitted, in any form or by any means electronic, mechanical, photocopying, recording, or otherwise, without the prior written permission of the author.

ISBN 978-1-952076-04-6 Paperback
ISBN 978-1-952076-05-3 Epub

Published by Katrina Pearls, LLC

# Dedication

This book is dedicated to the memory of my loving wife, who passed away in late 2019. Joycelyn Tippett was a fellow Apostle; my partner in service to God. She was the editor of my books and everything I have written since we married in 2006. She is greatly missed by a world that needs more like her. I am comforted by her continued spiritual presence with me and the insight to this series of books I owe to that presence.

# Table of Contents

From the Untrained Mind ............................................10
A Season Named Ordinary ........................................ 20

**Year A Sermons**

    Trinity Sunday ...................................................... 42
    Proper 7 ................................................................. 49
    Proper 8 ................................................................. 57
    Proper 9 ................................................................. 68
    Proper 10 ............................................................... 78
    Proper 11 ............................................................... 86
    Proper 12 ............................................................... 95
    Proper 13 ............................................................. 105
    Proper 14 ............................................................. 115
    Proper 15 ............................................................. 125
    Proper 16 ............................................................. 134
    Proper 17 ............................................................. 142
    Proper 18 ............................................................. 150
    Proper 19 ............................................................. 159
    Proper 20 ............................................................. 167
    Proper 21 ............................................................. 176
    Proper 22 ............................................................. 184
    Proper 23 ............................................................. 192
    Proper 24 ............................................................. 200
    Proper 25 ............................................................. 208
    All Saints Day, Proper 26 ................................. 217
    Proper 27 ............................................................. 226
    Proper 28 ............................................................. 233
    Christ the King Sunday ................................... 241

## Year B Sermons

Trinity Sunday ................................................. 252
Proper 5 .......................................................... 265
Proper 6 .......................................................... 279
Proper 7 .......................................................... 289
Proper 8 .......................................................... 297
Proper 9 .......................................................... 309
Proper 10 ........................................................ 319
Proper 11 ........................................................ 331
Proper 12 ........................................................ 340
Proper 13 ........................................................ 350
Proper 14 ........................................................ 360
Proper 15 ........................................................ 370
Proper 16 ........................................................ 379
Proper 17 ........................................................ 387
Proper 18 ........................................................ 398
Proper 19 ........................................................ 409
Proper 20 ........................................................ 420
Proper 21 ........................................................ 432
Proper 22 ........................................................ 443
Proper 23 ........................................................ 452
Proper 24 ........................................................ 462
Proper 25 ........................................................ 474
All Saints Day, Proper 26 ............................... 482
Proper 27 ........................................................ 495
Proper 28 ........................................................ 505
Christ the King Sunday ................................... 514

## Year C Sermons

Trinity Sunday ................................................. 523
Proper 4 .......................................................... 531
Proper 5 .......................................................... 541

Proper 6 ............................................................. 553
Proper 7 ............................................................. 558
Proper 8 ............................................................. 565
Proper 9 ............................................................. 571
Proper 10 ........................................................... 577
Proper 11 ........................................................... 584
Proper 12 ........................................................... 590
Proper 13 ........................................................... 598
Proper 14 ........................................................... 606
Proper 15 ........................................................... 613
Proper 16 ........................................................... 620
Proper 17 ........................................................... 630
Proper 18 ........................................................... 636
Proper 19 ........................................................... 644
Proper 20 ........................................................... 650
Proper 21 ........................................................... 658
Proper 22 ........................................................... 668
Proper 23 ........................................................... 674
Proper 24 ........................................................... 682
Proper 25 ........................................................... 689
All Saints Day, Proper 26 ............................... 698
Proper 27 ........................................................... 708
Proper 28 ........................................................... 715
Christ the King Sunday ................................... 725

# From the Untrained Mind

The sermons contained in this book are a collection of those offered up on my Wordpress blog, entitled "Bus Stop Sermons." The Ordinary after Pentecost sermons (including Trinity Sunday and All Saints Day sermons) total seventy-seven that have been collected from over one hundred seventy posts there. I have written all of the posts.

The totality of those posts cover every Sunday over a three-year span of time, with the motivation being the schedule of readings from the Holy Bible, as posted by the Episcopal Church's Lectionary. Included in that schedule are twenty-four to twenty-seven Sundays in the Ordinary season after Pentecost. The last Sunday in that season ends the liturgical year, with the following Sunday beginning a new year with Advent. Since the Episcopal Lectionary cycle takes three years before recycling (Years A, B, and C), roughly half the weeks in a year (on average 26) are considered Ordinary after Pentecost.

The disclaimer that must be understood is this: None of the words presented here (or any of those still there on Wordpress) have ever been spoken out loud before an audience of any kind. In that sense, they are imaginary orations.

My imagination stems from the movie *Forrest Gump* and the scenes where Forrest would be seen at a bus stop telling his life story to strangers. I imagine doing the same, only differently. I see my captive audience as one that is not forced to sit and wait for a bus to come take them some place they desire to be. Instead, they are seeking the goal of heaven, or at least some insight into Christian lessons. Christianity can be seen like a transit system that parallels public transportation.

Those who read my words will then be much like the ones Forrest talked with: patiently bored; interested while waiting, but getting to one's destination on a planned schedule is more important; embarrassed by the thought that an imbecile has anything worthwhile to offer; outright rejection with ridicule; or willing recipients of an engaging story. Over the past five years many people have visited at my bus stop. Several have actually liked what they read and a few have felt something I wrote demanded that they make a comment.

Like what Forrest shared at his bus stop, everything I offer is designed as a friendly exchange with strangers. It is my story, not the story of anyone else. The commonality of the lectionary readings and how they make me remember my life story makes me share what I saw, what I felt, and what I think needs to happen for me to get on that bus to heaven. After all, everyone going to a bus stop is there for the same purpose, even if the ends of their rides differ.

As I am waiting like everyone else, I remember my life with words, based on images passing before my mind's eye. The reality of my memories being expressed can seem like I am looking at someone sitting right next to me on the bus stop bench, talking to him or her. My memories of my life can become so vivid that it seems like I telling others what to do, when that is not the case at all. I have become God, through the Mind of Christ, telling myself what God wants me to do. It is like preaching to the choir, when preacher and choir are all the same person – a one man band form of church.

The history that had me write imaginary sermons is based on my relationship with my wife. My wife would become an Episcopal priest, but before she made that transformation she was a church-lady Episcopalian. She was raised in that religious denomination as a girl and had a renewed commitment, as to the depth of her involvement with that branch of Christianity, before we met. Thus, I found myself becoming acquainted with that form of religious worship.

I had been unchurched for roughly forty years, prior to being introduced to Episcopalianism. In that time I had not been heathen, in regards to belief in God and Jesus Christ. I had become disenchanted with organized religion at the age of sixteen and repulsed completely by my mid-twenties, due to the televangelism that so blatantly besmirched Christianity as a form of entertainment, with actors crying crocodile tears while they begged for money, promising ministries that offered Jesus theme parks to their paying fans. My first wife was raised a Methodist, and I set aside my dislike for churches on Christmas and Easter and whenever the nearby church offered reasonably priced softball leagues.

For as little as my church involvement had been, I never stopped feeling that I could talk with God at any time. My childhood religious upbringing had instilled a sense of closeness to God that made prayer be informal and constant. For as wayward as my life would roam, I always felt that God was with me, watching out for me. I never attempted to shame anyone for their religious beliefs or commitments to organized religion; but I rarely felt a need to go to a church, even though I often begged God for His forgiveness after feeling the guilt of sin.

My life changed completely in 2001. I began wandering down the path God had always planned for me to walk, knowing that I would wander the path I had taken to get to that point. Everything in my life began to be seen clearly as purposeful and necessary, grooming me for the road ahead. I suddenly was given an ability to understand the writings of Nostradamus, even though what I was shown was just the grand scope of view. It would take me another seven years to reach the microscopic level of detailed awareness.

It was during that time of my life that I began writing books that attempted to explain Nostradamus to the world. It was during that time of my life that I met the woman who would become my second wife. It was during that time of my life that I began regular attendance in Episcopalian churches.

God brought my wife and I together, for the purpose of walking our chosen paths that led to God. My wife had ideas of serving the Episcopalian Church as a priest. I had ideas about telling the world about Nostradamus being an Apostle of Jesus Christ. Once God joined our paths together, my wife had a plan to serve God as an ordained priest (Episcopalian schooled and metaphysically educated) and I had a plan to serve God as an unordained priest (metaphysically schooled and divinely educated). My wife and I, together, became like two sides of the same coin, as two souls with the same purpose, from different perspectives.

Sunday after Sunday my wife and I sat in a pew and listened to one lame sermon after another. As I read the handout bulletin that had the Scriptural readings printed on them, I was reading them with an ability to understand, based on the similarity of writing style I found in Scripture and that by Nostradamus. By being able to make sense of Nostradamus, the meanings of the Scripture readings became obvious to me. However, as obvious as it was to me, that clarity was not being expressed in pulpit oratory.

Each Sunday my wife and I would discuss this absence of explanation in church. My wife agreed with me. She confessed that she had never known so much was contained in the verses read aloud, as she had never placed great interest in reading the Holy Bible. The more we discussed these matters, the deeper our faith in God became. My wife wanted to fulfill an absence

## Ordinary after Pentecost Sermons: From the Untrained Mind

in the Episcopal Church with divine insight and holy knowledge. I wanted to tell the world that every book of the Holy Bible had been written by servants of God, just as Nostradamus had written a most holy book that was unrecognized as such.

My wife and I began a ministry of learning, where we attended bible study classes, lectionary classes, and began visiting a variety of Episcopal churches to listen to a variety of priests giving sermons. We found that the education of Episcopal priests did not allow them to see or promote the meaning that was found hidden in the Holy Scriptures, lingering at the origin language level, while demanding divine assistance in discerning the truth. Instead of the accepting my offerings (while my wife patiently observed and listened), my observations were often rejected outright, questioned as to where I had read such things, and tossed out like dirty bath water when I admitted I had no pedigree, such as a degree from a divinity school.

This was the same rejection I faced when telling others that Nostradamus was misunderstood, due to a mistaken desire to read divine syntax as paraphrased English. My wife, always the smarter of the two of us, saw that being able to attend seminary was dependent on not rocking the boat (or nave). She realized it would be impossible for her to serve God as an Episcopal priest, if the Episcopal Church banned her from seminary school. So, she was discerned, approved, and selected for official education (she already possessed a PhD from academia), meaning my wife was further down the path from church-lady to ordained priest. Meanwhile, I continued to focus on writing books about Nostradamus, leaving my religious interpretations for another time. Then, it was off to seminary together, my wife the student and me the spouse.

While in seminary, my wife and I lived in an enchanted land that was reminiscent of Disney World. Everywhere we turned there was someone in costume, with the whole campus like a movie set. Visiting for a week allows one to be mesmerized by the pretence, but living there and working there brought about an ugly sense of reality. The seminarians there proved, more often than not, to be reborn college drinking buddies and frat house pranksters. There were few who wanted to talk about their core faith after classes were over.

As a way to make three years pass by without screaming, "No! This can't be!" I wrote and self-published four books that explained Nostradamus and his prophecies. My busy work allowed my wife the luxury of not being distracted by my negativity.

In May 2013, my wife graduated from seminary and was soon after ordained as a deacon for the Episcopal Church, Diocese of Mississippi. She interviewed and was offered a medium-sized town's parish, which she gladly accepted. In the month before her official start, I began to write sermons that were based on the Episcopal Lectionary, from which my wife's sermons would be based. I determined that I would maintain this program for an entire three-year cycle. I not only had written a sermon for the first Sunday that my wife would officially begin ministering to her new flock, but I also had several sermons written for the following several Sundays.

I wrote those sermons for myself, but also as discussion material between me and my wife. My wife read every one of my sermons over that three-year cycle (completed in about 32 months). She occasionally used a snippet or a paraphrase from something I had written, never referencing me directly (per my request), in her own prepared sermons (the official ones). Because my sermons were written about my life, which is highly unique (as everyone's life is), they can only be presented by me. Still, my words had an influence on my wife, just as her words influenced me.

I originally posted my sermons on a GoDaddy website, but the expense to maintain it did not match the results. When I ended the idea of having a website for both Nostradamus and Christian writings (separately grouped), I created free Wordpress blogs and reposted them there. When the idea of a blog named "Bus Stop Sermons" came to be, I subtitled that name with "From the Untrained Mind." That subtitle is also placed on this book, with the reasoning being that I have no diploma that gives me an official pulpit, no official approval to lead a flock of followers, and no vast educational history of study that proves me intellectually adept at sermon writing. But, then, I don't believe Jesus, nor the first many waves of true Christian Apostles and Saints had sheepskins from the University of the Holy Spirit.

The subtitle should be obvious, because everything on my "Bus Stop Sermons" blog and everything from there republished here comes from one who has no training in preaching sermons. My wife, and all officially ordained priests, are "trained" to preach and also "trained" to follow ritual dogma and employer protocol. That education, more than giving theology students the secrets to obtaining the hidden meaning that Holy Scripture contains, "trains" them to do a sermon that is close to being only twelve minutes in length.

As I was rereading the sermons that I presented for the Ordinary after Pentecost season, it seems I also tried to keep away from any depth of explanation. By staying on a path that was based on my life and how the readings played out in my life's likes and experiences, I doubt anyone would walk out on me, if I were ordained and had a congregation to which I would preach my messages.

I once had a fellow parishioner confide to me that he became an Episcopalian simply because of the short sermons. He had been a member of a more 'southern' denomination, which had a preacher routinely present two hour sermons, with everyone expected to stay after church, to eat and get to know one another more. My wife also had to conform to those constraints; but like me, she had to prepare her sermons and print them out so she would not go off track and take too long. If I were to ad lib one of my sermons, I imagine I could wander for a couple of hours easy.

When I say "mind," I do that to differentiate the source of my knowledge. It is not from a brain that has studied the Holy Bible for decades. Like my wife had spent little time in her early history reading Scripture, I too was very Biblical illiterate. I knew the basic Bible Stories, but there was so much that the lectionary exposed me to that I barely recognized. When I took a course designed to educate laypersons for ministry, I was in a class of Episcopalians who knew just as little. However, I was better prepared from having studied before going to classes, and often from having written about what the course focused on each week, than were the other students in the class.

The point of an "untrained mind" is not to be a statement about how full of wisdom I am or how deeply I have read books about the meaning of Scripture, without ever getting a diploma (or even a gold star on a report), because there are not many people (if any) that see Scripture like I see it. Just as when I was learning to read the divine language that is ever-present in the writings of Nostradamus, there was no human being who was teaching a course in how to do that. The "untrained mind" is then metaphor for an openness to receive the Spirit of knowledge and speak the truth. While the brain functions in this process, it is not the organ originating higher thoughts. It simply receives them and then I have to figure the meaning by following impulses of insight.

As a twist of irony, I was raised in an Assembly of God church. That church is known for being in the "Pentecostal" branch of Christian denominations. The name "Pentecostal" is based on the Day of Pentecost, when disciples suddenly began "speaking in tongues." Many times I witnessed people (one woman more than others) stand up in church and begin making sudden, loud, unintelligible repetitive noises, with hands raised high. For some reason, Pentecostals believe making such noises constitutes being filled with the Holy Spirit. As I was sixteen when I voluntarily left that denomination, and had received some "training" in how to become tongue-tied and appear to be "speaking in tongues," I never believed making throat noises served any purpose; but then I was too young and ignorant to really know what was going on in church at that age.

Many years later, while in a church Bible study class, a young man said the unintelligible noises have to then be interpreted by someone who is fluent in "speaking in tongues." Supposedly, after a public display of noise making, someone then stands up and explains, "She said (this or that)." In all my youthful years of attending an Assembly of God church, where regularly the same woman would put on her display, I never heard anyone stand up and explain what she had said. All I heard were whispered "Praise the Lords" and then the pastor would continue where he left off. As such, I can assure everyone that "speaking in tongues" has absolutely nothing to do with making unintelligible noises.

What I do is the reality of "speaking in tongues," where the Greek word "*glōssais*" is translated as "tongues," but also can say "languages." Acts 2 sets up how pilgrims (Jews and Israelites) from many different places marvelled at how the Apostles suddenly began "speaking in other languages" (from the Greek "*lalein heterais glōssais*"), due to the Holy Spirit making them speak in the tongues of others. Understanding Nostradamus meant the Holy Spirit made me see the text of Nostradamus (the literal Old French, not the English paraphrases) and be led to see how vast the meaning was. Learning how to read in that divine "tongue" (via the Holy Spirit, as it must be with me to see the truth) means I interpret that which was spoken in tongues. Like the young man said, I prove that to be true. People read Holy Scripture and sit silently, not knowing what has been said (although some whisper "Praise the Lord"). I stand up to interpret what was stated.

I share this history not to make myself seem special. Anyone who devotes himself or herself to God and sincerely prays for His guidance, can likewise do what I do. Just remember what I said about seeing only the grand scope when I first started understanding Nostradamus. It took years of dedication and devotion to follow the whispers of insight and see the depth of truth that would be revealed through divine texts.

It then becomes a test at the bus stop. Like the one woman that told Forrest, after he said, "Isn't that your bus?" She just waved her hand and said, "There will be another one." She wanted to hear more about what Forrest had to say.

That is what a good sermon does. It lights a fire of interest. It burns within one's heart so they cannot ignore the call to "Look deeper" anymore. I pray these sermons will ignite others to be filled with the Holy Spirit and preach their own bus stop sermons.

# A Season Named Ordinary

For a long time I believed the name of the Ordinary season that follows Pentecost Sunday was called the Pentecost season. I came to that conclusion by seeing how each Sunday in the lectionary was identified as "after Pentecost." My assumptions included thinking Pentecost Sunday was the first week of this season named "after" it, only to discover it was technically the last Sunday in the Easter season.

I see that newfound knowledge as useful. Pentecost Sunday belongs in the Easter season as it marks a boundary that separates the learning from the learned. Equally, Easter Sunday marks a boundary on the other end of the seven Sundays in between, which is neither of the season named Lent or Easter. Both Easter Sunday and Pentecost Sunday represents walls that have an entrance gate (Easter Sunday) and an exit gate (Pentecost Sunday), with both gates being Jesus. That justifies Jesus' statement, "I am the gate.

In between the walls is the school of Jesus, where he taught his disciples for forty days. This makes the space between the two walls act like a seminary, with the gate on the wall of Pentecost Sunday being representative of graduation. Graduation is the culmination of learning, where one is prepared for ministry, but that ministry comes "after Pentecost."

The lesson taught from Acts 2 on Pentecost Sunday was Peter

and the eleven, along with the others who joined with them in prayer and devotion to the lessons taught by Jesus for forty days risen, was the Holy spirit filled them and they began to minister the truth to the public. From the spread of the Holy Spirit, through Apostles to those whose hearts were open to receiving the Spirit, "about three thousand souls were added to the number of the twelve." That is what lies beyond the gate of Pentecost Sunday; but to graduate and go beyond that gate, one has to become the gate, which is Jesus reborn.

The spread of Christianity is told in the Acts of the Apostles, which are standard reading selections for the Easter season. Part of the preparation process is to make a disciple ready to enter ministry, so stories of those who did it first are good training exercises. Unfortunately, that spread, for whatever reasons, slowed, probably when the Great Schism occurred and churches were created and divided, much like was the nation of Israel. Just as that division led to the eventual decline and fall of both Judah and Israel, the Western Church - the Church of Rome - has closed the school of Jesus and created false seminaries that no longer sends Apotles out into the world.

This change has created the walled in effect, where the space between Easter and Pentecost now acts like a fortress or a cloister based on belief. Belief alone is not enough to prepare Apostles to be lambs thrown to the wolves. This means Christians have stopped being reborn as Jesus Christ - like were Peter, the eleven, the women and family of Jesus, and the three thousand that became priests of Yahweh on that most eventual Pentecost Sunday.

The walls created by Easter and Pentecost no longer reflect the beliefs of people seeking to know God as the Father, based on the teachings of the Son. Rather than Easter representing a 'college entrance exam' into a school of learning (a most HOLY seminary that demands "receipt of the Spirit"), where knowledge of the risen Lord seeks to know more, Easter simply acts as a church door that is opened to let anyone inside. The far wall of

# Ordinary after Pentecost Sermons: A Season Named Ordinary

Pentecost is no longer an objective of ministry, but rather the acceptance that people have already 'been there and done that', so there is no longer a need to preach the truth (i.e.: the Gospel).

This makes the eight weeks between Easter and Pentecost become nothing more than a fortress, where the people within the walls believe they have found safety in numbers. Rather than seeking to receive the Spirit and be given precious knowledge of the meaning of Scripture, the Church has taken on the role of Lord, as the Great Protector of the followers of Jesus Christ. This is a training that is defensive in nature, seeking not to empower the common people, as the Church gains power through ignorance.

The Church is an institution (an organization of men and women) that has never ventured beyond the wall of Pentecost as true Prophets of Scripture. This means that the original concept of Apostles being filled with God's Holy Spirit, reborn as duplicates of His Son - the resurrection of Jesus of Nazareth in different bodies of human flesh (regardless of human gender) - who then go and touch the hearts and souls of new receivers of the Spirit has been lost. Rather than teach disciples how to commit in marriage to God Almighty, preparing to do the works of the Lord as His Son reborn, the denominations of Christianity now preach waiting for Jesus to return and that keeps the walls of Easter and Pentecost acting as sheepfold walls, with those running the churches as hired hands or (at worst) false shepherds.

This degradation is the same as happened to the children of Israel, when they were led away from Egypt by Moses, along with God's presence. This is where the number forty becomes a parallel and needs to be understood.

Jesus as the Christ needs to be seen as a parallel to Moses with Yahweh, with the difference being Moses talked with God, but God was external to him. Jesus talked with God, but God was within Jesus, making him become the Christ (or the Messiah).

The children of Israel are reflections of the disciples of Jesus, all of whom were given the expectation of priesthood. The children of Israel would become the priests of Yahweh in a land promised to them. The disciples of Jesus were promised to become priests in his name, just as Jesus was in the name of God the Father, as the Son. All would be given the reward of the Promised Land of Heaven. However, to reach that goal, both the children of Israel and the disciples of Jesus had to graduate from a process of learning, which means the walls of Easter (the Passover) and Pentecost (the Law) were the same parameters set before both, with forty being the timeframe between.

The forty years Moses with Yahweh kept the children of Israel in the wilderness is parallel to the forty days that the risen Lord, Jesus Christ spent with his disciples. The difference in years and days can be seen as relative to desire to be in those two similar, yet different, schools of priesthood. The children of Israel grumbled constantly, whereas the disciples of Jesus desired to be like him. The children of Israel were forced by circumstance to accept being cloistered, away from the civilization, for which their hearts still longed. Thus, two generations of Israelites were brought into a world that did not know the world of their fathers and fathers' fathers.

It is the story of the Israelites in the wilderness under Moses' guidance that is the parallel to Jesus in ministry with his disciples. All were chosen by God, but the Israelites were chosen by agreements made with their ancestors Abraham and Jacob, neither of whom followed Moses and Yahweh into a school of learning. The discciples of Jesus were willing followers, thus they had open hearts that desired to serve Yahweh. Still, it is important to see that graduation from either school of ministry cannot occur without lessons that prepare one for that ultimate goal - to be led as a student to become the teacher of students.

This is where the lesson of manna must be understood, in order for anyone to progress beyond always being a student or disciple, to become a rabbi or teacher. The manna was the truth taught to the Moses-led disciples in the wilderness, whereas Jesus was the manna fed to the disciples in Galilee and Judea. To better understand this, here is an article I recently published that explains this:

In Exodus 16:4-5 we read (NIV):

> "Then the Lord said to Moses, "I will rain down bread from heaven for you. The people are to go out each day and gather enough for that day. In this way I will test them and see whether they will follow my instructions. On the sixth day they are to prepare what they bring in, and that is to be twice as much as they gather on the other days.""

In Exodus 16:13-16 the story of manna continues:

> "That evening quail came and covered the camp, and in the morning there was a layer of dew around the camp. When the dew was gone, thin flakes like frost on the ground appeared on the desert floor. When the Israelites saw it, they said to each other, "What is it?" For they did not know what it was. Moses said to them, "It is the bread the Lord has given you to eat. This is what the Lord has commanded: 'Everyone is to gather as much as they need. Take an omer for each person you have in your tent.'""

Then, in Exodus 16:19-21 we are told:

> "Then Moses said to them, "No one is to keep any of it until morning." However, some of them paid no attention to Moses; they kept part of it until morning, but it was full of maggots and began to smell. So Moses was angry with them. Each morning everyone gathered as much as they needed, and when the sun grew hot, it

melted away."

With that history of manna originating, I need to make a few points that might allow you to grasp what manna is.

First, when an Episcopalian [or other similar denomination of the Christian religion] kneels at an altar for Communion, the priest hands him or her a wafer, saying, "The Body of Christ, the bread of heaven." This stems from John's first chapter, where he wrote of the Word (*Logos*) being made flesh, which is interpreted as "God made Jesus Christ" to spread the Word of God, like Jesus was a replacement for manna.

The point is not a lesson about how that childish interpretation is off the mark [which is is], but to focus on an understanding of manna from heaven, which might make understanding "the Word made flesh" have the broader implication of "Christianity," when that word refers to people actually reborn as Jesus Christ.

Jesus of Nazareth (born in Bethlehem) was the embodiment of how Exodus 16:32-34 states this:

> "Moses said, "This is what the Lord has commanded: 'Take an omer of manna and keep it for the generations to come, so they can see the bread I gave you to eat in the wilderness when I brought you out of Egypt.'" So Moses said to Aaron, "Take a jar and put an omer of manna in it. Then place it before the Lord to be kept for the generations to come." As the Lord commanded Moses, Aaron put the manna with the tablets of the covenant law, so that it might be preserved. "

Jesus was the jar. God's manna within Jesus was the Christ Spirit that filled Jesus. Jesus was the body of flesh that dispensed the Word of God, rather than God needing to let manna fall like rain from the sky.

Keep in mind that manna only fell where the Israelites were, and Jesus only became manna where the Jews of Judea and Galilee were, so manna in these days of everybody living in mixed neighborhoods and everybody being a hodgepodge of religious mythology means manna is restricted to only being available to those who God chooses. [God's chosen people.] You can't buy manna at the grocery store or pick it up at the drug store.

Manna from heaven now falls selectively and individually, not *en masse*. The call from God, through His Son, is to be likewise filled with the manna of the Christ, so one becomes a new jar that is Jesus reborn. Collectively, those are called Apostles [also Saints] and those are few and far between these days.

Second, Exodus says the Israelites asked, "What is it?" which is the Hebrew meaning of the word we English speaking people know as "manna" ["*man hu* "]. That was not a statement that expressed a lack of visual ability to see something unknown, but a question relative to their Spiritual hunger needs. The Hebrew that immediately follows says, "for they did not know "*man hu*."

That says manna was food for thought, not food for bellies. That food was relative to 'medicine for priests of Yahweh' and very similar these days to writings like this you are reading. Take a dose of this everyday and maybe, after forty years(?), you will become a priest of Yahweh. In the wilderness with Moses, the Israelites recited his orders from God from rote memory [before they had paper and pens], but then (just like all times since) the Word brings up the question, "What is it?" as a question about what the words mean.

After Moses died and after the manna stopped falling from heaven [and paper and pens were obtained], the Spiritual answers to those questions were only found in true Prophets of the Lord. The judges, and people like Samuel and Elijah, Jeremiah and Ezekiel, they became the manna from heaven for the Israelites. Jesus would become the manna from heaven for the lost children of Israel. Jesus offered the same Spiritual answers, but on a more direct - teacher-to-student - manner, where those offered that Spiritual food were those who voluntarily sought to be fed manna. The Jews of Jerusalem and elsewhere gave Jesus the same reaction: "We did not know '*man hu*.'"

Third, there are several places in Exodus that tell how many animals [livestock] the Israelites took with them from Egypt. When they bellyached about not having water, they said to Moses, "Why did you bring us up out of Egypt to make us and our children and livestock die of thirst?" (Exodus 17:3b) In a forty-year school of learning, at the Moses Camp for Israelites in the wilderness, they could have practiced sacrificial burning of livestock on altars [a good priestly duty back then] and as a result had plenty of belly food to keep them alive. The water kept them alive so they could make milk and cheese and chicken stew, *et al*. However, the Israelites were not in the wilderness like they were on some episode of *Survivor*. They were being trained to be God's priests. Therefore, in addition to belly food, they needed mental food that fed their spirits (souls). That is what manna from heaven is, with "mental" health [knowledge of God] going well beyond book learning.

In today's world where it is fashionable to grab as much as you can when something is freely offered, it is important to realize that is what Gentiles do. By "Gentiles," I means those who are run of the mill worldly sinners, who know what the laws are, but they break them none the less, as the only thing their pea brains understand is "Me! Me! Me!" The Israelites had been no different when they lived in Egypt, thus they had a lot of stuff that they took with them when they followed Moses out of town. It would take forty years of 'expanding their minds' as to what God expected out of them, before they were prepared to enter the Promised Land of Canaan.

Of course, after they got that reward of land, it was Katy bar the door, as far as forgetting everything they had been taught and reverting to "Me! Me! Me!" until their lack of faith had the Gentiles on the verge of killing all the Israelites. That is a lesson that never goes out of style: Without God's help IN YOU you will always revert to being a selfish little brat that could not care less for the wants and needs of others.

Guess what? [Read that as a "*man hu*" question.] God knew that human flaw was in His chosen people, so He laid down the "one day's worth at a time" law [with the only exception being "two days' worth at a time on Fridays"]. As soon as Moses passed that restriction on, the fools were doing the "Me! Me! Me!" again and ending up with maggots crawling around their huts and the tent stinking to high heaven.

When Jesus walked the face of the earth, his disciples asked him to teach them to pray. For all those Christians today, those who consider themselves disciples of Jesus, who put a lot of belief in the power of prayer, I wonder how much of that prayer today is not saying, "Me! Me! Me!", as in "Give me what I want God, even if what I want is for someone I love to stay healthy and with me!" I bet few Christians today recall [even though they say the words many times a week, perhaps] how Jesus told his disciples, "Pray to the Father, 'Give me this day my daily bread.'"

Don't let the plural pronouns "our" and "us" fool anyone. Jesus told the collective collective pronouns, but they meant "You pray singularly to God, so when I say, 'Give us this day our daily bread', I mean each of you says to the Father, "Give me today my daily bread."" That was an instruction from the Father through the Son that says, "If you want to call Me your Father, then you best be reborn as My Son. The only way to even begin to get there is to pray daily to Me, saying, "Please Sir, give me my Scriptural lesson.""

Now, there might be lots of well-intending Christians who understand that, clear as day. Look around the Internet, using the search term "Our Daily Bread" and see for yourself how many blogs and websites come up. There are lots of "Christians" offering "manna from heaven," from having been given a daily helping (an omer) from God. This then leads to that preponderance being explanatory and interpretative, because "manna" means asking God, "What is this?" in reference to something in Scripture. An "omer" is then the measure of understanding one is given by God. That probably is not all that can be understood, but it is enough for one day.

That then leads to the realization that snarfing up as much Scriptural meaning as one can, when one is taking more than one can conceivably grasp mentally, within one's soul-brain connection, grasping is only necessary for priests of God. That action of taking more than needed in one day stinks of profiteering, rather than seeking to know the truth. Is smells like the point is not to gain Spiritual insight, but to sell it to someone else, making monetary gains from nothing more than snarfing actions. Daily bread (manna from heaven) is only intended for those who are being trained as priests of Yahweh, who will then pass on understanding to others seeking to become priests of

God (children and maybe livestock).

So, one taking the "Me! Me! Me!" approach to writings about the meaning of Scripture makes, when the next sunrise comes around, one be identified by God as being "full of maggots and [beginning] to smell."

Keep in mind that maggots and bad body odor come when one is dead; and being born mortal means being born to death. So, trying to misuse the meaning of Scripture is bad for one's bodily health and a soul seeking to escape the failure of repeat and repeat again [reincarnation] can forget about it!

Once a day means what it says. It means not as much as can be freely grabbed and not only once a week ... for a couple of hours ... if the mind does not wander during that time. Daily bread from heaven helps save the soul and keep the flesh from stinking the place up.

[Published on the WordPress blog "*Apercevoir*," a.k.a. "Black Sheep Shepherding," on June 5, 2020.]

I hope this makes it clear that the concept of spiritual food does not come in the form of a ceremonial wafer. One cannot receive the Spirit by eating a wafer and sipping some red wine, even if a Church employee says a degree from a seminary and a the pageantry of a bishop leading a ceremony that officially puts a seminary graduate on the Church payroll, said to then be given the power to call down from Heaven and make Jesus Christ enter into wafers and wine. God does not get controlled by human beings in that way and neither does His Son.

Seminaries today are colleges of man that do not teach the Word. They cannot, so they do not attempt to teach the meaning of Scripture. Instead, they teach reverence to a Church of an institution, who will employ their 'priests' to stay within the walls of Easter and Pentecost, never going beyond the wall to the wilderness. To survive that exercise, the graduated students would have to become the gate (Jesus) through which others could enter, by receipt of the Spirit (the Easter gate of Jesus, through which one learns the truth). Institutional seminaries and schools of theology simply recycle disciples of the Church back into the sheepfold to overlord other disciples of the Church. No one has understanding of the truth, so no one is taught to receive the Spirit and seek the truth, in preparation to leave the sheepfold and enter the wilderness, spreading the truth.

It must be fully grasped that a season named "Ordinary" is a demand for ministry, by Apostles [Saints] "in the name of Jesus Christ," or there would be absolutely zero religion named "Christianity." This means grasping the meaning of that name, "Ordinary."

In the Church year there are two "Ordinary" seasons. One falls after the Epiphany, which is always on January 6th. Depending on the year and when Easter is scheduled to occur, the number of weeks in the Ordinary time "after the Epiphany" can vary. In the year 2020, there were seven Sundays in this period, which represented a longer than average length of time. The longest Ordinary season is the one following Pentecost; and, according to the Episcopal Church Dictionary, under "Ordinary Time," the Ordinary season after Pentecost is the true definition of "Ordinary."

That source states:

> "The Epiphany season, it should not be considered ordinary time." The focus is more on the season following Pentecost, as they define this as: "Ordinary time can be understood in terms of the living out of Christian faith and the meaning of Christ's resurrection in ordinary life. The term "ordinary time" is not used in the Prayer Book, but the season after Pentecost can

> be considered ordinary time. It may be referred to as the "green season," because green is the usual liturgical color for this period of the church year."

The Church does allow the color of green to be used during the season following Epiphany, and understands that color is an association to "Ordinary" time, but that association is not aptly applied to the season of Epiphany.

There is reasoning for this, which reflects the ministry of Jesus and his disciples. While the Church seasons during the year are not a mirror image of Jesus' ministry and life, the presence of two periods considered "Ordinary" reflect the two commissions of Jesus' disciples. Jesus sent out the twelve "and gave them authority to drive out impure spirits and to heal every disease and sickness." (Matthew 10:1, NIV - and also confirmed in Mark 6 and Luke 9) In Luke 10:1-20, we are told of Jesus sending out seventy-two in ministry. These commissions were temporary and separate from the Great Commission, which Matthew wrote of in his twenty-eighth chapter:

> "Therefore go and make disciples of all nations, baptizing them in the name of the Father and of the Son and of the Holy Spirit, and teaching them to obey everything I have commanded you. And surely I am with you always, to the very end of the age." (Matthew 28:19-20)

That states the differences between two "Ordinary" experiences, where one is temporary and limited, as an "internship," while the second would begin on Pentecost Sunday and last the remained of the Apostles' lives. For example, when my wife was in seminary, she spent a month at a small church and a hospital near that church, ministering as a "chaplain," as a "seminarian." That was her practice at ministry, in a program called Curricular Practical Training (CPT). When my wife graduated from seminary, the bishop of her diocese ordained her and other seminary graduates as a "deacon." Then, after she had served as a deacon for six months, the bishop came to her parish and ordained her a priest or rector (or vicar). That is how two "Ordinary" season should be recognized, with the "Ordinary time after the Epiphany" seen as not official ministry, being only practice.

While this appears to mean "Ordinary" refers to being sent out with some official arrangement and approval, the Church denies this is the meaning. Such a statement would be heresy, as only God commissions His priests and there is no head of a Church that comes close to being an equal to God. Thus, the Episcopal Church's definition of "Ordinary Time" is stated to mean: "The living out of Christian faith and the meaning of Christ's resurrection in ordinary life," where "ordinary" assumes the definition "normal."

No one in his or her right mind would even begin to think that being an Apostle of Christ [a Saint] is "normal" in any way. The better definition of "Ordinary" refers to the numerical application as "ordinal." An "ordinal number" is defined as such:

> "Also called ordinal numeral. any of the numbers that express degree, quality, or position in a series, as first, second, and third (distinguished from cardinal number)." (Dictionary.com)

Thus, the numbering of Sundays "after" a significant day (Epiphany or Pentecost) means "Ordinary" is simply a time in-between seasons, when it is customary to number the Sundays "ordinally."

Since that use of an adverb ("ordinally") cannot be the proper name (a noun) os a season or time, the term "Ordinary" then returns one to an understanding that it stems from the verb "ordain." That definition is then "to make (someone) a priest or minister; confer holy orders on." Because no Church can truly ordain a priest of God - only a priest of a Church - the true sense of "Ordinary time" is when God has deemed a disciple of His Son to be ready to be commissioned into the world as His priest, ordained by the highest authority.

In the eyes of all Churches, whose properties are theirs alone (church buildings), those ordained by God will be "living out of Christian faith and the meaning of Christ's resurrection in ordinary life," meaning "just not paid by the Church and preaching in one of their properties. This means a priest of God today (a true priest ordained by the Holy Spirit, reborn in the name of Jesus Christ) is like an Apostle in the original phase of Christianity.

God did not create a new religion when He sent His Son as promised - a Savior for the wayward. The religion of that day was Judaism. The Temple Jews owned all the synagogues in and around Judea and Galilee, so the first Christians became unwelcomed and cast out by those who did not accept Jesus as the Christ. They did not calculate, "We need to begin a new religion," as they were sent out in ministry to preach the truth as only Jesus reborn could do, with knowledge of meaning that goes beyond the surface meaning found in written text. Therefore, whatever denomination of Christianity one finds affiliation with today, it is no different than the affiliation the first century Jews had with a religion that had no connection with God Almighty. All religions are meaningless without the presence and support of Yahweh, the One God.

This mean the "Greater" Commission is beyond the powers of a Church, as an organization and institution of paid employees, which always remains within the fortress that is between the walls of Easter and Pentecost. Jesus is the gate to both walls, so one must believe the **truth** of Jesus resurrected and one must believe the **truth** of Pentecost.. The **truth** comes by **knowing** God as His Son reborn. When Jesus is resurrected within one's body of flesh, as the soul of Jesus merged with the soul of one's flesh, one becomes the gate of Easter. When that Jesus within has trained one to go forth as a priest of Yahweh, speaking the **truth** that comes from the Mind of Christ, one has become the gate of Pentecost. This is the **truth** of the Ordinary season that comes after Pentecost.

No Church of Chritianity today is led by a Saint, meaning no priests working for a Church has the ability to prepare anyone for minstry to the Lord. Rather than prepare students to graduate and depart into ministry, they lull them to sleep [a metaphor of mortal death] and keep them in the sheepfold, doing nothing beyond financing a Church, enabling the Church to pay a hired hand. The danger lies in when a Chruch rejects a true priest who has been truly Ordained by God and is Jesus Christ reborn.

The danger is not to the true priest, but to the Church. That warning was stated when Jesus gave thses instructions:

> Whatever town or village you enter, search there for some worthy person and stay at their house until you leave. As you enter the home, give it your greeting. If the home is deserving, let your peace rest on it; if it is not, let your peace return to you. If anyone will not welcome you or listen to your words, leave that home or town and shake the dust off your feet. Truly I tell you, it will be more bearable for Sodom and Gomorrah on the day of judgment than for that town. "I am sending you out like sheep among wolves. Therefore be as shrewd as snakes and as innocent as doves. Be on your guard; you will be handed over to the local councils and be flogged in the synagogues. On my account you will be brought before governors and kings as witnesses to them and to the Gentiles. But when they arrest you, do not worry about what to say or how to say it. At that time you will be given

> what to say, for it will not be you speaking, but the Spirit of your Father speaking through you. "Brother will betray brother to death, and a father his child; children will rebel against their parents and have them put to death. You will be hated by everyone because of me, but the one who stands firm to the end will be saved. (Matthew 10:11-22)

The ordinary season after Pentecost is an expectation of all who are true **Christ**ians. It is not 'vacation time', representing the warm weather months [Northern Hemisphere], when going to church is less important. If one is not called into ministry (meaning one refuses to heed the call), then one is not reborn in the name of Christ. If that is the case, then ponder the future being "more bearable for [those of] Sodom and Gomorrah on the day of judgment than for [you]."

With that said, let me restate the subtitle used in this series. "From the Untrained Mind" states the **truth**, such that I have no seminary training that tells me how to understand Scripture. In John's seventh chapter, Jesus was confronted by the Jews of Jerusalem [during the Sukkot festival], asking, "How did this man get such learning without having been taught?" (John 7:15)

Jesus responded by saying, "My teaching is not my own. It comes from the one who sent me. Anyone who chooses to do the will of God will find out whether my teaching comes from God or whether I speak on my own. Whoever speaks on their own does so to gain personal glory, but he who seeks the glory of the one who sent him is a man of **truth**; there is nothing false about him." (John 7:16-18)

The **truth** is not something learned from reading books, and there are no teachers who know the truth unless they are one with God.

I have come to the conclusion, from listening to many sermons given by priests in Episcopal churches I have attended and by watching television sermons (including Facebook and YouTube) by ministers of other religions, that the sermons of hired hands are little more than glorified 'children's church' understandings of Scripture. Priests today have not been taught to understand Scripture, beyond their having been taught Bible Stories as a child. Regardless of their good intentions, the churches have become politicized institutions, where the lessons taught have little to do with understanding the **truth** of Scripture. Instead, they attempt to teach adults to believe in childish fantasies that were not the intent of the writers of Holy Scripture. This means, by the time Pentecost Sunday rolls around, no one has been prepared to do anything more than badmouth anyone who does not agree with a priest's political agenda. Hatred is not the focus of the Ordinary season after Pentecost.

When my wife was ordained a deacon and assigned to serve as the rector of a small parish, I came out of the seminary experience ashamed of the religion calling itself Anglican or Episcopalian. Few seminarians acted as anything more than frat brothers and sisters, as college beer drinkers extrordinare. There were cliques and groups, few of which displayed any true holiness in character. Knowing my wife as one of only a handfull of sincere Christians being ordained from her class, and knowing my wife was restricted in what she could present to her first flock, I had a strong burning in my heart to preach the truth, even if I was to be the only one hearing it preached. I had entered the gate of Pentecost. I had become ordained by God, reborn in the name of Jesus Christ; so I began to write sermons.

I began to write sermons after the Ordinary season after Pentecost was underway. My first sermon addressed the writings listed by the lectionary for the Fourth Sunday after Pentecost, Year C, which was also deemed "Proper 6." That Sunday was May 26, 2013. After three years of writing the sermons presented in this book, the last one written finished the missing Sundays after

# Ordinary after Pentecost Sermons: A Season Named Ordinary

Pentecost, Year C. In the end, the sermons cover the Sundays that made up the missing Year C weeks fell on May 22, May 29, and June 5, 2016 (Proper 3, 4, and 5).

This separation in time can be seen in the sermons that are part of the section headed "Ordinary after Pentecost Sermons, Year C." When I first began, I was publishing on a Yahoo website. In addition to the sermons, I also published notes relative to each reading, including the Psalms. Often, the notes would be longer than the sermons, because when I first began I was trying to be "Episcopalian" and limit a sermon to twelve minutes. Thus, in the Year C section, it can be noticable how brief the sermons become, after the Third Sunday after Pentecost, Proper 5.

Relative to the after Pentecost season are "Tracks." This relates to the optional readings that are consistently presented, which pairs two Old Testament readings with two Paslms. Only one track is to be chosen for reading and preaching, but my attitude throughout was "If they all relate, preach them all." As I went along, I cared less about length of time and more about preaching the message, for which all readings created threads of support.

One of the problems I have with hired hands pretending to be ministers of the Word is their penchant for totally disregarding everything read aloud publicly, constructing a sermon on only one reading - usually the Gospel. That is not teaching the Word so the people in attendance can be led to understand and have their hearts burn with desire to learn more. That is a sign of ineptitude, especially when that one reading is bent and twisted to conform to some political message that stroke the back of some current event.

Holy Scripture is personal, eternal, and for all times, all places, and all things happening. Since most events that make human beings emotional are those evil, Jesus was niot sent by the Father to tell us to make the world magically turn into heaven. Evil things happen and evil things will alway be what defines this world we live in. Failing to preach the truth to the individuals, in a collective setting, only makes the world a place more inclined to be evil

My hope is that these sermons will project the **truth** that is being missed, by churches being too afraid to project the reality of an evil world as not being possible to change, but only possible to withstand by the presence of God within and the resurrection of Jesus Christ within one's being. Each human being that seeks to serve God - the **truth** of being **Christ**ian - must be moved deeply to a commitment of servitide.

The message found in all of these sermons (and those in the books of other seasons) say the same thing, repeatedly. That message is not taught by the hired hands in churches today. Many preach a childish version of commitment, but then turn around and say, "When Jesus comes at the end of days." Jesus ascended on the eve of Pentecost Sunday and returned twelve-fold (actually three thousand-fold) the next morning. The end of days means when one stops being too selfish to serve God, allowing God to reside in one's heart and let one's mind be controlled by His Son.

The repetitive message is marriage to God. God has proposed His love and He wants us to each, individually, say "Yes" to that proposal. Marriage to God means complete submission to His Will. The engagement period of time means showing one truly loves God and promises to do His Will. This engagement is then like the Ordinary season after the Epiphany. One needs to show God you desire Him as much as He desires you. There is no telling how long that will take. God knows each and every heart and when a heart is ready. That will be when God will be found coming within one, as "a sound like the blowing of a violent wind came from heaven."

Once that marriage between one's soul and God is secured, then the consummation of that marriage will bring forth the Son of

God (regardless of what human gender one's body of flesh is). When one has been reborn from that Spiritual union, then one has no desire but to please God, in the same way that Jesus had.

This is the true meaning of the Ordinary season after Pentecost. Please use this text in your engagement period with God, so you too will be prepared to be Ordained by Yahweh.

# Ordinary after Pentecost Sermons

# Year A

# FIRST SUNDAY AFTER PENTECOST

## Trinity Sunday

# YEAR A

**Relevant readings:**
Genesis 1:1-31 plus
   Genesis 2:1-4
Psalm 8
   *or* Canticle 13
    (Canticle 2)
2 Corinthians 13:11-13
Matthew 28:16-20

Robert Tippett

# Today God Creates Saints from the Heaven, Earth, and Firmament

Today, according to the Episcopal liturgical calendar, is Trinity Sunday. We recognize the Father, the Son, and the Holy Spirit today.

Symbolically, once one has been ordained as a priest for the Father – not a ceremony carried out by a religious institution, but an Ordination of Spirit – then one is the Son (regardless of human sex) through the Holy Spirit. Since we were all at the graduation ceremony for newly commissioned Saints last week, today we honor the Trinity that makes all Saints possible.

Let us all give a nice round of applause for the Father, the Son, and the Holy Spirit as one being.

<applaud>

Perhaps some of you were wondering why we sat through the Creation of the world, in the Old Testament reading this morning.

Certainly, the Trinity was in play throughout every step in that seven-"Day" time frame.

There is so much of value in Genesis 1 that it is impossible to make a short sermon about it all. Instead of letting this reading go unexplained, I invite everyone to take the time to pour over today's Genesis text and meditate on the meaning that is there. It is truly amazing. See me later if you need help understanding it all.

But, for now, let's take the most general view of what one finds there, which can be summed up in the very first line:

# After Pentecost Sermons: Trinity Sunday, Year A

"In the beginning created God heavens and earth."

You have to see that in a way that has your mind clear on the true meaning of "heavens." This is not alluding to outer space. We do not die and go to outer space. We go to the "heavens," where God lives … to the Father's house.

You also cannot see "earth" as our planet alone. The creation of "earth" includes the entire Universe, so it is our planet, all of deep space, and everything in between. The Hebrew word "*eretz*," meaning "land, earth," is better seen as a word referencing "substance," "matter," or "elements." In that way, "earth" is the opposite of "heavens."

Therefore, we should read how God created the spiritual. And then God created the material.

One is separated from the other, as two entirely different realms, with the physical realm having no way of accessing the spiritual realm by will.

In other words, we cannot go on a vacation to Heaven, and then come back to a 9 to 5 job in the earthly realm – with pictures and stories to tell our coworkers.

"Look! This is one of me at the foot of God. And this is me with the Archangel Michael. He was so nice."

While Disney World is a nice place to visit, it is not Heaven.

Heaven and Earth are two separate places created by God, but God can be both places at once.

When we then read about the Creation on Day two, we see a "dome" was created in the "midst of the waters."

Since Day one only produced "heavens" and "earth," or "the spiritual" and "the material," the use of "waters" must be seen as the "flows" or "springs" of Creation, with one spewing forth the "ethereal" and the other spewing forth the "elemental."

Between those two is placed a "dome," where the word written is "*raqia*." That word has often been translated as "vault" or "firmament," but literally means "expanse."

The reason we read "dome," "vault," or "firmament" into "expanse" is it is like the suspension system of a bridge, for a road over a river. It is a form of support that not only maintains separation, but acts as a connection between the two.

So, between the "spiritual" and the "material" is a "bridge of support."

That, my friends, is the Trinity: The Father, The Son, and The Holy Spirit. That represents the Heavens, the Earth, and the Firmament.

Again, there is so much more that can be gleaned from today's reading in Genesis. However, the purpose of Trinity Sunday is not to prove the Bible supports the premise of God, earthly beings, and the link between those two.

The purpose, as a follow-up to Pentecost Sunday, it to remind you that the Trinity is three parts, where one part is most often missing.

That missing part is you. Instead of the saying, "one brick short of a load," this is "one soul short of a Saint."

The Father and His Holy Spirit are always there, but it is up to you to reach out and connect, so the Trinity can be fully affected.

Thus, we read in the Book of Matthew today how Jesus told his

# After Pentecost Sermons: Trinity Sunday, Year A

disciples, "All authority in heaven and on earth has been given to me." All was given to Jesus by the Holy Spirit, the Firmament to which Jesus connected to Heaven, while on earth.

Jesus then instructed his disciples, "Go and make disciples of all nations, baptizing them in the name of the Father and of the Son and of the Holy Spirit." Jesus told them to do as he had done, so they would become the Son reincarnated, with Jesus Resurrected within them, through the Holy Spirit.

In turn, that would make eleven Jesus' rather than one. Those eleven would make disciples of all nations, just as Jesus had made disciples.

Jesus was telling them of the exponential power that was possible, if they would be found "teaching [others] to obey everything that I have commanded you." Just as I have told you to go and make disciples, you will tell your disciples to go and make disciples too.

Throughout all this process, into all times to come, Jesus said to the disciples, "I am with you always, to the end of the age."

The end of the age is when people stop passing the torch of the Holy Spirit, when people stop becoming Jesus and reaching out to new disciples.

In the reading from Matthew, we heard, "When [the disciples] saw [Jesus on the Mount of Olives], they worshipped him; but some doubted."

The Hebrew of that verse says, "*kai idontes auton prosekynesan; hoi de edistasan,*" which literally states, "And having seen him they worshipped; they moreover wavered."

To say "they worshipped" Jesus, that is a statement about how much the disciples honored Jesus, as the Son of God. Those who followed Jesus, as disciples, saw many reasons to have such faith in a man. They prayed to Jesus to give them that faith and ability. They were disciples, where a "disciple" is "a pupil" or "a learner," by definition, with that meaning coming from the Latin root word "*discere*." From that same word we get the word "discern," which puts a disciple on an intellectual plane, rather than a spiritual one.

If you recall last week, the Book of Acts referred to the pupils of Jesus as "Apostles." They had their graduation ceremony on the Day of Pentecost. They stopped being mental and let the force of God, the mind of Christ, take control.

Today's Gospel reading focuses on the day before the Day of Pentecost, as Jesus was about to Ascend to the Father. Matthew admitted the eleven were disciples, not yet apostles.

Matthew said, "They worshipped" Jesus, so they prayed to him and believed in him, because Jesus was doing amazingly worthy of belief things. The pupils loved Jesus as a deity, the Son of God.

However, "they wavered," "they doubted," "they hesitated."

When the translation says, "Some doubted," which is an error of translation, due to some seeing no reason to repeat the word "they," as meaning all of them. But that is wrong.

All the disciples hesitated thinking they could replace Jesus. They all doubted they could be like Jesus. They all wavered in their sense of security that they were ready to see Jesus leave them alone, no longer a man with them on the physical plane.

I believe there are many here among us who also "waver, hesitate, and doubt" that the time has come to step up and do as Jesus commanded his disciples: "Go and make disciples of others."

# After Pentecost Sermons: Trinity Sunday, Year A

Remember how there is a duality that has two separate parts that never physically touch – Heaven and Earth. Instead of saying Heaven and Earth, see this as Light and Darkness. See this as the Spiritual and the Physical. Know that there is Good and there is Evil.

As human beings, of matter, in darkness, surrounded and influenced by evil, that is all we can ever be … without some form of support … some bridge that can elevate us.

The "dome" that needs to separate us from the earthly, which can then connect us to the heavenly, is the Holy Spirit.

It is the hand of God, advocated by Christ, which comes to raise us to godly states of being, so we can bring a recreated Jesus into this dark world.

We are like matchsticks that wait striking, so the light can come upon us, so that others can be led.

Therefore, Trinity Sunday represents the fulfillment of the graduation ceremony that took place last Sunday, where all we learned has set in and taken effect, spiritually. We become the firmament for others of the Earth, to show them the light to Heaven.

We each should transform into Apostles through the faith of worship, letting our wavering, our doubting, and out hesitation drop like shackles and binding chains unloosed. We must see how freedom can only come when we cease following and become leaders.

May the power of the Holy Spirit have you walk in Light, to the glory of the Lord, with the eternal blessings of Christ.

Amen

# SECOND SUNDAY AFTER PENTECOST

# Proper 7

# YEAR A

**Relevant readings:**
Genesis 21:8-21
Psalm 86:1-10; 16-17
Jeremiah 20:7-13
Psalm 69: 8-20
Romans 6:1-11
Matthew 10:24-39

After Pentecost Sermons: Proper 7, Year A

# Maturing in Christ means weaning yourself from sin

In the Genesis reading today, we hear it beginning by making the statement about Isaac growing from birth "and was weaned." The Jewish custom thus applying to today's reading recognizes a Ceremony of Weaning, where the father begins to officially share in the raising of a child. A mother's breast is no longer a child's only source of nourishment and care.

Still, while that meaning applies in this reading, it is important to see the meaning of "weaning" as more than a baby ceasing to nurse. The word written, "*higamel*," also means this was a time of "ripening."

When one sees this duality of meaning, one can begin to understand how the child Isaac had matured. He had developed into a new state of being, from complete dependency on his mother's milk; to a state that was ripe for him to be able consume solid food – the bread of life.

But, in these verses read, we begin without naming Isaac, where all that was written was "The child grew." It does not say, "Isaac grew," because Isaac was not the only child in the picture.

Ishmael had likewise grown, and while he was not the focus of a "great feast," he too had "ripened" into a changed state. Ishmael "was weaned" from being a boy child, becoming a man child.

Isaac was like an apple on the tree, ready to be picked from its mother's branch. Ishmael had already been picked, and was beginning the feel the purpose of the fruit, which was to dispose of its seeds within.

Both children were at a stage of ripeness. Both children were being weaned from one stage to another. Isaac was beginning to explore the bounty of a world previously unknown. Ishmael was beginning to explore the pleasures of his sexuality previously unknown.

When we read that Sarah saw Ishmael "playing with her son Isaac," the word *"tsachaq"* is best understood when it is translated as "caressing" or "entertaining." Many use the translation as stating "mocking," "laughing," or "making sport of." A twelve-year old boy does not "play" with a twelve-month old (or younger) baby, in a normal sense of the word "play." Ishmael "entertained" himself, through "caressing," which means inappropriate "fondling" of Isaac, for personal pleasure.

As the saying goes, "Boys will be boys." However, Sarah would have nothing of that influence around Isaac, the heir of Abraham.

Isaac was born by the grace of God, through Sarah, as a priest-to-be. Sarah was protective of external influences on Isaac's growth and development, and the weaning celebration marked when Abraham would take on an equal or greater share in that protective raising process.

Ishmael's natural hormonal urges were too uncontrollable at that stage of life, as demonstrated. So, he represented a danger to Isaac ... not only physically, but emotionally and spiritually.

If it were anything less than that, then God would not have told Abraham to cast out his first-born son, as Sarah suggested.

God saved Hagar and Ishmael from death. Again, we see how water played a role.

The physical water inside an animal-skin canteen only keeps one wanting more water. When that runs out, dehydration occurs. However, God gave them a well of spiritual water.

After Pentecost Sermons: Proper 7, Year A

With that infusion, Hagar saw a physical well and got water to save herself and Ishmael.

When God told Hagar, "Lift up the boy and hold him fast with your hand," this is not a direction to reattach herself to her son, as an apple tree would do to its fallen fruit. The direction was to use parental influence on a pre-teen, so he would not be led astray. Ishmael needed to be guided to control his sexual urges.

When we see that Hagar found Ishmael a wife from Egypt, we then see how she was holding fast to Ishmael's development, to wean him from immature selfishness, leading him to adult responsibilities.

With his mother filled with the spirit of God, Ishmael grew out of that "experimental age," because of his mother's guidance.

Ishmael had children, as the Lord promised. When God said, "I will make a great nation of him," that nation became Arabia, the homeland of all Arabs.

Ishmael died, in a sense, and was reborn as his mother wished him to be.

In the reading from Romans, Paul asked the question, "How can we who died to sin go on living in it?" This reflects upon the death of Ishmael – as he was given up for dead, without physical water to survive in the wilderness. He was resurrected by spiritual water, through divine intervention, so he could fulfill his true purpose, as the father of a great nation.

We are all dead to sin, whatever "fill in the blank" sin most causes you to be "dead" to God. As human beings, we are all going to find something that delights our senses, which is sinful. Our personal experiences with sin makes us the worst people in the world to judge if something pleasureful is right or wrong. We need to call out to God ... just as "God heard the voice of the child."

You can see this Genesis reading as a statement about homosexual experimentation, where it results from a child's natural stage of sexual exuberance. But, as natural as it may seem, it is born of earthly darkness. Left unchecked, it can lead to an immature adult stage, where earthly sins and carnal delights blind one's self to the harm inflicted upon others and to oneself.

Sexuality, without the purpose of creating children, children who will be properly led by the hand to the light of maturity, is playtime. Selfishness is not a stage of light guiding one to grown-up time. It is immature ripeness, not purposeful ripeness. We call it the specific sin of "adultery," as "adulthood" is that stage of "ripening" that separates the mature from the immature.

Still, we all are born into a world of darkness, in need of light. We are reborn through the light of Christ, so once enlightened we must change. We cannot go back into the darkness to live, thinking the light always "has our back."

Knowing the light is there, but preferring to return to wallow in darkness means our "old self" never actually was crucified with Christ Jesus. So, we never died with him, and we are not going to be resurrected with him.

The "old self" is the apple on the branch, quite content just hanging there. The "old self" is then the apple too heavy to stay on the limb, falling and lying on the ground, turning from green, to red, and to dark brown, and feeling a need to release its seeds.

But, in order for a new stage to begin, the old stage must die.

The apple, once plucked, cannot reattach itself to the branch. Once eaten to the core, it can no longer be desirable as a fruit.

It must die to release the seeds, to be reborn as a provider of

# After Pentecost Sermons: Proper 7, Year A

plenty, much more than "one self."

This is the order of life.

You are born, you mature through stages, you die, and then you are resurrected through offspring.

You do not have any right to change that order, no matter how much it "entertains" you to do whatever it is that pleases you.

You do not have the right to "mock" tradition, or "laugh" at the ways that have always been, simply because your immaturity has not yet lived long enough to understand the greater importance of things beyond the here and now.

You do not have the right to "play" with your soul, as if it is something given to you to barter away; as if a soul were something selfishly "rewarding" (another translation for "*tsachaq*") when dangled at the end of a string, daring Satan to appear and snatch it up.

Jesus asked the question, "If they have called the master of the house Beelzebub, how much more will they malign those of his house?"

On one episode of *Seinfeld* the focus was on being "master of your domain." It was a challenge for self-control, at which all of the characters eventually failed.

Jesus is asking, who controls your domain? God? Or, Satan?

Jesus prefaced his question by stating, "It is enough for the disciple to be like the teacher, and the slave like the master."

That means Jesus said, "It is enough for **YOU** to be like **HIM**," but only if God is the master of your domain.

You have to be weaned from the earthly distractions. You have to grow in spirit. You have to demonstrate changes that prove you are not seeking self-pleasure, and you grow to tell others, "I could not have done this alone."

Just as Jesus said, "Fear him who can destroy both soul and body in hell," you have to realize that an empty animal skin will lead to death. Open your eyes and see the well provided by the Lord, and hold others fast by the hand so they too may be led to the light of Christ.

Because Jesus had previously said, "Have no fear of them" – the ones who call Satan the master – Jesus meant "Fear God." You should have no fear saying "No" to evil influences, because God can destroy both soul and body in hell, as the just "rewards" for those who love to wallow in a world of death, never dying, never serving a purpose for the Lord.

You are who you live with. An apple comes from an apple tree. An apple does not come from an Elm tree, or a Pecan tree, or a dog, or a house, or anything other than an apple tree.

Ishmael came from an Egyptian handmaiden, who did nothing to teach Ishmael proper manners and self-restraints … until they both died in the wilderness … to be resurrected with a purpose.

Sarah became set against her step-son, because he was upsetting the peace of Abraham's family.

She went to Abraham with a sword, not a dove. She knew what Jesus would mean when he said, "I have come to set a man against his father, and a daughter against her mother," and so on.

When you find love for sinful beings, as a personal choice over love of Christ, you become lost. Jesus said, "Take up the cross and follow me." If you are unwilling to do this, then you are "not worthy of" Christ.

# After Pentecost Sermons: Proper 7, Year A

As Barney Fife used to tell Andy, "You've got to nip it in the bud. NIP IT! NIP IT! Nip it in the bud!"

You do not lay down with dogs and expect to not wake up with fleas.

"Whoever loves son or daughter more than Jesus is not worthy of Jesus. Those who find their life will lose it, and those who lose their life for my sake will find it."

Translation: Teach your children to love Jesus above all. Those who go through stages of life will go through metamorphoses, with one death following another. We all are always looking back at our lives and seeing a version of ourselves who no longer lives.

When we look in the mirror and see someone we do not recognize, then we cling to death. When we look in the mirror and say, "Thank you Jesus," then we know we have been resurrected.

Those who die in the name of Christ will find a life full of purpose.

"So have no fear of them," when you have released your seeds into the world. When you have died in the name of Christ, then a forest of fruit-bearing trees will grow in his name after you.

Amen

# THIRD SUNDAY AFTER PENTECOST

# Proper 8

# YEAR A

**Relevant readings:**
Genesis 22:1-14
Psalm 13
   Jeremiah 28:5-9
     Psalm 89:1-4; 15-18
Romans 6:12-23
Matthew 10:40-42

After Pentecost Sermons: Proper 8, Year A

# As we ride into the valley of death, a shepherd watches over our souls

In 1854, in response to the events that occurred in the Crimean War, Lord Alfred Tennyson wrote these now famous words:

Half a league, half a league,

Half a league onward,

All in the valley of Death

Rode the six hundred.

"Forward, the Light Brigade!

"Charge for the guns!" he said:

Into the valley of Death

Rode the six hundred.

"Forward, the Light Brigade!"

Was there a man dismay'd?

Not tho' the soldier knew

Someone had blunder'd:

Theirs not to make reply,

Theirs not to reason why,

Theirs but to do and die:

Robert Tippett

Into the valley of Death

Rode the six hundred.

"Theirs not to make reply, theirs not to reason why, theirs but to do or die: Into the valley of Death." This is a statement about the role of soldiers, as dedicated servants to a nation and its philosophies, believing in its leaders.

Soldiers are trained to respond to orders, not question them. Thus, when a military leader speaks, his soldiers do as instructed.

That is a conditioned response, through drilling, voluntarily submitted to, from an initial position of faith – a faith that says, "Surely, my leaders will not send me to die for a bad cause. However, I am willing to die for my country."

We call our children who join the military "heroes." We decorate our young service men and women in ribbons and medals, to honor their dedication and service. Their loyalty and patriotism is valued.

Not long ago, we recognized Veteran's Day. Then we remembered D-Day. We salute the dead, the wounded, the scarred, and those who served.

For the most part, veterans leave the military barely older than children.

We say that those who serve – those who continue to serve, those who retire from active duty, those who retire wounded, and those who died in the name of our country, and those who gave their time for the protection of our nation's ideals: liberty, freedom, and justice – "Thank you for your service.".

To regularly maintain a supply of volunteered children to potentially put in harm's way, we prophesy a future filled with peace. Despite all the anxieties and worries that the enemies to our nation pose, as threats to our liberty, freedom, and justice, we believe our military will protect us.

In a way, when our country calls, we answer. We say, "Here I am." We stand up and salute.

Our faith in a system conditions us, just as Lord Alfred Tennyson wrote:

Ours is not to reason why,

Ours is but to do or die:

Into the valley of Death.

Many believe Tennyson wrote that last line as a direct reference to Psalm 23, verse 4, which states:

> Yea, though I walk through the valley of the shadow of death, I will fear no evil: for thou art with me; thy rod and thy staff they comfort me. (KJV)

The aspect of a valley also plays into today's Old Testament reading, although not so it is immediately seen.

God told Abraham, "Take your son and go to the land of Moriah and offer him there as a burnt offering on one of the mountains that I shall show you." Moriah is a name of a place, which stems from the Arabic word "*Marwah*," meaning any "Mountain range."

Where there are mountains, there are valleys.

If the valleys represent Death, the mountain top symbolizes Life – closer to Heaven. Keep that in mind.

Also, consider the symbolic parallel to what our national leaders have commanded: "Take you children to the land of mountain ranges and offer them there." Such a place – the *Marwah* or Moriah – is now named Afghanistan.

Keep that in mind also, if you will.

The scenario of dedication we read today in the story of Abraham and Isaac has one major difference to our national dedication to patriotism:

God saved Isaac's life. A ram was provided for the sacrifice, instead of Isaac.

That has not been the case with America's military involvement in Afghanistan. Many children have been sacrificed in the name of the United States of America.

We are so often tested through a willingness to sacrifice.

Do you believe in God? Prove it! Give your life for God!

Do you have belief in Democracy? Prove it! Give your life for America!

Do you believe we must march our children into the valley of Death? Prove it! Bury our children with flags, as we salute!

The world loves a hero.

Today's reading about Abraham volunteering Isaac to God is actually a repeated theme in the Old Testament.

When God calls, others also answer, "Here I am."

You might recall how the young prophet Samuel heard the voice

# After Pentecost Sermons: Proper 8, Year A

of God awaken him. He awoke thinking it was the judge Eli calling him.

Three times God called, "Samuel!" Each time Samuel ran to Eli and said, "Here I am."

You might remember how Isaiah had a vision, where God asked, "Who shall I send?" Isaiah answered, "Here I am. Send me."

If only we could hear the voice of God as clearly as the prophets heard that voice.

I once heard a dedicated Christian say, "What does the voice of God sound like? I have never heard it."

Perhaps he was listening for a voice that sounded like a politician? I don't know.

We tend to be more attentive to external authoritarian voices.

Patriotic Americans are willing to volunteer their services when they are still children. Adults who served as children tend to like the glory that continues to wrap around them, when they do as Abraham and offer up their children.

It has the feel of some 'rite of passage.'

We answer the call when we are young; but later we leave the volunteering up to the children.

Samuel was still a child when he answered the call.

Isaiah was still a young prophet when he volunteered to be sent by God.

We know David was anointed while still a boy shepherd and he went to battle against Goliath still a child.

That reminds me of another short story.

Do you remember the Aesop fable about the boy who cried wolf?

Here is a twist on what you have heard before.

Let's say we are in the land of Moriah – where there are mountains and valleys. The village is in the valley, by the stream. The villagers send their sheep to graze along the mountain side. They need a volunteer to watch over the flock.

A child is chosen.

The villagers need sheep for clothing and food, so they are valuable property. Because there is the danger of wolves preying on the sheep, they must be watched and cared for. But, a child is not much of a resistance against wolves.

So, we arm the shepherd boy with a horn and order him to yell in a loud voice, "**WOLF!!!**," should the flock be threatened.

Now in the story, as we know, the boy called "Wolf!" twice, when there was no real danger of wolves. Each time the villagers came running, as was the plan.

But, when the shepherd boy cried "**WOLF!!!**" for real, no one went to save the flock.

The sheep were lost, but that has no bearing on the moral of the story.

Rather than seeing how valuable property was lost … rather than focus on a failure of the villagers to respond to a call, as planned … rather than realize the villagers sent a boy to do the job of men too busy to do it … protect their sheep …

After Pentecost Sermons: Proper 8, Year A

We simply call the boy a liar.

No one trusts a liar.

Well think about what I am about to say, at least for the rest of the day today.

Imagine the flock of sheep as our souls. That is valuable property we possess.

Now, imagine our souls peacefully grazing under the watchful eye of Jesus: Our Lord and our Shepherd.

Let your mind's eye see the village in the valley below as the world and all its sin. Each day that we leave our souls to graze halfway up the mountain, we march into the valley of Death.

We fear no evil because Jesus has a rod and a staff to comfort us; but we still need to run when there is a call of danger.

Do we ever imagine Christ calling out, "Satan is coming!"?

Does our guilt from sin ever have us running up a hill to save our souls, only to find out our souls are still safe?

Thank God, it was only a test.

A test, just as we read today, "God tested Abraham."

Do we find moral conscience by calling Jesus a liar, if our souls are safe for now?

Do we see God as a prankster, when He had Abraham build an altar and place his only son, Isaac, on top of it ... only to have God then say, "I was only testing your faith?

Do we stop responding to an alarm because there is an unan-

Robert Tippett

Souls are saved by responding to tests ... unconditionally.

As we leave church today and head to our part of the village, here in the valley of Death, listen to your inner voice.

See if you can sense a child shepherd caring for his flock within you.

Amen

# FOURTH SUNDAY AFTER PENTECOST

## Proper 9

## YEAR A

**Relevant readings:**
Genesis 24:34-67
Psalm 45:11-18
 Song of Solomon 2:8-13
Zechariah 9:9-12
 *or* Psalm 145:8-15
Romans 7:15-25
Matthew 11:16-30

Robert Tippett

# Grow up and be an adult. A marriage proposal awaits your approval.

The Old Testament reading today is about marriage, like it was in the days of Abraham. Some gold jewelry was given as a way of announcing the engagement of Rebekah to Isaac, albeit the gifts were given by the father of the groom's slave – Laban.

Ladies … raise your hand if you received a nice golden nose ring from you husband, before you got married.

<Look for raised hands>

Some translations say Rebekah had an earring put on her face, but the word for "face" also means "nose" or "nostril." Besides, ears are on the head, but not the face. So, a nose ring was the gift put on the face.

The nose ring was half a shekel in gold weight. That is less than a fifth (.1826) of an ounce. She also got two bracelets, which were a total of ten shekels in gold weight. That is over 3 1/2 (3.646) ounces of gold. So, the ring for the nose was much smaller than the bracelets.

One would think it must have been a clip-on nose ring, since Laban put it on Rebekah. I doubt he had the tools to pierce her nose.

The giving of gifts was an official act of marriage proposal. The set of engagement rings is then later followed by Rebekah seeing Isaac for the first time and pulling a veil over her head.

This reading from the Book of Genesis is at the core of the Jewish marriage ceremony. It is why engagement rings are worn before a marriage and why brides wear veils still, to this day.

# After Pentecost Sermons: Proper 9, Year A

Regardless of the fact that nobody can adequately explain the symbolism behind nose rings and veils, as to what the reasoning was behind the ancient people of Abraham doing that, we still carry on the same tradition.

Following along with this marriage theme in Genesis is the lovey-dovey language of the Psalm. It sings of the "daughter" and her "beauty" and how that face will give "pleasure" to the "king." It speaks of the "princess" and her "bridesmaids" in a marriage "procession."

An optional reading for today is from the Song of Solomon, which is about the passion between two lovers, especially that love expressed in the marriage tent. That was where Isaac took Rebekah ... to consummate their marriage.

So, a strong vision of marriage is established today, but not only from a focus on love, but the willingness of a bride to serve her husband as her master. The submission of a wife to her husband is unspoken by Laban, but it is why Rebekah was asked by her family, "Will you go with this man?"

Knowing she would leave her family behind, to travel to a place she had never been, to meet some man she had never met, and to serve that man as his wife ...

Rebekah said, "I will."

Sounds a lot like "I do" doesn't it? More tradition carried on today.

With a strong marriage theme established, it then can become confusing when we turn to Paul's letter to the Romans, where sin and death are talked about. Paul even says, "Wretched man that I am! Who will rescue me from this body of death?" What does that have to do with marriage?

Then, we see Jesus talking to a crowd about people calling him a glutton and a drunkard. He thanks God for hiding things from the wise and intelligent.

Are we on the same page here?

It can seem to be mixed signals, but in reality all of the readings are focusing on marriage … just not that between a man and a woman. It is more than a physical bond and sensory delights.

I'm talking about a marriage to God.

When I was preparing to write today's sermon my mind quickly went to nuns. I had heard that Catholic nuns were married to Jesus.

When we were in seminary at Sewanee, one of the "tourist attractions" there ( at least a place where we would take visitors to see) was a convent of Episcopal nuns on the side of the mountain. It is Saint Mary's Convent. Before going to Sewanee, I had no idea there were nuns other than Catholic nuns.

According to Wikipedia, there are 2,500 "monks and nuns" in orders established by the Anglican-Episcopal Church.

Episcopal nuns are like Catholic nuns in that they are married to God. They wear a ring that symbolizes that commitment.

In short, being married to God is not expected to be a walk in the park or an automatic membership to an exclusive club. Expect a lot of hard work.

Raise your hand if you are married and never had to work at maintaining that relationship.

<Look for raised hands.>

# After Pentecost Sermons: Proper 9, Year A

There are requirements for being a Catholic nun: A woman over 18 must be single; and a woman must be physically fit (healthy).

Widows are considered single, but the health issue puts an upper age limit that is "40-ish." You can be a nun who has children, but they must be old enough to care for themselves (non-dependent).

Jesus said, "Take my yoke upon you, and learn from me; for I am gentle and humble in heart."

In other words, Jesus asked us to accept his nose ring and bracelet.

He asked, "Will you marry me?"

Nuns and monks have gone through this process, where the "engagement" period is a discernment of years. It is sort of like "living with Jesus" to see if you really want to get married.

The problem with nuns and monks marrying Christ, through cloistering and confinement, is that it makes it seem that Jesus is only to be the husband of a few.

A bride wears a veil to hide her face from other suitors. Only her husband will see her true beauty shine. Nuns wear habits. Monks wear robes with hoods. They are trying to keep others from being attracted to them because they are taken.

The aspect of a veil is not only for women. Moses had to wear a veil, after he talked with God, before he could talk to the Israelites. They would not be distracted by the bright glow that surrounded his face, so they could listen to what God had to say to them; but at the same time, seeing the veil meant Moses was all "lit up" by his relationship with God. His marriage to God required a veil.

In a way, God put a celestial "earring" on Moses' face. He wore a flashy gold piece right on the nose. The veil signalled that union. In art, they depict a golden ring over a saint's head – a halo. The same thing can be read into that.

In the Genesis story, Abraham had sent Laban, his servant, on a quest to find his son Isaac a bride. Valuable gifts were to be given to the bride-to-be as an "engagement" to the son, sight unseen. The bride-to-be would wear a veil before consummating the marriage to the son, the bridegroom. Once consummated, the two became husband and wife, forever married.

In the story of Jesus in the New Testament, God sends Apostles, His servants, on a quest to find the Son of God, Christ Jesus, many brides. The gifts of the Holy Spirit are to be given to the brides-to-be as an "engagement" to the Son, sight unseen. The brides-to-be cannot show these gifts before consummating the marriage to the Son, the bridegroom. Once consummated, the two become heart and soul, forever married as one.

Jesus thanked the Father by saying, "You have hidden these things from the wise and intelligent." You have placed a veil over the face of those filled with the Holy Spirit, so big-brained people cannot understand them by their physical senses.

Jesus said, "You have revealed them (the gifts of the Holy Spirit) to infants." An infant is a newborn. The gifts of the Holy Spirit have been revealed to those who have been Reborn anew, as infants who represent the Resurrection of Christ. They become newborns in a marriage of spirit and body.

The problem comes when we do not go to the well, as did Rebekah, with a commitment to serve anyone other than ourselves. If someone is there, like Laban, do you offer to not only get him a drink, but also water all the camels that come along with this stranger?

# After Pentecost Sermons: Proper 9, Year A

Are you going to the well like the Samaritan woman – regardless of what sex you are – having had five previous commitments that failed, so that now you are living with someone ... in case that fails too? Are you living a life of self-fulfilling prophecies of failure?

Do you resent having to go to the well? Would you answer, "I will," to the question, "Will you go with this man" if you knew it were Jesus? Do you have to hear him say he has living water that never needs re-dipping to quench your thirst?

Everyone sitting here today has a proposal from Christ. "Will you marry him?"

Christ is the husband. You are the wife.

For all males in the congregation, that is the only value of same sex marriage ... without any focus being on the physical union of two. A marriage to Christ is always a spiritual union.

There is no need for procreation in Heaven, so sex organs need not apply.

Paul was speaking of those who could not make a commitment ... those who could not say, "I will."

He lamented as one who is noncommittal, when he said, "I do not understand my own actions. For I do not do what I want, but I do the very thing I hate."

You want to commit. You like the idea of special gifts being given to you. You like the idea of marriage to God; but then you think, "I don't want to be a nun." Or, "I don't want to be a monk."

I like to have fun!

But … after you have "fun!" you hate yourself. You feel guilty. You feel dirty. You feel ashamed. "Fun" is like a 45-record ... after 3 minutes the song is over. What then?

Being married to Christ means you have to stay within the law. That means you can no longer "play the field." You have to maintain fidelity. You are an adult that likes to play adult games; but marriage means no more "adultery." No more **SIN!** No more **FUN!**

Being left at the altar is a lonely feeling.

Paul wrote, "For I know that nothing good dwells within me, that is, in my flesh. I can will what is right, but I cannot do it."

You cannot force yourself into marriage. You have to want it. If you have Christianity forced upon you, then "evil lies close at hand."

You imagine how being true to the LORD is too much hard work, with no real reward ... only promise.

Jesus compared his generation, where it is irrelevant when one reads his words, such that it is always "this generation" that he is referring to. Jesus said, "It is like children sitting in the marketplaces and calling to one another, "We played the flute for you, but you did not dance; we wailed, and you did not mourn."

"Children" means not being a mature adult.

"Sitting" means doing nothing of merit – idleness - all while the mind is filled with imaginative thoughts.

The "marketplace" is the mall, the ads on television, the ads on the Internet. It is all the distractions of a "gimme, gimme, gimme" world.

# After Pentecost Sermons: Proper 9, Year A

"Calling to one another" means staying in a child's world, only talking with other children. That does not mean actual children, but anyone. In today's age of hand attachments, called smart phones, are you not always "calling to one another"?

When we "play the flute" and people don't "dance," we want things to go our way, but we do not get it. That makes it become tantrum time.

When we "wail," we want people to feel sorry for us. We want people to be conditioned to please us or rue our tears. That is a child's way of acting.

The message today is "Grow up and be an adult. A marriage proposal awaits your approval."

A favorite band of mine is Tears For Fears. A song they did back in the 80's is named "Advice for the Young at Heart."

The lyrics to that song speak to the child in us all.

The song goes:

> "Soon we will be older
>
> When we gonna make it work?
>
> Love is promise
>
> Love is a souvenir
>
> Once given
>
> Never forgotten, never let it disappear
>
> This could be our last chance

When we gonna make it work ?"

Jesus said, "You will find rest for your souls. For my yoke is easy, and my burden is light."

Jesus wants to know when are we gonna say, "I will?"

Amen

# FIFTH SUNDAY AFTER PENTECOST

## Proper 10

## YEAR A

**Relevant readings:**
Genesis 25:19-34
Psalm 119:105-112
Isaiah 55:10-13
Psalm 65: 1-14
Romans 8:1-11
Matthew 13:1-23

Robert Tippett

# In a world full of choices, how much consideration do you give God?

Today's lessons focus on **choices**.

Esau **chose** to sell his birthright for a bowl of stew, because he was "famished."

Jacob **chose** to make a bargain of food to his hungry brother, rather than give him what he needed.

Paul told the Christians of Rome you have to **choose** between sin and righteousness, to pick either the flesh and death or the Spirit and eternity.

Jesus said you have to **choose** what you want to understand of the Word.

Do you **not** want to understand the meaning? Do you **not** want to only hear it, preferring to plead ignorance because of a lack of understanding?

Are you okay with receiving understanding with joy, as if allowed to hold something holy; but then have that joy fall away when troubles arise, all because you do not see how the holy meaning is applicable in today's world ... to you specifically?

Do you want hear the word and pretend to care for the world, by misunderstanding the intent of the word; so, you can then be lured away from caring by the choking hold of material goals and objectives?

Or, do you want to understand the Word so you can tell others and teach them how to understand and bear good fruit and yields?

The **choices** we make today are what will create our future. Choices are important.

Who here buys a car because you have the utmost faith that car manufacturers would never make an unsafe vehicle, would never overprice a vehicle unnecessarily, and would never lie and mislead in their advertising? Who walks in to a dealership, points to a car, and pays cash on the spot without even a test drive?

The answer is nobody.

We typically put much more time and effort into deciding what car to buy, which house we can afford, and what cell phone or computer we want, than we put into understanding what the Book of Genesis says … what the letter to the Romans means … or seeing how there are hungry birds, wilting heat, and choking thorns all around us.

"Why should I understand the Word, when I have a priest to tell me the meaning?" Some might think that.

Jesus said, "Let anyone with ears listen!" The exclamation point means that instruction should be emphasized.

It really says, <screaming> "**LISTEN UP PEOPLE!!!**"

"**HEAR THE PARABLE OF THE SOWER!!!**"

But, when we are born of sinful flesh … as everyone here is, as every human being on earth is … we have to deal with sin.

Paul wrote that Jesus, God's own Son, was made of sinful flesh, the same as we are. Jesus knew how to avoid all the mistakes of choosing sin … unlike everyone else during his life. We have the same difficulty everyone else had.

If only our sinful flesh came with a sensory organ that could make us so aware of sin. Then we would be repulsed and go away from it, rather than be attracted to and embrace it.

If only sin stunk to high heavens.

If only sin tasted sour and bitter.

If only sin felt slimy and dirty.

If only sin looked ugly and grotesque.

If only sin sounded alarms and made unwanted noises, like chalk on a blackboard or a vuvuzela's blast.

But, sin is not unattractive. It smells like perfume, tastes like candy, feels like satin, looks alluring, and sounds like what we want to hear.

Sinful flesh is found clinging to the bones of the politician you adore so much. Without having ever been close enough to understand exactly what he or she does behind closed doors, you give them votes of confidence.

Sinful flesh is found under the robes of the theologians whose books you read, who writes so many explanations about the meaning of Scripture, those that, no matter how hard you try, you can only memorize so many before you begin mixing up one story with another.

Sinful flesh is covered in makeup and costumes on the movie or television actors ... those you idolize so much that you can barely wait to see his or her new show. Sin surrounds the directors and script writers, whose interpretations and adaptations you would sit at a cafe for hours dissecting. If given the chance.

Sinful flesh is on everyone who follows false prophets, like the

After Pentecost Sermons: Proper 10, Year A

children of Hamlin followed the Pied Piper.

Never do any of those sinful flesh influencers grab you by the arm and force you to submit to their will.

You **choose** them, because they know what makes you tick. They know what allures you, so they promise you what they know you want. When you have studied what they have to offer and become filled with the imaginary selfish delights they propose, you **choose** them.

"Will it be the BMW? Or, the GM?" The **choice** is yours.

As the saying goes, "You get what you pay for."

As far as "understanding the Word" goes, you get back what you put in towards understanding. Just put in a little and find your seed has been sowed in all the wrong places. Put in a lot and find your seed has found good soil.

You get what you work for.

When you have been planted in good soil, you grow strong and tall, bearing good fruit, which turns into many seeds. Those seeds can then be planted and allowed to grow in the same good soil, themselves producing good fruit. The result is a bountiful yield, with crops that satisfy many.

So, the metaphor is this: God makes the first seeds – you ... us. You sow them where you see best – either in the world of sin or in the spirit of righteousness, which is Jesus Christ.

Jesus Christ is the good soil.

Wherever you plant your seed, you become a plant. We call plants "plants" because they do not have legs and feet, with which to walk about and travel from place to place.

When you place your seed in the good soil of Jesus Christ, you stay put. You grow as a true Christian. The nutrients you digest come from the Word. The understanding you generate comes from the living water that enters your roots. You produce the fruits of the Holy Spirit.

Now, human plants do have feet and legs, so it is possible for us to move all around the world. We can be globe-trotting plants, depending on how well we can afford the travel expenses. We can be local plants or international plants.

The analogy of us being plants then asks how deep our roots are in Christ. How deep does the Holy Spirit grow within us, so that we may endure the temptations of the sinful-flesh world, and still **choose** Spiritual life over worldly death?

Paul said, "There is no condemnation for those who are in Christ Jesus." "No condemnation" means we live "according to the Spirit." Paul wrote, "To set the mind on the flesh is death, but to set the mind on the Spirit is life and peace."

When he says "set the mind," we must have an "understanding of the Word," such that we realize "set the mind" is not meant as a declaration of will. It means more than simply **hearing** how living "according to the Spirit" must be, and believing what we **hear**. It means more than being filled with the joy of **hearing** how wonderful it is to live "according to the Spirit" …

… and then wandering out into the world, setting the mind on the flesh, and acting in deeds that are "hostile to God," and "cannot please God."

Paul clarified the meaning of "set the mind on the Spirit" by saying, "If Christ is in you, though the body is dead because of sin, **the Spirit is life** because of **righteousness**." Your mind can only be "set on the Spirit" if "Christ is in you." If Christ controls your thoughts, then your actions are **righteous**. Only if you are the resurrection of Jesus, in the flesh, can you be **righteous**.

That is why Paul said, "If the Spirit of him who raised Jesus from the dead dwells in you, he who raised Christ from the dead will give life to your mortal bodies also through his Spirit that dwells in you."

You are planted in the Holy Spirit, and you do not walk away from that soil … ever.

Now, take the example of Jacob. He was born of sinful flesh, so he tricked Esau into selling his birthright for stew. That is not having the mind set on the Spirit. It is having the mind set on the flesh.

Jacob did a lot of sinful deeds of the flesh. Jacob also faced one trial after another; including fearing that his brother Esau was hunting for him, wanting to kill him. Can you see that story being retold in the Israeli-Palestinian discontent?

We have to understand the Word and see how Jacob had an epiphany. He wrestled with an angel all night long. He came away a changed man. He took on the name Israel, to proclaim that change. He let Esau have the land of his original birthright, going into Egypt and dying there.

We read that Jacob was of a quiet nature. He wasn't always on the move and actively aggressive, like Esau. Because he was quiet, he was capable of listening. He had ears that could hear.

As Israel, his mind understood the word and his mind became set on the Spirit. He accepted that he must face his troubles, not run from them. He became the seed God would plant, which would produce fruit and yields.

We are sown from those seeds of Israel, which God sowed. Jesus was one of those seeds, through the fruit of Mary, a descendant of Jacob, Isaac, Abraham, and Adam. We are descended from the seed when our minds are set on the Spirit, through Christ.

Still, as human beings born of sinful flesh, it is ultimately up to us to **choose** our fate. We are not the firstborn. We come into this world clinging to someone else's heel. We have no birthright that will save us from death of the flesh.

We must wrestle with our own angel and come to the realization that we will be measured by the fruit and yield that comes from us. We must determine where our minds will be planted.

"Let anyone with ears listen! When anyone hears the Word of the kingdom and does **not understand** it, the **evil** one comes and **snatches away** what is sown in the **heart**."

"The one who hears the Word and understands it, [is him or her] who indeed bears fruit and yields," many times over. That is all who are planted in the Holy Spirit.

We need volunteers for Bible Studies next Sunday. We need those who understand the Word, and we need those who want to be taught to understand.

Will you be there? The **choice** is yours.

Amen

# SIXTH SUNDAY AFTER PENTECOST

# Proper 11

# YEAR A

**Relevant readings:**
Genesis 28:10-19
Psalm 139:1-23
 *or* Wisdom of Solomon
   12:16-19
Isaiah 44:6-8
Psalm 86:11-17
Matthew 13:24-43
Romans 8:12-25

Robert Tippett

# Sown as good seed amid weeds

In 1974 I had an accident where I had some compression fractures in three vertebrae of my upper back. The required healing process meant I had to learn to sleep on my back or side. Prior to that, I preferred sleeping on my stomach and sleeping on my back did not feel right. I could not sleep on my stomach and have my vertebrae grow properly, so I learned to sleep on my side; but I had to make sure I would not roll onto my stomach during sleep. To assist me in that, I began hugging a pillow when I went to bed.

In 2010 I had hip replacement surgery. The doctor told me I needed to sleep with a pillow between my legs, due to the artificial hip joint. The leg for that hip could not cross my other leg, and it could not even lean against the other leg while sleeping. As a result, I now sleep with three pillows: one under my head, one between my legs, and one "huggie pillow" that keeps me from sleeping on my stomach. It is okay for me to sleep on my stomach now, but I have simply grown accustomed to holding a pillow while I sleep that I can't give up.

According to Wikipedia, pillows date back to 7,000 BC. However, the article reports that a long time passed when, "only the wealthy and more fortunate people of the world were the ones who used pillows."

The article also said, "Pillows have always been produced around the world in order to help solve the old, reoccurring problem of neck, back, and shoulder pain while sleeping. The pillow was also used in order to keep bugs and insects out of people's hair, mouth, nose, and ears while sleeping."

It goes on to tell about the Egyptian development of pillows, saying, "Ancient Egyptian pillows were wooden or stone headrests."

# After Pentecost Sermons: Proper 11, Year A

Adding, "These pillows were mostly used by placing them under the heads of the deceased because the head of a human was considered to be the essence of life and sacred."

I remember watching a television show that showed what the homes of Pompeii revealed. The beds found in rooms of villas owned by wealthy people looked like they were carved in stone, with a stone bump at the head of the bed, like a stone pillow-roll. It was like a marble chaise lounge.

I remember thinking, "Surely, they put some blankets or straw on that, in order to get comfortable enough to fall asleep."

When the Jews dine for the Passover Seder meal, they practice a ritual called "leaning." They lay on their sides, on pillows, while eating. This is a symbol of the luxury of freedom. It is explained by them learning, "it was the custom of noble men to eat while reclining on a sofa or on cushions."

When we see how only the wealthy had pillows back in Biblical times, it is easier to see how natural it would be for Jacob to look for a stone to use as a pillow, when it came time for him to sleep.

It may be that Jacob was used to soft pillows to rest his head on, since he was the son of a priest, and maybe because he was not strong like Esau, having been a little pampered by his mother. Whatever the case, because he was travelling fast and lite, he obviously didn't take a pillow with him.

Sometimes, when I travel and stay in hotels, they only provide two pillows ... not my usual three. I never plan on travelling with a pillow, but when I find out I am one short, I always wish I had brought one with me.

I can tell you right now, if I had to use a rock as a pillow, I would not get any sleep at all. I am sure I am not the only one who would say that.

Maybe that is a curse of the luxury of freedom in this country? Perhaps we have grown too soft to sleep under the stars with our heads resting on stones?

Jacob was fleeing Beersheba, because Rebekah overheard Esau threaten to kill Jacob. Esau was mad over Jacob receiving Isaac's blessing, leaving him with nothing. She sent Jacob to travel to Haran, where her brother Laban lived. Haran was where Turkey and Syria meet today, using modern country names.

Jacob had travelled roughly 50 miles when the sun set and it was time to get some rest. Jacob slept under the stars that night, using a rock for his pillow. There had to have been some thought as to why Jacob chose that specific location.

There probably was a well nearby, as Jacob slept at a place named Luz. Named placed mean people live there, so water was necessary. The name chosen comes from a Hebrew verb, one that in the feminine can mean, "Almond wood." However, in the masculine, as "*luz*" is, it means, "Turn aside."

The masculine verb meaning is said to have a negative connotation, as: "an indication of turning away from wisdom; or a trait of deviation or crookedness in someone or something." Some think that meaning might indicate there was a crooked Almond tree near where Jacob stayed, in Luz.

Regardless of that name's meaning, we know that Jacob did not stay in an inn or at someone's house. If Esau sent people looking for him, he could have been identified by having made such contacts. So, Jacob was "on the lam."

The night that Jacob slept in the open, with his head on a stone, in the place known as "Turn aside," he dreamed of a stairway to heaven. He dreamed he stood beside God and heard his voice.

# After Pentecost Sermons: Proper 11, Year A

He dreamed he saw angels moving up and down steps connecting Heaven and earth.

When the dream was over it was the next morning. Jacob arose and stood the stone on one end. He then anointed the top of the stone with oil. That was a priestly function, where Jacob set a holy marker, a monument recognizing a place of spiritual significance.

And, from that act of recognition, we can begin to connect the story of Jacob's ladder to the parable told by Jesus, of the "Good Sower."

You see, Jacob was from good seed, not weeds. He was the son of Isaac, a descendant of Adam … a true child of God. He was a priest to the One God, and the birthright he received from Esau (regardless how) brought that distinction upon Jacob. The blessing of Isaac upon Jacob meant Jacob was seed that had been sown into the world's field.

Jacob and Esau were the seed of Isaac; but the holy lineage of Adam had come to a split in the road. Who would continue the tradition of righteousness? It would either be Esau, the first born, or it would be Jacob. Both were from good seed, but both were amid weeds sown by an enemy to God.

Jacob had deceived both his brother and his father. He had unjustly stolen his brother's blessing. He had put on the mantle of priesthood, gladly welcoming all the "things" that came with that; but he had acted in a "weedly" fashion, not like a "righteous dude."

When God stood beside Jacob at that place named "Turn aside," He told Jacob, "The land on which you lie I will give to you and to your offspring." God would seal that deal of birthright and all the possessions the birthright entailed. Nothing would transpire because Jacob stole from his brother, such that possession could be challenged in some court. After all, Esau knew he was not of priestly cloth. He loved the games of the world ... he loved lying in the weeds.

God then said to Jacob, "Your offspring will be like the dust of the earth, and you shall spread abroad to the west and to the east and to the north and to the south; and all the families of the earth shall be blessed by your offspring." That meant the children that were still to be born to Jacob would spread around the world, in all directions, beyond the boundaries of Canaan.

Finally, God said to Jacob, "Know that I am with you and will keep you wherever you go, and will bring you back to this land; for I will not leave you until I have done what I have promised you." That meant more than leaving Canaan and returning to Canaan, that land, or the much later nation that would take on the names: Israel ... Judea ... Palestine ... Israel. It meant God would bring Jacob back to this place where his head was then being supported by a stone, as he slept where there was a gateway to Heaven.

Jesus said that his parable included a field, which was the world. The field represents earth, dust, and land. The land of Canaan, no matter what name it would be called, was no more than a plot of field to be planted.

When Jesus said, "The good seed are the children of the kingdom," he did not mean everyone in the world is a child of God. They are not. Abraham sent Laban to Ur to find a wife for Isaac, so Isaac would not marry a Canaanite woman. The "children of the kingdom" are the priests dedicated to the LORD; and Jacob was "good seed."

At that time in his life, Jacob was just surrounded by too many weeds of influence, weeds of opportunity that seemed to offer things too good to let pass. He was running with the children of the evil one, who were the weeds representing a speedy life, too busy with selfish concerns to have hope for something unseen. Weeds do not require patience to reap, as do wheat fields.

God does not take up his good wheat because it is surrounded by evil weeds. That would destroy the good wheat along with the weeds. Instead, God lets everything grow to maturity, until when it is time for harvesting. Jacob was a young sprout of wheat, caught up in trying to compete with the weeds surrounding him. For a while, he must have thought like a weed, and acted like one of those sown by the evil one.

But, then Jacob had an epiphany. He slept and dreamed of God talking to him, promising him the world, through his children, those that were still some time away. Jacob began a transformation at that time; turning into the good seed and the good purpose he was sown to grow into, to become what he was meant to be … a child of the kingdom of Heaven … a priest for the One God.

When Jacob rested his head on that stone and dreamed of a ladder to Heaven, he was troubled in heart and mind. He was fearful about the many things going on in his life, which was not the first or last time troubled sleep has occurred. Jacob's worries then are no different than those anyone has ever had, based on current troubles and fears. We all are Jacob, in that sense, at some crossroad in life.

Paul wrote to the Christians of Rome, saying, "The sufferings of this present time are not worth comparing with the glory about to be revealed to us." Paul was writing to good seed, those who had transformed through Christ and become good seed, no longer distracted by the weeds surrounding them.

Those Christians were initially Jews, representing the children of Jacob, who would fulfil God's promise and go in all directions around the world. We are the good seed that has been spread from their wheat. The Christians of Paul's day, just like the followers of Jesus, and just like Jacob, all were mixed with evil bad seed, which was sown by the devil for the purpose of choking out the yield of the good seed. We are no different today; and by understanding that, we should see how Paul is also speaking to us in his letter.

Paul wrote, "All creation was subjected to futility, not of its own will but by the will of the one who subjected it, in hope that the creation itself will be set free from its bondage to decay and will obtain the freedom of the glory of the children of God." That means we are simply plants in a field, with no control over what grows beside us. All we can do is grow into what we were sown to become. Once the body has served its purpose, the hope is that the soul will return to God.

This is the "up and down" of the ladder Jacob saw. We come from Heaven, with the purpose being to return. The place of that ladder was named "Turn aside," where we are influenced to turn away from that return route, so that it is up to us to turn away from that distracting us.

Jacob renamed that place Beth-el, meaning "the House of God." It is about ten miles north of Jerusalem, which was then known as Salem. The King of Salem was Melchizedek, who is believed (according to the Midrash) to have given Abram the robes of Adam.

Think about that for a moment. Melchizedek, who was neither born nor died, ruled over a holy city just a few miles south of where a ladder goes to and from Heaven, named "Turn aside." How did Melchizedek come into possession of Adam's robes?

Was the place Jacob slept the same place where God turned aside Adam and Eve? Did Jacob choose to sleep where the portal to Heaven is? Was Salem the Holy City outside the gate to heaven? Was Melchizedek the physical embodiment of a Cherub, free to go up and down the ladder to Heaven at will?

## After Pentecost Sermons: Proper 11, Year A

Jacob awoke from his dream, saying, "Surely the LORD is in this place – and I did not know it!" It is a real stairway, but one that can only be seen through divine guidance.

That gate, guarded by cherubim and a flashing sword, is where good seed is gathered and taken to find their hope rewarded. That is where their souls will be laid in the barn of the master, while the weeds will be bound in bundles and burned at the end of an age.

We have to see how Christ is our rock, upon whom we lay our heads. We give to Jesus our minds and our thoughts. Christ provides needed support, but that might not be soft, fluffy, and easily molded to fit our big heads. Our dreams should not be of "the American dream," where visions of wealth, power, and the illusion of freedom are what we pray to see through wake-state eyes. Instead, we should desire the "Good Seed Dream," where we transform from a downward lean, towards weeds, and begin to stand tall and strong golden grains of wheat.

This dream can only be realized through the fulfillment of our prayers: that we will be adopted by the Holy Spirit. Once adopted, we become the children of God, His good seed, one with God and unable to ever change that arrangement. Christ is the mediator of those prayers, who takes our petitions, judges our hearts, and rules fairly on who will receive the Spirit. Adoption is not a speedy course. That dream must be our hope, and our hope can only be for an unseen reward.

We must wait for it with patience, just as a seed must rise towards the sun over a full season of growth. We must rise above the weeds and prove our worth.

Amen

# SEVENTH SUNDAY AFTER PENTECOST

# Proper 12

# YEAR A

**Relevant readings:**
Genesis 29:15-28
Psalm 105:1-11
 *or* Psalm 128
   1 Kings 3:5-12
    Psalm 119:129-136
Romans 8:26-39
Matthew 13:31-52

After Pentecost Sermons: Proper 12, Year A

# When your goal is what you love, you will work ceaselessly to make sure you reach that goal

Raise your hand if you married your first cousin.

<look for any raised hands>

That is what Jacob did. Laban was Rebekah's brother, making Rachel his first cousin.

Jerry Lee Lewis, of course, did marry his first cousin once removed; meaning one their grandparents was the great grandparent of the other. Maybe Jerry Lee Lewis's grandfather was also the great grandfather of Myra Gayle Brown; but maybe the grandmother was not the same great grandmother?

Whatever the details, that marriage did not go over very well for "the Killer," whereas it was okay for Jacob to not only marry cousin Rachel … but also cousin Leah.

We have already read about Abraham sending his servant to Ur to find a wife for Isaac. Laban brought back Rebekah, the daughter of Abraham's brother, so Isaac also married his first cousin.

Abraham did not want Isaac to marry one of those Canaanite women. That had nothing to do with the Canaanite women being uglier or more demanding. Instead, it had everything to do with pedigree. Abraham wanted Isaac to produce children through a woman of similar blood.

As they say, "Blood is thicker than water." That means, "family ties (blood) are always more important (thicker) than the ties you make among friends (water). It generally means that the bonds of family and common ancestry are stronger than the bonds between unrelated people (such as what friendships represent)." [from an Wikipedia article on the subject]

Abraham wanted a wife for Isaac that would maintain a holy bloodline. He wanted to keep everything "in the family tree."

These days we worry about the problems that might occur from "in-breeding." There are laws against marrying a first cousin in half of the states (25), with Mississippi one of them. Still, marriages of that nature are allowed in 19 states, plus the District of Columbia. It is allowed under certain conditions in seven other states, generally being when offspring will not result.

In the days of Abraham, Isaac, and Jacob, the same potential genetic problems might have existed, but we don't know about any such problems, because that has no bearing on the purpose of the books we read from the Holy Bible. We only know that which is relative to the history of our religion.

One problem that might have resulted, however, is a difficulty for the women to get pregnant. That is a common element repeated in that history.

It took a miracle for Sarah to have Isaac, after she had been "barren" for the first 90 years of her life. Rebekah was barren too, for the first 20 years of her marriage to Isaac. That led to Isaac asking God for some help having a child.

When you read a little further in Genesis (in chapter 35), you find out that Rachel not only had a difficult time conceiving, but she died after giving birth to Benjamin, the last of Jacob's 12 children, her second.

With all these stories of the women in the family tree of Adam having difficulty getting pregnant, you would think someone

# After Pentecost Sermons: Proper 12, Year A

would have figured out, "Maybe we do need to look for one of those Canaanite women as brides for our sons?"

God was speaking to them back then, and He never told them to go outside their family tree – their blood – "their kinsman," as Laban called Jacob – to find wives. God only said, "I will give this land to your descendants."

That family tree would lead to Jesus, and there are some who believe, one way or another, that the family tree was continued in Europe, after Jesus Ascended. That bloodline explanation is what the royal families of Europe have held dear, as it was what gave those of the last sixteen hundred years their birthrights to lead nations.

The way that system worked for a long time was simple: royalty had to marry royalty … their blood – "their kin" – in order to maintain the purity that made them worthy of being born to rule. They did not let their princes marry some pretty young commoner. They had arranged marriages, where marriage meant having children. It was the same reasoning that had Abraham say, "I don't want my son to marry one of those Canaanite women."

Regardless of how you think about that concept of royalty, the "family tree" of us "ordinary " human beings is a mess. It has evolved and devolved over the ages.

They say that in a short time down the road of America's future, "There will no longer be found physical traits in the populace that distinguish one race from another." Americans will have crossbred all of the unique features of its grandparents … Europeans, Africans, Chinese, Mexicans, Hawaiians, Eskimos, Cherokees, Mohicans, *et al*, into one generic composite, into a yet to be named breed. We call dogs of that mixture "Heinz 57's." In that sense, us Americans are losing any pedigree we had, making us mongrels and curs.

I imagine it will still be a preference among devout Jews to marry within their race. After all, their disdain of Samaritans was largely due to the Jews of Samaria having intermingled with their foreigner occupiers.

In the first parable we hear Jesus tell the crowd, he spoke of a specific seed … a mustard seed … which had a uniqueness that was understood by all who heard. A mustard seed is a very small seed.

I imagine **if** God wanted all seeds to be alike … as a generic "seed" for a generic "plant," bearing some generic "fruit" … then He would have changed everything at the Creation. Had God done that, the mention of a "mustard seed" would have gone over everyone's head.

"Mustard seed? What's that? I don't get the analogy."

By Jesus being able to specifically name one type of seed, he was able to create a clear picture in everyone's mind. A mustard seed was known to be very tiny.

As seemingly small and insignificant as a mustard seed is in appearance, if properly planted in good soil it can turn into a mighty tree. It can then live up to its special purpose. That special purpose is not only to produce more seeds, so more mustard trees can be grown, but it also has the purpose of spreading out many branches that allow the birds of the air to make their nests there.

That analogy was intended to touch each one who was listening, individually. Alone, outside of a crowd, as one of a whole race of people who "all look alike," everyone is important in the kingdom of heaven, even as one tiny seed of humanity.

Jacob was a tiny seed when he dreamed of a ladder to heaven. He was a tiny seed when he met his uncle Laban. So, being just

After Pentecost Sermons: Proper 12, Year A

one little seed of many does not mean you have no importance.

Then Jesus told of yeast, which is a unique microorganism. It is said to be "one of the earliest domesticated organisms." [Wikipedia] There are at least 1,500 species of yeast identified. Some yeast is used in the fermentation of fruit juices into wine, and grain juice into ales and beers. In measures of flour, especially those mixed with milk, eggs, and sugar, they produce gasses that make dough swell into large spongy loaves.

Yeast is tiny too!

Just as the small mustard seed grows into a mighty tree, so too does a little dough become leavened and rise to greater capacities ... just by mixing in a little yeast.

The mustard seed symbolizes us being planted into good soil, where the right environment allows us to draw the proper nutrients into us, allowing maximum growth potential. Yeast symbolizes an agent introduced into us, which raises us to greater proportions. Both good soil and yeast symbolizes the Holy Spirit. Without that agent, we only amount to a tiny seed or a measure of flour.

Now in the Genesis story we read how Laban let Jacob state what his wages for service would be. Jacob was the one who came up with his wage being a wife. Because Jacob so loved Rachel, he set the number of years of service for her hand in marriage at seven.

Laban asked, "What shall your wages be?" "Wages" come from as a justification for work and service. We work for pay. "The laborers deserve their pay." We are rewarded by wages; but the rewards only come after we have put in the required effort.

Jesus told the parable of "treasure hidden in a field, which someone found and hid." He then told of "a merchant in search of fine pearls finding one pearl of great value." We are told of the individual rewards each man had earned for work done, for services rendered. Both had amassed "everything they owned," from lifetimes of working for wages, and using wages to buy what they needed and wanted.

In the parables, one man joyfully sells everything he owns to buy the field with the hidden treasure, which he KNOWS is there. The merchant also "sold all that he had," so he could buy the "one pearl of great value." They had worked and served for all that they had, but they worked in a different way when they sold everything in order to get a greater reward.

Jacob worked to get Rachel. His personally set term of seven years earned him a wife – Leah. Laban told Jacob that traditions had greater value than personal wants. Thus, we work a lifetime to get rewarded by traditional means. Our efforts bring us wages to buy things. When Laban offered that Jacob could put in another seven years of service to get what he loved – Rachel - Jacob took up that challenge.

The first seven years went by quickly. That is how fast life passes us by, while we work to earn things to surround us ... things we need, and things we want. The second seven years was probably harder work. Still, Jacob did what it took to get the greater reward of Rachel. He did it because the wage was fair. The man sold everything for a field of promised riches, which was a fair cost. The merchant sold all he had to buy the perfect pearl, which was also a fair cost.

Selling everything you have to get what you love is a fair expense. Otherwise, what you thought was love was just infatuation.

Now Jesus then told a parable about fish caught in a net. The catch included "fish of every kind." This means there were different species of creatures that dwelled in water, with each recognized by a specific name. They were identified as "edible" and "inedible." They were sorted on the shore as "good fish" or "bad fish," where a "good fish" would be like a Tilapia, and a "bad fish" would be like eels and barbels (catfish).

The "good fish" get put in a basket for keeping, while the "bad fish" are thrown away.

This was an analogy of what happens to "good people" and "bad people" at "the end of an age." All of the parables were relative to attaining the "kingdom of heaven." So, either you plant yourself in the good soil of Christianity, become risen by the Holy Spirit of God, realize there is a treasure hidden for you in heaven, which is like a pearl of great value that you know about, so you work however long it may take to make sure you have earned the wage of the kingdom of heaven … or you get tossed in the furnace of fire, where all the "bad fish" go.

Of course, we all know that. After all, we are 21st century human beings, with big brains. We are confirmed Christians that, in the species of human fish, are called *Westernus episcopalyanis* … or something like that. So, we like to consider ourselves "good fish." We think we should go into the basket, not get thrown away.

So, Jesus asked the crowd who had just heard him tell a string of parables, "Have you understood all this?" They said, "Yes."

We say the same. "Sure, we get your point Jesus."

Jesus then heard that answer and said, "Every scribe who has been trained for the kingdom of heaven is like the master of a household who brings out of his treasure what is new and what is old."

"Every scribe who has been trained for the kingdom of heaven" is every prophet who has ever written a book in what we know as the Old Testament or the New Testament.

The word translated as "trained" is "*mathéteuó*," which in Greek also means, "made a disciple of" or "instructed." Those instructions come from God, through the Holy Spirit, to the disciples. The "scribes" wrote what the Holy Spirit filled them to write; and that is what we should understand. Being filled with the Holy Spirit is what actually makes anyone be "trained for the kingdom of heaven."

When we listen to Jesus, we must become disciples likewise trained. Understanding comes from being filled with the Holy Spirit. Understanding means doing what you understand must be done.

Then we need to realize that "the master of a household" is the same as God being the King of Heaven. He is the master over all his treasures … all his catches … all the fish in the seas.

When God "brings out of his treasure what is new and what is old," this is a reference only to the "good fish" sorted into the basket of the kingdom of heaven. There are the "old" treasures to be found, like those of the blood of Abraham, Isaac, Jacob, and Moses, who served God with all their hearts, selling everything they had, to earn that wage of Heaven.

Then there are the "new" treasures, who are those of the blood of Christ, who also serve God with all their hearts, selling everything to earn the same wage of heaven. We, just like the crowd that was listening to Jesus tell them parables, are not bloodline descendants of Jesus, so we all have to become descendants through his spiritual body and blood.

That means hard work, because we are not born into royalty, as instant residents of the kingdom of heaven. Still, our hard work becomes such a labor of love, through the Holy Spirit, that the time spent working passes quickly … like seven years seeming like a few days, or hours, or minutes.

Even if we think we have already earned the right to the kingdom of heaven, we might find out we still have work to do. Just like Jacob found out his reward was on the earthly plane, not the spiritual plane. When faced with more service, you do the work ... joyfully.

Paul wrote to the Christians of Rome, "All things work together for good for those who love God, who are called according to his purpose." Each of us is called to become "the firstborn of a large family," with the purpose of us individually "to be conformed to the image of His Son."

We are not asked to be a seed ... small and tiny. We are called to be a tree for Christ, as the resurrected Jesus. For that to happen, we have to remember what Jesus said, "The seed must die for it to take root." Just as Jesus died, we are called upon to let go of our petty selves and take root in the Holy Spirit and grow so that our branches can provide a home for the angels of God.

The wages of work have to be accepted as being what they are. Work is not play, although you can love the work you do. You receive a reward that is much greater than any "hardship, distress, persecution, famine, nakedness, peril, or sword" can threaten.

"We are not accounted as sheep to be slaughtered," because we willingly sacrifice all that we have earned in this world, for a hidden treasure in the next. We are to be accounted as true disciples trained for the kingdom of heaven.

Amen

# EIGHTH SUNDAY AFTER PENTECOST

# Proper 13

# YEAR A

**Relevant readings:**
Genesis 32:22-31
Psalm 17:1-7
  Isaiah 55:1-5
  Psalm 145: 8-22
Romans 9:1-5
Matthew 14:13-21

After Pentecost Sermons: Proper 13, Year A

# Wrestling with demons and feeding more than your ego

Today's readings bring to my mind my own personal sacrifices over the past thirteen years. If I had been able to put a box of tissues on each bench, I might spend the next half-hour telling you all the highs and lows I have experienced.

You would cry hard. You would laugh loudly. So, no dry eyes would be the result.

But, the lessons of today are not about me ... they are about you.

When asked about the Genesis story of Jacob reaching the point where he changed his name to Israel, most people would say that he wrestled with an angel. Others would say his struggle was with God.

I thought the same thing; but you have to ask yourself, "How could God wrestle with Jacob and not win? Why would an angel not be able to easily win in a fight? Why would either God or an angel not readily be identified by Jacob, who had seen them while sleeping on a stone pillow? Why would Jacob need to ask who it was fighting him? And, why would this stranger bless Jacob with a new name?"

The answer is that Jacob was wrestling with himself in a dream. Jacob wrestled with the Jacob who used his brother's hunger to take advantage of him. He wrestled with the Jacob who traded him stew that was rightfully Esau's, as a member of Isaac's family, for his rights as the first born.

Jacob struggled with the Jacob who had dressed up in animal fur, when his father lay blind and dying, tricking Isaac into giving him the blessing that was rightfully Esau's.

Jacob grappled with the Jacob who had stolen away from Laban, along with everything Jacob felt he deserved to keep as his own, without giving Laban the chance to argue differently.

Jacob fought with the Jacob who feared his brother Esau was going to kill him, if he ever got his hands on him.

The Jacob that was the son of Isaac, grandson of Abraham, and a rightful heir as a priest for God, hated the other Jacob.

God had reached out to that Jacob when he had dreamed of a ladder connecting heaven and earth. God stood beside that Jacob, as he watched angels going up and down the steps. God told that Jacob how He would give the land of Canaan to him and his descendants. That Jacob was told to depend on God being with him. That Jacob would be kept up by God.

This means Jacob was both Good Jacob and Bad Jacob. That was who wrestled one another that night.

The Hebrew says, "*lə-ḫad-dōw way-yê-'ā-ḇêq 'îš 'im-mōw*," which says, "alone there wrestled another with" or "him with." Jacob was "alone with himself." Therefore, Jacob "wrestled with himself."

The injured hip was Jacob's battle scar. His limp became a reminder of strong Jacob's victory over the weak Jacob, the alter ego who succumbed to influences that led him to feel alone and afraid.

His name change became a reminder that to be a true servant of God one has to be proved and tested. Jacob had contended. He grappled with that part of himself that would always turn its face away from God; and, by winning that fight, Jacob came away wearing the face of God.

# After Pentecost Sermons: Proper 13, Year A

As the sun rose, the man now named Israel held high the trophy won from a hard-fought struggle - the glow of redemption, along with the look of commitment.

We all are just like Jacob. We all have two personalities within us.

It is like the cartoons, where a tiny angel with a halo sits on our right shoulder, telling what good things to do. Then, a tiny red devil sits on our left shoulder, telling what bad things to do. It seems like those voices are external, but it is just like Jacob's wrestle.

This is an accurate depiction, as the angel is always over the right shoulder.

We all have to decide: Will I ever commit to only doing good? Or, Will I always be afraid my sins will bring me death and an eternity in Hell?

God is not going to appear to fight with you over your decision. God will not send any angels to hurt your hip and make you limp, as punishment for not always doing good.

You are the one in the ring … in two corners. God is watching. Christ is your trainer, in your corner, ready to wipe the cuts, towel the sweat, wave smelling salts under your nose, and give you water, as long as you don't give up the fight.

"Hang in there until dawn breaks, you can win the battle." is the encouragement.

Jacob was alone when he wrestled with himself. That is where no one can see the battle going on. Alone no showmanship helps, no style points are awarded for acting brave and mean, while running from the grasp of another. "Alone" means there is no "tag team" assistant waiting to come to the rescue.

In the Matthew reading today, we hear that Jesus wanted to be alone. He went by boat to a deserted place, by himself. A crowd of Jews heard he had left and walked to meet him. They met Jesus when he reached the shore.

In a way, Jesus wrestled with the crowd, curing their sick as he walked among them. We read that Jesus would eventually feed five thousand men that day. When you also read that "besides" the five thousand there were "the women and children," it makes sense that there could have been around twelve thousand people waiting for Jesus on the shore. That would be the count if it included five thousand husbands, five thousand wives, and two thousand children.

The people were there from out of town, because the Passover was near (John 6:4), so it wasn't like they all had homes to go to, where their own food was ready to be served. The people were visitors, on a pilgrimage. They were expected to find inns or relatives to stay with, meaning feeding themselves was not free. Many needed to find vendors to buy food from to feed themselves.

However, as visitors invited to stay with Jesus in a deserted field, it was "Jewish hospitality" that obligated Jesus to feed his guests. Perhaps the people expected Jesus to be their Messiah, like a new Moses who would lead them to regain the Promised Land. They would make an encampment on the flat area along the shore, like his army of volunteers preparing to settle in; and it was up to Jesus to feed his soldiers: men, women, and children.

With as many as twelve thousand sets of trusting eyes on Jesus, twelve disciples were frantic. "**NO, NO, NO!** Send them on their way, Jesus. All we have as far as food is five loaves and two fish a boy brought for us. We can't feed them all with that!"

The disciples had two tiny spirits wrestling on their shoulders.

# After Pentecost Sermons: Proper 13, Year A

The "It can be done" angels were having a hard time standing up to the "It cannot be done" devils. However, there was no wrestling for Jesus. He had complete faith in the Father.

Jesus "looked up to heaven," Matthew wrote; meaning Jesus did his "Penuel" (as Jacob named it), putting on the face of God. Then, with God upon him, Jesus blessed and broke the bread. Jesus then gave the bread to the disciples, who gave it to the people.

Now, the figure five thousand is the important number because each man represented his whole family. Give a loaf of bread to a husband and he will in turn give some to his wife and children. So, five loaves were "broken" into five thousand pieces of bread. Each piece became a full loaf of bread. That is a ratio of a thousand to one.

It means the gift was multiplied – in this case – a thousand-fold.

It is the principle taught by Jesus, "Give, and it will be given to you. A good measure, pressed down, shaken together and running over, will be poured into your lap. For with the measure you use, it will be measured to you." (Luke 6:38) The measure was five to five thousand, and it was measured to all the people.

Still, when every one of the twelve thousand had eaten their full, the leftovers filled twelve baskets – one basket of bread for each disciple, all of which had urged Jesus to send the crowd away. Not only was a multitude fed on five loaves and two fish, but the doubting disciples had more than they could eat left on their plates.

The disciples had been the voices of the devil. They were afraid, just like Jacob had been before he began to wrestle with himself and his doubt. The disciples wanted to follow Jesus, but their faith was weak. When the stuff hit the fan, they turned their faces away from God. Their inner demon always won the wrestling match.

Jesus never hesitated when the disciples showed their lack of faith. He said, "Bring [the multitude] here to me." God did not fail to support Jesus. The disciples were the instruments of God, passing the gifts of God, touched by Jesus, to the people, so all were fed solid food.

It was a miracle.

Still, the disciples were doubtful.

It is not easy exchanging old ways for new ones. Sure, Jesus could work miracles, but none of the disciples could do what he did. None of them could stop storms or walk on water. None could cure the sick, much less raise the dead.

Jesus was special.

But remember, Jesus taught that you can be special too. You can be just like Jesus, able to create miracles with the blessing of God. It just requires that you get alone and wrestle with that part of you that keeps yourself from becoming special.

Those kinds of fights are not easy. There will always be some pain. The scars of battle will always remain with you.

The way you walk today will not be the way you walk after you transform yourself into an Apostle of Christ. All the stuff you have now might disappear, causing you to limp along. All the ease you once knew will become harder to come by. Expect less money to pay for having things the way you want them. Expect fewer friends who favor your new path to righteousness. Expect to become dissatisfied with jobs that force you to regularly take advantage of others for your own benefit.

While we don't read it in the verses of today, Jacob's metamorphosis came after he voluntarily offered Esau a great number of his livestock … just giving it away to him. Jacob sent some of his servants to tell Esau, "Take all these animals as a gift from your servant Jacob." Jacob told his servants to let Esau know he would serve Esau as his master. Before God met with Jacob in a dream, Jacob had given, as an outward sign of repentance.

You have to give in order to receive.

The price you pay includes pains and struggles.

But, the pains of victory have a sunny side that makes all the hurt go away.

In Paul's letter to the Romans, it is important to realize that the first Christians of Rome were mostly Jews who believed God had sent Jesus as their Messiah. They were not pagan Roman citizens who fell in love with some strange religious cult and said they believed.

As Jewish Christians, they had a dual nature, the same as Jacob. Half of each of them was Jewish, while the other half was Christian. This identity was not easy to deal with. The Romans saw all Jews in the same light, with Christians simply a sect of Jews, followers of one specific Jew (Jesus). The Romans persecuted both Christians and Jews as being the worthless slum rats they thought they were, with both bad, and neither good. The Jews who did not believe in Jesus as their Messiah made Rome's Christians be targeted as worse than regular Jews, making them known as zealots, revolutionaries, misfits and outcasts. So, in Rome there was a struggle between Jews, as a self-identity crisis - Do we believe and change, or do we stay the same and live afraid.

Paul told them in his letter, "I could wish that I myself were accursed and cut off from Christ for the sake of my own people, my kindred according to the flesh."

That says Paul could wish to be a Jew, as he had been before he found Christ. After all, Jews were special people, chosen by God, with lots of perks and benefits coming to any Jews that recognized their covenants with God, maintained His Laws, went to the synagogue every Sabbath, and promised to stay pure, all while still waiting for the Messiah.

The twelve thousand Jews that went to meet Jesus all expected to be rewarded by God for following Jesus … **IF** he were really the Messiah. And "rewarded by God" meant things, like land, animals, and possessions. Jews, after all, were special.

Paul was telling the Roman Christians, "You have to wrestle with the old ways of thinking and realize the new way is the right way, even though it will bring "great sorrow and unceasing anguish."

Now, two thousand years later, as Christians long separated from our Jewish heritage, we think we are the special ones. Of course, the Jews still think the same thing. Thus, rather than wrestle with the Jews to see who God chooses more, we expect stuff to come to us, like it goes to them, because we too have followed Jesus to this flat place near Bethsaida. We expect to be fed things. We expect to be treated like honored guests.

The lessons today point to the battles we all face, but still fight because we have not defeated that way of thinking inside our minds.

We think we are special – as Americans – the greatest nation on earth, the most powerful – because we believe God has chosen us to run the world.

We think we are special – as Christians – the greatest religion in the world, the one truly supported by God – because we believe all other religions fear our Cross.

But, we are no different than Jacob, who feared his brother Esau – the father of the Edomites – would kill him because of hatred.

Don't people hate Americans and Christians today?

Certainly, they do.

Now, who caused hatred of Jacob?

If you see that answer, then you also know who caused America's and Christianity's haters.

We are no different than the disciples who urged Jesus to send the people away because they had no faith that they could afford to feed them all.

We each have to wrestle with the questions: Will I ever be capable of producing a miracle? And, will I always have fear that what I have is not enough?

Is your faith strong enough for you to give all you have, for the promise that you may receive a thousand-fold in return?

Amen

# NINTH SUNDAY AFTER PENTECOST

## Proper 14

## YEAR A

**Relevant readings:**
Genesis 37:1-4; 12-28
Psalm 105:1-22
1 Kings 19:9-18
Psalm 85:8-13
Romans 10:5-15
Matthew 14:22-33

---

en. We volunteer to do things so the younger folk can see what responsible people do. As the eldest child, that often means helping the parents with raising younger siblings.

Age does matter, and that is why I get the feel that Peter had that "firstborn" mentality about him. After all, Peter had been a follower of John the Baptist, so he had "disciple experience." Peter was one of the first to follow Jesus, in the initial group of four … so, he only had to be older than his brother Andrew, and James and John, the sons of Zebedee, in order to be the elder disciple.

Peter might have even been older than Jesus, causing him to constantly feel the urge to act as if his age made him a better disciple. He might have wanted Jesus to ask him for advice, from time to time.

But, when Peter stood up in the boat to show the others that it was okay to walk on water, because Jesus was doing it, he soon realized he was in over his head … even if he only sank up to his knees before Jesus pulled him to safety.

Does anyone remember the old cartoons Tooter Tortoise?

Each week Tooter would visit Mr. Wizard and tell Mr. Wizard what he wanted to be. It was always something different, something exciting yet dangerous, like a cowboy, a fireman, or a policeman. Mr. Wizard would always wave his wand and say a poem, sending Tooter off to his fantasy land.

Invariably, Tooter would find out that being a knight, or being a bull fighter, or being a football player was harder than it seemed. In fear, he would always cry out, "Save me, **MR. WIZARD!!!**"

Then, Mr. Wizard would say another poem and wave his wand and "Poof," Tooter was saved.

Likewise, Peter acted foolishly, and we read him crying out,

# Oh you of little faith ... why did you doubt?

"Oh ye of little faith ..."

"Why did you doubt?"

Raise your hand if you have ever been in a situation like Peter found himself, having boldly gone where you want to go, but when you get there you realize you have not prepared to be there. You realize you are "out of your league."

<look for raised hands>

Raise your hand if you have ever wanted to do something foolish like Peter, but instead you couldn't make yourself do it? Maybe, instead, you watched someone else volunteer to go first ... leaving you thinking, "Man, if he pulls this off I'm going to kick myself for not beating him or her to the punch." How often have you watched someone do something you were afraid of doing, seeing that someone embarrass himself or herself, so you think, "Whew, glad I didn't try"?

<look for raised hands>

Often our own failures, and knowing that others have failed, is what keeps us from trying a second time, or even trying at all. Thus Tennyson wrote, "Tis better to have loved and lost, than to have never loved at all."

When we are seeing failures in our Scripture, we have to see where passion plays a role.

It is hard to figure Peter's motivations some times. He did seem to be an emotional person. He cut the ear off the guard at Gethsemane, out of anger. He denied Jesus, out of fear. Jesus asked him three times, "Do you love me Peter?" if questioning his ability to be in touch with his heart tions.

In the Gospel story today, we see Peter jumping up to s alty to Jesus, and then crying out in fear from what he h

I believe Peter wanted to be the leader of the disciples, a imagine all the disciples looked up to him ... but ....

Perhaps Peter was trying too hard.

I get the feeling that Peter was a little older than the other d ples; and a little older meant being a little more respected. the eldest disciple, Peter would be allowed to do things first, it would be improper for a younger man to act openly before elder had his chance.

We see that importance of the firstborn of Biblical patriarchs, a repeated theme in the Old Testament. Just a couple of Sundays ago we read how Laban told Jacob, "We just don't marry the younger daughters before the older ones, around here." Birth order mattered.

Esau, the first of twins to be born, was supposed to get the birthright of Isaac, not Jacob. David, as the youngest, was out tending the flock, while his father, Jesse, let Samuel look over his seven older boys, as he sought the one God wanted him to anoint.

Today, we see how young Joseph had angered his older brothers, by telling of a couple of dreams he had. Those dreams angered them to the point they wanted to kill Joseph. He was Israel's favorite son, while being the youngest ... prior to Benjamin.

As adults, we feel it is important to be examples for the chil-

Robert Tippett

"Lord, save me!"

"Twizzle, Twazzle, Twozzle, Twome; time for this one to come home," as Mr. Wizard would say.

<make waving motion, like waving a wand>

In the Gospel reading today, the focus is mostly placed on Jesus walking on water.

This story is told by both Matthew and John, but not by Mark or Luke. Such an experience should have been remembered by Mark, as one of the disciples who was on the boat, sent by Jesus from the place where the multitude was fed.

All four Gospel writers told of the miracle of feeding the five thousand, but only two told of Jesus walking on water.

Matthew's perspective was from within the boat. John's perspective was from the shore, where Jesus had remained after he sent the disciples back across the sea, while he dispersed the crowd of five thousand men and then went into the mountains to pray.

It was dark, according to John's account. It was early in the morning, according to Matthew. Agreement between the two would put the time somewhere between 2 and 5 AM. I imagine both were telling the truth.

I can be found asleep at that time of morning. Maybe Mark was a heavier sleeper than the other disciples, so maybe he slept through Jesus walking on water?

But, then again, maybe the more important element of the story is not Jesus walking on the sea, but how Jesus rescued twelve fearful disciples. While the event is real, maybe Matthew recalled it as a witness that was in a half-asleep state ... like a dream surrounding reality ... not cognizant enough to fully understand what took place.

John, after all, tells a rather plain story, so "matter of fact" that one can see the possibility of amphibology (or double meaning) in effect, when he wrote, "They see Jesus walking on the sea."

"They" were the disciples, who were in a boat. John was walking with Jesus along the shore. The disciples were on the sea. So, "They see Jesus walking," but not from land (where John was), but from their perspective, "on the sea."

Some optical illusions seem like something they are not.

If you recall the morning after Jesus was resurrected, he appeared as an unrecognizable man on the shore, by the sea, while the disciples were fishing. Jesus recommended they cast their nets to a specific place, which they did; and they caught so many fish they struggled to get the boat to shore.

That was when Peter realized the unrecognizable man was Jesus, and he, "jumped into the water," the same as he did in today's story, after he recognized Jesus walking. This means Peter's role, as lead disciple or captain of the boat, was to jump out of the boat when it neared land, so he could tie the boat to a mooring.

Jesus walking on the water might then have been an optical illusion. Matthew said they thought they saw a ghost, and were frightened. John confirmed they displayed fear, but not from a ghost. In reality, John might have seen their boat close to the shore, so close to shore that Jesus walked towards the boat on a dock, while carrying a lantern in the dark. That could have seemed like a ghost, walking on the same plane as the water's waves.

John, from his perspective still on the shore, not the dock, wrote, "Then they were willing to take him into the boat, and immediately the boat reached the shore where they were heading."

Everything then happened as written, but the disciples were so drowsy, even with the wind and waves, that they imagined things that were not totally real. They were almost ashore, but they did not know it. They were fearful, so when they saw an illuminated Jesus coming towards them, they did not realize they were almost at the dock.

The importance of this reading is not so much the walking on the water, but what Matthew recalled Jesus saying to Peter (and to the others).

"You of little faith, why did you doubt?"

Before modern man grew big brains and became seemingly godlike in its ability to understand the Holy Bible, primitive man saw four basic elements in the world. Those four were: Air, Earth, Fire, and Water.

If you have a pencil and a piece of scratch paper, then write this down, because you can always use this information to help your brain interpret and understand Scripture better later …

Remembering that everything written was penned by those little brained people of antiquity.

Air is symbolic of ideas, thoughts and words, communications, etc.

Earth is symbolic of material things, things of value that can be touched, and in general, all the physical world.

Fire is symbolic of energy and action, especially those things that motivate us, change us, transform us, and urge us do things, even if it means running from someone else's actions.

After Pentecost Sermons: Proper 14, Year A

And finally, Water is symbolic of emotions, our feelings inside that make us love, hate, rage, care, worry, and be at peace (etc.).

Whenever you read Scripture and see these elements appear, individually or collectively, there is symbolic meaning meant to be gained.

In the story of Jesus walking on the water, when the wind was against the disciples, and they were far from land, three of the four basic elements are at play in this story.

We read the boat was "battered by the waves," which means they were very unsettled emotionally. They had just earlier handed out food to five thousand men, which was a miracle that shook them.

The wind being against them means their minds were causing doubts that led to their emotional instability. Their minds could understand symbolic washing away of sin, but not the magic of transforming five loaves of bread into "full meal deals" for possibly twelve thousand human beings (including women and children). All ideas were against all rationale they knew.

Being "far from land" means the disciples could not find anything of value to grab hold of for security. They were in their fishing boat, and fish was how they had earned a living before; but they were not doing as much fishing as they had been, following this guy Jesus around. They wanted to be on solid ground, but that seemed so far from their reach.

They had little faith and a lot of doubt.

In the Old Testament reading, the sons of Jacob-Israel had no faith in Joseph. They referred to him as "this dreamer." Joseph, they thought, did not understand his place as a boy among men. They threw Joseph in a pit that was dry, which says they were devoid of any emotions that would keep them from selling their own flesh and blood as a slave, to strangers.

Paul warned the Roman Christians that righteousness does not come from the Law – the Air of written material. Instead, righteousness comes from the heart – the emotional center, our Living Water source.

Paul said that righteousness says you "confess with your lips and believe in your heart." Peter said to his vision of Jesus, "If it is you, command me to come to you on the water," but once he got out of the boat, "he noticed a strong Wind," becoming "frightened."

There is no brain big enough to tell you how to be righteous. No Air ideas can command you. No Wind is going to make you realize you are outside of the laws of physics, causing you to sink any chance of emotional commitment to someone else's ideas.

You are righteous because your heart says, "Do this out of love of God and Christ." You are not righteous because someone tells you what to do. If you act righteous because of your heart, then the big brained people can see what you do and draft a Law about what makes you righteous. However, "righteousness" is not about "monkey see, monkey do."

Religion is more than the Earth that is represented by a church and the physical rewards that God sends our way for having faith.

Religion is more than the Air that is printed on your handouts each Sunday, or what words I speak explaining those words.

Religion is more than the Fire that causes us to act rashly, foolishly, and without preparation, simply because we cannot be still and we want instant transformation and gratification.

Religion is all about our emotional connection to God and Christ.

God speaks to us through our hearts; but to hear what God has to say, we have to be calm, still, and at peace. We have to trust our feelings and have faith that Christ will lead our thoughts and our actions in this world, for truly righteous purposes.

To have a lot of faith, we need to calm our sea.

Amen

# TENTH SUNDAY AFTER PENTECOST

# Proper 15

# YEAR A

**Relevant readings:**
Genesis 45:1-15
Psalm 133
  Isaiah 56:1-8
  Psalm 67
Romans 11:1-2; 29-32
Matthew 15: 10-28

After Pentecost Sermons: Proper 15, Year A

# What we always have here is a failure to want to communicate

In the movie *Cool Hand Luke*, the famous line was spoken by actor Strother Martin, when he said, "What we've got here is a failure to communicate."

What we've got here today, in these readings, is a theme of a failure to communicate.

In the story of Joseph telling his brothers, "Do not be distressed, or angry with yourselves, because you sold me here." They could not say anything. The guilty brothers were "so dismayed at [Joseph's] presence," they were failing to hear his words and believe them.

I imagine their minds were caught between, "Is this Egyptian prince going to kill us, or will dad kill us for selling his favorite son and lying to him that the lions ate Joseph?"

They heard words, but that could not have faith in them. They did not understand.

There was a failure to communicate.

In the first part of the reading from Matthew, we have entered into a setting that keeps us from realizing that the Pharisees had just complained to Jesus about his disciples eating food without washing their hands first. They complained that the tradition of the elders was not being maintained.

Jesus then "called the crowd to him and said, "It is not what goes in the mouth that defiles a person, but it is what comes out of the mouth that defiles."

The disciples then whisper to Jesus that the Pharisees took offense at what Jesus just told the crowd.

The Pharisees had missed the point of God's Law and had forgotten the warning of Isaiah.

The words of the Torah had been read, but the Pharisees had a failure to communicate the intended meaning properly.

Jesus then used a parable about the blind leading the blind, when he told the disciples why the Pharisees were offended.

Peter stood up and said to Jesus, "Explain this parable to us."

Obviously, there was a failure to communicate the precise reason how Pharisees with working eyesight and a crowd without any blind people could be called "blind."

What we've got here is another failure to communicate.

Even in the letter that Paul wrote to the Romans, there was doubt about how the Jews could still call themselves "the chosen ones of God," when they had screamed out that Jesus should be killed. They sold Jesus into the slavery of a punished prophet. Paul explained how disobedience today does not mean disobedience tomorrow; so even though the Jews killed Jesus, they are still called God's children **BECAUSE** of that disobedience.

Huh?

I imagine there were a few Roman Christians that had to read those words more than once, in order to understand how sin in the world is good, simply because sin is a requirement before one can receive mercy and forgiveness.

Jesus had explained to Peter and the disciples, "What comes out of the mouth proceeds from the heart." That statement reflected verbally and vocally that one's inner level of defilement - or righteousness - presence of or lack of either and both - comes out through the words you use. We speak from the heart - good or bad - as Jesus spoke; but his words did not sink into the disciples' hearts.

As they walked into Canaan, some crazy Canaanite woman began shouting at them. "Have mercy on me, Lord, Son of David."

The disciples urged Jesus to shoo her away, causing him to say, "I was sent only for the lost sheep of the house of Israel." Jesus was a Jew, with only Jews following him. He was, in essence, a Jewish ram leading twelve mindlessly lost sheep, who were now frightened by a woman that was not one of them.

Before anyone could tell the woman to shut up, she ran before them and knelt down before Jesus. She said, "Lord, help me."

She prayed for mercy. Her words spoke the truth of her heart.

Jesus told her, "It is not fair to take the children's food and throw it to dogs."

At that moment, Jesus had just come up with another parable. Peter had asked Jesus to explain the "blind leading the blind" analogy. Now, Jesus was talking about children, and food, and dogs, none of which were a part of that present reality.

Once again, what we've got here is a failure to communicate.

But, the Canaanite woman understood what Jesus was saying.

Her immediate response was, "Yes, Lord, yet even the dogs eat the crumbs that fall from the master's table."

She understood she was like a dog, begging for help, completely dependent on the master.

She understood that she was not invited (yet) to sit at the table with the master, able to have a full bowl of food (plenty replacing famine), meaning she was not allowed (yet) to follow Jesus as a disciple and be fed by his words so they filled her heart with understanding.

She understood that she would be happy if only one crumb would fall her way, a crumb that would save her daughter from demonic possession.

Jesus exclaimed, "Woman, great is your faith!"

Finally, someone who gets it! Jesus said (in essence), "You understand because my words have missed your mind and hit your heart. Therefore, we are communicating!"

We see how the outpouring of emotion, between Joseph and Benjamin, where there was hugging and weeping and kissing taking place in front of the other brothers, that was when the brothers could begin to talk to Joseph once again.

When they processed his words in their minds, they were speechless. There was a failure to communicate.

But, when their minds were triggered by their hearts, they cried, realizing their level of defilement, while **FEELING** how amazing it was to be forgiven for their sins.

The brothers wept before the words could come from their mouths. Their heart would then be the source of their confessions and repentance, realizing they had been dogs, blessed by a crumb of forgiveness from the master's table.

The focus that needs to come from today's readings is we are all in one or more states of being that the words of Scripture highlight.

# After Pentecost Sermons: Proper 15, Year A

We are blind, until our eyes are opened to see the truth.

We are headed to a fall in the pit, until we see the right path that must be taken.

We lead others to do as we do, as examples of failure, when we have no clue about what it is we should do.

We sell our souls because of hard hearts, led by evil intentions more often than by righteous emotions.

We take offense at those who understand things we misinterpret.

We like to feel special as lost sheep, crying out for our leaders to run off outsiders.

We ask Jesus to explain everything for us, rather than becoming emotionally one with God, so our mind speaks as Jesus, knowing in our hearts what God's plan is.

In the Gospel reading, it was a stranger that readily recognized Jesus as "Lord" and as a "Son of David." She knelt before this presence and prayed, not for herself directly, but for her daughter, whom she loved with her heart.

Her prayer was answered because of her faith.

I am sure we all have experiences where our prayers have been answered.

When we pray we pour out words from the heart. Still ...

Many times, we do not realize how well our prayers have been answered, until years after the fact. It is in hindsight that our eyes can be opened so we can see.

The length of time between prayer and realization of a crumb being within our grasp depends on how much failure to communicate with God we allow.

I once prayed earnestly to God for a sign that I was doing the right thing, making radical changes in my life, while trembling like a leaf that everything I was embarking upon would collapse in failure.

My prayer was answered.

It was answered so clearly that I was completely tickled with joy.

"This is so cool," I thought!

I am doing the right thing. Then I thought ... so everything will be smooth sailing from here on out.

What I had there was a failure to communicate God's intent, pretending that my fantasy was God's plan for me.

My future certainly had very little clear sailing in it, as for the next nine years it was like being on the Sea of Galilee during a terrible storm ... fighting to stay afloat ... fearing I was going to sink into oblivion.

By the time Hurricane Katrina came into my life ... a true storm of great magnitude and real destructive powers ... I already had been shaken like a rag doll in the jaws of a pit-bull.

Hurricane Katrina had the effect of tickling me just like the sign God had sent to me long before. As difficult as Katrina was to swallow, I could only laugh at how foolish I had been. I was no longer misunderstanding what my future would be, although I could see all those affected by Katrina's wrath believing it was a sign sent by God, implying "The future has to be better than this."

# After Pentecost Sermons: Proper 15, Year A

I no longer had a failure to communicate with God.

In the movie *Cool Hand Luke*, everyone remembers the Cap'n standing on the top of that hill, having just beat Luke into submission once again, saying, "What we've got here is a failure to communicate."

But later in that movie, shortly before Luke is shot, we glimpse a cycle completing. Luke finally gets to end his struggles that had begun years before ... when he cut the head of a parking meter off, while drunk. He was never going to earn freedom by obeying a system he did not believe in. Before finally being freed, through death, Luke stated the same words he had heard before, "What we've got here is a failure to communicate."

Luke's rebellious actions spoke like words from the heart, saying, "I do not believe in your rules."

Paul wrote, "For God has imprisoned all in disobedience so that he may be merciful to all."

Make sure you understand the conditional use of the verb "to be," as "may be."

There "may be mercy" granted, once your failure to communicate with your brain is replaced by a faithful heart. You effect the outcome.

Otherwise life will keep beating you down, keeping shackles around you ankles and wrists, so that what the law originally deems "to be" a two-year imprisonment "may be" changed into a death sentence.

Before you can be reborn, you must die.

Life must have the blind leading the blind towards the pit, due to a failure to communicate ... it is all part of a grand plan.

But for Salvation to be the surprise that leaves us speechless, we have to stop playing "follow the leader" and open up our hearts with faith.

Amen

# ELEVENTH SUNDAY AFTER PENTECOST

## Proper 16

## YEAR A

**Relevant readings:**
Exodus 1:8-22 and
 Exodus 2:1-10
Psalm 124
 Isaiah 51:1-6
 Psalm 138
Romans 12:1-8
Matthew 16:13-20

Robert Tippett

# When one plus one equals eleven

Today is the eleventh Sunday of the Pentecost season. In metaphysical thought, the number eleven is a "Master Number," which means it can symbolize the duality of base nature (a two, as 1 + 1) or it can be symbolize the duality of spiritual (eleven) elevation (as 11). The basic is representative of **one** plus a separate other **one**, as two. The higher is a reflection of **one** plus a heavenly **one**, as eleven.

If you recall, back on the Day of Pentecost, now 11 weeks ago, I said that was to be recognized as Graduation Day – when all good students would go out into the world and apply what they have learned.

The Ordinary season that follows Pentecost represents a time of ministry.

After all, as Christians we are admitted priests of Jesus Christ, regardless of how little (if anything) someone pays us to spread the Gospel, ministering our faith to the world. Priesthood is a vocation or calling, rather than an occupation or job.

You do not have to wear a collar to be a priest, and when the disciples stood up and began speaking with tongues of fire, they were not dressed any differently than the other Jews who filled Jerusalem that day.

Today we get a glimpse of what it means to truly be a Christian ... not just a student of Christianity. We see how basic twos all became elevens – each **one** with the **Holy Spirit**. Of course, we can remain a student at heart, forever spared any responsibility of being a priest simply because, "I still need to learn some more." That keeps one as a two, as **one** holding onto the **one** who was Christ, separately, and not as **one**.

# After Pentecost Sermons: Proper 16, Year A

Paul wrote a letter to the Christians of Rome, who were true Christians. They were priests to the One God, as Jews, who had been schooled in the Law of Moses, the Psalms of David, and the messages of the Prophets.

They were priests who had no clue how to serve Christ, but as Jews they thought they still had more to learn. They claimed belief, but they moaned, complained, lamented, and cried about not being able to control themselves and truly act like priests.

Paul told those true Christians, "Brothers and sisters, I appeal to you by the mercies of God to present your bodies as a living sacrifice." He made an emotional plea for them to stop trying to live like they had been living before. He told them, "You have to place yourself on the altar and offer your body to God, so you can become holy."

You do not become holy by wishing to become holy. You do not become holy by memorizing answers or going to places where the holy go.

You become holy through a spiritual transformation, "by the **renewing** of your **minds**, so that you will **discern** what is the **will of God**."

If you do not change the way your mind works - how you think - you will do the opposite of transforming, which Paul said was "**con**forming to the world." You do what other normal people do ... which is not holy.

So, how appropriate is it that on the eleventh Sunday of Pentecost we get a letter in the mail from Paul asking, "Are you a **two**, who conforms to the world – you plus an earthly existence? Or, are you an **eleven**, who transforms your mind to discern what the will of God is – God-inspired?"

Before you answer that question from Brother Paul, listen to the benchmarks he listed. We each need to be check off the one or ones that fit us. We need to be able to truthfully say, to one or more, "Yes, that's me!"

1. Are you able to **prophesy**? Meaning: Can you tell what the future holds or explain what the prophets meant, pertinent to our future?

2. Are you **ministering** to others? Meaning: Can you be found sitting with others, like Paul, making sure others are motivated and encouraged to keep serving God and Christ?

3. Are you **teaching** others? Meaning: Do you understand Scriptures well enough to explain the meaning to others, so they can see between the lines too?

4. Are you **exhorting** the Gospel [Good News of the Messiah]? Meaning: Do you display a sense of urgency in promoting a need for others to become ministers of Christ, because tomorrow may be too late?

5. Are you **giving** and generous? Meaning: Are you able to heal yourself of the sources of ill health, so your presence is freely given to others in order to help them to also be healed?

6. Are you diligently **leading**? Meaning: Do you seek out those who want to be Christians, but lack direction, becoming a beacon of light for them to be guided?

7. Are you cheerfully **compassionate**? Meaning: Do you spread a sense of understanding of forgiveness, while feeling the hearts of others still need some positive reinforcements to allow their minds to be transformed?

Before you answer if you are a two or an eleven, based on how many of these traits of the Holy Spirit you checked "yes" to, consider where the disciples were, before the Day of Pentecost found them transformed.

Jesus asked them, "Who do the people **think** I am?" They answered (basically), "A prophet like Elijah."

"Well, they see me doing miracles, and they hear me explaining the meaning of the Law," Jesus must have thought, leading him to then ask, "Who do you **think** I am?"

Simon Peter answered, "You are the Messiah, the Son of the living God."

Peter did not **think** that. Ordinarily, Peter **thought** just like one of the people. His mind **thought** just like those who conformed to this world. Peter's mind **reasoned**, "Jesus, you are a prophet;" but he said different than he thought.

Simon Peter transformed his mind for that one answer, as a disciple projecting to the Apostle he would become. His answer was discerning the will of God. Peter opened his mouth and God said, "You are the Messiah, the Son of the living God."

Jesus exclaimed, "**Blessed** are you, Simon son of Jonah!"

Peter was not "**Blessed**" because his mind knew the right answer. He was "**Blessed**" because God entered his mind and came out his lips.

Jesus said, "On this rock I will build my church." The fact that "Peter," in Greek, means "stone, rock" does not mean Jesus would have a stone church in his name built in Rome. The man name "Rock" spoke, symbolizing "This rock" of speaking from a holy source would be the foundation of Christianity.

That "Rock" was having one's mind transformed. It was no

longer conforming to the world, but sacrificing of self so that one's lips moved and the Holy Spirit flowed forth.

The "Rock" of Christianity means emotionally sensing the seven keys stated by Paul, which tell us today how we can know if we are truly Christian.

The reason Jesus "**sternly ordered** the disciples **not to tell** anyone that he was the Messiah" was because of this: If people said, "Jesus is the Messiah, the Son of the living God" simply because someone told them it was "blessed" to say such things, those people would be mistaking a **two** for an **eleven**.

You have to transform to an **eleven** and know from a changed mind what God wants you to know.

When we look at the Old Testament reading for Exodus, we see a seemingly non-relative story about the plight of the children of Israel in Egypt, up to the birth of Moses.

As a "**two**" we symbolize the children of Israel in captivity. In a world that conforms to hate people who are different, "number two" Christians are forced to struggle. They are slaves to building structures that defend the ruling class from the potential attacks that would expose just how frail our government and society is … without God, without Christ.

As "number **two** Christians," the government wants to take advantage of our willingness to cite self-sacrifice as a good thing. The government wants to kill any chance of us spreading the influence of a Christ mind to others. Because of blind faith we have no power to stop that planned genocide of the church's bodies. We do not have a clue how to stop trends that promote severe changes to what we were raised to respect and value. We are slaves to moaning, complaining, lamenting, and crying.

As an "**eleven**," we have the guts of a midwife, to go before the king and explain why we did not do as ordered. We say, "We did not kill Christianity because Christians are vigorous and do not need midwives to deliver their babies."

Christians are unlike the spiritless conformers of the world. Christians are willing to sacrifice themselves so they can discern "what is the will of God." They change so God will deal well with the midwives and so Christians will multiply and become very strong.

As members of a church, which itself only represents a "two" until it fills its seats with members who all check off one or more of the traits listed by Paul, we represent a mass of bodies tied together forming a wicker basket, which is then plastered with bitumen and pitch, or Scriptures from the Old and New Testaments. In that "two" form, we can carry the baby Jesus and keep him alive, just as Moses' unnamed mother saved the one who would save a nation of people later.

Just as Moses was named because he was drawn out of water, where water symbolizes our emotional being, so too must we each become Moses, able to lead our body from a world where we conform, to an unknown place that we know nothing about.

Rather than needing a boat to float on water ... remember how Jesus walked on water? We must heed the call and leave the boat, letting our emotions support our actions. We cannot do that by conforming to the world, because just as Peter found out, you sink and cry out for help.

We must go without knowing the answers, because our emotions have been elevated from "**two**" to "**eleven**." We care so much about preserving our faith that we sacrifice everything for a reward that cannot be seen.

The impossible must have an outlet through our sacrifice of self. That is the message today. We need to be emotionally recharged, so we are reassured our school days are well behind us.  There is nothing we can learn that will stop our palms from sweating, our knees from shaking, and our minds to be filled with doubt.

We can no longer rely on smarts to grow strong and become Apostles for Christ.

We are **one** as the body of the church, where **one** body is the sum of its parts.

We need a letter from Paul to touch our hearts, so emotionally we are reminded to keep the faith.  We can walk on water when we stop trying to be "ME," and start being transformed into Christ.

We need to give a heartfelt answer to who Jesus is to us, not just pretend to be something we have been afraid to surrender to.

Amen

# TWELFTH SUNDAY AFTER PENTECOST

# Proper 17

# YEAR A

**Relevant readings:**
Exodus 3:1-15
Psalm 105:1-6; 23-26
Jeremiah 15:15-21
Psalm 26:1-8
Romans 12:9-21
Matthew 16:21-28

Robert Tippett

# Take up your cross and then lead, follow, or get out of the way

When I was a student in college, as an advanced age senior seeking a bachelor's degree in psychology, one of my course instructors was asked about a doctoral candidate's chances of getting his doctorate.

The instructor laughed and implied it might still be a while.

I did not know who this doctoral student was, but I got the impression it was an almost mythical entity, one who was eternally on the threshold of producing a successful dissertation, but then equally eternally refusing to take that final step.

I was reminded of this thought while reading the lessons for today, as I see a theme of hesitation, or distraction, causing a lost goal.

Along the same train of thought, I see a similarity in this in news of Pope Francis making statements recently of his concerns that he may only have a few years left to live … either as an alive human being or as a serving pope.

It seems he may choose to retire from the rigors of heading the Church of Rome … I assume the plan would be for him to inhabit a villa next to the already retired pope, Benedict XVI, nee Joseph Ratzinger.

Maybe that is the same reason why that doctoral student can't take the step to become a doctor of psychology. Maybe actually being a PhD is too much work, too tiresome; or maybe something else has made him believe the prize of a doctorate is too unrewarding. In a case like that, simply putting on the clothes of a psychologist would feel like wearing the weight of the world, so much that it could only make one want to die or think of retirement.

That, in my opinion, is not what being a leader is about. A leader sets an example so others can follow that lead with enthusiasm, with hope and with affection. That makes a leader a mentor to the future leaders that will follow.

Pope Francis, in my opinion, is acting like Peter, who heard Jesus talking about suffering and death, only to call him aside and tell Jesus, "God forbid it, Lord! This must never happen to you."

It seems the human mind of Jorge Mario Bergoglio (the current pope) has been telling himself, "Don't let them see you frail, ill, and weak. God forbid it! This must never happen to you."

Today's lessons can then be summed up as being all about: Lead; Follow; or, Get out of the way.

Jesus was a leader. Paul was a leader. Moses was chosen to become a leader. Peter thought he was a leader. Satan is a leader for evil purposes. God is the ultimate leader for good purposes.

The disciples, including Peter, were followers of Jesus. Paul was a follower of Christ. Moses was a follower of God; and Jesus too followed God's will.

The same characters are seen to be in changing roles. A leader develops a follower to lead, so a follower becomes a leader ... and so on and so on.

The mythical doctoral student I heard of had followed a line of thought (education in psychology) to the point that he knew all there was to learn. All he had to do after reaching that point was apply that knowledge, by acting to present and defend his own ideas, opinions, and theories, based on the principles he had learned.

Instead, he chose to get out of the way. Rather than continue to follow behind a new and different course of study, or continue on and become a leader on his chosen path, he quit. However, the lore continues because he is always so close ... so maybe he will take that step this semester?

Pope Francis had followed the will of a church, accepting an appointment to be that church's leader. He followed, and he has been leading since early 2013; but ...

Now, he talks of getting out of the way, instead of leading like those he followed (previous popes). He followed by adhering to the principles that are part of the coursework for one following Christ, for one following God's call. He had (one would presume) a mindset on divine things, not human things ... like health and comfort.

Are we in that same "Get out of the way" category?

Is it just too hard to determine which leaders we should follow, because our faith in leaders is pretty much shot?

Is it just to exhausting to even think about leading others, when we have a hard enough time leading ourselves to church once a week (or month, or year), for a couple of hours?

Is it too frightening to think we would be expected to lead someone other than ourselves, because for all the following we have done, we still don't feel prepared to take that last leap of faith?

If we answer "yes" to any of these questions, then, like Peter, we are "setting our minds on human things and not on divine things."

Moses, when he first saw the spectacle of a burning thorn bush, had his mind set on "human things," things of the physical world. He thought, "Why is that combustible material burning with fire but not being consumed by the flames?"

The disciples were told by Jesus, "If you want to follow me [rather than Mr. Simon Peter here], then deny yourself." That means, "Suspend your 'human things' brains, so they don't wander onto that type of thinking."

Jesus said, "Take up your cross and follow me."

When we think of this reference to a "cross" as Jesus purposefully taking the opportunity to inject prophecy of his crucifixion into minds that struggled going beyond 'human things' thinking, you miss the obvious.

The Greek word "*stauron*" has been translated as "cross." I have discussed this before, as that word in a non-crucifixion conversation is commonly understood as a reference to a "stake" or "pole," such as would be a "T-shaped support" for grapevines to be suspended along.

As a "cross" that is "T-shaped" or even built as an "X," we see that the "stake" had become stuck in the ground, fixed into position at an intersection. The group had come to a fork in the road, where a point of indecision had been reached. Who do the disciples follow?

Do the disciples go left (follow Peter's rebuke of Jesus, as the leader of the disciples who follow Jesus), or right (follow Jesus's rebuke of Peter, as the leader of Peter)? Peter had caused everything to come to a halt, as far as leading, following, or getting out of the way was concerned.

"Pick up your stake and follow me," means, "If you stake your claims on Peter, then you are no longer my followers. I am no longer your leader."

When Jesus then said, "Truly I tell you, there are some standing here (not the forward movement of walking) who will not taste death before they see the Son of Man coming in his kingdom," the plural number is stated. "Some are" means more than one, so knowing that Judas was one, Jesus just identified Peter as in the same boat with Judas.

By "not tasting death," Jesus meant there would be no inkling of thought about what Jesus' death would be, in terms of divine things. Because Peter and Judas, and perhaps even Thomas (where "Seeing was believing" was a reflection of his mind), their minds were set on death being the end … not the beginning.

Their faith was not in following a leader who was now talking about death. The divinity of resurrection meant nothing to them. They wanted a strong, healthy, "live long and prosper" leader, one who rewarded his underlings with cushy appointments and free visits to the palatial estate. New leaders would be something to think about many years away from that point in time. After all, Jesus was only in his thirties, with plenty of life left … so they thought.

In the "Moses and the burning bush" story, we hear how "he had turned aside to see … this great sight," the vision of a dried shrub not being destroyed by flames. Likewise, the disciples of Jesus were turned aside by Peter acting like he knew what was good for Jesus.

"Here I am!" said God. "Here I am as the Son of Man," said Jesus. "Here I AM That I AM," said Moses.

When both Moses and Jesus were to say, "I AM That I AM," they said God leads my mind. My mind is set on divine things because I stopped thinking in terms of human things.

"Here I am of a mind set on divine things," said Paul.

After Pentecost Sermons: Proper 17, Year A

These are the bold things God says through humans who have God within them.

When God called Moses' name, twice, God was not within the thorn bush, where "the angel of the LORD appeared to [Moses] in a flame of fire out of a bush."

The Hebrew word "*mit-tō-vek*" says "amid," such that the angel was "amid" the bush. When God called, "Moses, here I am," God was "amid, within, inside, and internal" to Moses, not the bush. God called Moses away "from the bush," as a voice spoken to him and heard by him … internally.

Moses followed God's voice. He stopped, and where he stood then was holy ground, because God was within him. Moses removed his sandals in honor of that presence.

As a follower of the LORD, Moses became a leader of the LORD. Moses walked, God talked.

As a follower of the LORD, Jesus became a leader of the LORD. Jesus walked, God talked.

As followers of Jesus, most disciples became leaders of the Christ mind, with the angel of the Holy Spirit burning amid them without destroying their bodies, with God genuinely in their hearts. The Apostles walked, God talked.

The lesson today is to stop hearing the command, "Lead, Follow, or Get out of the way" as giving you only one option.

Lead as an Apostle of Christ, with a mind set on divine things.

Follow the teachings of Christ, through a mind set on divine things.

And finally, tell that mind set on human things to "Get behind me, Satan!"

You have some leading and following to do.

Amen

# THIRTEENTH SUNDAY AFTER PENTECOST

## Proper 18

## YEAR A

**Relevant readings:**
Exodus 12:1-14
Psalm 149
 Ezekiel 33:7-11
 Psalm 119:33-40
Romans 13:8-14
Matthew 18:15-20

Robert Tippett

# Freedom from sin does not come by changing the rules

Freedom is an ideal in which Americans place a lot of value.

We are the Land of the Free. We have the Liberty Bell and the Statue of Liberty.

We pride ourselves in a doctrine that includes the Freedom to worship as we please, and a Freedom from one Church being required to approve our civil laws.

Freedom walks hand-in-hand with Democracy, where the people are Free to decide what is best for the people.

In the Exodus reading today, we remember the original Passover, where the Freedom of the children of Israel, from the bondage of the Egyptians, came with specific requirements made by God.

That lesson says Freedom comes at a price.

The firstborn of Egyptian animals and humans had to die so the Israelites could go Free. More Egyptians would die later, chasing after those who were Freed. While meandering for forty years in the wilderness, countless followers of Moses would die, for various reasons, all so God's people could be Free to find the Promised Land.

America's creation came with similar costs.

The Freedom of Independence cost lives. The British suffered loses, as well as the Colonial Americans. Once Freedom was gained, other wars would later be fought to ensure that hard-fought for Freedom remained America's greatest trait.

# After Pentecost Sermons: Proper 18, Year A

In our case, Freedom demanded a Union. So, when some states tried to split that Union, that Freedom was denied ... again, at the cost of many lives.

Once the Israelites had been Freed from Egypt, Moses brought them the Law of God, which they agreed to uphold. It was non-negotiable. Their Freedom would from then on be restricted within the walls of that Law.

This is how Freedom must be seen as a state of mind ... an Ideal ... where the reality is, will be, and has always been ... an illusion.

When one delves into the concept of Freedom of religion, most of us here today think only in terms of Christianity. That was the original intent. That was and is our religion, as Americans, so that Americans would be Free to worship God and Jesus Christ, without fear of oppression by the State or other religious groups.

We like to think our societal laws are based on Christian principles ... and while the vast majority of our laws have been established from that premise, the trend for the past several decades has been to separate our laws from all religious influence.

The concept of a separation of Church and State has become so challenged in our court systems that about the only laws Christians can count on today, as being truly Christian, are those governing the various Christian churches. The Episcopalian Church is one of the many.

Most of those churches have come under attack, with stronger and stronger suggestions, recommendations, and demands for the Christian churches to change their laws to match those of society.

And many churches are doing just that.

For whatever justification they use, the changes are motivated by fear - fear of losing membership, fear of being persecuted, fear of not being able to ably defend why not to change.

This erosion has seemed justified because the Laws of the Old Testament no longer seem to fit our New Freedom lifestyles. We modify everything these days, in order to keep up with changing times; and the times are changing much faster now.

Maybe sponsors will be the way of the future?

We read how God told the children of Israel, "You must do these things for eternity."

Eternity includes our modern times, meaning the remnants of the Israelites ... the Jews ... are sadly stuck with the dilemma of having to decide, "Which laws of God do we keep, which do we change, and which do we chunk into the trash?"

Us Christians tend to think, "Whew. Glad we don't have to worry about more than the Ten Commandments." We are not Jewish, after all.

The problem with that way of thinking is it is wrong.

The Jews were the remnants of the children of Israel because they had failed to maintain the Laws of Moses ... all of them to some degree ... as they were originally commanded.

Still, it was Jews who became the first Christians, while other Jews continue to memorize Laws and fail to live up to them. Christians do not have to be, nor should they want to be, like the Jews who are not Christians. However, Christians are expected to be like Jews who were Christians. Christians **ARE** the descendants of the children of Abraham, Isaac, and Jacob. We are Israelites by faith.

Paul was one of those Jews for Jesus, as an Apostle in the first wave of Christianity.

In his letter to the Romans, those early Christians who were primarily other Jews for Jesus, Paul told them, "You still have to obey all the Laws." He said that to Christians.

That means we too have to obey all the Laws of Moses, as written, for eternity, without thinking we can change one word or drop one clause.

The walls of restriction imposed by the Law sent by God will always seem to tightly wrap around us, like a boa constrictor, squeezing the life out of us ... when we live on the edge of our religion and not in the midst of it.

When we stand on the towers affixed to those walls of Law and look out over the land of sin beyond, where all the rest of society is happily going about, we begin to long for what they have, feeling like the Law needs to be modified.

Paul said, "Love your neighbor as yourself." As long as you love, all the perimeters of the Laws are so far away from your heart that you do not know what all the complaining is about.

The problem is getting people to fully understanding what "loving your neighbor" means. It does not mean accepting the sins of your neighbor as your own, as if having safety in numbers justifies changing God's Laws.

If the walls of the Law were just taken down and rebuilt a few miles out, just look at how many more we would have standing with us, within the new walls of the law!!!

It doesn't work that way folks.

We do not have the Freedom to play God, making up the laws.

Matthew told us how Jesus gave a series of instructions about what to do when you, as a disciple of his, find another disciple bringing sin upon you.

What does that mean, for one disciple of Christ to bring sin upon another disciple of Christ?

It means that if a disciple of Christ (a Jew for Jesus) breaks any of the 613 laws written by Moses in the Torah, in the presence of another Jew or Christian, then that sin is brought upon the one who has not broken that sin. It means that "sin" is based on those religious laws (Judeo-Christian), not any Roman laws or any government's laws, unless their laws match the religious laws of Moses. Therefore, if a government allows a sin to be legally acceptable – by law - then one must choose between one world and the other. Do I serve God or government?

You cannot be a priest for God while wearing a filthy robe.

You have to understand that at the point in time when Matthew was writing, Jesus had already told his disciples, "Do not sin. Live by the Law by following me." So the instructions are pertaining to one trying not to sin, as a disciple of Jesus. Still, stuff happens; so if one disciple sins and another disciple knows of this, it would be a sin to witness it and do nothing about it.

The first step, according to Jesus, is to directly confront the sinner, one-on-one. If that does not correct the sinning, then two or three members of the assembly of disciples following Jesus are to see this person continuing to sin and then collectively confront him. If that does not correct the sinning, then the sinner is to be brought before the whole congregation of Christians, for them all to demand the sinning cease. Finally, if none of those steps correct the sinning, the sinner is to be excommunicated ... treated as if that member were a Gentile of no religion, or a tax collector, a Jew who follows none of Moses' laws.

# After Pentecost Sermons: Proper 18, Year A

At no point in these instructions does Jesus say, "Well, if the sinner is a well-to-do member who puts a lot of money into the church coffers or volunteers to do more church service than most others, then give him some slack. If that happens you guys probably need to write some new laws or change the old ones."

No. Jesus said, "Where two or three are gathered in my name, I am there among them." That means, the Church of Jesus Christ is to have no sinners at all. If that means only two or three can go without sinning, then so be it. Jesus will be with those two or three.

Of course, Jesus would love the whole world to be devoted followers of his, all Free of sin.

That is what Freedom is about, and the Freedom from bondage God gave to the Israelites ... of whom Christians are descendants.

We are Freed from having to worry about sin because God set the rules for us to follow, so we will be without sin. Jesus came to take us one step further.

You cannot be Free of sin as long as you think you are that one who can sin every once in a while, in front of other Christians, and still get by because you make up for those sins with some extra credit stuff.

That is selfishness. It will not work in the long run. It destroys, not maintains the Law.

Paul, by saying all you have to do is love your neighbor, is saying that all you have to do is be truly filled with the Holy Spirit, receive the mind of Christ, and never again ever consider doing anything but what it takes to be a good Christian.

If only Christian neighborhoods were outwardly recognizable as such.

That means if you see a fellow Christian struggling to maintain acceptance of the Holy Spirit within, then you confront them with the fact that it is better to lean on me until you regain your strength, than it is to stand alone and succumb to sin. You love you neighbor as yourself, because you are just like your neighbor and you want the same help in return.

That kind of love does not come from will power or wanting to be a good Christian. It can only come from receiving God in your heart, so your love is God. Your thoughts are only like those of Jesus. You are then a reborn Jesus, unable to sin, and only desire to help your neighbors. Your neighbors are **only** those who are other Christians filled with the Holy Spirit or progressing to that point.

But, you do not fall in love with your neighbor's sin, and think wrapping your arms around that sin, covering it up will act as forgiveness. You do not have the authority to forgive sins by accepting them, as if you can make sin go away through blindness.

You forgive others by confronting them, not letting them go on sinning without an offer to help. You cannot have neighbors that continuously sin. You don't change the laws.

It is that simple.

It is that hard.

Whatever you wrap yourself in on earth, you will be wrapped within in heaven. Whatever you let loose on earth, you will let loose in heaven.

That means: If you change the laws to allow sin, you will **not** have the blessings of Christ or God. If you bind yourself to Christ while on earth, the Holy Spirit will be sent to you to assist you.

Or, as God instructed the children of Israel: Gird your loins with a priestly robe, be prepared to walk a righteous path for the rest of your life, hold the staff of the Holy Spirit as your crutch, and hurriedly consume the Lamb of God, so you will be capable of loving your neighbors as yourself.

Amen

# FOURTEENTH SUNDAY AFTER PENTECOST

## Proper 19

## YEAR A

**Relevant readings:**
Exodus 14:19-31
Psalm 114
  *or* Exodus 15:1-11
   Genesis 50:15-21
   Psalm 103:1-13
Romans 14:1-12
Matthew 18:21-35

After Pentecost Sermons: Proper 19, Year A

# Once you walk into the parted sea, on dry ground, it is too late to start thinking about swimming lessons

When I was young and first in college, taking physical education classes was mandatory. Besides a classroom course on health, where a book was read and tests on how well the students learned a book yielded a grade, five elective P.E. classes had to be taken. Each student got to choose which sports or exercises they wanted to sign up for; and then they learned the rules of that activity, with the grade based on one's participation on a field, in a bowling alley, or on a court.

One that I chose was Beginner Swimming, which took place in the school's swimming pool.

I learned how to swim long before I went to college, but I figured taking beginning swimming would be like an easy A. It was.

It was designed for people who had never learned how to swim, and the first weeks of the class we stood in the shallow end, held onto the side of the pool and practiced placing our faces in the water while blowing bubbles.

After three months of learning how to do the breast stroke and breathe while swimming, without drowning as we swam across the shallow end, never venturing out into the deep end, the final exam meant jumping into the deep end, off a diving board.

For us more advanced beginners, we had to **jump** off the high diving board (not dive), surface, and then swim the length of the pool, touching the edge at the shallow end.

For those who were still beginning swimmers, with less strength in swimming and breathing developed, they only had to jump off the low dive and swim, or dog paddle to the side of the pool, at the ladder to in the deep end.

Everyone did this, to varying degrees of apprehension, except one girl.

She walked out onto the low dive, looked at the deep water and fear overtook her. She would not jump into the water.

The coach pleaded with her. He told her that she would fail the course if she did not jump into the water. He assured her it was safe: he had positioned a few of his assistants – I assume members of the swimming team – dog paddling in the water with life preservers in their hands, ready to immediately come to her aid after she jumped in. There were other assistants standing along the end and side of the pool with long poles, which they held over the water ... for her to grab hold of, if need be.

They gave her a life vest to put on, so she would not sink after getting into the water.

She walked slowed out to near the end of the diving board. She leaned over and looked at the water. Her legs trembled. She had fear written all over her face. Everyone was encouraging her that it would be okay. Her saviors were in position and nothing bad would happen to her.

The girl refused to take the leap. She hurriedly got off the diving board and curled up in tears. The coach slammed his clipboard down on the tiles surrounding the pool and stormed off, saying, "You get an F!"

I remember that story while reading the Exodus story of Moses leading the children of Israel into the sea, with its waters parted, and dry land for them to walk across.

# After Pentecost Sermons: Proper 19, Year A

I imagine if I had been in a camp by the sea, I would have some sense of direction, knowing which way the sea was. Seas usually have a breeze, a scent and a sound associated with them. So, when Moses told everyone, "Get up. It's time to head out," they had to know he was marching them towards the sea, if not into it.

It was night when they left, but the pillar of cloud and fire stood between their camp and the Egyptian army, lighting up the darkness, preventing an attack. I presume that light was what allowed them to follow Moses into the sea, so they would not stumble on any rocks that might have been in their path.

Still, I imagine the darkness kept them from seeing that there was a wall of water to their left and their right, walls that towered over their heads.

They were walking where deep waters had been, on a level much deeper than the deep end of a swimming pool. They did this not because they knew how to swim, nor because they were brave. They did not march after Moses because he offered them a passing grade.

They followed Moses blindly, with faith. I imagine none of the children of Israel even saw the walls of water; but if they did see them, there certainly were no knees knocking or crying about how dangerous it all seemed.

The path seemed so safe, even the Egyptians took the same course into the sea, chasing after the Israelites. At first, the path was dry, and I imagine they were too busy hurrying to catch the rear of the Israelite column to see there were walls of water on their left and right, towering higher and higher over their heads, the further they pursued.

Today we read that, "The Egyptians pursued, and went into the sea after them, all of Pharaoh's horses, chariots, and chariot drivers." In Exodus 14:7 we know the number of chariots was six hundred, and the drivers were the best he had."

I imagine, if a horse and chariot were ten feet in length, and five feet in width, then the path wide enough for three chariots to be safely side-by-side, with a safe following distance of twenty feet and a safe passing lane – should one lose a wheel and need to be by-passed – there would be thirty foot wide road, twenty feet deep, just for three chariots at a time entering the sea. There were then two hundred such distances, the Egyptians would have gone at least six thousand feet into the sea; and that assumes a nice flat area uncovered, without any large boulders that were previously underwater.

That calculates to 1.1364 miles. Since it is safe to assume the Egyptians were in the sea at the same time the Israelites were in the sea, I imagine it would be safe to project a minimum of two miles across the sea floor had been travelled by the Israelites.

If you walk a mile out into the deep end, there is no quick way out of the water, even if the ground below your feet is dry.

When dawn came, and light made the situation known, the Egyptians realized where they were. The dry ground began to turn to mud. They were seized by fear. They wanted to run away; but it was too late.

"At dawn the sea returned to its normal depth." It "covered the chariots and the chariot drivers, the entire army of Pharaoh." We then read, "Not one of them survived."

Still, as the waters were overwhelming the Egyptians, those Israelites still walking along the sea floor were safe. They "walked on dry ground through the sea, (with) the waters forming a wall for them on their right and on their left."

Those who had reached the shore, along with Moses, they watched as this miracle unfolded – Egyptians tossed and drowned in the rush of water, while Israelites still walked between unmoving walls of water. The Israelites saw the dead bodies wash ashore and "the people feared the LORD and believed the LORD was with Moses."

Some say, "Seeing is believing," but the Israelites did not see the miracle as it was happening. If they had seen where they were going ... if they knew how impossible that was ... they would have been like that girl on the low diving board in my P.E. class ... frozen with fear ... unable to move beyond the shore, into the water ... regardless of how many promises of safety were presented.

If you remember the story of Jesus walking on the Sea of Galilee, the disciples were in a boat and fearful for their lives. Peter said to Jesus, "Call me to walk on the water and I will come." Jesus said, "Come!"

Peter took steps in response to that instruction from Jesus. The same can be said of the children of Israel, after they heard Moses say, "Come!"

But, Peter began to see the impossibility of water being a safe place to take a walk. He became like an Egyptian, sinking into the waves ... until Jesus pulled him out.

Jesus said, "Oh you of little faith. Why did you doubt?"

It is all about faith. It is all about hearing the call and responding to the call without thought.

Thinking only gets you in trouble.

Paul's letter to the Christians of Rome points to those with weak faith. He was talking about Christians criticizing other Christians for not knowing when the Sabbath was, or what to eat and not eat, or when to fast and when to feast. Too much thinking was going on, about what other people were doing, rather than simply doing as instructed by the voice within.

In the Gospel reading today, Matthew told how Peter went to Jesus and asked how many times he needed to forgive one of those who made up the assembly of followers – the church led by Jesus. Peter wanted to know when he could stop forgiving and start finger pointing, if he saw some of the followers were not doing something right, according to the Law of Moses.

Both of these readings point out issues of faith, as focusing on Christians judging other Christians, and not about Christians judging anyone not a Christian.

As Christians, we are all members of the same family, but we are each on different levels of spiritual attainment. It is like all of us are in a Beginner Swimming class, but some of know how to swim and others are just learning. Some of us are symbolically eleven times seven (77*), meaning we already know how to breathe as we stroke, blowing out air with our face in the water, and breathing in air as we turn our heads to the surface, all as we stroke with our arms and kick with our feet. Some of us are symbolically sevens, meaning we know where the pool is, but we still are not sure about going into the water.

If you recall when I explained the symbolism of the number "eleven," Jesus is saying how those simply following the law forgive seven times. However, those who have been elevated by the Holy Spirit, as "eleven" people, they forgive by teaching those in need of forgiveness how to receive the spirit. True Christians then become the teaching instructors for the beginners.

We are all either teaching or learning how to trust in God and not drown in the sea of misery that surrounds us in the world. We are all either teaching or learning to follow Christ whenever he calls, without fear, doubt, or question.

We are all either filled with the Holy Spirit or seeking to be so filled. Without that commonality we have no meaningful relationship.

As family, we have all embarked on the path of Christianity, just like the Israelites entered into the sea, with walls of water on the right and on the left. Our enemies are on our heels.

Our lives are now completely dependent on faith.

We should all help each other to the other side, rather than complain about how impossible things seem.

We must not get tired of holding the pole of salvation out to yet another one who has ventured out on the diving board, but has little faith and too many doubts.

Amen

\* The reading says Jesus told Peter to forgive "seventy times seven." This means "seventy times" (7 X 10), with another "seven" then added, making eleven times seven be the instruction. It does not means 70 X 7 = 490.

# FIFTEENTH SUNDAY AFTER PENTECOST

# Proper 20

# YEAR A

**Relevant readings:**
Exodus 16:2-15
Psalm 105:1-6; 37-45
Jonah 3:10-4:11
Psalm 145:1-8
Philippians 1:21-30
Matthew 20:1-16

After Pentecost Sermons: Proper 20, Year A

# In the company of God, you are expected to provide customer service

Everyone has heard of "customer service." As customers, we expect to be served. Businesses depend on customers, so they have to be concerned about "customer service."

There are two basic ways companies serve their customers. The first way is to sell them a product – they serve the customer what the customer wants.

You go to a restaurant and order a meal, which is then brought to you … in a bag or on a plate. Dinner is served.

You go to a phone store and listen to a clerk tell you about all the different features of service their phones have. Then you buy one and the clerk sets up your phone so it works. A new customer leaves with a shiny new phone and phone service.

You go to the mall store and find some piece of clothing you like, and you ask the clerk to let you try the clothing on. If it fits well and looks well, then you buy the piece of clothing. Certain stores actually measure you and make tailored adjustments, to fit the customer's needs.

Every business serves its customers by making sales.

Then there is the second way customers are served by companies: they respond to complaints.

"This steak is over-cooked."

"My bag of food was short something."

"I just got a $500 bill for my phone service and I want to know how that happened."

"I need to return this piece of clothing because it makes me itchy when I wear it."

Overall, the complainers far outnumber those who take the time to tell a company just how pleased they are with the product or service they received.

The failure of companies to provide as much attention to complaints as they do when making a sale makes customers complain about the difficulties they face filing complaints. Sometimes, trying to get a cable company to stop your service, due to poor customer service, does not solve the problems. It makes it worse.

That lack of attention makes people more prone to be geared up to complain, rather than always expecting to be pleasantly surprised by a company following up on a sale. No one expects a company's customer service department to be calling them before they can find reason, asking them to think hard ... "Are sure you cannot find any complaints?"

That kind of customer service does not exist, in part because we human beings love an outlet for expressing our opinions on anything and everything in the world that does not meet our personal expectations.

We are natural born complainers.

In the readings today, we see evidence of that human trait.

The children of Israel complain, "If only we had died by the hand of the LORD in the land of Egypt, when we sat by the fleshpots and ate our fill of bread; for you have brought us out into this wilderness to kill the whole assembly with hunger."

# After Pentecost Sermons: Proper 20, Year A

In the parable told by Jesus, we hear the first hired laborers complain, "These last worked only an hour, and you have made them equal to us who have borne the burden of the day and the scorching heat."

This theme of complaining has become a caricature of being Jewish. Jewish comedians joke about hearing their uncles complaining, "Your knee? My back!"

In reality, we are all crying out about something we complain about; but because no one wants to listen, we learn it is best to keep our complaints to ourselves. We suffer in silence.

For that reason, open a complaint department, then just sit back and watch the lines form.

"Finally! Someone is willing to listen."

However, companies want to make our complaining as difficult as possible, so we will revert to silent suffering.

Eating the over-cooked steak is better than waiting an extra thirty minutes and making the cook mad.

Go without the fries you just paid for and split the fries you did get.

Pay the phone bill regardless of the hidden costs that were unexpected.

Give the piece of clothing to someone who is not allergic to the material.

Move on with your life. Realize stuff happens. Get over it.

This, in a way, is the message of Paul. He wrote to the Philippians from his Roman prison cell, as he was awaiting his eventual execution.

If anyone had reason to complain, it was Paul. Instead, he wrote (and I paraphrase), "I am hard pressed between my desire to depart and be with Christ , begging my jailers to go ahead and execute me; and my natural fight to survive, seeking to remain in the flesh so I can continue to be available for you." The Philippians, like the Israelites Moses led, needed leadership they could tell their pains to, and know their complaints would be given careful consideration.

The Israelites were complaining about their possible deaths, from starvation. Moses was in the same position of need, but he was responsible for those who followed his lead.

Paul was seeing the beauty of death, but did not want to leave young Christians without a shoulder to cry their complaints upon.

The Israelites had Moses and Aaron, who listened like Paul. They heard reasonable complaints ... the complaints everyone has. Those customer service reps were middlemen for the Big Boss upstairs, and the complaints were heard at the top.

We all need food to live, otherwise we die. The Israelites complained about basic needs not being met. They feared the worst, probably still far from starvation. We all need someone to care about our pains and suffering, someone who keeps checking in on us to make sure we are okay. Like the figurative babies they were, they cried at the first twinge of hunger, because that was all they knew to do in order to get what they needed. Knowing someone is paying attention means we can endure silently, without worrying others needlessly.

In the parable told by Jesus, the complaints by the laborers were not about needs being met. The first hired laborers had agreed with the landowner about their wages. After each had been paid that wage, their complaint was not about not getting what they bargained for; but, instead it was about not receiving preferential treatment. The first hired suddenly desired more than they bought in for.

In all of these examples of complaints and potential complaints, the "company" has to be seen as God. God runs a company the way one should be run. God's "customer service department" listens to complaints and responds correctly and in a timely manner. It cares ... something human business struggles with.

To the children of Israel, they were right to complain about a lack of food. Food is a need. They were given meat in the evening (via quails) and bread in the morning (via manna). Service with a smile.

Their needs were met because they had followed Moses and Aaron into a wilderness through faith in the LORD. Only the LORD could meet their needs in such a hostile environment; and as such, they needed to experience a miracle to have their faith increased. They had to cry first, in order to feel the impact of receiving their nourishment.

Paul was meeting that same need in the faith of the Philippians. He was providing them with "customer service," telling them that it can seem like everything would be better off, if only you could die and go to Heaven. But, your faith is needed here, in the flesh, as a model of faith, so the faith of others can be elevated.

In the Gospel of Matthew, we read of Jesus telling how the landowner (God) told the complaining laborers (the Pharisees of the Temple), "the last will be first, and the first will be last."

The "last" who "will be first" are those of true faith, the followers of Christ, the new laborers for a new covenant. Those of true faith will be "first" in line to the kingdom of heaven.

The "heavenly kingdom company" of God is all about selling a good product and following up on that sale, making sure everyone is happy with that product.

The "first" who "will be last" are those of little faith, those who do lip service for the LORD. The Israelites were the first, as those who agreed to the Covenant presented by Moses, who then lost everything from negligence. They had come back from exile in hopes God would forgive them one more time.

The representatives of the "first" were then the Pharisees and Temple priests. The first hired laborers agreed to a wage (the Covenant), but then they did so little work that the landowner had to keep hiring more and more workers. The "first" result was nothing being done, more than them just hanging around until quitting time, expecting to be paid for their "customer no-service." They had no true faith, so they would be "last" in line to the kingdom of God.

The same model applies today, just as well as it did in the past. If you have faith in God, your complaints about needs will be heard and promptly dealt with. You might not get what you want, but you will at least get a flash of understanding about what you do have, so you can see that is worth more than you thought.

If you are saying you have faith, while doing little more than signing up for the "reward points," then don't be surprised if your efforts to redeem them in the earthly plane finds little acceptance. If you complain about not getting extras and perks, then you may find it is like calling out to God and reaching his "toll free number," with a computerized voice command program that constantly says, "I'm sorry. I did not understand that. Let's try again. Say or enter your complaint."

It is always easier to build yourself a "Good Christian Booth" to sit in.  Relaxing and wiling away the time, rather than doing the actual work of a true good Christian.  Your sign is all that gives the impression that you are as you advertise.  Avoiding the scorching heat of the day in a relatively comfortable place, while making plans to go to Heaven when you die, is not part of the wages you agreed to.  Sure, you said you would work for Heaven, so you were hired to fill the position of priest; but how come God had to keep finding other laborers to actually complete the harvest?

It was because you failed to do the work you promised.

If people were to mistake your booth as a "Complaints Department Counter," coming to you so their faith in God could be revived, do not be surprised.  Good Christians are known to seek customer satisfaction, advertising, "We Listen."

The problem comes when other Christians find you nonresponsive or unavailable, because you do not know how to help people.  You get exposed for what you truly are and what company you really work for, which isn't one devoted to God or Christ.

If you are **not** living in the flesh, instead living as one "standing firm in one spirit, striving side by side with one mind for the faith of the gospel, in no way intimidated by your opponents," then you are an encouragement for "salvation," not "destruction."  You provide customer service as a priest, a minister, a pastor, a good shepherd.

Good Christian Customer Service helps save souls, which is a need.

God has "graciously granted you the privilege **not only of believing in Christ**, but of suffering for him as well."  By believing in Christ, you welcome the complaints of fellow Christians and you help soothe their pains by demonstrating the strength that faith brings.

Being "first" is not all it is cracked up to be; but being "last" is not as bad as it seems.

You just need to choose which position you want to be in ... wisely.

Amen

# SIXTEENTH SUNDAY AFTER PENTECOST

## Proper 21

## YEAR A

**Relevant readings:**
Exodus 17:1-7
Psalm 78:1-4; 12-16
　Ezekiel 18:1-4; 25-32
　Psalm 25:1-8
Philippians 2:1-13
Matthew 21:23-32

Robert Tippett

# Growing from innocent babies into responsible adult Christians

When I was a driver for United Parcel Service, my route was in a rural community. The town's Main Street was on the line between two counties, so half the community was in one county, with the other half in another.

One of the counties used street numbers for all addresses, while the other county only used Rural Route addresses. That means everyone who lives on one rural route road has the same address.

For example, one road was Center Hill Church Road. The Route 3 part of that road was a four-mile long road, between two state highways (which the road crossed at both ends, but was no longer Route 3). That particular stretch of road got its name because the Center Hill Baptist Church was on it, about two miles from either end.

Over that four-mile span, there were probably fifty to seventy-five houses, with each having a mailbox. The address for every one of those mailboxes was Rt. 3 Center Hill Church Rd.

That means anyone delivering packages to the people who live on Center Hill Church Road needs to know who lives in each house. That is a learning process that takes time.

One good thing about a rural community is people know most of the other people around them. So, in the hunt and peck method of learning, a driver sees someone, stops and then asks, "Do you know where so and so lives?"

You find out that one four-mile road, like Center Hill Church Road, only has about five different family names that live in about forty of those houses. On top of that, those five families most likely sold the land that the rest of the houses were built on, so they have an idea who lives in those houses.

One family I quickly came to know owned five houses (or trailers), all on one side of the road. I first met the parents of three children, each of who lived on Center Hill Church Road. One son had a garage, which could generally be called "next door," although it and his house were a quarter-mile down the road. Their son worked on cars in his garage, but it wasn't like a business that was open every day, at certain hours. It was open on an "as needed" basis. The son's mother pointed out the garage to me, and told me that he lived in the trailer just on the other side of the garage, in a stand of pine trees ... next door.

I made regular deliveries to that trailer, about once a week. I eventually met the son who worked on cars, and his wife, because they would receive C.O.D packages, which the parents were not going to pay for. Over time, I met their daughter, who was around twelve or thirteen when I began learning the people of that rural community.

One day, heavy rain was pouring down. It was one of those "all day rains." In my young history as a U.P.S. driver, I had always thanked God when it rained, because no matter how hard it rained while I was driving the package car, when I stopped to make a delivery the rain always seemed to slack off.

That was important in those days because drivers still used paper delivery record pads, on clipboards, and were required to get signatures for all deliveries. It was hard to make a ball-point pen write on wet paper.

That day I had a delivery for the man in the trailer, next door to the garage on Center Hill Church Road. It was raining when I rolled to a stop as hard as it had been all day. Despite the pine tree cover, the rain was pelting hard on the vehicle. As I opened the bulkhead door, I thought my luck had finally run out. I was prepared to get soaked making that delivery.

However, by the time it took to take the package off the shelf and turned around to step back into the cab (less than 30 seconds), the teenage daughter of the man was standing in the cab of my package car, smiling, and drenched with rain. She had on no coat or hat, and she had no umbrella. She obviously saw me pull up and then she immediately ran out to meet me, unprepared for heavy rain.

I was shocked. I asked, "Why did you run out in the rain? You're soaked."

She said, "So you wouldn't get wet. I don't mind."

I shook my head and wrote up the package info on the paper log and handed it to her to sign. She did, following my instructions … "first initial, last name."

I thanked her and she immediately took the package, an envelope, and ran back into the pouring rain, into the trailer … soaking wet from head to foot.

About four or five years later, after I had gone into management at U.P.S. and stopped being the U.P.S. driver for that rural community, I was shocked by the news I saw on television.

That sweet girl had shot and killed both her mother and father, in that trailer. The reason was said to be because the girl was not allowed to use the father's Mustang on a Friday night.

Because the girl was then seventeen, she was tried as an adult and sentenced to many years in prison for her crime.

It is a sad ending to that story.

I tell you this story because we all have been children, and many of us have children of our own, and most of those children have grown into adulthood, with some having children of their own, our grandchildren.

The readings for today focus on that element of childhood, where the point of responsibility for one's actions is reached, after stages of growth and development having prepared us for that day.

In the Exodus story today, we read how Moses led the children of Israel into the wilderness, where they complained about their not having water to drink. Last week, they complained about not having food to eat. Rather than see them as bellyachers and complainers, we need to think of the Israelites as an infant child. We need to realize they were completely dependent on Moses, just as a baby has no means of doing anything for itself. A baby is totally dependent on the parents for life, so a baby cries when it needs something.

The baby Israelites cried. God, the Father, and Moses, the nurturer of the baby, provided for the baby's needs. Quails and manna fed them, with Moses making water spring from rocks. Each miracle act was a natural response to the child's demands.

It is this miracle working that makes babies see their parents as super-heroes. Caring for children creates a strong emotional bond, one that makes children believe in their parent's abilities to teach them the truth, unconditionally.

Regardless of that blissful relationship, when children reach certain ages they get tired of being cared for and they want to be all grown up.

We did not read from the Book of Ezekiel today, but the optional alternate Old Testament reading that has been set aside for us tells of God speaking to Ezekiel in a dream, telling him to stop using the proverb, "The parents have eaten sour grapes, and the children's teeth are set on edge."

Most of us have heard or read that before, but few have the ability to explain what that proverb of Ezekiel means.

The Hebrew proverb that most likely fits, as the source of Ezekiel's comparison, is: "Grapes picked too soon don't even make good vinegar."

Ezekiel was saying the children of Israel (and Judah) had grown into parents too soon. Because they wanted to be adults before they were ready … to make their own decisions about what was good and what was bad … they were setting their children up to fail. The parents had tasted the sour grapes of exile, with their land overrun by the Babylonians. Their children were about to bite into the sour grapes of their parents, born in a foreign land.

The immature Israelites had wanted to be like other nations; and even though God was supposed to be their king, they started making bad choices in kings and queens, to the point of losing it all. They were too young to be making grown-up decisions, but once made, if of age, you pay for the crime.

Paul, wrote to his disciples in Philippi … his children, who he had raised to become good Christians. He encouraged them to remember all the things he had taught them. Remember about the holiness of Christ, he wrote. Remember everything about Christ, because they were soon to be "of age," when Paul would no longer be around to "father" them and they would be responsible for their own actions.

And then we read how Jesus asked the chief priests and teachers of the temple to answer which son did what the father instructed, either the lazy son who said "No," but then went to work in the vineyard, or the lying son who gave all the right answers, only to do none of what he said he would do. They answered correctly, recognizing the lazy son was the one who actually did the will of the father.

# After Pentecost Sermons: Proper 21, Year A

Jesus then told those elders that sinners were closer to the kingdom of heaven than they were. They were metaphorically called the lying sons of the Father. Because of their lies, all of Judaism believed they were the children of God (as opposed to the Gentiles), as if they were still infants, too young to do anything for themselves. The people did not know how to be responsible for their sins.

Or, they acted as if they were school-age children, still learning the mistakes of their ways, thus always deserving of another chance.

Believing they were children, and not adults, would make any extreme punishment for their sins come as a shock ... when tried as adults and not those cute children of God.

But all children have to grow up and take responsibility for their own actions ... and inaction. The lazy son knew all the work involved in tending to a vineyard, and he did not want to work. He said what he felt, "No!"

But, then a voice inside his head spoke to him. He knew it was not a matter of choice. He had a role of responsibility to play; so he went to the fields and did the work required.

I'm sure he grumbled the whole time ... but he went to work.

Jesus pointed out to the Pharisees and priests, "The tax collectors and prostitutes believed in John the Baptist." That meant, even though they each were saying, "No!" to the right things to do, they at least heard the voice inside their heads telling them they were wrong to refuse a bath with water that symbolically cleansed them of their sins.

Feeling guilt made them closer to heaven, although they still had said, "No!" None of them had yet gone to do the work the Father instructed. Therefore, they were the same as the lying son, as far as present-time salvation was concerned.

The lying son, on the other hand, knew the work was hard and long, and felt no guilt in having none of it. He just knew lying would make it appear he was Mr. Obedience.

We are no different than those two sons of the father in that parable. At times we are lazy. At times we are liars.

But, we are no longer babies, incapable of being held responsible. We have come of age and have the freedom to do whatever we choose is best, right or wrong.

Our judgment will be fair, based on our actions.

In the Lord's vision before Ezekiel, God mentioned how the house of Israel complained about "The way of the Lord is unfair." God asked back, "Is it not your ways that are unfair?"

God then said the punishment for iniquity will be harsh. He advised, "Get yourselves a new heart and a new spirit!"

God ended by saying, "I have no pleasure in the death of anyone. Turn, then, and live."

Be adults. Be all grown-up; but as Paul encouraged his teenager Christians, "Let the same mind be in you that was in Christ Jesus."

Amen

# SEVENTEENTH SUNDAY AFTER PENTECOST

## Proper 22

## YEAR A

**Relevant readings:**
Exodus 20:1-20
Psalm 19
  Isaiah 5:1-7
  Psalm 80:7-14
Philippians 3:4-14
Matthew 21:33-46

Robert Tippett

# Knowing the laws is only the first step in God's plan

I was born in the capitol city of my home state. I spent the first three years of my life living in an urban, midtown apartment, where there was much hustle and bustle about.

There were streets that had cars passing by, which made crossing the street a hazard.

I was taught, "Do not cross the street without looking both ways for cars AND THEN cross only with an adult holding your hand."

For the most part, I obeyed this law. It made sense to my young two and a half-year-old mind. I sure did not want to get run over by a car.

Still, when an urge to explore would hit me and there were no adults around, I would sometimes bend the rules and cross the street alone. I looked left and right before running across.

No one told me to look back. That was where my mother was watching me break the law. When I got back home I found out what happens to lawbreakers.

When I was about 4 years old, we moved out of the city into the suburbs. There was not as much hustle-bustle there; but, still, there was the law about not crossing the street alone.

I was the only kid who lived on the side of the road our house was on. There were many kids who lived on the opposite side, and at times all us kids on the road would stand across from one another, unable to cross to all be on the same side.

# After Pentecost Sermons: Proper 22, Year A

The subdivision was still in a developmental stage, as paved roads, the kind with deep tar, rather than gravel with surface tar spray, had not yet come to the neighborhood. Back then, the road had clay clods along the edge of the road. That was where the local government planned to later come and put in granite curbs.

As kids looking for fun things to do, we would throw clay clods at one another, across the road. Our young arms were not able to actually throw a ball of dirt twenty-to-thirty feet, so the road would be where most of the dirt ended up. After one of our "battles" the black road would be covered with red clay streaks. No eyes were ever put out.

One day, after the granite curbs had been set in place, and fresh dirt clods were about, one kid and I faced off, kiddo a kiddo. He had more ammunition than I did, so he did more throwing. Besides, he was probably only 3, while I was going on 5. So, he was out of my league. I just stood there and watched him miss me, laughing at him.

Then, that boy's mother saw him throwing dirt at me and she ran out of the house scooped him up in her arms and she then began laying down the law on his behind. New law for him to remember: "You do not throw things at other children!"

I laughed some more.

I sat down on that new granite curb and laughed and laughed. I laughed until I found out another new law.

"Thou shalt not sit down in an ant hill, lest thou get bit."

I jumped up and looked down. I saw the anthill and ants on my legs. I ran crying, "Momma, momma, momma!"

I tell you this story because the children of Israel were like babies, kids who knew nothing on their own. They were like kids who would cross the road dangerously, hurt others with stones without realizing what they were doing, and laugh at other people's misery, while expecting their own miseries to be immediately soothed by motherly care.

They were like babies that needed to be told what to do and what not to do.

For that reason, they were told the Law of Moses. And, when God made noises that put exclamation points on those Laws, they feared what would happen if they should ever break one.

Just like I had never been run over by a car, I feared that happening ... because I broke the law.

God told Moses to let them know, "Do not be afraid; for God has come only to test you and to put the fear of him upon you so that you do not sin."

That's right! I never did get run over by a car; but I sure did get whacked by my mother for breaking the law.

Fear God. God is like those eyes watching you sin when you don't realize it. God is like a bed of ants waiting for your butt to sit with them, after sinning.

In Psalm 19, David used metaphor to tell how constant the Laws of God were. Regardless of where you are on the time line of faith, if it was wrong long ago, then it is still wrong today.

"One day tells its tale to another," David sang.

"It goes forth from the uttermost edge of the heavens and runs about to the end of it again."

What goes around always comes around, again and again.

Once we grow to understand these laws we are taught as children, having seen the same result repeat time and time again, we become mature. It finally dawns on us why it was our parents told us laws and rules.

It was so we would not mess our lives up, if not end them completely by accident. It was for our own good, although ... like the saying goes, "no pain, no gain."

In Paul's letter to the Philippians, he talks metaphorically about death. He told of his own change from Saul, the man he used to be, who thought he deserved a standing of "righteousness under the law." Saul became Paul when he suddenly became aware that he had misunderstood the Laws that had been taught him.

Paul wrote about how he thought he had "reason to be confident in the flesh."

Now, let's review what "reason" means. By definition, the meaning for the infinitive verb "to reason" is: "To think logically." In actuality, the Greek word written by Paul was "*dokei*," which translates as, "to think, to suppose." So, "reason" means "using the ole noggin." Paul **thought** he had confidence in the flesh.

What Paul was then pointing out, about his realizing he was wrong about what he thought it meant to be chosen by God as special, was that learning the Laws of God was only a baby step towards being truly special. It was wrong to think more into that.

It was faulty thinking, bad logic, wrongful supposing.

Now, knowing that David wrote a song about how laws always remain constant, repeating over and over, Paul understood that there were Christians in Philippi who were just like Saul ...

thinking they were special because they were Jews, God's chosen special breed of human being.

He warned them not to think in such ways, but to feel the presence of the Lord, through the Holy Spirit, and let the mind of Christ bring them true understanding of the Laws.

Raise your hands if you have figured all this out and your personal sense of well-being is because you think you are God's chosen special person, based on "confidence in the flesh."

<look for raised hands>

Do you think being Episcopalian is better than being Roman Catholic, Baptist, or Methodist, or Assemblies of God?

Do you think you are a Christian because you follow rules your parents taught you?

Don't be embarrassed if you find a tingling on your legs, or a bite or two on your butt … in case your pew has a concealed anthill. Remember, Paul wrote, "I want to know Christ and the power of his resurrection and the sharing of his sufferings by becoming like him in his death."

You see, when Jesus told his parable, the one that we read this morning, those listening were the chief priests and elders of the temple. He was talking to those who thought they knew "righteousness under the law." They thought they were "blameless."

If anyone had asked them, "Raise your hand if you think you are special in the eyes of God, having figured everything out," they would have all stood while raising their hands high.

It is human nature to want to cross the street when the urge hits you, to laugh at the misery of others when they are caught doing wrong, and to cry to God for salvation when things don't go the way you planned. It is human nature to want to be the best ... the teacher's pet ... the chosen one.

We look at our "confidence in the flesh" and thank God he made us special, and not like those kids across the street.

Then, some kid named Jesus came along and started making everyone look like a fool for thinking they were special.

They rejected the cornerstone that was the Lord's doing.

Matthew wrote, "They wanted to arrest (Jesus), but they feared the crowds."

They feared the crowds ... not like the instruction God gave to Moses, explaining the reason He gave His children Laws and made loud noises that scared them. It was "to put the fear of (God) upon you ... so you do not sin."

But, the chief priests and elders of the temple feared the crowd, who thought Jesus was a prophet. Matthew did not say the reason they did not arrest Jesus was they feared God.

What everyone here today needs to go home pondering is this:

Do you have "confidence in the flesh" because you do everything the crowd does; and because you learned to do that so well, you feel special?

Do you call following the crowd being Christian, because the crowd calls itself Christian?

Could you give up all that you have today, and look back tomorrow on what you once had, seeing those things lost as rubbish?

Try pondering these things from your heart, and not you minds.

Robert Tippett

Amen

# EIGHTEENTH SUNDAY AFTER PENTECOST

# Proper 23

# YEAR A

**Relevant readings:**
Exodus 32:1-14
Psalm 106:1-6; 19-23
Isaiah 25:1-9
Psalm 23
Philippians 4:1-9
Matthew 22:1-14

Robert Tippett

# Wedding crashers sometimes get caught and thrown out of the banquet

Years ago, when I was young and wild, I happened to be in southern Florida. Because I knew a friend who had moved there, close to where I was visiting, I decided to pay him a visit. It was unexpected, but I was welcomed to drop by and stay with him for a while.

As we were catching up on how each of our lives had unfolded since we last were able to pal around, my friend told me he had to go to a wedding party. He asked me if I wanted to go with him, and I said, "Sure."

He wasn't dressed formally, and neither was I. We met up with some of his Florida friends, and none of them were dressed any differently than we were. In several cars (none mine, as I had flown to Florida), we drove to some place that I had never been before in my life; and we got out and met a couple of adult males on a sidewalk. Everyone was happy to see one another.

Then, one adult male headed towards a building, followed by my friend and his friends, but the other adult male came up to me and said, "I'm sorry, but this is a Jewish wedding party. You are not an invited guest, plus you are not Jewish, so you cannot go inside."

Before he left, he said, "I'm sure you understand."

Then, I was left alone on the sidewalk; with no idea how long a Jewish wedding party lasted. So, I went to a pay phone and called for a cab. I took a taxi to the airport and I flew back home. My trip to Florida was over.

I remembered this flash from my past because of the parable

# After Pentecost Sermons: Proper 23, Year A

Jesus told the people of the temple in Jerusalem. I imagine, had I been allowed to attend that wedding party in Florida, I might have stood out as uninvited. I might have been asked questions by whoever was paying for everyone to have a nice time, which I could not answer well enough to justify my being there. In essence, I would have been a wedding crasher.

It was best I leave on my own accord. Better that than be kicked out.

Still, the point Jesus was making was not about someone being uninvited, as the king had sent his messenger out into the streets to invite everyone to come – good and bad.

The "one man" who stood out, did so because he was the only one not wearing a "wedding robe." He was spotted by the king because he did not desire to be part of the celebration. By not putting on a "wedding robe," he was refusing to be "married" to the king's son. By not putting on a "wedding robe," the one man was stating he was not a priest to the king's son.

When Jesus said at the end of the parable, which can be taken as the moral of the story, "For many are called, but few are chosen," this can be somewhat confusing to some.

It sounds a lot like when Jesus said, "The harvest is plentiful, but the laborers are few," where many are called to pick the grapes, but few volunteered to do that work. It is that being restated, but the word "chosen" can seem difficult to grasp, when compared to "few laborers."

The Greek word written is "*eklektoí*" ("ἐκλεκτοί") can translate as, "chosen out, elected, picked, or selected." Keep in mind that this parable follows the one we read a few weeks back, where the master of a vineyard hired laborers for the vineyard, at several times during the day, paying all the workers the same wage.

"The last will be first, and the first will be last," was the moral of that story.

Maybe God likes people who don't stand in lines to buy stuff ... the first with the new gadgets, or the first with Black Friday deals?

After the parable reading today, we can see how "many laborers were hired, but few chose to do the work." They showed up, but they probably were not dressed to work. Because the vineyard owner kept seeing no work was being done, he kept sending for more workers. That means that the last workers hired did, in one hour, what the first workers took all day not accomplishing. The first did nothing at all.

This means "chosen" is an act of the wedding guest, and also of the laborers, but not of the king or of the vineyard master.

"Many are called" to attend a marriage between the king's son and those who would become his dedicated workers – the marriage banquet was planned for those who would put on the robes of marriage – as priests, servants to the king. However, those invited did not care to go that far.

"Few are chosen" means, "few choose to answer the call."

For the vineyard owner, only those hired at 5:00 PM were motivated to do hard labor, thankful for that opportunity. They chose to work, such that even being the last called to work they saw an urgency. They chose to actually pick the grapes, to gather the harvest, thus they were most deserving of a full day's wages.

In Paul's letter to the Philippians, he points out the names of three who were called to the king's wedding, as all Christians have been. All who knew Paul personally, through his ministry, had put on the wedding robes, as priests married to Jesus Christ. Because the invitations had gone out to everyone – both those good and those bad – Jews and Gentiles, sinners being repentant – it seems the minds of Euodia and Syntyche were two choosing to do the work. However, each did their work differently.

Paul pointed out in his letter, "I plead with Euodia and I plead with Syntyche to be of the same mind in the Lord."

Thus, this bad element was showing through their robing, as some form of bickering and complaining about each other. The two were women, and because Paul addressed this chapter to his "brothers and sisters" the early church recognized the laborers were both males and females.

The implication of Paul pointing these two women out may be because women are more prone to be emotionally committed to their relationships and strive more for perfection. This sense of feeling might have made both become blinded to there being more than one way to do the same work. Thus, these two women were not of the same mind, and the one mind they needed was the mind of Jesus Christ.

Paul recommended that Clement help them out; and there are those who believe Clement of Philippi would later become Pope Clement I. He is believed to be either the second or third Bishop of Rome, following Saint Peter.

Now, that history is well and fine, but it does little to have us stand up and put on our wedding robes, having us be filled with the Holy Spirit as those married to Christ in mind and heart.

This means understanding the symbolism found in names can help a little towards that goal.

The name Euodia means, "Good road" or "Good trip." It is something like the saying, "Have a nice day!"

The name Syntyche means, "With chance" or "Good fortune,"

but because it meant luck more than skill, it's common use in Greece implied "Ill fortune."

So, we need to hear Paul saying there was some "cat fighting" going on between two brides of Christ, as they may have entered into that holy matrimony because being Christian meant (to one woman) "Everything would be easy going." Contrarily, one might have complained because the "Good fortune that was expected as a reward for being Christian" was not panning out, seeing there were way too many grapes to pick.

The name Clement means, "Peace" or Calm." This is representing someone who is truly married to Jesus, with the "mind of Christ" taking over and leading him. Clement represents one who truly chooses to serve the king, married to his son in heart and mind.

Thus, Paul was pointing out attendees at the wedding banquet who have to be seen as paralleling today's Christians.

Now, the "one man" at the parable's wedding party stood out because he had attended for all the wrong reasons. He flat out rejected the son. He certainly was not going to marry him nor promise to love, honor and obey his commands. There was no "Peace" within "one man," such that it showed.

In the Exodus reading, we see Moses talking God out of destroying all of those back-sliding Israelites who God had "chosen" as his own priests. As much as God "chose" them, it was supposed to be a mutual choosing. However, it was apparent, while they were worshiping their gold jewelry, formed into a bull-calf, that they had not yet put on the wedding robe and chosen only one God to whom to be married.

At that time, they must have only been engaged.

The Israelites pleaded with Aaron to make them some "gods" to worship, who would take the place of the God of Moses. They were happy to have a speechless idol – the golden calf – lead them. Speechless idols are easier to follow than a God that repeatedly orders and commands His people to wander around in godforsaken wildernesses, having to worry and fret over everything.

The Israelites stood out then, as they would stand out when Israel and Judah fell, and as Jesus told a parable that reflected the same "one man" standing out, as the one who refused to even make the simplest of gestures of willingness to serve the king.

The condemnation of God, as spoken to Moses, was still in force – although delayed. The reason was this: The Israelites never found "Peace" or "Calm" as God's servants.

They would show up in the vineyard early, for pay, and then do no work.

They would say, "Yes," to the father, only to do nothing they promised to do.

They would try to steal the land his vineyard was on, even killing his son, thinking God would never come to reclaim what they had been allowed to rent.

They would show up at a wedding banquet showing no respect whatsoever.

It is easy to read the Bible and see times so long gone as if those times bear no consequence today. We like to think we are wearing the wedding robes proudly, as Christians dressed up in our Sunday finest. We like to believe we are hard at work picking grapes for the Father, by putting an offering into the tray. We like to see ourselves as the arms of the master, who are ready to receive the orders, to go in and destroy those sinners, and to leave nothing standing.

However, we do not read old books to find fault with those long gone.

We are every failure of which we read ... until we find peace and calm and choose to marry our bodies to the spirit of Christ.

Anything less than that will make us each stand out as pretenders at the king's wedding banquet. Anything less than saying "I do" will make us identifiable as the "one" not wearing a wedding robe.

No one can put that robe on for us. It is up to each one of us ... alone.

For many are called, but few choose to say, "I do."

Amen

# NINETEENTH SUNDAY AFTER PENTECOST

## Proper 24

## YEAR A

**Relevant readings:**
Exodus 33:12-23
Psalm 99
 Isaiah 45:1-7
 Psalm 96:1-13
1 Thessalonians 1:1-10
Matthew 22:15-22

Robert Tippett

# The reality dramas of the Bible stories are like reruns that never stop entertaining

In the Exodus reading today, you have to think of it as a serial movie or television show: "Previously on Exodus, Moses comes down from Mount Horeb and finds the children of Israel worshiping a golden calf. Angrily, he broke the two tablets given to him by the LORD. The LORD sends a plague upon the sinful Israelites."

In episode 33, the LORD instructed Moses, saying "Go on. Take these people and give them the land of milk and honey I promised; but I will not go with them or I will get angry and kill them all, because they are a stiff-necked bunch."

Moses then told the Israelites to strip off all their ornaments and be sad, which they did. He then went into the "tent of meeting" to talk to God.

Thus, we catch up today in that private conversation, where Moses is telling God, "You can't leave us now. Why would the people follow me? They can't see me as being anything special. You are the one who is special. Without you to control them, these stiff-necked people will run amok."

We find out today that the LORD has come up with a plan. He tells Moses to go up the mountain again and stand in the "cleft on the rock" and wait for Him to pass by. Moses will be allowed to see the back of the LORD, but not His face.

Now, this last part is interesting in the sense that in chapter 33, verse 11, while Moses is in the tent of meeting chatting with God, we read, "The Lord would speak to Moses face to face, as one speaks to a friend." From that one would assume that Moses had already seen the face of God; but this new information could mean only seeing God's back is a form of punishment …

Or, Moses really had not met the LORD face to face in a material, physical sense. Remember, God told Moses, "For no one shall see me and live."

Now, that too can seem like God kills people who try to look upon his face, but the reality is this: Look as close as you want, but you will never see the true face of God while you are alive, in a fleshy body, on the earthly plane. You only get to face the LORD when your soul leaves that body, after death. Thus, no one shall see the LORD and still be alive in body.

This makes seeing **the back** of God important to understand. In one way, it is referring to <u>hindsight</u>, where we see all kinds of miracles unfold before our eyes, throughout our lives, but we cannot see God at work at that time when God was making things happen. The Lord's hand covers us while he is passing in front, and it is only afterwards that we know it was God at work.

Still, the point of today's conversation was not about convincing the Israelites to follow Moses and to always see the LORD as being with them in hindsight. Instead, the point is to show the Israelites proof that God was with Moses while they followed him, knowing that God was with him. When they saw Moses, they saw God, but they could not see Moses' face.

In another episode from the show Exodus, we find that Moses came down the mountain with replacement tablets, with his face aglow from the presence of the LORD upon him. Moses began to wear a veil because the glow was so strongly emitted from him. From the glow, the people had proof that God was with them, as long as Moses was with them and aglow.

Now you can see this show Exodus like you see a television

show, such as *Bonanza*, or *M\*A\*S\*H*, or *Leave it to Beaver*. Those shows were all filmed long ago, with stars like Loren Greene, Harry Morgan and Hugh Beaumont since departed; but, we still see them alive in reruns. Today's reading is also a rerun. It is nothing new. We have all seen this one before.

BUT ... if you look carefully at the play before your eyes, you can see some nuances you missed before.

Perhaps you see how this rerun is similar to the rerun of Elisha going to a mountain cleft, asking the LORD to take his life because things have gone so terribly wrong (worse than worshiping a golden calf). In response to that drama, the LORD told Elisha to stand outside the cave and wait for Him to pass by.

That is a similar theme, right? It is a rerun of a rerun. It is a repeating of something done before.

How about the show Matthew, where Jesus goes up a high mountain along with Peter and the brothers of Zebedee, to have the spirits of Moses and Elijah appear talking with Jesus? They were all aglow ... Transfigured. Then, the LORD spoke to Peter, who was thinking of things he would like to do, saying, "Shut up and listen!"

That is the same kind of theme being repeated again. The Bible Network does that a lot. Still, we are entertained.

Now, it may be difficult to see how Jesus, when he confronted the Pharisees about taxation, is repeating this theme. There is a nuance, which is glimpsed by knowing the character Jesus.

Of course, from our perspective two thousand years after this confrontation,and as regular viewers of the Bible Network, we know Jesus is filled with the Holy Spirit. Because we know that we aren't surprised when he turns the tables on the Pharisees' and Herodians' plan to trick Jesus into saying something they can use against him.

We feel like we are as smart as Jesus. We think we would have said the same thing. We laugh and applaud Jesus making them walk away speechless; but, we miss how the Pharisees and Herodians could not see what we see.

Likewise, we miss how the people of the Northern Kingdom would kill all the prophets of God (except Elisha) and then look to kill him. We miss how the Israelites in the wilderness of Sinai would give up on Moses and God, to worship idols of gold. We miss how Peter would even dare to stand up and make a suggestion to holy ghosts.

The rerun … the repeating theme … is God was with Moses, Elisha, and Jesus. We know of this presence from having watched these Bible shows over and over, from the pew that substitutes as our living room sofa; but none of the supporting characters, none of the guest stars, ever see the face of the LORD being on each hero's face.

We miss how easy it is for us to play the role of Israelite, Peter, and/or Pharisee … all **thinking** they could tell the presence of the LORD, only to find out you only see **the back** of the LORD, after the fact. We are looking at the LORD now, but we cannot see Him.

The reason Jesus could not be seen as holy – with God inside him, upon him, as him – is he too wore a veil. Moses wore a veil to hide the glow. That veil hid the face of God so well that the Israelites kept forgetting God was with them, in Moses, repeatedly over the next 40 years.

We don't read that about Elisha, although we know he was given the mantle of Elijah and was a true prophet of Israel, one who could talk to God, "face to face, as one would speak to a friend." But, it was obvious Ahab and Jezebel could not see God in Elisha.

Peter, John and James saw Jesus as a prophet, based on what he did, more than how he looked, so Jesus didn't appear to be the face of God to the Pharisees or the Herodians.

This is the veil all Apostles wear. You cannot go around wearing the face of the LORD for everyone to see, lest they all drop dead.

Think of how you would react if you were in the Walmart and standing next to you was Brad Pitt, or George Clooney, or some other big name idol you love to watch in movies and shows. We know their names and faces because they pretend to be some character from a play, or book, or idea. You would probably think that person was a god and drop to your knees (figuratively) in worship and adoration. You would dance and praise their performances, putting on all sorts of ornaments of praise for their works you enjoyed so much.

If you ever act in that way, then you just angered the LORD, just as had the Israelites and Peter. "Shut up! Jesus is my Son in whom I am well pleased! Listen to him!"

But, do not worship him.

Jesus is a man wearing a veil so you cannot see the magnificence of Jesus is actually the LORD.

In the letter of encouragement sent by Paul to the Thessalonians, he alluded to this veil all Apostles must wear; but, you have to use the pause button, rewind and replay, to hear that.

We get the part where they are filled with the Holy Spirit of God, when Paul wrote, "He has chosen you, because (Paul, Silvanus, and Timothy took you the) message of the gospel (which dawned upon) you not in word only, but also in power and in the Holy Spirit and with full conviction."

# After Pentecost Sermons: Proper 24, Year A

Paul recognized that they were no longer the people who other people saw them to be, but they were God as those normal-looking people. Paul said they "became imitators of us and the LORD." They were not pretending to be Paul, Silvanus, or Timothy, but the Christian Apostles of Thessalonica were duplicating that model.

As others also filled with the Holy Spirit, walking about the populace looking as normal people, they would become proof for others to know that God was with them. The Apostles of Thessalonica would be "examples to all the believers in Macedonia and in Achaia."

That duplicated how the Israelites knew God was with them, in Moses, even though Moses wore a veil. It is how the disciples and others knew God was with Jesus, even though he looked like a normal Galilean to the big wigs in Jerusalem.

Paul wrote, "Every place your faith in God has become known, so that we have no need to speak about it."

Did you catch that?

"We have no need to speak about it" is reference to the veil.

Paul then wrote how they had heard word from people they had seen, who told them, "How you turned from idols, to serve a living and true God."

That says the Apostles of Thessalonica stopped looking for God to come up to them, in another human being or as the spirit of God … something external to them. Instead, God became a living and true God as them. People could not see them as God, but as living examples of how God would be if God were human.

It isn't something that comes instantly, as Paul wrote, "To wait for God's Son from heaven, whom God raised from the dead." That means Jesus is raised within the Apostles, as God within them. It takes time to prove to God you are a worthy resting place for His Spirit. Once you prove your metal, then you can become Jesus.

But, you have to cover that face when in public. Then, you let your actions speak louder than words.

Amen

# TWENTIETH SUNDAY AFTER PENTECOST

# Proper 25

# YEAR A

**Relevant readings:**
Deuteronomy 34:1-12
Psalm 90:1-17
   Leviticus 19:1-2; 15-18
   Psalm 1
1 Thessalonians 2:1-8
Matthew 22:34-46

Robert Tippett

# God is a loving God, but it helps to understand God's love

Raise your hands if you love "love."

Good. Now, raise your hands if you have children … or were ever a child.

Now there is a combination – children and love – the two truly go together.

Still, I know some people who would gather in a reverent setting, such as in a church on Sunday, and get a little peeved if someone else's little bundles of love and joy had not yet learned the discipline of silence.

Children can become as distracting as children are distracted. It is only natural.

Still, there is a proper place for everything. In Ecclesiastes this is written: "For there is a proper time and procedure for every matter."

When we hear the word "love," especially the women folk, our minds drift off into warm and fuzzy memories of everything cute, cuddly, and that which is all smiles and kisses. So often we relate God to this definition of "love" and translate it as meaning His willingness to forgive and forget. Aaaaahh. Love.

Still, for the men folk, the word "love" often means less outwards displays of emotions and romantic embraces; but instead, a sense of duty, commitment, and responsibility. I love, therefore I work. As such, "love" can come across cold and unfeeling. Grrrrrrrrr. Love.

# After Pentecost Sermons: Proper 25, Year A

We see this "love" expressed by God's protection of His children in the Old Testament stories of the "wrath of God." One can find it difficult to see God's "love" displayed in actions that some might not see as loving, in any way. Likewise, some might call the Department of Family Services if they ever saw a parent spank the diapered bottom of their own child, for that child having done something wrong.

This is where we miss the point of "love" including the aspect of "tough love." That is the source of the proverb, "If you spare the rod, then you spoil the child."

As terrible as that sounds, a "rod" is a shepherding tool. We speak of it lovingly when we recit the twenty-third Psalm: Thy **rod** and thy staff they comfort me. Spare that rod and the sheep get lost.

Please, do not get me wrong and think I am promoting going home and beating someone you love with a switch (another way of reading the Latin word translated as "rod"). That is not the point. The point is that "love" very often means saying or doing something that makes a sinner know he or she is sinning, so he or she will realize that and stop sinning.

In television commercials, this concept is presented when they imply the power of a Snicker's candy bar can change personalities. Someone not acting himself comes back to reality after getting a chocolaty-caramel, peanut-nougat sugar rush. Thus, the Mars Corporation represents "love" as being when you help a friend snap out of bad behavior, into good.

In the Gospel reading today, we see a "love" competition. We begin reading where the Sadducees have been silenced. What silenced them was Jesus answering their question about whose wife a widow would be in heaven, if she married seven brothers while alive on earth. The Sadducees did not believe in any Resurrection to heaven, so they made fun of that possibility.

Jesus shut them up by saying, "God is not the God of the dead but of the living."

The "love" competition is each squaring off to help the other to understand the error of one's way, with each holding a position of error-free holiness. Jesus won that match of "love."

It is "love" because **if** Jesus did not love the Sadducees, **then** he would never have made himself known to them. They would have never cared to pose a question to one like Jesus, who so loved the Sadducees that he cared. Because of his love, they should know the truth and be set straight.

Then, the "love match" between the Pharisees and Jesus followed. Those "lawyers" prided themselves on knowing every one of the 613 laws of Moses. With that many, the Pharisees thought it was impossible to see any one of them as more important than another.

Because Jesus loved them, he told them plainly that the foremost law for YAHWEH's priests was, "You shall love the Lord your God with all your heart, and with all your soul, and with all your mind." He then added a second law that was important to add to the first, which was, "You shall love your neighbor as yourself."

That one-two "love" punch was followed with the *coup de grâce*, which was Jesus lovingly adding, "On these two commandments hang all the law and the prophets."

The Pharisees were speechless. They were not expecting Jesus to "love" them in that direct way of teaching them what they should have known, but had not realized. They were cold from Jesus' blows of "love."

While they were backed onto the ropes of the "love" ring, dazed, wondering what hit them, Jesus then lovingly asked them, "What do you think of the Messiah? Whose son is he?"

It was their duty to fight back lovingly, so they responded truthfully, saying what they believed the answer to be. They said, "The son of David." However, Jesus slapped them with one more "love" revelation.

Jesus told them that a son of David would certainly be flesh, like Jesus was, but also like the Pharisees were. The difference was how you saw the flesh as a meaningless point to defend. The Pharisees expected the Messiah to be the son of a king, and bow to no one; but King David bowed down before his King, addressing God as Lord. So the Son of God could not be descended from one lesser than God.

That means the Messiah would not be the son of an earthly ruler, but the Son of God, Israel's King and LORD. A true Son of God would have greater abilities than David had … as a prophet, as one without sin, as one able to perform miracles.

The "love" bout was over. Jesus had more love that came out of his lips, from his heart, than those on the temple steps could counter. The Pharisees and Sadducees were done in. They realized their "love" was of **self**, centered in their **minds** only.

There they were, pretending to be descended of Judean royalty, waiting for a Messiah king who would love them by handing them the riches of the Roman Empire, securing property titles in their names, simply because they wore purple robes and made sure the Temple was neat and clean.

Their "love" was not the warm and fuzzy kind that is emotionally based in a mother, nor was it the serious and responsible love of a father, who teaches as well as disciplines. Jesus had just shown to them a Father's love, to set them straight. Their "love" was worldly, not spiritual; and they needed to realize that.

Now, the laws that Jesus quoted to the Pharisees might sound like one of the Ten Commandments, but it is not. It is actually from the Book of Deuteronomy, as that is where we read how Moses told the Israelites, "Love the LORD your God with all your heart and with all your soul and with all your strength." You can find that in chapter six, verse five.

The second law that Jesus told the Pharisees, "Love your neighbor as yourself," that is found in the Book of Leviticus, chapter nineteen, verse eighteen. The whole verse says, "You shall not take vengeance or bear a grudge against any of your people, but you shall love your neighbor as yourself: I am the LORD."

When Jesus said, "On those two commandments hang all the law and the prophets," that means none of the laws of Moses can ever be meaningfully maintained without "love" in the heart, through the Holy Spirit.

When Moses said, "Love the Lord your God with all your heart," you have to understand that this meant "with all your soul," which is God's breath sent into your flesh and bones. It also means "with all your mind," which can only be part of the equation **AFTER** your heart has received God, and your soul has been raised by the Holy Spirit.

You cannot "love" on a spiritual level when you try to limit "love" to an encyclopedia article or dictionary definition, or some minuscule essence of thought, as if "love" can truly be captured in a Harlequin romance novel or a Lifetime cable-channel movie.

When you grasp this concept correctly, and if you then read Leviticus 19 (an alternate reading choice for today) closely, you see that this "love of God," in "heart, soul, and mind," is how Apostles are made. An Apostle must be realized as one filled with the Holy Spirit, and it must be seen that **EVERY LAW** hangs on that presence. A "prophet" is one so filled. The people and the

After Pentecost Sermons: Proper 25, Year A

Pharisees saw Jesus as a "prophet," but they did not know how to become a "prophet" themselves.

That is because they all misunderstood "**LOVE**."

In Paul's first letter to the Thessalonians, he wrote, "We had already suffered and been shamefully mistreated at Philippi."

That reference was to the persecution Paul (an Apostle of Christ) and his co-Apostles suffered at the hand of the local Jews, in the synagogues of Philippi. Paul wrote about having a "love" match with them and being run out of town.

While Jesus won his "love" bout with both the Sadducees and Pharisees, remember he too was persecuted. Both Paul and Jesus would be killed because their Jewish "neighbors" failed to maintain the foremost law of being themselves Apostles, and then the second foremost law, which was "love you neighbor as an Apostle," not as someone whose heart isn't loving properly.

In Leviticus (which is the book of rules for God's priests to follow), Moses passed on these commandments:

"You shall not render an unjust judgment."

Ooops. That rule did not favor the Pharisees and Sadducees judgment of Jesus.

"You shall not be partial to the poor or defer to the great."

That means do not favor the poor by ignoring their poverty and do not look away from those who you love, simply because they provide you with the butter you love to spread on your bread.

Ooops. That was another rule pointing out the failure of

the Sadducees and Pharisees, because they made the poor outcasts and saw themselves as great.

Moses continued, saying: "With **justice** you shall judge your neighbor."

This is important to realize, as "justice" means fair judgment, rooted in a heartfelt "love" of God, with one's soul and mind tagging along with God's Holy Spirit.

Ooops. That was another failure of the lawyers to maintain this. They certainly were judgmental, but Jesus regularly exposed the errors of their judgments.

Moses wrote, "You shall not hate in your heart anyone of your kin."

That means (since all of the Israelites were descended from Jacob), "do not hate any other Jews."

Ooops. The Sadducees, Pharisees and Jews of Philippi seemed to have some hearts hating, at least towards Jesus and Paul.

Finally (but not all that was written), Moses said, "you shall reprove your neighbor, or you will incur guilt yourself."

That means it is your responsibility and duty, from a "love" of God in your whole heart, to point out the mistakes, trespasses, and sins of your neighbors (i.e.: your fellow Jews or Christians).

I mean, if you see someone making an honest mistake, you tell him, right?

If you have a child forgetting to be quiet in church, you take him or her to the nursery for some "love" lessons, right? Not as punishment, but as a commandment to reprove, lest you get blamed (rightfully) for raising loud, distracting babies.

# After Pentecost Sermons: Proper 25, Year A

"Love" means never having to say you're sorry for being responsible for someone else's sins.

You won't be, as long as you "love" them as you would want them to "love" you back.

Thus, "Love" also means never having to say you're sorry for not listening to a neighbor (a fellow Christian, who is an Apostle of Christ), who expresses his or her "love" for you, by pointing out your sins.

Tell me where I'm going wrong, so I may go right; but do it with a purity of "love."

Amen

# TWENTY-FIRST SUNDAY AFTER PENTECOST

# All Souls [Saints] Day - Proper 26

# YEAR A

**Relevant readings:**
Joshua 3:7-17
Psalm 107:1-7; 33-37
  Micah 3:5-12
  Psalm 43
1 Thessalonians 2:9-13
Matthew 23:1-12

After Pentecost Sermons: Proper 26, Year A

# The benefits you enjoy today are due the efforts of those before you

I used to drive a package car for U.P.S. United Parcel Service had, at that time, such a reputation that they did not advertise in **ANY** way. This included nothing on the drivers' uniforms (hat excluded) that said "UPS." It was just a plain brown uniform – shirt and pants – both "UPS brown," which was all the customer needed to see to know who we were.

The package car, also UPS brown, had the only evidence that a driver worked for that company, as applied to each front side of the vehicle was the gold U.P.S. shield. If you wore a cap (which I did not), there was a UPS gold shield on the front of those. That was the extent of their advertising back then.

Each driver was trained to approach a delivery and shout out, "UPS!" That gets attention. People come meet the driver sometimes, saving them steps and time. People did that out of respect for the name of the company and the uniforms the drivers wore.

On my route, which was largely rural, I had one really big business. It was a clothing manufacturer, one that produced men's suits and shipped them all around the country. It was a big place, with a dock in the back that had room for four tractor trailers. The dock was always full, so there were often ready and waiting tractor-trailers staged in the dock area, left idling along the gravel perimeters of the shipping zone. The drivers would be found inside, waiting for their turn on the dock.

I say the dock was always full because for the first half of each business day that manufacturer was very busy shipping and receiving – basic suit materials in, and finished suits out. Still, until I came in the morning – in my small U.P.S. package car (in comparison to normal U.P.S. package cars and much smaller than a huge trailer) – one dock position was left open. It was left open for me to back up to it, so I could deliver however many packages I had on my vehicle for that company, shipped through U.P.S.

I remember one day sliding all the packages for that delivery on the dock and then hopping up on the dock to record them all on a paper pad with my Bic pen. There were three tractor trailer drivers sitting in three folding chairs lined up along the wall, with each driver waiting for his turn to get a dock position. They were all fine, country-raised gentlemen, with each seeing an opportunity to tell a young U.P.S. driver how special he was.

"Oh, there is the special one that they reserve a dock spot for. So glad you could drop by and not have to wait … like we have been," one said.

"I hear you U.P.S. drivers all got big fat Teamster raises last year. I used to be a Teamster, but my old company got run out of business. Could you spot a brother a few bucks?" another asked.

"Look how this business sends someone to help him. They pick up all the boxes and move them for him. We have to unload our trucks AND put it where they want it," the last one said.

I finished recording all the package numbers, asked for and received an official signature, and then left … walking by the lineup of chairs with the tractor-trailer drivers who were ribbing me. I saluted them as I walked by, without saying a word.

I tell you this story because I, personally, did nothing to warrant that special behavior. Years, even decades of grooming by managers, supervisors, customer service reps, and trained drivers before me had conditioned that company to suspend its standard method of doing business and favor United Parcel Service.

I was given a position of honor because of my predecessors,

without having to do anything myself, other than show up and reap the reward. I enjoyed the reward, even took it for granted and depended on it, because I had to get those bulky suit packages off my little truck before I could begin my route. Since I could not wait in line, like a tractor-trailer driver, I would have had to do many times more work, in order to make that delivery by walking a couple of the packages at a time up the steps to the back door, then recording each package, until everything was delivered. That would have been exhaustive work; but I did not have to face that. Favoritism made my job easier.

In the Gospel reading today, we hear how Matthew remembered Jesus telling the crowds and his disciples that being a Jew was like being a typical tractor-trailer driver, one who has to work for a living. Jews had to wait in line like the next guy … first come, first served.

That means in this reading we should understand how Jesus was telling them that being Jewish did not mean God had a dock door left open, waiting only for them. A Jew still had to do what it took to deserve a chance, an opportunity, to make the most of what opening came available.

Because it was Jesus telling his followers and listeners – who were all Jewish then – his instruction about expectations of special favor then means us, as Christians, need to hear the same advice as if it were intended for us. It is intended for us.

Jesus is then saying, "Being Christian is not some fancy suit you put on that makes people stand by in awe. Being Christian is not some club you join so you can get special recognition when you stop by big time suit manufacturers. And, being Christian is not a guarantee to get free coffee and doughnuts at Krispy-Kreme."

In other words, being Christian is **MUCH MORE** than saying you go to church somewhere, and that you believe "in Jesus and God."

Now, it is easy to get confused by Jesus telling the crowds and disciples to watch out for "Scribes and Pharisees." When you look around you do not see any of those here, or in the local environment.

Raise your hand if you are a "Scribe or Pharisee."

<pause to count hands>

See? No such people are here today. But, how are "scribes and Pharisees" to be translated from an ancient Jewish setting, so we can recognize them in a modern Christian society?

The key to answering that question comes from what Jesus said next. He told those who were listening, "Do whatever they teach you" about the Law, about the Scriptures, about the verses – such as, "Go ahead and memorize things like "The Lord is my shepherd" and "Our Father who art in Heaven."

Do all those things that the Holy Bible says to do. To do that, you have to first learn what that is.

Is there anyone telling us to do what the Holy Bible says to do today?

Certainly there are. They are all around us. I am one. You should be too. In that sense – as Christians – we should all be able to write about and interpret what it is we say we believe. We become the equivalent of scribes and Pharisees.

So, what is the problem today that becomes a reflection of the problem then?

Again, look at what Jesus said. He told the students, "They do not practice what they teach. They tie up heavy burdens, hard to bear, and lay them on the shoulders of others; but they themselves are unwilling to lift a finger to move them."

We have plenty of people telling us what we should be doing, but not that many who are actually doing as told ... demonstrating what **doing** means. This is not only the preachers who place the guilt of sin on everyone's back, while wearing a collar or robe or high hat, as if they are not just a normal human being underneath all that garb; but, it is someone wearing overalls too, if that one begins casting a condemnation of sin on someone else, based on words written in the Holy Bible.

Anyone with a lot of guilt heaped upon their shoulders needs help with not sinning, more than they need condemnations for being a sinner added to their guilt. Sinners don't just need words of guilt, because they can read the words of the Bible books and figure out for themselves that result. Instead, sinners need demonstrations showing them how to remove all the guilt of sins; **BECAUSE** we are **all** naturally born sinners.

These days, there seems to be a trend to accept sin. That becomes a way for removing the guilt that sin brings, as far as reclassifying something that used to be a sin to something acceptable, no longer being heaped on one's shoulders to bear.

Oh? You do this sin that preachers used to say would send you to hell? Well now, we don't say that is a sin any more. After all, who are we to go loading up your shoulders with guilt over something that you probably can never stop doing? Heck, most of you with huge personal guilt were born with a predisposition to sin ... some unknown genetics thing ... so it is natural to sin that way. Go ahead!

When you hear that, you are forgetting that Jesus said, "Do whatever they teach you **and follow it**." In order to justify that modern, self-serving approval of sin, one has to back-up genetic waivers with Scripture that says any form of sin is approved, and therefore comes without guilt.

The problem is twofold, as I see it. First, there is a whole lotta preaching going on with not a whole lotta explaining. If you are going to preach, you have to teach. If you are going to learn, you have to apply yourself to the teaching. Simply because you sign up for a class that comes with a textbook (call it Bible Reading 101) does not mean you automatically make the grade.

Second, there is a whole lotta skipping of step one. Teaching requires having actually learned something well enough to teach that which has been learned. However, as it was in the days of Jesus, the teachers were more self-proclaimed readers than bona fide experts.

Simply because no one had truly applied themselves, Jesus found unskilled, hired hands watching over the flocks. Today, the same problem exists. Without true teachers, everyone just jumps ahead to, "We're all saved because we believe in Jesus and he died for our sins." We think that because we read it in a book.

When you take that approach to Christianity, you pull up to the dock expecting a dock door to be waiting on you. All the special privilege is yours, because of all the work done by Jesus and a long list of Apostles and Saints. Just come on in and walk by the lineup of regular folk who have to actually show patience and do all the hard work to get in.

In the words of Dana Carvey, when he would play "Church Lady" on Saturday Night Live, "Well, isn't that special?"

Paul wrote to the Thessalonians, saying, "As you know, we dealt with each one of you like a father with his children, urging and encouraging you and pleading that you lead a life worthy of God."

Did you catch that word?

After Pentecost Sermons: Proper 26, Year A

"Father?" The Apostle Paul and his co-teacher friends "dealt with each one like a father with his children."

Raise your hands if you are a father of a child or children.

<look for raised hands>

Did being a father ever mean doing no work at all? I doubt it.

Did it mean getting up in the middle of the night to calm a crying baby? Did it mean years of hard labor at some job or profession, so you could earn money to provide for the child's upbringing?

Did it mean worrying and wondering, "Did I do enough training and teaching, so my baby can grow up and walk on its own two feet?"

Christians are all God's children. God is our Father who art in Heaven. God watches all of us Christians down here, each child bearing a huge load of guilt on its shoulders, and He knows which ones are applying themselves to the lessons of His word.

They apply themselves by going to school and listening to the teachers; but beyond listening, they do homework and personal projects. They apply what they hear and read, through personal acts and experiences.

As such, all those who teach us can never call themselves "instructor." The only "instructor" is the "Messiah," or the "Christ." That is not the human man that was Jesus; but the Holy Spirit within, which Jesus Christ will advocate for us to receive.

You see, **you** become the "instructor" when you are able to walk on your own two feet. When all that the Father has sent for you to learn has become a part of your nature, then you become a child of God, with the Mind of Christ.

You cannot observe how holy people feel inside, seeing what motivates holy acts.  You can interpret the actions of others as holy; and you can try to mimic such acts, pretending to be holy, imagining other people will see your good gestures as divinely motivated.  No good act goes unnoticed; but, be careful not to be doing good for self-serving reasons.

You cannot be found longing for all the **things** that you think accompany the acts of a holy person, thinking being holy deserves earthly favoritism.

God's favoritism means hard work, with exhausting hours, day in and day out, at all times.  You can only maintain this schedule if God has sent you the "instructor" within.  That is how God removes all the burden of guilt from past sins, from an application called penance.

Certainly, you will find no dock doors open just for you and that will make you humbled.  However, all who humble themselves here will be exalted in the end.

Amen

# TWENTY-SECOND SUNDAY AFTER PENTECOST

## Proper 27

## YEAR A

**Relevant readings:**
Joshua 24:1-3; 14-25
Psalm 78:1-7
   Wisdom of Solomon 6:12-16
   *or* Amos 5:18-24
   Wisdom of Solomon 6:17-20
   *or* Psalm 70
1 Thessalonians 4:13-18
Matthew 25:1-13

Robert Tippett

# Being prepared for when it is time to be with God

When I was a child, I was a Cub Scout. For a short time I was a Boy Scout. I quit scouting because it did not seem like fun; and, I preferred to watch what was on television on the night of the week that our troop meetings were scheduled.

I was thirteen and without any close adult guidance, so I took the lazy way out.

In hind sight, I can say I wish I had kept going, but knowing what I know now, I probably did the right thing ... for the wrong reasons. Scouting was not cool when I was in high school and the last thing I needed was another reason to be deemed uncool.

Still, the oaths taken by all scouts, boys, girls, cubs and brownies, include the promises, "to love God," "to serve God," and "to do my duty to God."

The motto for both Boy Scouts and Girl Scouts is "Be prepared." When I heard that motto, I figured it meant scouts were prepared to start fires with flint rocks, pitch tents, treat snake bites, whittle chains out of blocks of pine, cook on Coleman camping equipment, and how to spot old ladies needing help crossing streets.

The Scouts have merit badges that are awarded for many fields of preparedness. Still, their motto leaves it open to meaning anything and everything that one can find worthwhile to be prepared to encounter.

Be prepared ... for everything.

All of the readings today address that state of preparedness, in the sense that our preparation must be towards death. Jesus said,

# After Pentecost Sermons: Proper 27, Year A

"You know neither the day nor the hour" when death will arrive to escort your soul to Heaven. So, be prepared at all times.

In the Old Testament reading from the Book of Joshua, we might not realize that when Joshua gathered all the tribes of Israel to Shechem, his time on this earth was almost up. Chapter 24 is considered (according to the article on Wikipedia) to be part of Joshua's "farewell" to the Israelites. Joshua was preparing them for their continued life as God's people, after Joshua would be dead and gone.

That Wikipedia article also draws attention to some parallels between Moses and Joshua, where both presented farewell speeches to the Israelites; and, both parted waters before crossing the children of Israel - out of Egypt and into the Promised Land. The point is also made that the Israelites celebrated the Passover upon entry into their new land, whereas they celebrated the first Passover before departing Egypt.

The article does not discuss how those parallels can indicate a repetition of holiness; but instead, the article leads one to assume that Jewish tradition might be made up, as a fictional recreation of Moses in the man named Joshua. However, it can all be explained as God using all of His devoted servants in the same manner.

The aspect of the Law being brought down to the Israelites by Moses, at Mount Horeb, is then paralleled to this account of Joshua making up a covenant, statutes and ordinances for the Israelites to agree to and follow. Joshua did that at Shechem. There is a difference between the two events, even if the two are quite similar.

It is important to understand that Shechem was seen as a most holy place in Canaan. To call the tribes of Israel to Shechem is then a statement of the holiness of God delivering on a promise, after having met in the shadow of the Mountain of God, agreeing to follow the LORD's servant to that place promised.

Prior to this farewell warning by Joshua, not to forget to only worship the One God – YAHWEH - the land of Israel had been subdued by warfare. Once conquered by force, the land was divided amongst the tribes. God had given His blessing for all those victories, and now it was time to renew the agreement that had led the Israelites to that point.

Joshua pointed out that the Israelites came from a lineage that worshiped more than one god. Abraham was originally from Sumer, a polytheistic society, which was the culture that spread to Babylon and Assyria. Joshua called that the polytheism of the Amorites. Additionally, the Israelites (those who originally left Egypt) had come from a polytheistic land, Egypt, such that their ancestors themselves knew of many gods who were worshiped.

Jacob's wife Rachel had stolen her father's "household idols," which were of gods lesser than YAHWEH (the roots of Ba'als) because Rachel believe those gods would protect them.

There was no doubt that many gods were known and worshiped many places. Joshua admitted that. However, the children of Abraham, Isaac, and Jacob - the Israelites - were not chosen by the One God, the LORD, YAHWEH, because God liked how stiff their necks got when things didn't go their way.

They were not special human beings. Only if they agreed to serve the One God, and no other, doing everything that had been drawn up for them to learn and act upon, would they then receive a special blessing from God. God blesses all His priests who serve him and only him.

It then becomes important to repeat what Joshua told the Israelites, as it has not faded with time. The same applies today, just as it did then. "You cannot serve the LORD," which is best stated as conditional.

Read his words as saying, "**If** you cannot serve the LORD, as you have committed to serve only Him," **then** you need to understand that "He is a holy God."

If God were not holy, then it would be okay to serve more than one god. However, "He is a jealous God; he will not forgive your transgressions or your sins. If you forsake the LORD and serve foreign gods, then he will turn and do you harm, and consume you, after having done you good."

That is not a threat, it is a promise.

It is a Law of physics, just as Boy Scouts know: Face a burning campfire on a cold winter night and your face will become so warm it burns; but turn away from the fire and the cold air will soon turn that burning face into frozen cheeks. Thus, turning away from God (sinning) will consume you and do you harm (self-inflicted pain that God will not prevent), after you were fine facing God (not sinning).

You also have to realize that Jesus did not come to be another God. There can only be One God in this religion passed to the Israelites. Jesus was filled with the Holy Spirit of that One God, wilfully acting as commanded by that God whose Spirit resided within Jesus' human body. Thus, God did not come as Jesus, making God in Heaven and God on earth, which becomes two Gods.

That would make Joshua seem like a liar, and lead some to think it would be okay to forget all about that vengeful, harming, consuming God, since Jesus was such a loving God.

In the reading from Matthew, we hear Jesus tell the parable of the ten bridesmaids, where five were not good scouts, having run out of lamp oil. They were not prepared. After they went to the market to buy some more oil, by the time they got back they were left behind. They cried out, "Lord, lord, open to us." In response, God said, "Truly I tell you, I do not know you."

The moral of that parable is the same as what Joshua told all the people of Israel, "Keep awake therefore, for you know neither the day nor the hour." Be prepared at all times. Do not be caught worshiping more than One God.

The five unprepared bridesmaids thought all they had to do was ask the five 'good scout' bridesmaids, who had prepared and brought oil with them, to **forgive** their lack of preparedness, and to **give** oil to them – as if they had mistaken the teachings of Jesus, seeing Jesus as God on earth. Jesus' parable of the bridesmaids, in effect, says, "Be like me. Be always prepared, because only the One God knows when He will come for His children."

This same warning is given by Paul, as an encouragement to all Christians who were filled by the Holy Spirit. He told them not to lose their faith and become fearful because other Christians were becoming martyrs all around them. Paul told them that facing death was part of the course.

Those saints had all died long before they were martyred, giving up their egos (selves) so Christ could take over their bodies. As such, anyone who maintained the covenant, statutes and ordinances, did so because they were filled with the Mind of Christ. If persecuted to death, then those would be raised like Christ was raised.

Paul was encouraging Christians to make sure they we prepared to die for Christ, just as he died for them. They too were bridesmaids with lamps filled with the oil of the Holy Spirit, which (like living water) never runs out. Thus, they stayed awake and alert for the door's opening and their bridegroom's arrival, ready to attend the wedding banquet at any given moment. They were good scouts.

# After Pentecost Sermons: Proper 27, Year A

The five bridesmaids whose lamps went dark, they did not have this eternal fuel that represented the light of Christ. Their "engagement" to Christ was based on the material and physical, not the spiritual. They had to run to the store to buy some more lamp oil, the kind that eventually always runs out. That was a sign of their lack of true commitment, a sign that they worshiped other gods (such as Jesus, the 'household idol' version).

Perhaps, they worshiped the building that represented the LORD's house, more than Christ as the LORD. Perhaps, they worshiped how everyone gave them honors as always going to church, or always knowing the right things to say; but, they never became a church for Christ themselves, thus they never realized the true meaning of the things they said.

It is important for us to realize that the only way any of us can ever fully follow all the agreements made with the One God, and the only way to ever completely adhere to the letter of all the rules and ordinances, is to let God into our hearts. We must die and rise again as Jesus Christ. Only when we gain the same mind that Jesus had can we ever truly worship only one LORD.

If we keep God and Christ external to us, we worship self as a god; and that will keep God from knowing who we are when our end comes.

Moses, Joshua, Jesus, and Paul all said the same thing as David, when he sang, "So that they might put their trust in God, and not forget the deeds of God, but keep his commandments." We can only have trust in the LORD and never forget His deeds and commandments when we sacrifice ourselves to His will.

Only then will we truly be prepared.

Amen

# TWENTY-THIRD SUNDAY AFTER PENTECOST

## Proper 28

## YEAR A

**Relevant readings:**
Judges 4:1-7
Psalm 123
   Zephaniah 1:7-18
   Psalm 90:1-12
1 Thessalonians 5:1-11
Matthew 25:14-30

After Pentecost Sermons: Proper 28, Year A

# Understanding the parable of the talents

For any church, in any place, that schedules their "Stewardship Drive" for pledges to fund the budget for the coming year, based on the parable of the talents …

**SHAME ON YOU!**

In my opinion, the parable of the talents is greatly important and must be fully grasped by all want-to-be Christians. It has nothing to do with money, and anyone who points out that a "talent" represented a "year's wages" in ancient Judea is not capable of preaching about spiritual matters.

A "parable," to use the most appropriate definition, is "a statement or comment that conveys a meaning indirectly by the use of comparison, analogy, or the like."

It is, therefore, a metaphor, such that being like something means a reference to another thing entirely.

Thus, if the parable of the talents is telling of something like a year's wages (like five year's wages, or like ten year's wages), the metaphor is **NOT** on material value, but on spiritual value.

So, by all means, sign a card and promise to give 100% of your spiritual value to a church. Commit to give 100% of your spiritual value to God and Christ.

But, if no one ever preaches about the meaning of the metaphor in the parable of the talents, then no one ever realizes it is about spiritual value and not about money. Thus, priests and ministers will always be begging church-goers to give money out of guilt, rather than spiritual enlightenment.

God is like the master who goes away, leaving his slaves who are like us in charge of various degrees of spiritual value, which is like lots of money.  **CHRIST** is like the talent, as the advocate for the Holy Spirit of God to the faithful.  Christ is (like the commercials say) so valuable he is priceless.

Now, with that basic understanding, and keeping in mind that everything in the world requires funds to keep everything working to some degree of fluidity, let's move on from the filthiness of money and address the theme of today's readings.

Every year the prophetess Deborah gets completely lost in the efforts to misrepresent the parable of the talents.  What does a female judge of Israel have to do with that story told by Jesus?

In these modern ages, since "equality" took on such importance and women have sought to be recognized as worthy of holding down work positions, worthy of being elected officials, and worthy of being priests in churches, Deborah has been trivialized as some kind of "Women's Lib activist," and not seen as she actually was.

Even if you read the translation that says, "Deborah, a prophetess, wife of Lappidoth, was judging Israel.  She used to sit under the palm of Deborah between Ramah and Bethel in the hill country of Ephraim" (which is confusing at best and ridiculously meaningless at worst), you still come away thinking she was a judge of Israel.

You can see how Deborah heard the pleas of the children of Israel (those in the upper regions – Naphtali and Zebulun) and she heard God's commandment to save his children, which she passed along (presumably while still sitting under a tree). Therefore, everyone who reads these verses comes away with the idea that Deborah prophesied and led the children of Israel back to God's protection.

As a "prophetess," she was filled with the Holy Spirit. Deborah had a God-given talent. That is the link to the parable of the talents, told by Jesus.

Now, being a prophet or a prophetess is not a talent most people possess. If we have any prophets or prophetesses here today, please raise your hands.

<look for raised hands>

Being a prophet, according to Paul's list of the "gifts" of the Holy Spirit, is one of the seven he named. A "gift" is like a "talent" of a spiritual value, and ability to prophesy is an important ability. In that list of Paul's, which he wrote of more than once (in differing explanatory words but with the same seven listed), there are differing "talents" than can be possessed. Some, one or all, can be put in one's care by the master, God.

Thus, one slave can be given "five talents," with "another two," and still another one. This means some true Apostles of Jesus Christ could conceivably receive the following abilities: to heal, to prophesy, to understand prophecy, to minister, and to give heartfelt care to others. Other Apostles may only have these abilities: to understand prophecy and to minister. Still, some may only be given one power of the Holy Spirit: to understand prophecy. That is the meaning of five, two, and one "talents" left to slaves.

Notice how I listed all of these three fictional Apostles (slaves to the Master) as having the ability to understand prophecy. You have to realize that everything in the Holy Bible is prophecy, so through the talent of God, the Holy Spirit, with the gift of the Mind of Christ, the words of the books of the Holy Bible are realized by those with this gift – the talent of understanding.

In the case of Deborah, **ALL** of the children making up **ALL** of the tribes of Israel were responsible for learning the Torah – the books of Moses, and the Law. That is not a gift, as a recognized talent of God. Simply because you have a big brain and spend the time to memorize what it is you say you believe, if you do not understand what you believe, then you end up like the people crying out to a judge to save them. Knowing what you believe in and believing what you understand are two different things.

Knowing things, as possessing intelligence, is available to any normal human beings in a public school and to anyone who can gain entrance into a college or university. Knowing is even available to children in Sunday school; and as children grow up, their knowledge grows in Adult Bible Studies. The talent of understanding is available to everyone too, but only through Jesus Christ. You have to welcome God into your heart, who then replaces your ego with the Mind of His Son, and then you become the reproduction of Jesus, capable of knowing without having been taught. However, like the tribes of Israel, most people were not ready, willing, or able to make that commitment to receive the wisdom of God.

So, most people have no true God-given talents to waste. They depended then, just as now, on those who had talents, like Deborah. Deborah saved the Israelites because Deborah did not bury her talent in the ground and do nothing to help anyone but herself.

That is the message today, and that is why it is so important to understand. The parable of the talents is about helping others, through being filled with the Holy Spirit. That talent awaits your actions - that of going to God requesting to receive it, and then using it to help others do the same. God is not impressed with those who ask for personal gratification. However, ask for the ability to help other and God answers.

The problem is then how few people there are who are willing to lift a finger to help anyone who will not help them in return, twofold. How many read the parable of the talents and dream of being given a gift of money that multiplies, making one richer than their wildest dreams?

We miss the point of how five abilities given by the Master means that one needs to then report back to God how five others also got abilities of the Holy Spirit from their help. Or, it may be where the one with two gifts from God has seen the need to pass those gifts on to two others, so they too were filled with the Spirit.

Imagine how easily that can happen to you, if you seek and receive the talent to understand the books of the Holy Bible. Look at the potential you then have, for passing that knowledge onto to others through Bible Studies, Lectionary classes, or simply not being afraid of discussing your religious understanding with anyone who poses a religious question. Your willingness to share your gift can lead to others also being inspired to receive the Holy Spirit of understanding.

But we get selfish. We get lazy. We get apathetic.

Then, when our time in life is up and the Master comes for our soul, He asks, "What did you do with the talent I left you to use?"

At that time there will be no lies, no cover-ups, no excuses allowed in response. Only the truth can be told then.

To tell the LORD, "I never used it. I left it untouched, buried where no one could ever know it was there" is an admission of failure, of selfishness, of a lack of caring for anyone other than yourself. Then you can expect to hear God reply, "You are a worthless slave. You will not enter into my realm of Heaven. Your soul will be thrown into the outer darkness, where there will be weeping and gnashing of teeth."

None of us wants that future, if we think about it. But, how many people put off using their brains to come to a realization of sacrifice for the benefit of others? So many put off that commitment for as long as they can ... until it is too late.

That makes Paul's letter to the Thessalonians important to understand, as he warns about that end to those who decide to live in darkness, without the light of Christ leading their actions. Paul wrote:

> "For you yourselves know very well that the day of the Lord will come like a thief in the night. When they say, "There is peace and security," then sudden destruction will come upon them, as labor pains come upon a pregnant woman, and there will be no escape!"

Paul (according to the New Revised Standard Version) ended that last statement with an exclamation point. He emphasized that statement of doom, where there will be no more time left to put off.

Christians filled with talents of understanding know not to let the light of Christ go out. Being filled with the Holy Spirit is **NEVER** about you having a wonderful life on planet earth, so you can retire early and live long, possessing more than your neighbor.

It is **ALL** about passing what the Lord gives to you on to others and making God's investment in you pay dividends through others. Your reward will be based on how well you sacrificed of yourself, so that others could be saved.

When you know that, then you see how ridiculous it is to beg people to give some small percentage of their money to keep the church alive for another year. A true Christian church does not beg for earthly comforts, depending on the talent of human generosity, as measured in currency and monetary notes. It is about being **ALL-IN** spiritually, with faith in the LORD and actions led by the mind of Christ. All true churches survive because God and Christ know their works.

Amen

# LAST SUNDAY AFTER PENTECOST

# Christ the King Sunday

# YEAR A

**Relevant readings:**
Ezekiel 34:11-24
Psalm 100
  [Ezekiel 34:11-24]
  Psalm 95:1-7
Ephesians 1:15-23
Matthew 25:31-46

After Pentecost Sermons: Christ the King, Proper 29, Year A

# Sheep and goats in the pasture of Christianity

When I first began understanding Nostradamus, I was amazed with what I was seeing. I **felt** how important it was for everyone in the world to understand a document that some people were interested in, but none realized the whole truth it contained. I was filled with a sense of urgency.

In hindsight, after reading the readings for today and the focus on prophecy of the end times, I see how easy it would have been for me to **feel** the first slap of rejection and stop trying to tell anyone anything about Nostradamus, anymore.

"I have this book you might want to publish," stated the querry letters I mailed out.

"Not interested," was the reply over fifty times.

"I have this book I self-published, if you would like to buy it. I am available to help you understand any confusing parts," was my self-promotion, offering a willingness to speak about what I felt was vitally important to know.

"Not interested," has been the most prevalent reply for the past thirteen years [in 2017].

"I can teach anyone who is interested in learning how to understand Nostradamus, if you just make the time to learn it as a course," was my offer when a wrote a book explaining the syntax of prophecy [2010].

"Not interested," has been the resounding response.

"I can tell anyone how to read the books of the Holy Bible, based on what I have been able to understand from reading the Book of Nostradamus (*The Prophecies*), as long as someone comes to Bible Studies and wants to learn the truth of the Word," has been my offering since my wife became an ordained priest.

While not said, I **feel** people hear what I have to say and want to say, "I have never before heard anyone say what you say, therefore you must be a liar and I will stop coming to Bible Studies as long as you come."

While not stated that directly or that specifically, that is how I read the responses I have encountered over the last eight years. Bible Studies is an exercise few have an interest in taking part in to begin with; and, I tend to make those who falsely come want to cease coming.

One of the things I have pointed out recently, to both gasps and silence, is how I "see" the Gospel of John in a light that exposes John's experiences were as a child, not an adult. I read what John wrote, and the longer I look at his words, the more it says between the lines, "Jesus may have been married to Mary Magdalene. Jesus was related to Lazarus, Martha, and John, through that marriage."

I have recently, within the last few months, come to the realization that John was actually the son of Jesus; and I have made that known, because it does me no good to see that and remain silent about it.* I see that revelation as spiritually uplifting. I see it as more reason to believe, rather than reason to think lesser of Jesus or Christianity.

I have heard people speak about John's Gospel as if there may be reason to doubt John's words, seeing how his Gospel does not seem to match the other three. Reading it as the memories of a man recalling his childhood explains this.

I have heard the disbelief of others, aghast that I would even suggest such a thing. I have **felt** the rejection. Not once has anyone come to me asking, "Robert, will you help me understand more about how you see what you see?"

Recently, the news has reported a book is about to be published and available on the market, one that proclaims an ancient biblical text has been translated for the first time. In it, Jesus is said to have been married to Mary Magdalene and that marriage is said to have produced two children.

The response to that news has been quite negative. No one wants a married Jesus. No one wants a Jesus with children. No one wants a Jesus that was human, just like us. A godly Jesus is less likely to be duplicated, so keep him that way and let his followers be blind to ever thinking they could possibly be like a human Jesus.

Even the name for this last Sunday of Pentecost – as Christ the King Sunday – makes the man Jesus seem elevated to a level that is well above what normal people can aspire to become. After all, kings are few and far between. The title, however, actually comes from the Roman Catholic Church, as the name of a Feast Day in honor of Christ. The readings have nothing to do with recognizing that feast.

With that understood, let us look at what we have just heard read.

In the prophecy of Ezekiel that we read today, it says, "the Lord GOD will search for his sheep, and will seek them out." God told Ezekiel, "I will rescue them from all the places to which they have been scattered on the day of clouds and thick darkness."

I see the words of Nostradamus as being cloudy, with them telling a theme that is thick with darkness; because *The Prophecies* tells of the end of the world. That end is not pretty; and, thus, a parallel can be drawn to *The Apocalypse* of John. Thus, from knowing that it is clear to me that God told Ezekiel to prophecy of the end times, when all God's sheep will be gathered for safe keeping.

In Ezekiel we read, "I will bind up the injured, and I will strengthen the weak, but the fat and the strong I will destroy. I will feed them with justice." It later says, "I will judge between sheep and sheep."

That relates to the prophecy told by Jesus, as told in the Gospel of Matthew; but, Ezekiel's "sheep and sheep" are restated by Jesus as "sheep and goats."

To many people reading a difference stated as "sheep and goats," the brain leads one to conclude that sheep are different from goats. They are different species, easily distinguishable as one apart from the other, when seen in a field or pasture. This thinking then leads one to think that Jesus is telling us about believers and nonbelievers, which could be read as Christians on the right hand of God and those of all the other religions on the left side.

The problem with that thinking is it fails to read how Jesus spoke to both sheep and goats as having a relationship with Jesus Christ. One group helped Jesus, while the other group denied Jesus. To deny Jesus is to claim to know him, believe in him and even love him, as did Simon Peter, only to deny him when the going gets tough. Therefore, both groups can be seen as calling themselves "Christians," but only the sheep acted Christian.

That is who will be gathered when Jesus comes at the end times.

When you can see this, you can then re-read Ezekiel and see how the fat and strong sheep that God will destroy are parallel to the goats of Jesus. That symbolizes those who have profited by claiming to be Christians, when they will not in truth be Christian in their actions. Those "goats" are who "will go away into eternal punishment."

The thing that makes a sheep a sheep and a goat not a sheep is the Holy Spirit. That is what, as Paul wrote, makes one a "saint."

A "saint" is a sheep that serves the Lord, to the point of being persecuted to death. True Christians make that sacrifice so their souls can attain Heaven. A "saint" is one who receives the "spirit of wisdom and revelation," and who walks the earth as the resurrected "body" of Jesus, so that "the fullness of him fills all in all."

That means not just the mind ("I believe. Therefore, I am Christian."), but every nook and cranny of the human being - mind, body, and soul - full, **ALL** in every place. "I am Jesus. Therefore, I am Christian."

Paul wrote that to the yet to be filled Christians of Ephesus, praying that they would open their hearts and receive the Spirit.

Of course, hoping, praying, and telling people, "You can do it, if you just apply yourself," does not always gain the desired result.

Perhaps, all the Ephesians did as Paul wished and all became true Apostles of Christ. Perhaps, their sacrifices then are why there are still Christians around today.

Paul also wrote, "Above every name that is named, not only in this age but also in the age to come," which means all who change their names to Jesus, via the presence of the Christ Mind from the Holy Spirit. No matter when that happens, the same result will bring about complete compliance with God's Law, with no more sinning done.

In other words, every goat that stops being a goat and becomes a reproduction of Jesus, as the Lamb of God in Spirit, becomes a sheep that will be gathered by Jesus. Those transformations were seen to begin in Age of Pisces and have lasted into the "new age," the Age of Aquarius.

We are in that age now … the age of information, technology, and instant global connections. The Age of Aquarius is the Age of the Big Brain, when "tastes great and less filling" can be seen as the worldly mantra, as opposed to the mantra of the Holy Spirit. Christians lose their desires for sensual delights, opting to be more filled with the Spirit of God.

But, it is also the Age of Goats, or the Age of Fat and Strong Sheep.

It is also the Age of the End Times.

If you remember, Matthew began this prophecy of Jesus by remembering how Jesus told them of the time of his return in glory, with angels. That return will be when Judgment comes to the sheep and goats. The Judgment will be based on how each individual helped Jesus, by feeding him, giving him drink, welcoming him, clothing him, healing him, and visiting him in prison.

Neither the sheep nor the goats knew they had ever met Jesus. After all, when the age of return comes, the man named Jesus will have been long gone, not seen in the flesh for nearly two thousand years. His return will have him find a world of all new sheep and goats.

How could either sheep or goats have done any of those things mentioned by Jesus?

The answer is by becoming Jesus, through the Holy Spirit being received. They feed Jesus by eating while Jesus is them. They give Jesus drink by being Jesus and quenching their own thirsts. They welcome Jesus by receiving his mind through the Holy Spirit, becoming Jesus. They clothe Jesus by dressing themselves, as Jesus resurrected. They heal Jesus and care for his illness, by letting Jesus come within them and do what is necessary to cure their bodies. They visit Jesus in prison by understanding the earthly realm is everyone's prison, such that Jesus inside one's heart is visiting him before freedom from the earthly realm allows a return to Heaven.

The sheep also consume the bread of the Holy Word. They drink the blood of Christ, as the Holy Spirit. They dress in attire that says, "I am not led by earthly lusts." They cure themselves of an addiction to sins. They minister to others in their various states of persecutions and rejections.

The goats reject all of that. They are too concerned with how others will see them. They think (not **feel**) that if they start acting like a "Jesus freak," then they will lose contacts and their important network of worldly securities.

The fat and strong sheep reject all that too, while lapping up all the luxuries of being deemed holy, by pretending to be religious, all while getting rich on earthly delights given them by the lost who seek to be found.

There is nothing new exposed in today's readings. It is the same song sung, just one more added verse. The message has long been how it is easier to do nothing than it is to receive the Holy Spirit and be led to a life that has people reject those who say, "Jesus was a married man with children, just like us. So, why can't we be like him?"

It is easier to ignore those who say, "Nostradamus wrote a prophecy the same as did Ezekiel, saying the same things as those said by Matthew and Jesus."

But the clock is ticking. We have entered the "age to come," the time when Jesus will return and Judge the living and the dead.

The message is always the same as we close this Ordinary season after Pentecost season, and come to the end of another Church cycle. On the eve of Advent, we have to ask ourselves, sincerely and honestly …

Am I living with the Holy Spirit or living for all the possessions I can grab?

Am I dead and reborn in Christ, as Jesus resurrected, helping others; or, am I dead to belief in God and Christ, rejecting being a servant, a priest, a minister to those lost?

Am I ready for the Advent of Jesus' birth long ago?

Am I ready for the Second Coming of Jesus … the meaning of Advent?

Am I ready to finally have the Advent of Jesus born within me?

Is Christ my King today, or am I waiting until the last minute to decide?

Only you can answer those questions.

Amen

\* To clarify this aspect of "marriage" and having a "son," this does not necessarily mean Jesus had sex with anyone. Although I firmly believe the DNA of Jesus was in John the Beloved, the possibility is John was a Divine offspring. Jesus was the product of a miracle birth, so there is no reason why John could not have been likewise conceived by holy means. I also do not expect anyone to adopt my **feeling** about this matter, as I have no proof. Remember, Adam was the Son of God and his mating with Eve was a holy exchange, for a Divine purpose, resulting in multiple children. Jesus referred to himself as the Son of Man, where the Hebrew word for "man" is "*adam*." The only reason

Jesus would likewise have a blood offspring would be for the purpose of generating both "body" and "blood" Christians – the kings of Europe and the Apostles who would lead the churches of Christ.

# Ordinary after Pentecost Sermons

# Year B

# FIRST SUNDAY AFTER PENTECOST

# Trinity Sunday

# YEAR B

**Relevant readings:**
Isaiah 6:1-8
Psalm 29
  *or* Canticle 13
  (*or* Canticle 2)
Romans 8:12-17
John 3:1-17

Robert Tippett

# Ordinary time is when the poisonous snakes are exposed

A long time ago, when I was in my early twenties – very early twenties – I responded to a want-ad in the newspaper.

I wore my only suit and applied for a job that promised great financial rewards ... as long as I was dedicated and hard-working.

The job offered "free training," requiring "no experience." Since I met that requirement the job sounded like money in the bank to me.

I applied and sat through a high-powered pitch, along with about twelve other young men, that said I could earn more money than I would know what to do with. That income would be based on the commission potential of sales. I was offered the job and I took it. I began on Monday.

For four days I showed up for the "free training." That meant I had to memorize a sales pitch and practice it on others applicants for thirty-two class hours, with me receiving no pay.

On Friday morning they said we were ready to go door-to-door, using the sales pitch on real customers.

The trainers - probably men of twenty-eight years of age, or so - "volunteered" a couple of the applicants, those who had large cars, to load up about ten of us (along with the trainers) and use the gas in the cars of those "volunteers" to drive us all about one hundred twenty miles away to another city. There we were to look for "matchbox subdivisions" to be dropped off in, because that was where door-to-door salesmen were best able to find buyers.

After Pentecost Sermons: Trinity Sunday, Year B

Our product being pitched - as far as we were told - was a membership to a buying club, similar to what Costco and Sam's Club are today. However, this was well before that type of business became well known and popular.

This was well before the Internet and smart phones.

The cost for a membership was $750 per family, which was a lot of money back then.

BUT ... you could save more than that cost in a year, simply by buying all the things you regularly bought, but at discounted rates through that club.

AND ... the $750 was a one-time fee, with the yearly payments after only $12.

AND ... you got a FREE set of the best encyclopedias mankind had known to that time to boot! The encyclopedia company even offered a service that would even send your child a printed report on any topic requested, even if that topic was not found in their books!

All I had to do was rake in the sales.

<pause>

We reached that target city around 11:00 AM, made a stop at McDonald's, and then cruised the town for places to drop us trainees off. This being in the middle of a southern summer.

The trainer dropped me off in a nice subdivision. I was wearing my suit - from my high school dance days - and I was carrying a briefcase they gave me, holding all the promo material and sales forms inside.

<pause>

By 2:00 PM, I had sweated through my suit coat and pants. I looked like a drowned rat.

Few people were home during a weekday, and those who were slammed doors in my face ... time after time.

Finally, one kind man welcomed me inside his home, where the air conditioning felt wonderful.

I began to give him the sales pitch, but the kind man quickly said, "Shut up. I don't care what you are selling. You look like you are about to have a heat stroke."

The kind man told his wife to pour me a tall glass of iced tea. He gave it to me to drink and told me to sit and rest.

I sat there for about twenty minutes, and when I thought, "Now is the time to make the pitch," he showed me the door.

I thanked him for his generosity.

About 5:00 PM the trainer found me walking in another subdivision – he was driving one of the trainees' car, someone whom he had dropped off like I had been.

He asked me how many sales I had made. I told him none. He told me he was going to show me how to do it; so I walked door-to-door with him, and he got us inside a couple of homes. People were home from work by then. His pitch almost hooked a couple of people, but the cost was just too high ... although they admitted it sure sounded great!

About 8:00 PM, five of us and the trainer sat in that car the trainer had taken over and we waited in the parking lot of an apartment complex where the last trainee was inside. He was trying to close out a deal.

# After Pentecost Sermons: Trinity Sunday, Year B

The trainer had gone by a package store and was handing out bottles of beer for us hot and tired trainees. We were all very hungry and had little to drink since early that morning.

It was twilight; and under the cover of darkness, with a couple of beers in him, the trainer said, "Man, this is the best scam I have ever worked."

"What do you mean?" I asked.

He explained: "The $750 is for the encyclopedia set and the first year of a buyer's club membership. The buyer's club only costs $12 a year. People would rather spend that much for the opportunity to save money spending on nice things, thinking the encyclopedia set is free."

The last trainee came back ... without making a sale ... with no one in our group making a sale ... and still a two-hour drive back to the training office. I did not get back home until after 11:00 PM that night.

I decided not to ever go back to that job.

I receive no pay, but I did get a free educational experience ... as long as you see "free" as how much money I paid to be taught a lesson. Because I never wore that suit again, that was a cost to me, but it was an old suit.

I tell you this story because, in my mind, regardless of what some may say about him, I see the Pharisee named Nicodemus as no more trustworthy as that trainer who passed out beers in someone else's car, under the cover of darkness.

It would be so easy for me to preach about how Nicodemus can be a reflection of every American Christian, especially those who give credit to God for living in the greatest land the world has ever known. I could preach how American Christians should give credit to God for all the opportunity America offers to everyone who is industrious, and especially give credit to God for having been made rich.

Nicodemus would see matchbox subdivisions as Jewish settlements, placed in the world for the benefit of those who memorized sales pitches.

It is unfortunate that so many Christians are religious only under the cover of darkness. Too many profess faith, only letting the truth slip out ... telling strangers where their heart really lies ... after a few beers. However, to preach about Nicodemus would be to waste the opportunity to focus on what Jesus told him.

Jesus first said, "No one has ascended into heaven except the one who descended from heaven, the Son of Man."

Then Jesus told Nicodemus, "And just as Moses lifted up the serpent in the wilderness, so must the Son of Man be lifted up, that whoever believes in him may have eternal life."

Both of those statements speak of the history of the people who God had chosen ... those committed to serving only Him, in return for a promised reward. Both of those statements made by Jesus, referring to the Son of Man, were made prior to Jesus regularly calling himself that.

In Hebrew, the word for "man" is "*adam*." Thus, the Greek words written by John, "*Huis tou anthrōpou*," are akin to the Hebrew words, "*Ben adam*." That title implies a "Descendant of (the) Man (named Adam)."

In Ezekiel, the Hebrew text shows God addressing him as "*ben adam*." Ezekiel wrote that he was called that by God a total of **ninety-four times** (according to Wikipedia). As such, for Nicodemus to hear Jesus use that reference, Nicodemus (a Pharisee of

After Pentecost Sermons: Trinity Sunday, Year B

high ranking) would have heard Jesus referring to Ezekiel – the only prophet who used that title.

Possibly, Nicodemus heard Jesus hinting that Jesus considered himself to be a prophet equal to Ezekiel. After all, Nicodemus told Jesus, "No one can do the things you do apart from God."

Whatever Nicodemus took from Jesus telling him about the ascension of the descended Son of Man, the reference was to Adam - the first priest sent to earth by God, "in order that the world might be saved through him."

"Through him," means, "through the descendants of Adam," in particular those significant leaders who were groomed to generate the multitudes who became God's chosen people. That path "through Adam" went through Abraham, Isaac, and Jacob. The path then into the wilderness with Moses and into the land and nation of Israel. Then it went through the separate Judah ... and then Roman Judea, where the Jews returned from exile, after having lost their land.

Jesus was then a descendant of Adam ... and this lineage is confirmed in the Gospel of Luke [Luke 3:38]. Ezekiel was also of that lineage ... as a prophet of Judah ... as one who kept the fire of service to God alive when Judah fell.

This means that being a Son of Man is more than a blood relative distinction. Both Jesus and Nicodemus were Jews, but only Jesus was purified by a altar coal placed on his lips by a seraph of God.

Being the Son of Man requires the Holy Spirit ... being able to talk to God ... like Adam, like Ezekiel, like Moses, like Jesus ... like the Apostles of Christ.

The Son of Man is the Son of God, in the form of a man, filled with a devotion to God and belief in the Christ Spirit.

So, when Jesus told Nicodemus that the Son of Man had to be lifted up like Moses lifted up the serpent in the wilderness, so that all the Israelites believed the cure for snakebite was faith, Jesus was to be what that bronze serpent symbolized, lifted up so the people would not perish. Jesus was therefore telling Nicodemus that Nicodemus was one of the many poisonous snakes in Jerusalem that were biting the Jews of Judea, causing them to die **spiritually**.

When we then read John 3:16, we need to see how Jesus had just begun his ministry. At that time he was alive and well. There was no hint of Jesus being threatened by stoning or crucifixion. No one was yet plotting his death.

This means that when Jesus then said, "For God so loved the world that he gave his only son, so that everyone who believes in him may not perish but have everlasting life," Jesus was prophesying.

God's only Son was Adam, as far as Nicodemus would have understood. Adam was whom God had given to the world.

That meant God made Adam to give Adam to the world to save a world without religion … a world without faith.

Adam would begin a bloodline that was also a spiritual line – of Patriarchs, Judges, Kings, Prophets, and Jesus …

And the Apostles of Jesus …

And those Apostles still present in the world today …

Who all were, are, and will be priests of the One God, re-embodiments as the Son of Man – as God within a faithfully devoted human form.

# After Pentecost Sermons: Trinity Sunday, Year B

We see this in the Old Testament story from Isaiah.

King Uzziah had been a devoted king for decades, but then he made a grave error.

His error was why Isaiah cried out, "I am lost, for I am a man of unclean lips, and I live among people of unclean lips." Uzziah sinned, and all the people of Judah suffered.

But, then an angel of the LORD placed a burning coal from the altar and touched Isaiah's mouth. He was told, "Your guilt has departed and your sin is blotted out." That red-hot coal burned away the lips of flesh, leaving only lips of Spirit.

That was the same thing as an Israelite being bitten by a poisonous snake in the wilderness looking upon the raised bronze serpent.

That would be the same as being a disciple of Jesus in hiding, after his death, who then looked up to see the raised Jesus.

They all were expected to repay that salvation with eternal dedication.

Thus, God asked in Isaiah's presence, "Who shall I send, and who will go for us?"

Those who have been saved from death … given eternal life … they owe big time.

That is why Paul wrote to the Christian Jews of Rome, saying, "Brothers and sisters, we are debtors."

Anyone who has been saved by God's Holy Spirit …

Anyone who has been removed from the "born to die in the flesh" list, to be given a place in heaven, has to say to God,

"Here I am; send me!"

Last week was the Day of Pentecost, when the coals from the altar were placed on the mouths of the disciples of Jesus. They stood up and began speaking in foreign languages.

They all said, "Here I am; send me!"

Today is the beginning of Ordinary Time, when those who are ordained by the Holy Spirit begin their ministries.

It is a time to remember how Jesus said, "The harvest is plentiful, but the workers are few."

Christ needs workers; and God is again calling out, "Who shall we send, and who will go for us?"

How will you answer?

When will you feel it is time to trade in guilt and sin for eternal life?

The problem that has always been present, which always keeps the "labor force of God" under-staffed, is too many people getting bitten by the snakes that keep them mortal and living according to the flesh; and, thus, guaranteed to die.

Born ... live ... die ... repeat. No eternity in heaven. All because of so many poisonous snakes being about.

Nicodemus and his Pharisees buddies, the Temple priests and scribes, they were the poisonous snakes that killed the Jews and kept them from eternal life. Even if Nicodemus secretly supported Jesus the rabbi, he represented one who would not openly risk his own position, much less his life, for that of another human being.

# After Pentecost Sermons: Trinity Sunday, Year B

Certainly, the ruling council of Jerusalem ordered some stoned to death; they had the Romans crucify others, but more than having the power to bring about one's physical pain, suffering and immediate death, they caused the people to fear **them** – the snakes – and not God. Their fangs injected the poison of fear into the people ... a fear of serving God ... simply because their venom never allowed anyone to know how to serve God properly.

The same poisonous snakes are all around us today. We don't call them Pharisees or High Priests, however.

Instead, we call them by names that seem just as honorable as those titles seemed then. There are still those men and women - respected leaders - who we bow down before. They are those humans that we fear **if** we are to make them angry and those who we know there is no reason to fear **if** they are behind us.

The snakes today are those who gain our trust and confidence with promises of worldly gains, social solutions, and national prominence. They play the games of politics and philosophy, using the pretense of equality, freedom, and justice to divide the people ... rather than unite ... to confuse the people ... rather than teach the people self-sufficiency through God's Holy Spirit. The poisonous snakes are the false shepherds who see the people as property.

Has someone like Nicodemus ever come to see you secretly, asking for your support ... asking you to join his or her team? Does that one-on-one visit come off as so important that you feel you owe that person your support?

When these snakes bite us, too often we sell our souls and do what Paul warned the Romans not to be trapped by. He said, "If you live according to the flesh, you will die."

Paul continued to say, "You did not receive a spirit of slavery to fall back into fear."

Think about that for a moment ... **a spirit of slavery**. We hear the word "slavery" and instantly think it is the opposite of the beloved **FREEDOM** that makes America so great in the eyes of so many.

But, with all the hype about **FREEDOM**, who is truly free?

If you are wholly free, then make yourself float and deny gravity. Are there not the laws of our nation holding us as slaves, just like there are laws of gravity that keep us bound?

Does not the Law of Moses act in the same way? Certainly, we are free to break all those laws; but, are we Christians free from suffering the consequences of that freedom, just like the Assyrians and Babylonians punished the wayward Israelites and Jews?

Today, American Christians fear so many things, that fear indicates they are **slaves** according to the flesh. They reject a slavery to the spirit. Most Americans have debt owed to banks and credit card companies; but, who attempts to pay a monthly bill from Heaven, from God's collector Jesus Christ, which says, "You promised to serve Me"?

If one has not received a spirit of slavery, which is a devotion to service to the LORD ... with a loving desire **for** that **slavery** to God ... then one is a slave of the flesh and only takes delight in self. There is nothing left in the spiritual checking account that can be used for helping others.

Today, the snake bite victims can be seen when they get loose after a few beers, under the cover of darkness ... like my trainer did so many years ago.

They see life as a series of scams ... always trying to take care of self, at the expense of others.

## After Pentecost Sermons: Trinity Sunday, Year B

We all get duped into their schemes, at one time or another.

We all have to make the decision, once our eyes are opened and we know "I made a mistake." We either keep going or we quit – never to go back and lie with snakes again.

It might cost us the suit off our backs, but the education you get is a free test in the wilderness, when it is just you and Satan.

You either answer his call, saying, "Here I am, make me rich."

Or, you answer God's call and tell Satan, "Get behind me. You're history."

Amen

# SECOND SUNDAY AFTER PENTECOST

# Proper 5

# YEAR B

**Relevant readings:**
1 Samuel 8:4-20 and
　1 Samuel 11:14-15
Psalm 138
　Genesis 3:8-15
　Psalm 130
2 Corinthians 4:13-5:1
Mark 3:20-35

After Pentecost Sermons: Proper 5, Year B

# In the chess game of life, the pawns are those pieces "greatly afflicted"

In the story we read today from the first book of Samuel, where the Israelites went to him and asked God to give them a king … to be like other nations … we see how God granted their wish.

From the ancient Chinese proverb that Judge Ito was known to quote during the O.J. trial: "Be careful what you wish for … you just might get it."

God gave Samuel a "laundry list" of commands, which focuses on what serving a human king entailed for the Israelites.

By then, none of the Israelites had ever breathed the air of a nation ruled by sovereign power … such as that surrounding the Pharaoh of Egypt.

Egypt was one of those "other nations" that the Israelites wanted to be like.

God told Samuel to tell the regular Israelites what they could expect was sacrifice:

> You must sacrifice your sons, so they will be on the front lines of any danger surrounding the king.
>
> You must sacrifice your able body to plow the king's fields and reap his harvest – then do the same for your own field.
>
> You must use precious metals to make weapons, leaving little ores left over to make the implements that make rustic, farm life easier.
>
> You must sacrifice your daughters to do all the household

chores of maintaining the king's home.

You must sacrifice the best of what you possess, just so the king can impress foreign visitors.

You must sacrifice 1/10th of your farm animals.

You must sacrifice yourself to be a slave to the king.

To put that in chess pieces terms: You become a pawn – to be sacrificed when need be; and, when sacrificed, that is seen as little lost.

There is a saying many Americans say from time to time: "God, Family, & Country."

Based on what God told Samuel, choosing to let a human leader command your allegiance would place "Family" last on that list.

What a human king would invariably do is place "God" after "Country," because the human king equates to "Country," and after all – the celebration held by the Israelites at Gilgal, when Saul was made King of Israel, meant Saul had replaced God.

That is why God's first response to Samuel was, "They have rejected me from being king over them."

But, the problem the Israelites saw was not having a king, because in their minds a nation was identified by its leader. Without a **visible** king over them, that absence only invited people to see their land as open territory to squat on.

Think about that for a moment.

Envision the whole world as a large map where individuals are standing in the places where each nation is. Imagine how each individual represents the leader of that nation.

# After Pentecost Sermons: Proper 5, Year B

Imagine how a tall individual reflects how the size and power the nation is greater. Some are giants. Some are like elves. But, places without representation appear to be vacant lots, land where expansion can take place.

With that image in mind, see then how "The Promised Land of Canaan," which was filled with many people of different roots, in addition to those Israelites who had divided out segments of Canaan to its twelve tribes … they had no human king that represented the whole of that one place.

That place would appear to have no one standing in place, <u>because God is invisible</u> and God was their King.

The Israelites wanted the world to see they had a ruler, as a physical warning for others to beware.

And, even though God had been their ruler, and even though God had secured their Promised Land for them, and even though God had sent them Judges and Prophets to rescue them from all the squatters who came thinking their land was unsettled, God gave the Israelites an instrument of power that no other nation possessed – the Ark.

Still, with all that history, the Israelites wanted a human king to be responsible for their lives and safety.

Of course, God warned the Israelites that a day would eventually come when they would "cry out because of your king, whom you have chosen for yourselves; but the LORD will not answer you on that day."

That is a heavy warning.

However, the Israelites saw it like their Father saying the reason you cannot have "an official Red Ryder carbine action

200-range-shot model air rifle" is because "you'll shoot your eye out kid."

Once they woke up the day after the sacrificial offering made at Gilgal and found they had the gift they wanted so much, "The Israelites rejoiced greatly." They got their wish.

Now, Gilgal was where Joshua led the Israelites into Canaan, after Moses died. Joshua then circumcising the Israelite men there, with circumcision being a symbol of marriage to God. That act was concluded by Joshua placing stones in a circle – the meaning of the name Gilgal. Joshua did that as he stated, "God had **rolled away** the reproach of Egypt," where the reproach came from the "king" of Egypt.

The symbolism meant that the people were no longer bound to the Pharaoh. They were instead bound to God.

God was their king, and all the Israelite males agreed to be circumcised as a way of saying "I do" to God.

Samuel took the Israelites to that same place, once the elders of the Israelites chose a human king instead of God. Gilgal then served as the place for the divorce decree AND the new marriage agreement between the Israelites and their human king, Saul.

What we do not see in what we read today is how **nothing** that was agreed upon when Moses came down from the mountain, how **none** of the laws that bound the Israelites to God **forever** as His chosen people had become part of that divorce decree.

Even with a human king, the people were still expected to maintain that Covenant – at all times – **AND** the king was expected to keep all those laws on the books, so they continually governed the nation of Israel.

God's warning came true – of course – and the people cried out because of their king; but the LORD did not answer.

The Israelites lost their nation – their precious land and standing in the world – because the kings they approved kept breaking the laws, ignoring the Prophets, and mixing and mingling with all the people "of other nations," whose gods had different concepts of law.

It was the realization that they had messed up with this king thing so bad that they had slacked off greatly on the Covenant part, which led to the law having a renewed importance to the Jews in captivity in Babylon.

They re-recorded all the scrolls of the Torah, the Psalms and the books of the Prophets and "laid down the law" to all who would seek to regain the LORD's favor.

By the time they had been granted their freedom and returned to the lands their ancestors had once called home, they had no king of their own and no nation of their own …

But, they agreed to be slaves to whoever ruled over their lost lands … the Babylonians, the Persians, the Herodians, and then the Romans.

They agreed to be slaves to those overseers, as long as it was understood that their religion and their dedication to the laws of Moses meant they were primarily God's servants, as He was their supreme ruler.

Now, in the laws the Jews followed they were expected to stay away from those who did not have a Covenant with God … as much as possible.

That meant they lived in clusters of their own people, so when they were supposed to "love their neighbor," it was understood that "their neighbor" meant a fellow Jew - not just anybody, or everybody.

We read this not long ago, where Peter, the Jewish Apostle, explained that to Cornelius, the Roman centurion, saying, "You know how unlawful it is for a Jewish man to keep company with or go to one of another nation."

In the big city where I was raised, there was a known "Jewish neighborhood." If one's travels happened to take one through that part of town on the Jewish Sabbath, you would see lines of them walking down the sidewalks leading to the synagogue.

The Jews of that city made up only a small percentage of the total population, but they made it a point of obeying their law and not place themselves openly among the Gentiles, those who do not know or understand their laws.

You have to realize that the law AND the Jews being compliant to that particular law was a result of kings telling their ancestors, "It is okay to live among people with different religious values and experience what they call important."

They had lost everything because of not following the letter of **their** pact with God.

The renewal of the Temple of Jerusalem – only for the Jews, and no one else – brought about the rise of lawmen ... the policemen of all the sacred texts: the Temple priests & scribes; and the Pharisees & rabbis.

Not only did the Jews have to stay to themselves, but they also had to learn all the laws and scriptures. They could not be allowed to lose the only thing the Jews hoped to regain ... the favor of God.

It was within that setting that we find Jesus and his disciples today, as read in the Gospel of Mark.

# After Pentecost Sermons: Proper 5, Year B

At that time, Jesus had only recently begun his ministry. Jesus officially chose the twelve who would follow him throughout his travels just before this story told by Mark. The twelve disciples had followed Jesus into a home in Galilee, for the purpose of having dinner.

Prior to that, Jesus had healed a man of his withered hand, having performed that miracle on the Sabbath and in front of witnesses.

That particular act had two consequences: 1.) Crowds began following Jesus wherever he went; and 2.) The lawmen were alarmed that healing on the Sabbath was breaking the law.

At this point, it becomes important to see that EVERYONE in the story told today – Jesus, his disciples, the crowd following Jesus, the people saying Jesus has gone out of his mind, the scribes who came down from Jerusalem, and Jesus' mother and brothers – they were **ALL** Jews.

While in a land of mixed-faith people, this gathering took place in a setting that excluded Romans, Samaritans, Greeks, Arabs, Parthians, and anyone else not Jewish.

In that way, when we read how Jesus' "**family** heard [the commotion of the crowd following Jesus], so they went out to restrain him," this "**family**" was more than simply mom and his siblings.

The Jews are a "**family**" because they keep themselves separate from those who are not part of the "family" of Jews.

The Jews are considered to be both the followers of a specific religion **AND** a race of people, where "race" means "a group of people of common ancestry" – a "family."

In this way, that **family** was divided into two parts: those who believed Jesus was special; and those who feared Jesus was possessed.

The scene plays out like an intervention, where someone's family member has joined a cult and has disassociated one's self from his relatives and neighbors, which has caused the relatives and neighbors to attempt a rescue.

As such, the family and neighbors wanted to save Jesus from himself. Rather than being under the influence of a guru or charismatic cult leader, they saw him possessed by evil spirits, causing him to go against his **family**. They saw Jesus as the news has projected Jim Jones and David Koresh, as becoming a dangerous cult leader.

The difference was that the family and neighbors were the ones caught up in cult worship, with Jesus and his followers being the ones led by the true light of God …

And … that turns the focus back on who truly is one's king … who does one serve?

The king of Jesus is <u>God</u>.

The king of the scribes who came up from Jerusalem was <u>the law</u>, which their leaders had deemed meant, "No healing shall be done on the Sabbath."

The scribes could hold up a scroll for all to see. "Look here! This is God's word!"

Jesus could not hold up anything visible that proved he was the Son of God … of the "**family**" of God the Father.

Paul wrote to the Christians of Corinth – Jews and Gentiles who believed in Jesus as Christ, as those who were filled with the

Holy Spirit of God – saying, "We look not at what can be seen but at what cannot be seen; for what can be seen is temporary, but what cannot be seen is eternal."

The mother and brothers of Jesus believed in God. They believed in the Law of Moses. They saw the need for lawmen to police the people. Because of that need being seen, they feared not having leaders who would act like kings, to rule the people and make them obey the laws sent by God. And actual delivery of **THE** Messiah ... they feared that too, as that represented another human king.

Jesus also believed in God; but his belief ... his faith ... was not because he could see a scroll. His faith would not force anyone physically to do what is right. He believed in the Law because it was written on his heart, where it could not be seen by anyone. It could only be felt by Jesus. As such, Jesus was himself the lawman of the **nation** of **Jesus**, who's King was God. Thus, **THE** Messiah was not one human king, but a duplication of one nation into many individuals whose total allegiance was to One God.

But none of that could be seen.

When this presence within Jesus brought about the accusation that he was filled with "an unclean spirit," he told those surrounding him, "Truly I tell you, people will be forgiven for their sins and whatever blasphemies they utter; but whoever blasphemes against the Holy Spirit can never have forgiveness, but is guilty of an eternal sin."

When Jesus was told his mother and brothers were trembling outside the house he was in, afraid that the lawmen of Jerusalem would use the scrolls to condemn Jesus – all while **knowing** Jesus was of holy origin – Jesus said, "Here [surrounding me] are my mother and my brothers!"

The **family** of Jesus encircled him like the stones of Gilgal … those married to God through the symbolic act of circumcision.

Your true "**family**" is composed of those who seek guidance how to find God, they are those who readily receive the Holy Spirit, and they are those who encourage others to seek and maintain God as their only King.

"Whoever does the will of God is my **family**," said Jesus.

The moral of these stories today is that **WE** are no different than the Jews were during the days of Jesus' earthly ministry.

We live in a land of mixed-faiths. We have elected rulers, to whom we willingly commit ourselves, as their slaves. We hold up legal documents that we allow lawmen to enforce. We tremble with fear whenever one of our own is found breaking those laws.

If the lawmen judge that we must eat the food of idols or respect the rights of those who have no religious beliefs - those who serve no gods at all - then we submit to that will, rather than be persecuted for separating ourselves from that influence. We sell our souls for membership in a national family, rather than stay with Christ - no matter how many shout, "Come out and go home with us. Stop acting like you're not just like us!"

Today, anyone who speaks the truth of sin to others, inspired by the Holy Spirit to speak publicly, they are called "out of their minds" and "possessed with an unclean spirit." They may see Christians as legally being in need of government intervention.

Today, we stand two thousand years and half a globe away from where Jesus stood and we think we know it all. If anyone comes to us, as one of us – one within the "**family**" of Christians – and tells us, "You have it all wrong! You are going the wrong way!" then what …

Do we not disown them?

Is Facebook and other social media nothing more than the playground of those who tell us what we want to hear … or we "unfollow" what they say?

Have you ever stopped seeing the religious posts of "friends and family," simply because those messages weigh on your conscience?

Do we not stand in fear and shake like leaves in a strong wind, when one of our own is letting the Holy Spirit speak, leading us to call out for that dear one to "please stop embarrassing us!" God does not walk about the population looking like God.

God is unseen …

God does not make himself appear as a human king, president, prime minister, pope, or cult leader.

God can only be seen as looking like **us**, when we have God within, when we let God's presence be known to others by our acting as Jesus did.

How often have you seen God and thought, "Well, there is another fanatic"?

In the reading from Paul's first letter to the Corinthians, Paul quoted Scripture, saying, "I believed, and so I spoke."

That "Scripture" is actually Psalm 116:10, which states, "I trusted in the LORD when I said, "**I am greatly afflicted**."

That means one's faith comes when one realizes, "I am greatly afflicted," and not when one thinks, "Man, I am so loved by the LORD because I have this and that and a bunch of those."

Robert Tippett

In this Ordinary season, when the priests of Christ serve God by showing their belief by speaking so others can hear, think about how your present life fits into the scenes projected today.

Can you see how you might need to admit, "I am greatly afflicted," before you can begin your own ministry?

Can you see how you have to honestly ask yourself, "Who do I serve? Who is my King?"

Amen

# After Pentecost Sermons: Proper 5, Year B

# THIRD SUNDAY AFTER PENTECOST

# Proper 6

# YEAR B

**Relevant readings:**
1 Samuel 15:34-35 and
   1 Samuel 16:13
Psalm 20
   Ezekiel 17:22-24
   Psalm 92:1-4; 11-14
2 Corinthians 5:6-17,
Mark 4:26-34

After Pentecost Sermons: Proper 6, Year B

# A quest to answer the question, "Who do you serve?"

One of my all-time favorite movies is *Excalibur*.

It is a movie about King Arthur, who (in my mind at least) symbolizes Christianity. More than Jesus and his twelve Apostles, Arthur and his Knights of the Round Table symbolize the wholeness of Christianity, with the knights being all who are filled with the Holy Spirit.

The Kingdom of Camelot then represents the earthly realm; and, at the end of the movie when Arthur has died and set sail to the island of Avalon, that represents the return of Christ and the defeat of evil in the final battle.

God's ultimate purpose of Christ, and thus the ultimate purpose of Christianity is to defeat evil. It is not to make certain people be seen as special ... above all the rest ... as such a purpose would only divide the land ... not unify it with Heaven.

Avalon was a mythical island, which comes from Welch, meaning, "place of fruit trees." Thus, Christ is shown returning to the Garden of Eden, where Heaven and Earth are one.

The Knights of the Round Table represent the Apostles of Christ, as well as all the Apostles who would lead others by the acts of chivalry, brought on by the Holy Spirit.

In the movie, one knight, Sir Percival, was knighted by King Arthur so he could stand in and defend Guinevere's honor. He had been a squire prior to that.

Percival, in a sense, is like the Apostle Paul. He was anointed by Jesus Christ ... after Jesus had died, when he then became King.

The name "Percival" is believed to be rooted in Old French words "*Percer val*," meaning, "To pierce the valley." That can be seen in the terms of "scraping the bottom of the barrel," where the valley is an earthly low point; also keeping in mind how Ezekiel was shown dried bones filling a valley.

As such, "Percival" personifies how the weak shall become strong, through Christ. The squires shall become knights is this same principle.

Sir Percival, like all the Knights of the Round Table, was sent out to seek the Grail after King Arthur fell into despair and Camelot fell into ruin.

In the reading today from the first book of Samuel, we read how "the elders of the city [Bethlehem] came to meet [Samuel] trembling." They asked Samuel a question that was rooted in their fear, "Do you come peaceably?"

Israel had fallen upon hard times, due to the despair Saul had fallen into … because "the LORD was sorry that he had made Saul king."

Many of the Apostles of Christ … just as did the Knights of Arthur … found their deaths in a quest for the Holy Grail … seeking to return the land to belief in the One God, the one true King.

Sir Percival, in his quest, encountered the evil boy-prince Mordred … the illegitimate son of Arthur and his half-sister Morgana … who asked Sir Percival if he sought the Grail. Percival said, "I do," and Mordred led Percival to a tree where there were many rotting corpses of knights hanging from the tree's limbs.

This symbolizes the persecution of Jesus **and** his Apostles; and that is why we read so often how the Apostles recalled, "They hung him from a tree."

Mordred told Percival, "They [the dead knights] were looking for [the Holy Grail] too. But they weren't good enough." That says they were "good," but martyrdom alone will not return a land to peace. There must be a steady flow ... a renewal of knights ... so more will come to replace those fallen.

Sir Percival was hung from the same tree by the servants of Prince Mordred; but, near death, Percival experienced a vision. He saw a God-like figure in a king's castle, sitting on a throne, high atop a flight of stairs.

The scene evokes imagery of Jacob's ladder, where angels went up and down, to and from heaven.

This kingly figure and Percival have this exchange in the movie, after which Percival glimpses the Holy Grail:

> **Grail figure**: "What is the secret of the Grail? Who does it serve?"
>
> **Percival**: "You, my lord."
>
> **Grail Figure**: "Who am I?"
>
> **Percival**: "You are my lord and king. You are Arthur."
>
> **Grail Figure**: "Have you found the secret that I have lost?"
>
> **Percival**: "Yes. You and the land are one."

The Grail itself is symbolic of the cup that held the wine that Jesus shared with his disciples ... it symbolizes the cup of salvation from which we drink each Eucharist service we hold, in honor of Christ. We drink from that cup so we can serve the

LORD ... so we can serve our King filled with the Holy Spirit ... so we can be one with God and Christ.

At that point in the movie when that vision ended, Sir Percival was saved from suffering and death on that tree, falling to the ground. Once saved, he returned to Camelot and immediately took a royal chalice with wine to Arthur. The following exchange takes place:

**Percival**: [holding the Grail to Arthur's lips] "You and the land are one. Drink."

**Arthur**: "I am wasting away. I cannot die and I cannot live."

**Percival**: "Drink from the chalice. You will be reborn and the land with you."

**Arthur**: [drinks] "Percival... I didn't know how empty was my soul... until it was filled."

It is important to see the immediacy of Salvation comes from receipt of the Holy Spirit ... not from physically drinking wine from a pretty cup. It is our souls that thirst for the Holy Spirit. Without that Spirit, we are empty.

Now, these lines of dialogue come from a 1981 movie, and not the 12th-14th century tales of King Arthur. The script was molded from *Le Morte d'Arthur*, by Sir Thomas Mallory (published in 1485). However, other versions have text that differs from the movie script; with not all in agreement ... such as some texts call Mordred the nephew of Arthur, rather than his illegitimate son.

As much as it interests me, my intention is not to preach about *Excalibur*, but to use those scenes to illuminate the message I see in the readings this week. Those images came to my mind as I read about the failure of Saul to lead the Israelites as Samuel told him, as God had commanded him.

The details of that failure precede what we read today, but we understand "the LORD was sorry that he had made Saul king over Israel."

We then read how Samuel listened for God to tell him which of Jesse's sons would be chosen as the next king of Israel. David being anointed as a boy parallels young Arthur pulling the sword from the stone.

In Psalm 20, David sings praise to the LORD: "Now I know that the LORD gives victory to his anointed; he will answer him out of his holy heaven, with the victorious strength of his right hand."

Victory comes from God. Both Saul and David would know that personally from both ends of the "victory" spectrum, where every victor yields a loser.

The answer that Percival gave to the LORD, "You and the land are one," is like how Paul wrote in his letter to the Corinthians:

> "If anyone is in Christ, there is a new creation: everything old has passed away; see, everything has become new!"

When an Apostle is "in Christ," then Christ is in the Apostle.

Heaven and earth are one. The physical (land) and the Spirit are one. God the Father is in His Son and the Son is in the Father, as one. So too is anyone who is "in Christ," as those are reborn as the Son of God.

Still, the element of youth abounds.

David was a boy king. Arthur was a boy who had to be knighted before he could officially [legally] become king. Percival was a squire who had to be knighted before he could officially defend the honor of Guinevere ... the woman who I see as symbolic of the Church of Christ [Rome].

From youth comes the exuberance of devotion. When we are reborn with the Holy Spirit and "everything has become new," we are like children ... young at heart.

Saul failed because he was trying to fit an old earthly model ... to be like a strong king, which identified with those kings of other nations of significance. With maturity comes experience and with experience comes the realization that being the king always brings challenges to that authority. Experience knows how hard it is to always be physically the strongest, so wise kings surround themselves with strong young arms.

That is the old earthly model ...

But, this old model always fails; and we see that in Saul's failures before God, as well as David's failures of his older life. Even wise Solomon fell victim to "believing his own press clippings," thinking it was okay to marry women who practiced other religious rituals, and then sanctioning the worship of other gods in Israel.

The failures come from thinking (as king) that one has the authority to introduce a perversion into the general rites of the population of God's children. Saul thought he would be adding to his strength, if he pleased his young generals by giving them forbidden booty that was not his to give.

Not long ago, when we read from Isaiah, we read how he saw a vision of smoke in the Temple, which made him cry out that he was of a people with unclean lips. His cries caused a seraph to bring a coal from the Temple and place it to his lips - to purify him. That dream was symbolic of the failure of King Uzziah, who after many years of devoted service before the LORD, he then thought he was holy enough to do no wrong.

He was wrong to think that.

So, the Arthurian tale of King Arthur falling into despair, so that his kingdom also suffered, is a repeated theme in the Old Testament stories of our heritage.

Over time it is natural for the earthly to break down and fail.

We live in times … twenty centuries after Christianity was born, so that we no longer represent those times when "there [was] a new creation: [when] everything old [had] passed away; [and] everything [had] become new!" You have lost the Spirit we [Christianity] once had.

We live in a time that is representative of the young Prince Mordred … whose name means "We are bitten," implying a "Painful" bite [like that of a snake, causing us to fear our mortality] … when the weakness that has befallen Christianity brings about the Painful tests of the devotion of the faithful … expecting them to "tremble" with fear, as did the elders of Bethlehem when Samuel arrived.

We want peace, but we fear war so much that there is no true peace.

It is the natural way of earthly things. As we age, we become weaker, less able to wear all the armor and lift all the heavy weapons.

But what we need to see today is how the answer to this present danger comes from the words spoken by Jesus, recounted in the Gospel reading in Mark.

Christianity today is just like when Arthur said to Percival, "I am wasting away. I cannot die and I cannot live."

Arthur needed a champion like Percival to revive him.

It is up to **us** to give Christianity rebirth.

Jesus said, "With what can we compare the kingdom of God, or what parable will we use for it?"

He then answered, "It is like a mustard seed, which, when sown into the ground, is the smallest of all the seeds on earth."

Each one of us is like a mustard seed, individually of complete insignificance, of no importance, in no way capable of rescuing or protecting anyone or anything … including ourselves. Still, it is **within us** tiny mustard seeds where the kingdom of heaven can be found.

Jesus then continued, saying, "When [a mustard seed] is sown it grows up and become the greatest of all shrubs, and puts forth large branches, so that the birds of the air can make nests in its shade."

That says, "Small people grow into the strength of God's faith – that which avows Christ is King – that which produces Knights as Apostles, with large branches of denominations – each devoted believers, whose faith is rooted in the strength of God, advocated by Christ to receive the Holy Spirit – the wine of power from the Holy Grail."

Heaven and Earth are one, when the Holy Spirit takes root and grows in You.

Christians are the protectors of the earth, because the arms of Christ – the nations and lands under Christian kings – provide homes where all can see the peace that is brought forth by the LORD.

# After Pentecost Sermons: Proper 6, Year B

In this Church calendar period, known as Ordinary Time, we are asked to kneel before Christ our King and be knighted as defenders of the faith … as those who are sworn to die in self and be reborn as Jesus. Thus, we should see the urgency for our individual ordinations as priests, with our LORD sending us out on a quest to make the land and the King whole again.

Ordinary Time is a renewal of the Great Commission, when we must answer, just like everyone else, "Who do you serve?"

Jesus said, "The kingdom of God is as if someone would scatter seed on the ground, and would sleep and rise night and day, and the seed would sprout and grow."

We are those who are sowing the seeds of God's love through Christ.

The "greatest of all shrubs" must be a strong sanctuary for the faithful … or it will become where the faithful will be hung, for "not being good enough."

Amen

# FOURTH SUNDAY AFTER PENTECOST

# Proper 7

# YEAR B

**Relevant readings:**
1 Samuel 17:4-11; 19-23; 32-49
Psalm 9:9-20
  *or*
  1 Samuel 17:57-58 and 18:5; 10-16
  Psalm 133
      Job 38:1-11
      Psalm 107:1-3; 23-32
2 Corinthians 6:1-13
Mark 4:35-41

After Pentecost Sermons: Proper 7, Year B

# At war against those who promote fears

Most of us here today have heard the sound bite of President Franklin Roosevelt saying, "The only thing we have to fear is fear itself."

Roosevelt spoke those words in the first paragraph of his 1933 Inaugural Address, when he was sworn in as president for the first of his four terms elected.

I had wrongly presumed that he spoke those words about the threat of World War II; but, instead, he was referring to the Great Depression that had enveloped the nation, beginning in 1929.

While being somewhat of a religious theme, the "fear" Roosevelt spoke of was not religious. He spoke or the fear of financial instability nationally … a "fear" that businesses and people would be shy about making material investments. Those fears arose due to the losses that had ruined so many "easy money" millionaires, bankrupted so many small businesses, and put so many hard-working common people in soup lines.

"Brother, can you spare a dime?" was a question heard often in those days.

The answer to that question was 'Big Government'. The fears of the people would be assuaged by Roosevelt's New Deal federal work programs, farm subsidies, anti-poverty welfare initiatives and the passing of the Social Security Act of 1935.

The safety and security of Americans was placed in the hands of a government that grew into a protective giant.

Today, our Federal government stands "six cubits and a span," fully dressed in armor and weaponry. The shield-bearer that runs out before it is its underling – that which can be summed up as all the support functions of the politics identifying with Washington D. C.

Our government has long boasted to the world, the same as it boasts to its own citizens still, "You shall be our servants and serve us."

Just as Goliath bellowed those words before the Israelite armies, we likewise stand today, "dismayed and greatly afraid" of the giant our government has become.

The only thing that makes Big Government unchallenged is fear.

It was fear that gave rise to <u>other</u> Big Governments, primarily those which led to, or were greatly affected by World War II.

World War II and the Great Depression were the offspring of the fears that followed World War I - the fear that it must be the war to end all wars.

It wasn't.

The League of Nations and the subsequent United Nations are institutions that fight fear with fear.

It was fear that led to the Cold War, where two equal 'Goliath' giants were afraid of "pushing the red button" and beginning the end of the world.

It is fear that defines the current war our Big Government is mired in – a War on Terrorism.

"Terrorism" can be defined as "A state of **fear** produced by acts of violence and threats to intimidate or coerce, especially for political purposes."

# After Pentecost Sermons: Proper 7, Year B

The distinction of "political purposes" reverts one back to government directed "fears," where the "political" can then equally infer Democracy, or Communism, or Radical Islam (all as philosophical-religious motivations), simply because each **giant** uses acts of violence and words of intimidation as its ways of forcing its will upon peoples.

Today's readings speak loudly about the effects fear has on people.

Young David heard the boasts of Goliath and immediately went to Saul, saying, "Let no one's heart fail because of [that giant braggart]."

Fear lurks in the hearts of people.

Jesus was asleep on a boat that was being tossed wildly about in the waves of the Sea of Galilee, when his disciples awoke him, frightened. Their fears made them think they were about to die. Jesus simply commanded the environment, "Peace! Be still!"

And ... it was so.

Fear of death is strong in people who know they are mortal creatures.

Paul wrote the Corinthians saying, "We are treated as impostors, and are yet true; as unknown, and yet we are well known; as dying, and see – we are alive; as punished, and yet not killed; as sorrowful, yet always rejoicing; as poor, yet making many rich; as having nothing, yet possessing everything."

Those who are without fear are either evil or good: Goliath or David; Materialist or Spiritualist; Scientist or Cleric; Warrior or Healer. One's reason for being fearless is clear to see, while the other is not.

Being fearless because of an unseen God causes people to lash out against those whose faith is not founded in natural, physical powers, but in the spiritual ones.

"The only thing you have to fear is God," as everything else is just some over-dressed giant that is trying to make sure you tremble like a leaf, because your fears give that giant complete control over you. Fears cause you to submit to the gods of the world, because you forget there is only One True God.

We read how Goliath, upon seeing young David coming towards him – basically unprotected and unarmed – "cursed David by his gods." The "gods" of Goliath were clearly visible: his size, his strength, his armor, his weapons, and his allies. Goliath worshipped the "gods" of nature, those who awarded their faithful with physical abundance and worldly riches.

We read how Jesus' disciples saw, "A great windstorm arose, and the waves beat into the boat, so that the boat was already swamped." After Jesus calmed the situation by a command, the disciples wondered, "Who then is this, that even the wind and the sea obey him?"

The disciples, like the Philistines **AND** the Israelites, worshipped the "gods" of nature, who punished the faithful through random acts of physical violence. The "gods" of nature always stand before us with super stature - compared to our feeble selves.

"Who am I to do battle with those giants?" we meekly ask.

I remember moving to coastal Mississippi on August 1, 2005. In the months prior to that date (in hurricane season), there had been three hurricanes that made landfall on the gulf coast: Cindy (Cat. 1 – LA.); Dennis (Cat. 4 – FLA.); and, Emily (which hit two places: Cat. 4 – Yucatan and Cat. 3 – Mexico coast)

# After Pentecost Sermons: Proper 7, Year B

Due to Cindy and Dennis, the people of Waveland, Pass Christian and Bay Saint Louis had already been sent to shelters twice before, in preparation for potential landfalls there.

Both times the hurricanes missed that area of Mississippi.

I had never experienced the wrath of a tornado before in my life, much less a hurricane. As Hurricane Katrina developed in the Caribbean and then hit southern Florida, as a Cat. 1, few were listening to the warnings and fears projecting that Katrina would regroup and hit the Gulf Coast as a greater storm.

People went about their business as usual, thinking another false alarm would have them needlessly packing up a few things for an overnight stay at some secure location, with maybe a few limbs in the yard to clean up the day after.

I was not afraid of Katrina because no one I came in contact with was afraid. Even though the television was screaming "**FEAR!**" Everyone was saying, "They always make it seem worse than it ever is."

We all know the reality now.

In a way, Hurricane Katrina was like the Great Depression of 1929, as both came about because of nature. Depressions, like hurricanes, come and go, leaving messes in their wakes. People are used to tragedy striking randomly. While there is fear, there are prayers for God's help, regardless of the outcome.

The greatest fears are not for salvation, but for recovery.

The true fears that Hurricane Katrina exposed (and since then - Sandy, in 2012) came when the people expected the government to come save the day and make all the hurts and wounds go away quickly. God saved the lives of most people; but the government that boasted it was the Greatest Nation in the World was found to be run by liars and cheats.

The government is a lower-case "g" god. All it is good for is blowing hot air and using fear as its means of growth in power.

What we need to listen to today ... what we need to hear from these scripture readings, is David asking **us**, "Why does your heart fail from fear, because of terrorism?"

What we need to hear is Jesus asking **us**, "Why are you afraid? Have you still no faith?"

What we need to hear is Paul asking **us**, "Why do you restrict the affections of your heart from God and Christ?"

"Why do you only pray for salvation when all hell is breaking loose?"

What **we** need to realize today is that which speaks to **us** from the psalm, where it sings, "The ungodly have fallen into the pit they dug, and in the snare they set is their own foot caught."

The snare we set is worshiping little-g gods Monday through Saturday (and half of Sunday), while acting fearless only on Sunday.

Fear is promoted in everything we see on television these days – in the news, in the entertainment, in the sports and competitions.

We, like the Israelites, tremble at the thought of having to be the one chosen to champion a cause. We gladly give up all our beliefs for the anonymity of watching someone else fight our battles for us.

We, like the disciples, find no solace in the fact that Jesus sleeps in the face of our fears, when it is our fears of lesser "gods" that have kept Jesus from being watchfully protecting us.

We, like Paul pointed out, fail to see how Isaiah heard God say, "In the time of my favor I will answer you, and in the day of salvation I will help you."

Instead, we demand that God must meet our schedule. We are blinded to the realization that "**NOW** is the acceptable time; and **NOW** is the day of salvation!"

All our fears disappear when our hearts have been opened wide for the LORD.

Indeed ... "The only thing we have to fear is fear itself."

Amen

# FIFTH SUNDAY AFTER PENTECOST

## Proper 8

## YEAR B

**Relevant readings:**
2 Samuel 1:17-27
Psalm 130
    Wisdom of Solomon
       1:13-15; 2:23-24
      Lamentations 3:21-33
    *or* Psalm 30
2 Corinthians 8:7-15
Mark 5:21-43

After Pentecost Sermons: Proper 8, Year B

# Don't let your faith be slain upon high places

The readings today place a focus on faith.

In David's poem, *The Song of the Bow*, we see how Saul and Jonathan died because their faith was placed more on their abilities as leaders of warriors, than a faith that followed the commands of God.

Of that level of faith, David repeated the lyric, "How the mighty have fallen!"

That song was ordered to be placed in the Book of <u>Jashar</u> … meaning the Book of <u>What is Right</u> … <u>What is Just</u> … <u>What is Upright</u>.

Their deaths were not mistakes but examples of what will always be found to be fair and impartial justice.

The justice of faith placed in the sword is double-edged … you live by the sword, you die by the sword.

In Paul's second letter to the Corinthians, he stated that "faith" was one area of growth that comes into one's life, once receipt of the Holy Spirit has occurred.

Paul's suggestion to those new Apostles was to spread their excelled faith by letting others see that they indeed had tremendous faith.

Increased faith cannot be kept private. It must be made public … as Luke wrote, "No one lights a lamp and puts it in a place where it will be hidden, or under a bowl. Instead they put it on its stand, so that those who come in may see the light."

In the Gospel of Mark, we read the story of Jesus, Jairus and the woman in the crowd. This story is steeped in faith.

Jesus openly displayed his faith so all could see … so those in need were attracted to him. Jesus was a lampstand of light for those who came to him.

Jairus showed faith in Jesus, as a man who was known for having had produced miracles.

The hemorrhaging woman also showed faith; but, in more ways than is readily obvious, such as when she sneaked a healing touch upon the cloak of Jesus.

The story in Mark's Gospel is like an onion, with layers of deeper meaning … all concerning faith.

We first see the faith of Jesus having attracted "a great crowd," which "gathered around him" after he landed on the Galilee side of the sea. His light of faith was radiantly attractive, like the flame that draws in the moths.

We then meet Jairus, who is said to be "one of the leaders of the synagogue." The Greek word written is "*archi-sunagógos*," which is a title often used to denote **THE** elder of a synagogue.

Then and now, many synagogues only have one leader, such that a lone rabbi is deemed an "*archisunagógos*," just as is the head rabbi at a large synagogue. In that position, he is the one who oversees many lower rabbis. Both leaders are given the same title of respect.

It makes sense to assume Jesus landed in a large place along the shores of the Sea of Galilee – like Capernaum – where large crowds could quickly be gathered upon his arrival. A place like Capernaum would be where multiple synagogues existed, with some having several rabbis, making Jairus more of an important figure in such a place.

Now, when we read, "Jairus came and, when he saw [Jesus], fell at his feet and begged him repeatedly," that posturing <u>before</u> Jesus and pleading for help was certainly a sign of his faith in Jesus … albeit one born out of the desperation, from having a "little daughter at the point of death."

Upon Jairus pleading for Jesus' help, it is then important to see that Jesus had faith in Jairus. We can assume that, when Mark wrote, "[Jesus] went with [Jairus]."

Jesus' faith was that Jairus would receive the Holy Spirit and assist – as an elder of the synagogue – in supporting the Messianic message later. The faith Jesus had was confidence in a future gain, by helping Jairus then, at his time of need.

Jairus sought the bread of life from Heaven and Jesus saw Jairus' faith as deserving his omer of manna.

Then we read about the hemorrhaging woman in the crowd. Mark told us that she "had been suffering from hemorrhages for twelve years."

That is not an insignificant number, as we see when Mark later tells us Jairus' "little daughter" "was twelve years of age."

Twelve is a metaphysical number, with meanings too deep to get into more right now. Just know twelve represents "completeness." It represents the end of a cycle of life. It represents a higher octave of the number three … a spiritual awakening, ending a period of wandering.

Still, you have to peel down another layer and realize that for as long as the woman "had been suffering," and had "endured much," during that time she "had spent all she had," only to get worse in the care of physicians. Over the same span of time, Jairus had enjoyed the pleasures of a daughter. For twelve years, Jairus had known the blessing that was she, who he still called his "little daughter."

As an elder in that place (logically Capernaum), it goes without doubt that Jairus had encountered the hemorrhaging woman before, as she also was a Jew there. Not once, I imagine, had Jairus seen the woman as someone else's "little daughter," a girl who had grown into a problem that was representative of her change from girl into womanhood, with ceaseless blame coming because she was suddenly seen as being full of constant sin, as a woman no longer a girl.

In a way, the woman had been a "little daughter" that had died twelve years prior.

The faith of Jairus would have led him to learn the Pentateuch, having him spend many years deeply studying the laws that told how such maladies would outcast the woman … as a sinner.

The faith of the woman had her try for twelve years to cease her uncleanliness, so she would be able to do all the things that normal young women yearned to do … including attend a synagogue, so she could openly pray to God. If cured, she could demonstrate how strong her faith had remained through it all, such that the past twelve years would prove that she was not a sinner, as she had not spent the years ignoring the laws in the scrolls.

Jairus and the woman had both placed their faith in physicians, seeing men who knew the arts of healing … knowing what herbs to eat, what salves to spread over wounds, what salts to soak in water for cleansing … as instruments of God. They took on the importance of the snake lifted up by Moses, to whom all eyes were then raised.

# After Pentecost Sermons: Proper 8, Year B

But that faith had been weakened in both Jairus and the woman, by this day they both encountered Jesus.

For Jairus, the failures of his personal physicians, unable to save his daughter, had driven him out into the crowd in desperation. In a panic Jairus was seeking a man, Jesus, who had a record of miracle working. Jairus sought out Jesus as a last resort.

The woman had lost her faith in medicine men long before; but she had no other recourse, because of her religious faith. She was told what hoops she had to jump through, as steps towards her possibly regaining good standing within the Jewish population.

She, we read, had said to herself, "If I but touch [Jesus'] clothes, I will be made well." That was a statement of faith.

Mark told us that Jesus was, "immediately aware that power had gone forth from him," after the woman touched his cloak. This caused Jesus to turn and ask, "Who touched my clothes?"

The response of Jesus' disciples tells how ridiculous that question seemed to them.

They must have thought, "Um … hello? There is a large crowd gathered and following you here. We are so squeezed in around you that it might have been I who bumped into you by accident."

Still, you have to see the question of Jesus as faith related, because he **felt** how the Holy Spirit's power had been transferred to someone in his presence. Jesus asked who it was, from his faith allowing him to **KNOW** that there was a spiritual need present.

Jesus wanted to know who also had the faith of need. It was someone other than Jairus.

Now, it is important to understand that an unclean person – like the hemorrhaging woman – touching **ANY** clean Jews (as Jesus, the disciples and Jairus were), meant that touch would have caused them to be unclean also … simply by them coming in contact with an unclean person.

Some, who have written about this story from Mark's Gospel say that Jesus did not care about such laws that called for purification after encounters with the unclean. They argue that Jesus regularly touched them, as a necessary part of their healing. However, that actually is not the case.

Jesus did not break any laws set forth by God, through Moses. An unclean woman had not actually touched his robe, although an unclean woman planned to go beyond that legal barrier. But, it was a miraculously healed (cleaned) woman that touched Jesus.

You see, when she had said to herself, "If I touch him I will be healed," God immediately healed her, via His Holy Spirit. As such, when Jesus told her, "your faith has made you well," it was to make sure she did not run off happily telling everyone that Jesus had healed her.

Knowing she was clean, the woman could approach Jesus as had Jairus - from the front - displaying the same posturing of respect, begging before Jesus for forgiveness, offering her confession.

To have her go out saying, "Jesus healed me," would have been the wrong message for Jesus to allow into the world. If only Jesus could heal, then how lost would the world be after Jesus' death?

Jesus asked, "Who touched me," so he could tell the mystery person in the crowd, "I did not make you well … your faith was known by God, so God healed you."

It is so extremely important to then realize that amid this conversation held by Jesus, with the woman … whom Jesus called, "**Daughter**," telling her to "go in peace, and forever be healed of your disease" … Jairus was there … eyes wide open and mouth probably agape. He had personally witnessed a miracle!

Jairus <u>knew</u> this woman and <u>knew</u> how long she had suffered. He <u>knew</u> how little the physicians had helped her … and now look at her! She has been healed.

Realizing that, Mark then wrote, "While [Jesus] was still speaking [to the healed woman], some people came from [Jairus'] house to say, "[Jairus,] your daughter is dead."

When those messengers saw how Jairus had found Jesus, they then asked him privately, "Why trouble the teacher any further?"

Now the Greek word used to identify Jesus as a "teacher" was not "*Rabbouni*," but "*di-dask-a-los*," which means an "instructor with an acknowledged mastery in a field." This identification is important to grasp.

As an elder of the synagogue, the first treatment Jairus would have sought for his daughter's health would have been faith-based – as prayer. Certainly, Jairus and many other friends and family had prayed for the girl to return to health. But, in addition to the prayer group, such a high-ranking citizen would have had a team of physicians come into his home, doing all that the advancements of medicine allowed them to do.

One can then be assured that the people who came from Jairus' house were armed with an official diagnosis – pronounced by a lead doctor – that Jairus' daughter was indeed dead.

They would have put a mirror under her nose. They would have felt her pulse. They might have even pricked her body with a pin. Thus, the news sent to Jairus had come from the mouths of professionals, not people who were clueless about how to determine death.

This means they addressed Jesus as if he was known to have been sought by Jairus, as being a man who could give some miracle working <u>instructions</u> to Jairus' doctors, or that Jesus was recognized as a **master** miracle worker, who had studied magical arts well enough to have learned "tricks" that could heal and prevent death.

But ... raising people from death?  Nobody could do that!

They recommended that Jairus no longer needed those "services," the kind offered by one lesser-respected, less-trusted than were those men of the cloth and medicine.

It was then from overhearing this message to Jairus that Jesus immediately told Jairus, "Do not fear, only believe."

Now, that is not a recommendation, as much as it is a command. It was **THE instruction** of utmost importance, which came from this **master** whom Jairus had sought.  "<u>Do not fear</u>" says, "Do not have any doubts."  Thus, "<u>only believe</u>" says, "Have **faith**."

After seeing the hemorrhaging woman – a "**daughter** suffering for twelve years" - healed before his very eyes, Jesus told Jairus to have faith that his twelve year old **daughter**, who had suffered only recently, would likewise be healed.

Having just heard Jesus say to the healed woman, "Your <u>faith</u> has made you well," Jarius' love of his daughter, his love of his God, and the love he now had for Jesus and someone else's daughter who Jesus had just healed – that **LOVE** gave him also the faith to heal his daughter.

By the time Jesus, Jairus, the girl's mother, Peter, and James and John of Zebedee had gone into the bedroom of the "little girl," she had already come back to life.  She was no longer dead.

Jairus' faith had healed his daughter, while the group of men still walked to his home.

So, Jesus spoke the truth when he said to the family and friends lamenting the daughter's passing, "Why do you make a commotion and weep? The child is not dead but sleeping."

Their laughing was a sign that they lacked faith in miracles, having put all their faith in physicians, prayer and scrolls that tell Jews the proper way to mourn a death.

Their lack of faith had them removed from the house.

That was Jesus practicing the Jewish law that forbids the faithful from mingling with those without faith – sinners who hemorrhaged laughter uncontrollably at the idea of faith. The same law had banished the hemorrhaging woman from the synagogues of which Jairus was an elder.

Again, some writers of the meaning of this story say that Jesus disregarded the cleanliness protocol by touching the hand of a dead girl. That defies belief in the purity of Jesus, as the Son of God.

The girl was **not** dead, just as the woman's hemorrhaging had stopped immediately **before** she touched Jesus' garment.

The moral of this story, which falls in line with the faith theme of the second book of Samuel reading, is Saul and Jonathan had misplaced their faith and suffered. They had become the unclean who were banished from Israel.

Likewise, the hemorrhaging woman had placed her faith in those who would not allow her in the synagogues, while telling her to go put her faith in physicians … not God. She had faith in blind rabbis and blind doctors, neither of which could see how to save one's soul.

Their failures are no different than the deaths of Saul and Jonathan, as the seemingly high mountains of priesthood and medicine men had failed.

"How the mighty have fallen!"

Jairus knew firsthand how his faith in men meant the death of his baby girl, but his faith in God's Holy Spirit meant the rebirth to his "little daughter."

In Paul's letter to his Christian children in Corinth, he advised them not to forget how Jesus was rich with the Holy Spirit, but had willingly become poor – through sacrificing his physical life, so others could be rich with the Holy Spirit. Paul knew the Holy Spirit made its recipients excel "in faith."

That presence of the Holy Spirit meant those Apostles had to go serve others, just as had Jesus served … "in order that there may be a fair balance."

Those who have faith, but have not yet received the Holy Spirit, they must have faith that the Holy Spirit has already been sent by God. It will come in the hands of those who are trusted to go to others and share that wealth – those riches of God's power – to spread the feel of increased faith.

In that spirit of sharing, Paul then quoted Exodus, as Moses had said after God had given the Israelites His manna – His bread from Heaven. Manna was God's food of life to those starving to death in the wilderness (from lack of faith), just as Jesus was manna to Jairus and the hemorrhaging woman.

Moses wrote, as Paul remembered, "The one who had much did not have too much." That was because his gifts were the amount needed, for those whom he would return to serve that bread too … fairly. Jairus, as an elder, would serve many through that which he had gathered for the needy.

"The one who had little did not have too little," was representative of the woman, who had to begin anew, from her life of banishment, where her closeness was only to a few in need.

If you have the Holy Spirit, then share with those in need.

If you are in need of the Holy Spirit, then have faith that God will send your fair share through one of His couriers.

Ask and you shall receive, but by all means, "Do not fear, only believe."

Amen

# SIXTH SUNDAY AFTER PENTECOST

# Proper 9

# YEAR B

**Relevant readings:**
2 Samuel 5:1-5; 9-10
Psalm 48
   Ezekiel 2:1-5
   Psalm 123
2 Corinthians 12:2-10
Mark 6:1-13

After Pentecost Sermons: Proper 9, Year B

# A citizen of the city of God

When I try to let people know how to be filled with the Holy Spirit, I enjoy using fictitious characters from movies.

The common theme there is: Slow-brained, not Big Brained; Simpleton, not whiz kid; and, Overly trusting, not always on guard.

You could even say those characteristics mean people who are filled with the Holy Spirit are more easily used and abused – (if for nothing else) due to a perceived lack of protective senses and defensive skills in them. The Holy Spirit makes them come across more like children, not as the adults they are.

They project like lambs, not the wolves the world turns so many people into.

This nature of naiveté leads me to compare Biblical figures and parable roles to characters like Chance Gardener (*Being There*), Forrest Gump (*Forrest Gump*), Navin R. Johnson (*The Jerk*), John Coffey ("like the drink, only not spelled the same" – *The Green Mile*), Lloyd Christmas and Harry Dunne (*Dumb & Dumber*) and even, to some extent, Karl Childers (*Sling Blade*).

Still, those fictitious characters are just that – FICTITIOUS.

They are not real. The characters are not the actors who portray human beings that possess those characteristics of innocence. Neither are the authors who created the characters portrayed as innocent and pure. Presumably, the characters come from their imaginations of how easily the weak are abused. The characters are lovable because they fall down, but bounce back without lasting anger.

They, like the stories of the Holy Bible, project how universal justice always triumphs over injustice. They reflect how God is the power that holds such pure fools up, into places of honor, while they themselves have no concept of their position.

The characters strike a nerve in each of us because of their childlike innocence; and we were all once children. We have since grown and matured; but, we all have histories where we were taught lessons about how cruel the world can be.

We identify with those characters because they represent the innocent child in each of us; and, it is the children who are closer to God and under the watchful eye of Jesus.

The reality of life, however, is real life does not always have a happy ending. That is the difference between fiction and nonfiction, between fairy tales and history.

In the reading choices for today, the Episcopal Lectionary presents options – as far as the Old Testament and Psalms are concerned. This occurs routinely, in particular each week during the Ordinary Time season. One option is read aloud in church, along with the fixed Epistle and Gospel passages, while the others are set aside for some other time in the spotlight.

It is important to realize that all reading choices have been selected by purpose. The choices reflect how the Gospel's lesson can often be found reflected in more than one lesson from the Old Testament. The Epistle is the New Testament's compliment, as support to the Gospel.

Today is read aloud the story of David being chosen by the elders of the Twelve Tribes, to replace Saul as the King of Israel. David's history as the King of Israel is then summed up as lasting forty years, telling how he build the City of David, made Jerusalem the capital, and how Israel thrived because God was with David.

# After Pentecost Sermons: Proper 9, Year B

The reading not read aloud is from Ezekiel, where God told the prophet, "Mortal, Stand up on your feet, and I will talk with you." God spoke to Ezekiel at a time when Israel was in the throes of utter collapse and pending ruin.

Therefore, the second book of Samuel's reading focuses on the beginning – when all was well and fine with Israel – while the Ezekiel reading focuses on the end – when God said, "They and their ancestors have transgressed against me to this very day. The descendants are impudent and stubborn. I am sending you to them, and you shall say to them, "Thus says the Lord GOD." Whether they hear or refuse to hear, they shall know that there has been a prophet among them."

This reading more loudly proclaims the message of the Gospel from Mark today, where Jesus preached in the synagogue of his hometown – Nazareth – and then called his disciples to "Stand up," so God could speak through them, just as God spoke through Ezekiel.

The disciples were instructed to be seen ONLY as **simple characters**, as they went in pairs through Galilee; and, it is not hard to see, throughout the Gospels, just how much the pairs headed out like Lloyd Christmas & Harry Dunne ... sans the carpeted dog truck.

Still, the message of Second Samuel echoes why those simple agents of God were sent to tell the people: "a prophet has been among you." The simplicity of appearance - their lack of grandeur - reflects how David did not elbow his way to the throne of Israel.

David did not proclaim a right to rule because of his own personal feats, or his own powers of significance. He did not boast of his "exceptional character," saying, "Look at me and see how blessed I am!"

We heard it read, "All the tribes of Israel came to David at Hebron," not the other way around. David was sought out because of his devotion to the God of Israel. It was his faith in God and God's recognition of that faith that had made David readily known to the Israelites.

With the death of Saul, Samuel had the power of king, as the prophet of Israel. Samuel was the mortal who regularly "Stood up so that God could talk with him." Samuel had ruled like a judge prior to Saul; so after Saul died, Samuel again rose to that same role.

David, meanwhile, had been leading the troops of Israel out to defend the nation and back, time and again. He was seen as one who was fearless, because he also "Stood up," so God could talk with him.

When the elders went to David and convinced him to be their king, he did not rest on his laurels. He began the work of building the city of David. That work never stopped being required, for as long as David ruled.

The work never stops.

There is always more to do. Ask Queen Elizabeth. She knows. Buckingham Palace has not been updated since she took the throne in 1952. The news recently says it needs $270-million in repairs, just to remain livable.

Relative to this constant need for work in order to avoid collapse, we heard read how Paul prayed, asking God to repair his weaknesses, due to "the messenger of Satan" tormenting him.

Paul wrote to the Christians of Corinth and told them: "Three times I appealed to the Lord about that thorn in my flesh, that it would leave me."

Paul prayed to God, "Make it stop, please. Let the work be finished."

But, God spoke with Paul, because he had "Stood up." God talked with him and said, "My grace is sufficient for you, for power is made perfect in weakness."

If you think you have built a perfect home, one that will never need repairs, and will never need maintenance … then think again.

Your "citadels" can only provide "sure refuge" when God is in them. The city of the LORD of hosts … the city of our God, where God is established forever … is not some buildings made of stone and filler. The City of David - which is still being sought archaeologically, uncovering evidence of ancient ruins - might have been more a work in progress within David himself … more than things he built in Hebron and Jerusalem.

The true city of God is made of bone and flesh, just as the Israelites told David they were the bone and flesh surrounding their king. The City of David would then be built so God's throne within that "city" would be in the heart of that place, where the constant pumping of life blood circulated. From within David's heart, every inch of all Israel could be revitalized with Spirit.

High atop the watchtower of that city now sits Christ, who not only is vigilant of that which is outside the city, but who also is constantly at work sending orders to all that is within. The Christ Mind constantly sends out repair and maintenance orders, to the systems built within the body that houses God … its bones and flesh.

That is where the childish mentality of fictitious characters symbolizes how ineffective the "bone and flesh" city of God becomes, when an adult brain replaces Christ as the overseer.

The work of David was left to Solomon, but Solomon's wisdom was not enough to keep the body of Israel whole. Israel split in two after Solomon's death; and following a series of Big Brained rulers, none of which had God in the heart of any city once overseen by David, Israel and Judah fell upon ruin.

God sent Jesus to the valley of dried bones, which had lost all flesh. God had Jesus "Stand up" and spread His word, much like Ezekiel had. It was time to tear down the old stone and fill structures [*Millo*] and rebuild Israel with flesh and bone. The bodies of the new faithful would each surround God and His new King, who had descended from the House of David - the stump of Jesse.

In Mark, we read of Jesus being rejected by the Nazarenes. The people of the village where Jesus was raised saw Jesus as "the carpenter, the son of Mary and brother" to brothers and sisters ... all of whom were common human beings and not gifts from God.

That was their Big Brains speaking, which was similar to the reaction Ezekiel heard. The same rejection would be repeated when the disciples were sent out in pairs, to enter villages looking purposefully as common Jews ... not wearing the tunics of rabbis, much less anything that could hint at their needing the accompaniment of a procession like that was suitable for holy prophets.

The "hometown" of all Jews was Israel ... that land which had collapsed and was then under Roman occupation and domination. Therefore, Jesus ... and later his Apostles ... would find rejection throughout the lands they travelled, wherever they found other Jews ... their brothers and sisters in faith.

Still, there were many who listened and heard their message ... "The kingdom of God has come near." Some had demons cast out and illnesses cured ... because they listened AND because they believed

"The City of the LORD of hosts was in your presence." "It is now in you, so your faith has healed you ... so God may have a good home in which to reside."

Now, as much as we can sit on the bus stop bench today and shake our heads at how stupid, blind, and terrible THOSE JEWS were back then ... the Big Brain keeps us from realizing the same presence of the City of God needs to be <u>built and maintained</u> within **US**.

Ezekiel comes to us all the time with a message to do better, to try harder. We are too impudent and stubborn to listen.

Paul comes to us frequently telling us, "be content with weaknesses, insults, hardships, persecutions, and calamities for the sake of Christ." We rebel from such advice.

Evangelists come to our door regularly and we tell them, "I'm sorry, but all I have is excuses why I cannot listen to you."

Too often, the Kingdom of God comes near to us, and we don't even suggest, "Please, as you leave at my request, would you at least keep the dust of my doorstep on your sandals ... to remember me by?"

The untold blessing in today's Gospel is that Mark recounted Jesus' **second** rejection by the people of Nazareth. Luke told how Jesus spoke in the synagogue there previously, before he chose his disciples. After that event, the people of Nazareth wanted to throw Jesus off a cliff.

Instead of Jesus getting mad, he simply walked through them and went on his way.

**BUT** ... he came back, only to be rejected again.

The moral of that story is this: Only a fool would come back for seconds of punishment.

That is, unless the **REAL** fool is the one who keeps thinking he or she is smarter than God, continually refusing to hear a message sent ... if it does not tell one what one wants to hear.

After all, we are descendant of those impudent and stubborn ... those from a rebellious house.

God believes in second chances, however. Heck ... God even believes in third chances.

<pause>

But, don't tell anyone that.

Perhaps, that was the secret kept by the person who Paul knew, who was in Christ, and who told Paul he "was caught up in the third heaven"?

Ssssssshhhhh.

"Refrain from [telling that secret], so that no one may think better than what is seen or heard [openly], even considering the exceptional character of the revelations."

Instead, "boast all the more gladly of [your] weaknesses, so the power of Christ may dwell in [you]."

Let Christ do the thinking for you and let God sit on His throne in your heart. God placed that throne there, but work has to be done before God can be seated.

Offer yourself up to be rebuilt into the city of the God.

# After Pentecost Sermons: Proper 9, Year B

The less you THINK you know, the better you are, because God knows how much more you need His help ... when you play the simpleton.

If you want to "Stand up on your feet, so God will speak with you" in the third heaven - the Heaven of Heaven - then you have to keep it a secret that you are filled with God's Holy Spirit ... until you have led others to realize their own secret.

Amen

# SEVENTH SUNDAY AFTER PENTECOST

# Proper 10

# YEAR B

**Relevant readings:**
2 Samuel 6:1-5; 12-19
Psalm 24
  Amos 7:7-1
    Psalm 85:8-13
Ephesians 1:3-14
Mark 6:14-29

After Pentecost Sermons: Proper 10, Year B

# Judgment of the quick and the dead

In the older Episcopal Prayer Book (1928), which we still read from on occasion, from the Apostle's Creed we say aloud, "And he shall come again, with glory, to judge both the **quick** and the dead."

That is a statement of belief, as an Apostle, as one filled with God's Holy Spirit understands.

The use of "**quick** and the dead" is an idiom that is found three times in the New Testament and that is why it was placed in the Apostle's Creed … understanding (of course) that "quick" is an Old English term, as found in the King James Version of the Holy Bible.

The Greek words written, "*zōntōn*" (Acts 10:42) and "*zōntas*" (2 Timothy 4:1 and 1 Peter 4:5) mean "living," in our present day vernacular.

Today, when we read the Nicene Creed aloud we will say, "He will come again, with glory, to judge both the living and the dead." But, there is a subtlety that has to be grasped, relative to that older usage of "**quick**."

This subtlety might make more sense to you after reading how Paul wrote, in his first epistle to the Christians of Corinth, "This, indeed, is what is written: "The first man, Adam, became a **living being**." The last Adam became a **life-giving** spirit."

The "last Adam" is, of course, Jesus, but also all Apostles of Christ (as was Paul), until this line reaches the ultimate "last Adam."

Still, in Paul's text we find the Greek words for "**living** being" to be "*psychēn zōsan*," which also means a "soul alive." A "soul alive" then means a body of flesh, one breathing in the air of life; and the word "***zōsan***" shares the same root verb as do "*zōntōn*" and "*zōntas*," which is "*zaó*" ("I live, I am alive").

In contrast, Paul used the Greek words "*pneuma **zōopoioun***," meaning "spirit **life-giving**" or "a **quickening** spirit." The same root verb, "*zaó*," as "I live," becomes elevated to an ability "to make live." Adam became alive as an embodied mortal soul. Jesus became an embodied mortal soul who could "give new life."

This means there is MORE to life than simply being alive.

In the news this past year, the daughter of Whitney Houston and Bobby Brown was found unconscious and rushed to the hospital. Recently, she was moved to an extended care facility, where she (for all intent and purposes) is kept **alive** by her basic brain functions still being capable of making her muscles move so her lungs can respire ... make her breathe in the oxygen of life. Meanwhile, she is in a coma that keeps her without the **life** she once lived.

Thus, when we **believe** that Jesus Christ will come again, with the glory of God, to judge the living and the dead ... the **quick** and the dead ... that means Jesus will come as a "quickening" upon us who breathe in air AND who **believe** in God and Christ. The judgment that will come upon each of us, individually, will be in respect to whether we have accepted "a quickening spirit," or if we are just as dead as Bobbi Kristina Brown ... breathing air, but spiritually lifeless ... as far as serving God and Christ is concerned.

Now, I realize this is something most people do not know, as not many tell you the meanings of things like I tell them. The Jews who served within the Temple during Jesus' days believed there was neither Heaven nor Sheol for souls. They believed there was only the living souls, who could be divided into Jews and

## After Pentecost Sermons: Proper 10, Year B

Gentiles, and then further into good Jews and bad Jews. The Pharisees believed there was a Sheol, which was a purgatory-like place, where the souls of the dead kind of wandered around, waiting for Judgement Day. That would be one view of the "living and the dead," but that ceased to have merit once Jesus was named the Messiah, assumedly spending a day in Sheol, saying, "You, you, and you over there ... come with me. The rest of you go to Hell."

Today, most Christians believe they will go to Heaven, as long as they do a few good things before they die, with all the vermin of the earth going to roast in Hell upon death.

I do not see it that way, as waiting until the death bed to say "I'm sorry" is not a ticket to Heaven. That is what I hear from reading what Jesus and the Apostles wrote (not based on what the best educated guess is). One's gifts and charitable donations to a church might play a role in such determinations as to who goes to Heaven and who does not, but I do not believe that alone is the key to Heaven. I do not get **all** of my knowledge from books and Internet searches, which imply Heaven can be 'bought,' so I stand alone, as an island of interpretation, seeing things differently.

I was told recently that I have no right to preach, because I have not passed many tests on Christian topics and have not been given a document that says I can be hired as an official priest. Certainly not in any highly regarded denominational institution. But, that makes me wonder who tested and certified Paul, whose letters are studied by scholars today?

I digress. Just know, it is always wise to beware of bus stop preachers; but, it is never wise to **fear** a warning that false shepherds are (and will be always) among us. As long as one is led by the Holy Spirit, the false will be exposed and the truth will set one free to challenge and expose the false.

I only know what I hear myself think, and I trust those thoughts … although those thoughts often lead me to seek out a semblance of "quickie education." Books and Internet searches help, when the voice points me in the right direction. Once I find the truth, I can gather some data in my basket, to back up some of my thoughts with facts and figures. That may come across as if I am properly educated in spiritual matters.

Still, I do not ask anyone to believe in **me**. There is no Church of Robert that I represent. I only speak my mind openly, so that your mind will be enabled to listen for the voice inside your heads, which leads you to test everything told openly. Tests will prove the truth to you, so your beliefs are your own, and not simply the thoughts of others you mindlessly hear or read, believe and repeat, leading you to blindly trust others without question.

It is my role, I believe, to help others understand what the words in the books of the Holy Bible wholly represent, beyond what is commonly and most readily seen on the surface. Everyone can navigate upon smooth waters and calm seas, but it is more important to be able to calm the rough waters, which much of Scripture can become, so fear and panic does not overcome anyone on board the bark of Christianity.

Now, from my thoughts I feel the need to tell you the meaning of "**quick**" and "**quickening**." This is because of the story in the Gospel of Mark, about King Herod beheading John the Baptist.

Some of you may recall a movie series, which spun off into a television series called *Highlander*. The premise of all of them was constant, such that a group of semi-immortal humans walked the earth, forever looking like they were thirty-two, strong and fit, while being in relationships with mere mortals. Some of these characters were trying to help the mortals, while others tried to abuse them, seeking positions of wealth and power. All the while, the bad semi-immortals were trying to kill the good semi-immortals, and vice versa.

# After Pentecost Sermons: Proper 10, Year B

According to the script line, the only way to kill one of these "heroes" was by cutting one's head off, with his own sword preferably. That would release the dead Highlander's spirit, which was visually depicted as an eruption of power, like that of an electrical storm. That energy would leave the killed being's body, and then be absorbed into the killer's body, giving him additional strength.

That release of Spiritual energy was called "the quickening."

It was much like the "*pneuma zōopoioun*" Paul wrote of, as it acted as an enhancement of life, as "life-giving spirit."

Now, there is nothing I could find on the Internet that said this movie-TV concept was historically based, such that it may have been a belief once held in antiquity. So, it is only be presented now as modern fiction; but like all things … if it can be thought, it can be reality; and, it could have been thought of before by others, at different times, in different places. It could be "life imitating art," in reverse.

In the Mark reading, you may have noticed how the news of Jesus' following of Jews and the works Jesus was doing had reached King Herod after John the Baptist had been beheaded. That news then leads to a "flashback," as if Herod then remembered the history that led to John's beheading.

I like to refer to Mark as the Sergeant Friday (a *Dragnet* television show character name) of the Gospels, such that Mark's book frequently does not seem to offer much more than, "Just the facts ma'am. Just the facts."

In the "facts" of today's reading, Mark simply says, "Some were saying, "John the baptizer has been raised from the dead; and for this reason these powers [those of a ghost] are at work in him [Jesus]." But others said, "It is Elijah.""

Now this could make it seem that King Herod (Herod Antipas) heard this as the scuttlebutt in the air, as he took leisurely strolls around town. Upon hearing the rumors spreading, Herod then decided, "John, whom I beheaded, has been raised," as if Herod believed in ghosts, more than immortal prophets coming down from the sky.

According to an article on Wikipedia, entitled "Ghost," it states, "The ancient Romans believed a ghost could be used to exact revenge on an enemy by scratching a curse on a piece of lead or pottery and placing it into a grave." At the end of this reading from Mark's Gospel today, we read, "[John's] disciples heard about [his death by beheading], [so] they came and took his body, and laid it in a tomb."

Obviously, John's disciples could be the ones "scratching a curse on a piece of lead or pottery and placing it" in John's tomb, so John could come back and exact revenge on Herod.

But, this is not how I read "the facts."

It makes sense that King Herod would not stroll about town, especially in an occupied land where the dangers of revolt had to constantly be squashed by Roman soldiers. A king, like Herod, would remain busy administering to the business of government; and, in that capacity, he would have trusted advisers come to him and report all the news of importance, giving Herod "the pulse of the town" on a regular basis.

Thus, those who would warn about the spirit of John rising, they would be his aides of Roman heritage and religious traditions; while those who would say Jesus was Elijah, they would be of Jewish roots, as priests and scribes of the Temple who were loyal to the king. Both offered the counsel of their wisdom, such that what Mark reports is an "educated guess," and not simply some unfounded and biased opinions.

However, King Herod was also wise as king; and in that wisdom, he knew the importance of recognizing the wisdom of holy men: Roman, Jewish, and even the likes of a Jewish prophet, as was John.

By Mark telling of Herod's talks with John, knowing King Herod "feared John, knowing that he was a righteous and holy man," one he protected while keeping imprisoned, we see how Herod's wisdom meant that when he heard of Elijah's return, Herod saw John as Elijah. Herod's intrigue of John led him to conclude that this great Prophet of Israel had indeed returned, only to be placed into the hands of Herod for fate to initiate the future.

The man whose actions since John's death were producing all the new rumors and gossip (Jesus) Herod saw as actions coming from a Jewish warrior Messiah, one with mystical powers. By saying "John has been raised," Herod meant the threat of John the Baptist had been exponentially raised in this new person, Jesus. Herod's wisdom heard the thoughts in his mind say, "Jesus is the one who was prophesied to come after Elijah," so Herod expected the future to bring about the threat of Jewish justice, as an attempt to destroy the presence of Rome in Palestine.

Just like from a *Highlander* movie script, King Herod saw his beheading ordered as one done to a semi-immortal – John the baptizer as the prophet Elijah – thus releasing a **quickening** … sending out an increased ability of Spirit, which then settled within the life force of another. Jesus was undoubtedly the beneficiary of that release; and the Greek name for Jesus (*Jose*) means "Increases / Increaser," so Herod would have factored that meaning into his calculations.

As such, when Herod said, "John has been raised," he meant the power of John had been released upon his execution, which then elevated Jesus to immortal prophet status … one who would exact the prophesied revenge.

Because Mark flashed back in Herod's mind, after Herod had that inkling of royal wisdom causing him to draw the conclusion he did, it was to show how King Herod realized he had signed his own death sentence. By killing a man he found intriguing, a prophet he found much wiser than himself, and a man of God whom he feared, even while John was behind the bars of a prison, Herod had empowered an enemy.

The memory of Herod's meant he sought the wisdom of hindsight, as well as the excuse for blame. He saw it was all because of royal women.

Aaaaaahhh ... if only men didn't need women "to complete them," then perhaps the Trojan War would have never been waged and perhaps Herod Antipas would have lived to a ripe old age, rather than dying at the age of thirty-nine ... only nine years later.

This, then, becomes the link to the Old Testament story of David dancing wildly before the ark, while Saul's daughter (Michal - David's wife) watched that display from her palace window.

While this is not read aloud today, Michal is recorded as having said to David, "How the king of Israel has distinguished himself today, going around half-naked in full view of the slave girls of his servants as any vulgar fellow would!"

I imagine that display was the male equivalent of Salome's sensual dance before King Herod, which caused Herod to make promises he should not have made. However, David danced feverishly to show God he was filled with the spirit of excitement for God and His ark. Because of David's selfless actions, God granted Israel the gift of safe-keeping.

Herod, on the other hand, acted as a god by granting a wish that should have been rejected, due to his wife manipulating their daughter. Herod knew the request was not Salome's; but, still he ordered an unjust death, to one he had been keeping safe, to satisfy the anger of a woman called a sinner.

Instead of taking part in the parade for the ark, as did "all the house of Israel," Michal stayed at a distance, watching secretly. Undoubtedly, Herodias sat silently watching the interaction between her daughter and husband. Both Michal and Herodias were royally aloof ... dead to the Spirit of God.

God's judgment of Michal was to make her barren, never to give birth to an heir she would rather see rise to the throne. God's judgment of Herodias was to have her watch Salome fall through weak ice on a pool, reaching to grab hold of her just as the ice decapitated her. Herodias stood holding the head of her daughter in her hands, as justice served in return.

David saw God "enthroned on the cherubim" atop the ark. He showed God how much **quick** was in his steps. That same Spirit spoke to John as he told prophetic words to King Herod, which Herod would realize after the fact. David danced with just a loin cloth and rebuked the unholy criticisms of his wife. John the Baptist wore animal skins and ate locusts as a sign of his refusal to be bought by the finer things offered in life. Herod was a shrewd ruler; but he was also royally aloof, which allowed him to be influenced by the women in his life.

David knew the dangers of going against God. The ark, after all, was returning home after having been lost by Saul, who took it without God's approval, bringing a King of Israel defeat in battle. Saul sentenced himself to die, by falling on his own sword after his son Jonathan was killed in action. John knew the dangers that faced all Jews who pretended to maintain the laws, but who felt they were above any justice that could come against them, for doing as they pleased.

David wrote in his poetic reminder, "How the mighty have

fallen."

I imagine if King Herod knew that song, a lump must have come up in his throat then. He must have gulped hard when he realized he should not have done what a little girl (coached by her mother) had asked him to do. Sometimes, being royally aloof can put one into a cold and lonely position.

Herod had released a serious **quickening** … at least he thought. He feared making another mistake.

David responded to Michal by saying, "I will celebrate before the Lord. I will become even more undignified than this, and I will be humiliated in my own eyes. But by these slave girls you spoke of, I will be held in honor." David heard a louder voice in his mind, which let him know what truly dignified a king.

That was the wisdom of the Holy Spirit speaking, the voice of the "**life-giving** spirit" that separates "the **quick** from the dead." David had it, thus he was "living." Herod did not have it, thus he was "dead."

"Dead man walking," as they say in prisons holding the condemned.

Paul wrote in his letter to the Ephesians, "With all wisdom and insight [Christ, through God's Holy Spirit] has made known to us the mystery of his will."

It is that Wisdom that makes us **quick**.

All other wisdom comes through hindsight. Herod's wisdom was hind-sighted, which gave him a cold chill running down his spine because he could not undo what had been done.

Foresight is wisdom that speaks to us within our heads … before the parade or song and dance begins. Those who are **quick** follow those leads.

Amen

# EIGHTH SUNDAY AFTER PENTECOST

# Proper 11

# YEAR B

**Relevant readings:**
2 Samuel 7:1-14
Psalm 89:20-37
  Jeremiah 23:1-6
  Psalm 23
Ephesians 2:11-22
Mark 6:30-34; 53-56

After Pentecost Sermons: Proper 11, Year B

# Building the temple of the Lord

Everyone here knows the fable / fairy tale of <u>The Three Little Pigs</u>.  One built a house of straw, another built a house of sticks, and the third built a house of bricks.

The Big Bad Wolf came looking to eat some pigs, so he blew down the houses made of straw and sticks, but after those two pigs escaped to the brick house, the wolf could not blow that house down and the three little pigs were saved.

We are left to wonder if the two who lost their houses rebuilt in brick or stone … or if they all lived happily ever after in the one brick house.

In the Gospel of Matthew (which we do not read today), Jesus told a parable about two men who built houses.

The "wise man built his house on the rock," while the "foolish man built his house on sand."

Now, there were no wolf attacks but Mother Nature played the same role, "huffing and puffing" rain and wind, with flooding waters, all pounding each house.

The house built on rock survived, while the house built on sand did not.

I imagine much of Waveland, Mississippi was built on sand, because when Hurricane Katrina came ashore it blew away many houses.

Only the concrete slabs stayed in place, while the homes washed away.  Even the boulder ballast of the railroad tracks was washed away, with the metal rails left mangled and twisted.

All of this paints a picture that if you are going to build something, build it right … build it sturdy … build it strong and durable.

That was what was in David's mind when he looked at the ark, which had just been brought into the city of David, and he saw it was only in a tent … a portable tabernacle.

Certainly, it was a large tent, but have you ever seen what strong winds and rain can do to a tent?

Not long ago, at a Major League Baseball game in Pittsburgh, the grounds crew had to roll out the tarp to cover the infield because a storm came up quickly. That big, heavy tarp – which is not too different from tent material – was lifted up in the air by heavy winds. It took many crew members and even some players to keep it from flying away.

That long and wide tarp was being raised like a hotdog wrapper can be, by normal winds.

So, David was thinking, "You know what? I have this study cedar house to live in. We need to build a big sturdy building to put the ark in, because it is so important and we wouldn't want it to be blown away."

It was wise of David to think that … and the Temple would be built by wise Solomon, after David had passed away.

So, the most important part of the second Samuel reading is when God told Nathan, "Go tell David, 'The LORD will make you a house.'"

Last week, I pointed out how the City of God is not a place with buildings, but a place in each person's heart. Each of us has to do the work to make ourselves open for God's presence; and then

After Pentecost Sermons: Proper 11, Year B

we have to maintain that "building" in honor of God.

The readings this week confirm that message; but it is easy to get confused and look at the beauty and magnificence of buildings - cathedrals, mega-churches, and even the Temple of Solomon - and think in terms of the physical, and not the spiritual.

The Temple in Jerusalem was torn down by invaders ... twice. Again using the lyrics from David's song of sadness, written into the Book of Jashar - "How the mighty have fallen!"

I was raised in a cathedral-style church, one originally home to a Methodist Episcopal denomination, which was sold to my mother's denomination - Assemblies of God. That religious group eventually declined in number and vacated the building. It was sold several years later and transformed into a Renaissance-theme restaurant. That church had fallen ... but so too since has the restaurant.

Satan has a way of coming and huffing and puffing and blowing buildings built of weak materials down.

That is why it is so important to realize why David wanted to build a suitable building for the ark to be housed. The ark was the power of the **House** of Israel.

Inside the ark was the Law ... the sacred tablets of Moses.

Memorize those laws ... know them by heart ... and whenever times get tough, your adherence to the Law will save you. The Law is then like pallets of bricks delivered to a building site. Still, God would have to tell His prophets how and when to use the powers of the ark, to defeat an enemy that threatened the House of Israel. The "blueprints" then called for more than just bricks.

As this external protection of the Israelites was all part of God's plan, we should be able to look back on that history and see how the Law was placed inside an ark, which was itself then placed inside a tent or building, which was then placed inside a city of people, who were all inside the boundaries of a nation of people - those who all shared in one religious faith. This environment established by God was then a **place** where all the chosen people of God went <u>to learn about their religion</u>.

In the wilderness with Moses ... in Canaan with judges ... in Israel with kings ... in exile with Pharisees ... in Jerusalem with Temple Priests ... in Judea and Galilee with Jesus ... that whole history, with thousands of years of learning, all while maintaining the Sabbath as a mandatory holy day of rest and religious observance ... all that made the House of Israel the equivalent of one huge, expansive, and historic **seminary**.

Only the descendants of Abraham, through Isaac, and through Jacob received acceptance letters to attend that "school building," that "college" for priests, who would serve the true One God.

Before Jesus visited that "campus," no one had ever "graduated" from the House of Israel, as far as being ordained to serve the whole world.

That was because the external environment was one kept from them, so the Israelites were protected by the pretense that no one ever needed to graduate. Once acceptance into that prestigious "university" was granted (by birthright), then that "Disney Land" environment produced the fantasy of religion. Admission meant everyone there only had to study texts, memorize the laws, and attend classes held by parents and rabbis ... with *Shabbat* services mandatory.

This created a constant hostility between those inhabitants of that religious "Fantasy Island" and those of the real world.

# After Pentecost Sermons: Proper 11, Year B

As Paul wrote to the Ephesians, the two sides consisted of those identified as "the uncircumcision" and "the circumcision." The Gentiles were "aliens from the commonwealth of Israel" – the **House** of Israel – and the Gentiles were "strangers to the covenants of promise."

In essence, Jews had all that in their private "building," and they posted signs outside that said, "No Gentiles Allowed." Thus, there was a "dividing wall," with that invisible "structure" being the cause of the hostility between Jews and Gentiles ... between seminarians and laity ... priests and heathens ... between shepherds and sheep.

Paul pointed out how Jesus came to tear down that wall that divided the two groups. As such, Paul wrote, "So [Jesus] came and proclaimed peace to you who were far off and peace to those who were near; for through him both of us have access in one Spirit to the Father."

If you recall, Jesus said, "Destroy this temple, and I will raise it again in three days." Those words were used against Jesus in his trial before Pilate. Those words had Jesus convicted and crucified.

Since history proves the Second Temple was destroyed – by the Romans, in 70 AD – we hear Jesus say, "Destroy this temple" and we think that history made those words prophetic ... which they were.

**BUT** ... Jesus was not referring to a building of stone and mortar being destroyed. He was not referring specifically to the Temple of Jerusalem ... a "house" built to replicate the one Solomon built to "house" the ark ... from David's plan.

Jesus was referring to the whole campus of Judaism. In essence, Jesus said, "Destroy this educational institution ... this seminary of religious studies, which has never before graduated a priest that served any purpose for the real world."

When you hear Jesus make that statement, it is more understandable that raising a replacement for **THAT INSTITUTION**, in three days, happened when Jesus died, was dead for three days, and then resurrected. "That institution" changed from being Judaism to the new identity of Christianity, even though everything still looked the same.

Jesus was not speaking of building any physical structures, from inanimate materials, like straw, sticks and stone. Jesus meant he would use spiritual parts. Thus, Paul wrote how Jesus, "built upon the foundation of the apostles and prophets, with Christ Jesus himself as the cornerstone."

Jesus provided for a new building be set upon a solid foundation – like rock - and not a weak one - like sand. In three days, a perfectly square stone became available, allowing for a new temple to be raised on that rock.

But, again, the new temple would be built of flesh and bones, with Jesus's cornerstone being the life blood within that structure - the Holy Spirit.

"In him," Paul wrote, "the whole structure is joined together and grows into a holy temple in the Lord."

Thus, as Paul continued to tell his fellow apostles – both Gentile and Jewish – "You also are built together spiritually into a dwelling place for God."

**YOU** are each temples that have been rebuilt for God … **YOU** just have to sweep out all the trash and do the work of sprucing up and washing windows first.

Just like a cathedral for Methodist Episcopalians was cleaned, so it was attractive to the Assemblies of God buyers, so too do we have to look marvelous to God.

In the seminary that I visited, I saw how the fantasy world prepared the would-be graduates for the real world. Student-priests were assigned to assist real priests, who served real congregations.

This same "practice run experience" is found in today's reading from the Gospel of Mark. We read how, "the apostles gathered around Jesus, and told him all that they had done and taught."

Jesus **WAS** and still **IS** the seminary for his disciples, who would be graduate priests one day, ordained to be sent forth into the real world. Once in the real world, the Apostles would themselves become temples, amid people in need of religious shelter, protection, and teaching.

Before that could happen, Jesus listened to the apostles joyfully tell about how wonderful it was to be filled with a power that placed them in a position of importance among the ordinary folk.

He told them, "Come away to a deserted place all by yourselves and rest a while." After all, "many were coming and going, and they had no leisure even to eat." However, Jesus was not asking his students to take a much needed break from all the work of priesthood ... as if walking with the "great unwashed" was hard work and tiresome.

Jesus was telling his disciples to learn to stop trying to remember everything they had been taught in his seminary AND the seminary of Judaism. They were thinking so much they forgot to do the basic stuff, like eat and rest. Therefore, Jesus was laying the foundation for them to set their simple brains aside and let the Mind of God take over the operations of His temple.

God NEVER grows old and weary, unable to listen to a prayer or offer the warmth of a smile. God does not "retire," like modern popes do.

That is why so many people flocked to Jesus and his apostles-in-training. The sick and lost did not see people they wanted to touch ... they saw temples they could have access to, ones they could touch without being beaten away, treated like criminals who were breaking the law simply because they wanted the light of religion to shine upon them.

There was a great divide between Jews and Gentiles, while there was an equal divide between clean Jews and unclean Jews. All the unclean Jews – the sick brought on mats to Jesus – were like lost sheep ... sheep without a shepherd ... Jews without a Temple ... the first two little pigs without a home left standing because of the Big Bad Wolf.

Those unclean Jews were the practice congregations for a new order of priests ... those who would go into the real world as temples of the Lord.

To be a temple of the Lord, you have to learn, you have to practice what you learn, you have to experience the value of that learning – both in your own personal sense of fulfilment and you sense of joy from fulfilling the needs of other – and you have to stop being a student and transform into a teacher (a rabbi). You have to stop being a sheep and become a shepherd.

You have to graduate from being a "take it down, move it, and set it back up" tabernacle, to becoming a shining new temple that beacons to all who are lost, and in need of being found.

You know you have been ordained to be a temple of God, when the ark has been placed in your heart, so that the Law has been written upon the cornerstone of you, making you a temple in Christ Jesus.

Amen

# NINTH SUNDAY AFTER PENTECOST

# Proper 12

# YEAR B

**Relevant readings:**
2 Samuel 11:1-15
Psalm 14
  2 Kings 4:42-44
    Psalm 145:10-19
Ephesians 3:14-21
John 6:1-21

Robert Tippett

# As your soul lives

I watched a cable news show back around the 4th of July weekend, where a reporter was sent out to ask ordinary people easy American history questions: (for example) Who fought the Revolutionary War? Who was the general who led the colonial military? What year was the Declaration of Independence signed?

Although the reporter said most of the presented video of the "On the Street" segment was the filming of the stupidest responses, he added that overall most everyone did poorly answering the questions.

One question that I remember was, "Who was the king of England in 1776?"

One woman guessed, "King Tut?"

She then added, "I don't know many kings."

A young lady interviewed on the show, who incorrectly answered several basic history questions, said, "I hated history in school. It is so boring!"

Many people feel the same way.

Perhaps that is why there is the adage: "Those who do not learn from history are doomed to repeat it."

The fact that history repeats is not in question, as babies are born, they mature, they pair up an have babies of their own … so life continues because of repetition.

However, if most people fail to remember the mistakes of life … if most people do not stay awake in history class and enjoy learning what mistakes history teaches …

then most people doom themselves (and those living with them) to repeat colossal mistakes … time and time again.

Over the course of history, we find nations and empires rising and falling, just as human beings are born, then grow in size and strength, only to have them grow old and weak, before an end comes.

Nations and empires are not immortal because they are run by mortals, regardless of how strong, influential and driven are the leaders of nations and empires: presidents, prime ministers, chancellors, czars, sultans, pharaohs, emperors, queens … and kings.

We see today the first flaw of King David … the greatest King of Israel. David could not control his lusts, those which are so easily accommodated by being in such a position of power. King David was mortal.

David made the same mistake as did King Saul … who thought God blessed him by making him a god on earth, able to do whatever pleased him … like use the ark without God's permission.

David's mistake was a model of history for Solomon to follow … like father, like son … so, Solomon did as he pleased and when he died Israel and Judah split.

Things did not get better … because things did not change, based on knowing the mistakes of the past. History repeated, time and time again, until both Israel and Judah were dead.

History believes Saul began the Kingdom of Israel in 1020 BC. In 586 BC, the Babylonians put to death the last holdout of that original kingdom.

That means Israel lasted four hundred thirty-four years as king-ruled entity. History says that is about average, with some of the most ancient dynasties (those in India and in the Near East) lasting as long as eleven hundred years. More modern empires have lasted as little as fifteen to eighty years.

The "Classical Greek Civilization" (ending with Alexander the Great) lasted three hundred fifty years. The "Roman Republic" (ending with the assassination of Julius Caesar) lasted four hundred fifty years. The British Empire (ending with its surrender of Palestine in 1949) lasted three hundred forty-six years.

Our nation has lasted, until now, two hundred thirty-nine years ... so in "Great Nations years" (calculated like "dog years") we are about to turn sixty.

The downhill slide has begun, with retirement age (sixty-five) coming in less than twenty-five calendar years (2040).

Just in case you think our nation's Constitution could make us capable of having one of those "Thousand Year Dynasties" ...

The Israelites lasted three hundred ninety-six years under Moses, Joshua and judges, before they asked for a king: "To be like other nations."

Saul, David and Solomon added one hundred twenty years to that total (five hundred sixteen years) and the split nations eked out another three hundred forty-four years. In all, they lasted eight hundred sixty years before death.

BUT ... that was based on a COVENANT with God, not a pact with "the people."

Now I am boring you with all this history because the link between a reading telling of the sins of King David and two of Jesus' greatest miracles – feeding the five thousand and walking on water – comes when you hear read, "When Jesus realized that they were about to come and take him by force to make him king, he withdrew again to the mountain by himself."

Jesus knew a human king was not what the people of Galilee and Judea needed.

"Been there. Done that."

That history lesson again. Jesus was not doomed to repeat failure.

It all goes back to the first time, when the Israelites went to Samuel about having a king lead them, when God told Samuel, "I am their king."

God was the king of Jesus. Jesus knew that every one of the five thousand adult Jewish males he just fed with miracle food needed to have the same king within their hearts ... God.

The last thing the Jews needed was another human being getting swept up in all the hoopla ... all the finery of possessions and all the luxuries of power ... all the responsibility of being "god on earth," so all the priests of God's god could sweet-talk a man into forgiving others who know what it feels like to be a man ... because that is what destroys kingdoms.

It wasn't long ago that we were reading of the miracle of little David defeating the mighty giant, Goliath.

We read the lesson of how David saw in the history of Saul and Jonathan's deaths, moving him to wrote the song with the repeated lyric, "How the mighty have fallen!" He had that song written into a "Lest they forget" book.

Now we see how "in the spring of the year, the time when kings go out to battle ... David remained in Jerusalem."

He remained to be a "peeping Tom," to be an adulterer, and to become one who connived a way to not be caught as a sinner, by Uriah, whose wife David had made pregnant.

In the Gospel reading from John, we read how Jesus went from one miracle to another, where his going up the mountain to avoid being made king allowed him that ability.

Without speaking to the crowd, Jesus said (in essence), "As you live, and as your soul lives, I will not do such a thing."

That is what Uriah said to King David, when King David told Uriah, basically, "Go on down to your house and be the king of that castle and enjoy all the comforts of home, while others do all the dirty work."

Uriah refused gifts, beds, and companionship, just as Jesus refused the thought of turning his focus on God to that of focus on the people ... which always, in turn, becomes a focus of self.

Did you know the name Uriah means, "Light of the Lord."

We recognize Jesus as the Light of the World. He said that, adding, "Whoever follows me will not walk in darkness, but will have the light of life." (John 8:12)

The Light of Jesus is the LORD, which shines through him, so we may see and not walk in darkness.

When Uriah said, "As you live, **AND** as your soul lives," he spoke of the Holy Spirit of the LORD, which lit his path, which had lit David's path, and which would light Jesus' path so that our paths could also be lit by the Holy Spirit.

We all have life. We all have blood pumping through our veins and oxygen filling our lungs. Our brains do not consciously

After Pentecost Sermons: Proper 12, Year B

focus on those bodily functions of life. God made our brains so God could function subconsciously – instinctively and naturally – because God gives us life.

Still, our souls have life when we consciously submit our will to serve the LORD. Our soul lives when we bring God into our hearts and let God not only lead our functions of life, but also lead our actions of life.

You see, David was instinctively aroused by watching the women of Jerusalem disrobe and bathe themselves in the purification pool that was conveniently visible from the rooftop of his palace.

It was spring time, when new life is astir – with the birds and bees and lesser animals all instinctively led to mate. Man, after all, is still an animal.

That is the battle kings go out to do in the spring … especially a king like David, who had said to Michal (his wife) after dancing half-naked before the procession of the ark, "I will become even more undignified than this, and I will be humiliated in my own eyes." The "battle" was staying faithful to God in his mind, and not bowing before the instincts of his primal nature.

Paul wrote to the Christians of Ephesus, saying, "I bow my knees before the Father. I pray that, according to the riches of his glory, he may grant that you may be strengthened in your inner being with power through his Spirit."

"As you live, **AND** as your soul lives" means inner strength through the Holy Spirit, which is prayerfully sought and not a natural birthright, but a gift received from God, which is what Paul knew.

Paul then continued to state how his prayers were, "that Christ may dwell in your hearts through faith, as you are rooted and grounded in love." Through the love of God in your hearts, with the Christ mind ruling your conscious thoughts, you become **fixed** and **constant** in your devotion to God, so much so that selfish, instinctual and biological desires can be discerned from true actions that are based on love. One's conscious actions are rooted in love ... not lusts.

"As you live, **AND** as your soul lives, you will not do anything that God does not approve of."

Paul then continued to add, "I pray that you may have the power to comprehend, with all the saints, what is the breadth and length and height and depth, and to know the love of Christ that surpasses knowledge, so that you may be filled with all the fullness of God." This means the mind of Christ is the mind of God in the brain of a human, through the Holy Spirit.

You cannot forget the history lessons of life, when Jesus is wide-awake in your understanding center, giving you all the correct answers to the most difficult questions life has to offer.

Uriah had the power to comprehend. He knew how, "The ark and Israel and Judah remain in booths; and my lord Joab and the servants of my lord are camping in the open field." Uriah comprehended all that while he saw David in his home, offering the luxury of a king to a commoner.

Regardless of whether or not Uriah comprehended what David had done with his wife, he comprehended that what David offered to him was a trap ... a test ... a temptation that only a saint would reject. That's all Uriah needed to know.

The comprehension of Uriah was so saintly that he held in his hand his own death sentence as he went back to join with Joab and his fellow soldiers. Yet, he was not even tempted to read the note. He faithfully went to his death ... just as Jesus would do centuries later ... just like a sacrificial lamb.

After Pentecost Sermons: Proper 12, Year B

Both Uriah and Jesus served the same King, whose kingdom has not once failed ... and never will.

David had served that King, but he fell prey to basic human urges and worldly temptations, those readily available to men of means.

God spoke to David about this, as we read in his Psalm 14:

> "The fool has said in his heart, "There is no God."
>
> "All are corrupt and commit abominable acts;
>
> "there is none who does any good."

There is only one heart each person knows. No one by God knows the heart of more than one mortal human. Therefore, there is only one citizen in the kingdom of **self**. The throne of God resides in every heart; but, only fools force God the King from taking His seat, because it seems like too much work keeping one's heart clean enough for God to remain present.

Everyone loves to be like King David ... Master of One's Own Domain.

The temptation is to be "king for a day" ... as Satan told Jesus in the wilderness:

> "The devil took him to a very high mountain and showed him all the kingdoms of the world and their splendor. "All this I will give you," he said, "if you will bow down and worship me."" (Matthew 4:8-9)

But, it is better to reject that role and ascend to a higher place, where it is just you and God.

Where you can live **AND** where your soul can live in honor of the only true King.

Amen

# TENTH SUNDAY AFTER PENTECOST

## Proper 13

## YEAR B

**Relevant readings:**
2 Samuel 11:26-12:13
Psalm 51:1-13
   Exodus 16:2-4; 9-15
   Psalm 78:23-29
Ephesians 4:1-16
John 6:24-35

Robert Tippett

# Children of God at the all-you-can-eat buffet

I had a black cat once. After visiting a friend at his apartment, a kitten was at his door when my wife and I were about to leave. My friend said, "Oh that's 'dumpster kitty.' It's a stray. You can have it if you want."

We did want it, so my wife and I took it home with us.

I named the kitten Idi Ali – after two "black cats" whose names were in the news in the 1970's – Idi Amen and Mohammed Ali. We just called the cat Idi.

In time, we had four cats in our house, all totalled. We set down four cat food bowls in a line and called the cats when it was feeding time. Each cat always went to the same bowl. They ate in the same order every day, from left to right: Idi – Windphred – Leo – Sam.

They all would begin eating at the same time, but Idi took eating like it was a challenge. He acted as if he had to eat as much as he could.

Idi would finish the food in his bowl; and then shoulder Windphred out of the way, who had only eaten half of what was put down for him. Windphred would walk away and let Idi finish his allotment.

Then Idi would finish that bowl and shoulder Leo out of the way. Leo would have eaten three-quarters of his allotment; but, having eaten his fill, he too would walk away and let Idi finish up.

By the time Leo's bowl was licked clean, Sam would finish his allotment, so Idi and Sam would walk away in unison, leaving

# After Pentecost Sermons: Proper 13, Year B

four cleaned bowls behind.

We saw Idi's eating habit as stemming from his days as a kitten, when he never knew when a meal would be set before him – in the dumpster. He had learned to eat as much as he could find, as a survival instinct.

That same instinct seems to be in human beings as well.

We see it come out when God tested the Israelites with their daily manna. The men were instructed to get one omer of manna per household members – and no more.

Some took more anyway, only to find it wasting in their pockets, before they could eat it.

Today, we Americans have the luxury of "all you can eat" restaurants. They represent the reality of the dream that the Israelites had, when they were hunger-struck and had no more food. They complained, "When we lived near such plenty that large vats could be filled with meaty stew for us to eat, along with our fill of bread to sop our bowls clean."

"Aahh, the memories of 'all you can eat' Egypt."

Of course, thoughts of plenty are always stronger when one is confronted with the reality of little-to-nothing.

In the case of the Israelites, "all you can eat" was not a statement of "see how much food you can force your body to take in" – like a July 4th Coney Island hot dog eating contest. Instead, it meant, "This is all you are allowed to eat."

I remember when I went to church as a child in a Pentecostal denomination environment, the preacher would walk about the pulpit-altar carrying a Bible in his hand. Every week he would tell the congregation to turn to a specific book, chapter and verse

– then he would pause, for all the members to do as he said, before continuing his sermon.

The people in the pews all brought their Bibles with them to church.

To an Assembly of God congregation or to a Baptist congregation, "all you can eat" of Scripture would take an hour to an hour and a half sermon to serve. The partaking of food was so important, people would write notes in their Bibles … as if writing down recipes to try later at home.

To Episcopalians, "all you can eat" only takes ten to fifteen minutes to serve. It is the "dieter's platter," so to speak. No need to bring your own Bible. Everything needed is on the menu at the front door.

The Jews of Jesus' day were starving spiritually. The Temple and the synagogues offered "all you can stomach," which left them as dissatisfied as the Israelites became, after they got tired of the same ole same ole:

"What?!?! Manna?!?!? Again!!!"

The people of Galilee had enjoyed going to that new spiritual restaurant down by the river – John's "Dunk and Shine" – but Herod Antipas had closed that place forever. So, when they went to the "Jesus Dinner Theater by the Sea," where "all you can eat" was accompanied by magical entertainment AND a sermon. Five thousand men with their families ate their fill, but the next day some wanted even more.

Jesus told those Galileans, "Do not work for food that perishes, but for food that endures for eternal life, which the Son of Man will give to you."

In other words, gathering as much manna as you greedily can

get your hands on, only to have all the excess gathered become wasted, that waste serves no one for the better.

It is like waiting in line at a popular "all you can eat" restaurant and noticing you are the thinnest person there. It is the epiphany of understanding that excessive eating only leads to feeling like you need to eat excessively again and again. That leads to stored body fat, which leads to all kinds of diseases and ailments developing in one's body as life goes on.

So, Jesus was saying, "Exercise! Work for food that endures; as energy coming in, it in turn can be converted into actions that keep the body fit and tone."

In Spiritual terms, that means, "Take in a lesson taught in Scripture and then convert that into one's routine of life. Do not let that lesson become stored away as a layer of fatty knowledge that wraps around one's heart, leaving one feeling run down. The cure is not from going to "eat" another helping of Scripture, or "working for food that perishes."

Jesus then told the Galileans what Paul told the Ephesians, while using different words. Paul said, "Each of us is given grace according to the measure of Christ's gift."

That means "all you can eat" is based on your "metabolism" – or how well you can "burn off" that grace by working to pass what you have digested on to others.

Jesus called that "the work of God," which comes to those "who believe in him who [God] has sent."

Moses was sent by God. Jesus was sent by God. Paul was sent by God and you are called to be sent by God.

You have to answer the "dinner bell" that calls you to the table; but you have to understand that the call is not to lead anyone to a form of Christian obesity, known as the Big Brain Syndrome. Instead, it is to create fit servants of God.

A "fit servant" is then detailed by Paul when he wrote, "The gifts (Christ Jesus) gave were that some would be apostles, some prophets, some evangelists, some pastors and rabbis, [all necessary gifts] to equip the **saints** for the work of ministry."

Nowhere did Paul say it is a gift of God to be able to quote Scripture and then not know how that quote **is** a morsel of manna, with **purpose**.

Many might be able to point to a flab of flesh and remember, "Oh yes. I remember being fed this on the tenth Sunday of Pentecost, Year B, 2015. All I remember about it is it was so delectable."

In the Second Samuel reading today, where David has stolen another man's wife, impregnated her, ordered her husband killed, and then brought her into his house as his wife, we see David no longer lean and hungry to serve the Lord. Instead, he dines at the "all you can desire to eat" buffet of Israel … his land of plenty.

From a Big Brain perspective – three thousand years later – it is easy to see how Nathan told David a parable about himself. Well before David realized he had done anything wrong, we shout out loud along with Nathan, when he yelled, "You are the (rich) man (in the story)!"

But … we are just like David all the time. We have a blind spot for our sins … such as over-eating, while others starve.

The reason we are just like David and unable to admit our wrongs is we have a child-like mentality about why we go to the spiritual table on Sundays.

Because is it routine, ritual, custom, and "the way it has always been done before," we see "going to church" as just part of the ceremonial activities that go along with "going to church." For many, church is followed by the "all you can eat" Sunday lunch buffet. We identify Sundays as special because in our youth Sunday was when we all dressed up for church and then came home where mom had made pot roast and we all dined like kings.

This is why the "**children**" of Israel never could get it. They never figured out that they were "chosen" by God to become priests for the world. They did not understand that God sent manna as one's daily sustenance towards learning to act **priestly**.

They always thought like children, thinking: "God chose me because I am special."

Jesus knew the Galileans were not asking him, "When did you come here?" because they saw the signs of priestliness as something they should digest and exercise on their own. They saw his miracle of feeding five thousand men with five loaves of bread and two fish as entertainment, which they would love to see again.

They saw Jesus as a free "all you can eat" restaurant.

That was a childish mental perception. It was an immature mindset.

Paul wrote about how we are only served portions of Christ's "gifts" of the Holy Spirit. Those "gifts" were "all **some** can eat" and "all **others** can eat," as long as their consumption was purposeful, "for building up the body of Christ." That means the "gifted" will exercise what they are fed, so they deserve more spiritual food, in order to do more spiritual labors.

The "buffet" of Christ is for training, development and conditioning, "until all of us come to the unity of the faith and the knowledge of the Son of God, **to maturity**, to the measure of the full stature of Christ." This means each of us is designed to be a part of the whole – an arm, a hand, a thigh, a shoulder, *et al* body parts – with Christ being the guide in our brain in our heads. We have to strengthen our individual parts, so the whole body is strong, while being led by the mind of Christ, for the will of God.

Paul then stated clearly, "We must no longer be children, tossed to and fro and blown about by every wind of doctrine, by people's trickery, by their craftiness in deceitful scheming."

In other words, we cannot be distracted by that which has flashing neon lights advertising, "All you can eat served here," when no one there will (or can) tell you what the purpose is behind the food they serve.

We cannot see the food given by Scripture and think, "Woe is me! I long for the days when the church offered a $7 "all you can eat" breakfast buffet before church. It was so much easier getting out of bed early on Sunday for that!"

My black cat Idi Ali had some tricks and craftiness, beyond eating more than his fair share, which caused the other cats to sacrifice.

I had a neighbor come up to me one day, admitting that she had been leaving food in a bowl on her back porch for him. She said, "I have been feeding your pregnant cat." She thought Idi was Eydie (as in Gormé), and she thought his girth was due to being close to delivering a litter.

Fat cats have a way of making people think they are something other than what they really are. Some may not show their fat as the gluttony of "all you can eat" buffets, however. Some show their fat in fancy shoes and suits, haircuts and make-up, cars and jet planes. We fall for wanting to help them be fatter, thinking they need our help, so they can help others - rather than tell them, "Shame on you!"

But, the truth will always find a way to surface, just as the parable told by Nathan seemed to David, at first, to be about other people, far away from him.

We need to hear Nathan say to us, "**You** are that man!" How often do you take care of self first and only think of others when they are those who can potentially benefit you. The lamb of the poor man is stolen and sacrificed every day – past, present, and future – by those who are rich by worldly means.

The <u>lamb</u> is Jesus. The <u>poor man</u> is the Scriptures.

We routinely offer up a buffet of opinions about what our faith teaches us and how blessed we are by God and Christ – all while we cannot point to anything of our own lives that we have sacrificed, so others can learn to be Jesus and to see him throughout the Scriptures.

In this tenth Sunday of the Ordinary Time season, which symbolizes how each and every true Christian is called to be a priest, beyond simply being a "child of God." It is time to understand that ordination call, which is to **ALL** would-be Christians.

A priest is one who daily serves the LORD and takes whatever gift-crumbs fall from that master's table, as "all one needs" to eat. A priest performs the works of God daily, which is what Jesus told the Galileans.

To be a priest, one has to grow up, stop being a child and mature in Christ.

One has to be able to see the dumpster as where one used to search for food, out of childish fears. One has to realize that "all you can eat" is readily available, based on "all you can show" you are ready, willing, and able to make use of.

Robert Tippett

Amen

# ELEVENTH SUNDAY AFTER PENTECOST

## Proper 14

## YEAR B

**Relevant readings:**
2 Samuel 18:5-33
Psalm 130
  1 Kings 19:4-8
  Psalm 34:1-8
Ephesians 4:25-5:2
John 6:35-51

# Neighbors are members of the same body

In 2003, when I was a neophyte interpreter of Nostradamus, I volunteered to speak about my findings on the prophet's work to an organized group of "skeptics."

The meaning of the word "skeptic" has to be understood as the definition states: "A person who questions the validity, authenticity, or truth of something purporting to be factual, especially religion or religious tenets." This means any group of skeptics will always include atheists.

After my presentation was completed and during the question and answer period, I made a general comment that the future exposed by Nostradamus was of a Holy War between Islam and Christianity. I said the United States would be attacked as a Christian nation.

One woman in attendance raised her hand and objected that the United States was not a Christian nation, because the founders were not religious leaders and the Constitution was written so that a nation was created with no religious affiliation.

Without thinking how her objection was way off the focus of Nostradamus, my emotions led me to immediately tell her (in a somewhat bellowing voice), "That is the most ridiculous thing I have ever heard! The laws of America were Judeo-Christian based and the first thirteen colonies were English, made up of Christians of various Reformation sects, escaping the persecution of the Church of England. There were no Muslims, Hindus, or Jews who founded this nation!"

She did not wish to argue her point further, so the questioning then returned to focus on some things I had stated in my speech.

# After Pentecost Sermons: Proper 14, Year B

When it was all over, the group applauded – I imagine because I was brave enough to present my views on something they completely did not believe in, but in a way that was logically addressed.

I am reminded of this past experience because of how Paul advised the Ephesians, "Putting away falsehood, let all of us speak the truth to our neighbors, for we are members of one another."

I attempted to address the false opinions that were commonly held about Nostradamus (the illogical), by presenting the truth of views that were based on plain evidence. I did so because this truth (the message of Nostradamus) was necessary for all Americans to know. After all, we are neighbors in this country, even if we are parts, sects and groups of differing views, making up the whole of our nation.

When I erupted at the woman's question, I was angry – but I did not sin because I responded with the truth – and after I left the meeting I felt good about the whole experience, with no animosity towards anyone there. That was even though I knew everyone in that group saw me as another example of ridicule – some crazy person who will believe in anything.

Still, my willingness to stand before a group of people who disbelieved in me as much as I disbelieve in their worship of doubt was a necessary step towards my deeper understanding of Nostradamus. It was later that I came fully to the realization that Nostradamus was a true prophet of Jesus Christ.

That developmental path has led me to write sermons and preach before strangers waiting for their bus to arrive. My Nostradamus voice has lost it urgency; but my Christian sermons have found a place for that importance.

Still, this process in my life, which has now grown significantly over the past thirteen years, has led me to realize that our "neighbors" are not just anybody breathing air. We are not "members of one another," as Paul wrote, such that all human beings collectively make up the "body" of the animal called "Man." Paul meant more by stating that.

As Christians we are "neighbors" with other Christians. We are "neighbors" with other parts, sects and groups making up the "body" of the Judeo-Christian believers in the One God – Yahweh. Those who are not Christians are then not united with us. Non-Christians are not the "neighbors" of true Christians.

In the Second Samuel reading, where David's son, Absalom, was leading an insurrection against his father, to take over the throne of Israel, his defeat needs to be seen in the light of a former neighbor, one who moved away from the neighborhood and ceased being a "member" of David's Judah. Absalom did not seek to unite. Instead, he sought to divide and then conquer.

Absalom led at least twenty thousand soldiers against "the servants of David." All who Absalom led were lost from the whole of David's Israel. Because David still saw Absalom as a "member" of his household, he still saw his son and the army of Israel as "neighbors" and "members of one another." David instructed his soldiers to deal lightly with Absalom, and when the battle was over he waited for news of Absalom's fate.

When we read, "The Cushite [said], "May the enemies of my lord the king, and all who rise up to do you harm, be like that young man," the meaning was, "may death come to all who are not "neighbors" of David's nation" The Cushite messenger did not see those left dead as "one" with his army.

If you listened carefully, we read that "the slaughter ["in the forest of Ephraim"] was great that day," but "the forest claimed more victims that day than the sword." Israel [the enemy] and Judah [David's "servants"] were "neighbors," as "members of one another" – the nation of Israel. However, anger had set in and the two sides viewed each other with "bitterness and wrath and wrangling and slander, together with all malice."

They had become enemies to one another.

Still, it was the forest that claimed more victims in this decisive battle. Absalom is said to have caught his head in a low branch of a great oak tree, where he hung suspended after his mule kept running. It can be assumed that many other soldiers died from such accidents, as the noise of battle struck fear in both man and beast.

The symbolism of so many deaths coming by accidentally getting caught in tree branches can be seen as an indication that Israel could not split (branch out), as that would take it on a course short of heaven. Tree branches have mystically been seen as holding up the sky, by many cultures, thus they are symbols as spiritually uplifting links to heaven and the divine.

As such, God protected David's Israel from being overrun by Absalom's Israel. The battle was fought there because God knew it would unify Israel under David, doing it in a way that limited how much killing by the sword was necessary.

In that same light, one can see how Jesus was amid a group of Galileans, some of whom were Nazarenes who recognized Jesus as just some local boy. That recognition turned that crowd gathered around Jesus into very forgetful people. After having Jesus miraculously feed them with bread and fish (they might not have been aware that was a miracle, although the disciples knew it was), they were now angered that Jesus said, "I am the bread that came down from heaven."

Just as Absalom led twenty thousand soldiers who had forgotten that King David was king because of God's will, they all died because they were not ready to commit to being servants of God. Jesus pointed out how Moses had led multitudes of Israelites into the Wilderness and God fed them with the manna from heaven, but they too all died because they were not ready to eat eternal bread and fully serve God.

None of those Galileans were ready to see Jesus as sent by the Father to be the living bread he said he was.

Likewise, none of those skeptics I talked to were ready to see Nostradamus as a Christian prophet, shown a future Holy War.

The Galileans saw Jesus as "the son of Joseph, whose father and mother they knew." They concluded that children raised in Nazareth do not come from heaven, nor are they the offspring of God.

The skeptics saw Nostradamus as a charlatan, because throughout history charlatans have regularly been uncovered; and, skeptics deny that those claiming to have psychic abilities can prove them.

About this disbelief, which is based on faith in only the observable universe, Jesus quoted Isaiah – Isaiah 54:13 – when he said, "And they shall all be taught by God." Chapter 54 of Isaiah is a song called "The Future Glory of Zion," which is believed to have been written in exile. Thus, the song focuses on the rebirth of that which had died.

Skeptics can only see proof that they allow God to expose to them – individually. But, they would have to convert from skeptics to believers, for that realization of God's teaching to take place.

In the verse that follows the one Jesus quoted, Isaiah wrote, "In righteousness you will be established." You cannot be established as worthy of heaven until you are taught by God. You cannot come to Jesus until you are taught by God.

# After Pentecost Sermons: Proper 14, Year B

This means that our "neighbor" is **not** someone who does not believe in God. While our "neighbor" **is** someone who claims to be Christian, we should not simply take that at face value. We should be "putting away falsehood," so we "speak the truth to our neighbors," because those who believe in Jesus as Christ and are filled with the Holy Spirit are strong "members" of that body. However, those who are only hanging onto Christianity because of the "free bread and fish," they are like palsied "members."

Paul wrote, "Thieves must give up stealing; rather let them labor and work honestly with their own hands, so as to have something to share with the needy." To claim the values of Christianity without doing any of the works, this amounts to taking something without paying – thievery.

When we come across those who have indeed been taught by God, they have been filled with the Holy Spirit. Those Christians are the best neighbors as they give strength and comfort to others of like mind.

That is who we need to seek out. We need to lay our eyes on and lend our mutual support towards those who keep our mind in Christ and our hearts open for God. That environment – that "neighborhood" – is what allows us to "be imitators of God, as beloved children, and live in love."

The world outside that sphere of influence is where we come in touch with anger and temptations to sin. If we focus on our families and neighbors, we will shine a light so bright the outside world will come to us. They will come and see neighborhoods that "let no evil talk come out of their mouths, but only what is useful for building up, as there is need, so that their words may give grace to those who hear."

The saying goes, "You can lead a horse to water but you cannot make it drink." Another way of saying that – we find today – is "And they shall be taught by God." We lead them to the living waters, but God will teach them how to drink.

Set the example and let God teach conversion. Once converted, a neighbor will start a new neighborhood elsewhere – one added to one whole body, connected as a Christian network of neighbors.

Still, just as Jesus told the Galileans, "The bread that I will give for the life of the world is my flesh," there are many in the world who hate neighborhoods that they do not fit well among.

Nostradamus was led by Christ to see and write about a future when that hatred will become intense. There are evil groups who seek to take a pound of flesh through acts of revenge. They are like Absalom's army, seeking to divide, then conquer.

The only way to avert that end is to light up the world with a massive network of truly Christian neighborhoods. However, in America now, as that objection made by that woman in a group of skeptics proves, we doubt that the United States of America was really set up to be a Christian nation.

That lack of commitment to a religion, to Jesus Christ, and to the One God of all, will find this nation in a great battle where "the forest will claim more victims than the sword."

America and its Western allies – those who claim to be Christian by birth – will be led by Absalom-like leaders. America was founded without a king, claiming individual **rights** over righteousness, having learned nothing from God. The land tried to split, between 1861 and 1865, only to be reunified by force, with retribution creating many cracks in the armor carried by subsequent leaders. Thus, like the story of Israel, America will be killed by the many seeds of evil that our history shows we have long ago planted around the world. Those seeds have now grown into forests of hatred, great oaks with strong limbs that are no longer neighborly, as allied members one with another.

## After Pentecost Sermons: Proper 14, Year B

David, whose sinful acts had cursed his house, still felt strong emotions for his child-gone-awry, Absalom. This is how we hold fond affections for the founding principles that created our nation, even as the lack of God and Christ was always an intentional flaw. By not making a nation where state and religion are one, choosing instead to give birth to a nation of the people of equal heritage, there is no heavenly goal. By design, the people (who are always easily influenced by evil) were intended to shape our nation's future course towards ruin.

Our hopes, like David's, are that we will be dealt with gently, for the sake of our ideals: freedom, equality, and democracy. After the battle is fought, the answer to the question, "How well are those ideals?" will be, "Not well."

In the alternate Old Testament reading, which was not read aloud today, the lesson is of Elijah running from a death threat made against his life by Jezebel. He stopped to rest under a shade tree, where he prayed, "It is enough; now, O LORD, take away my life, for I am no better than my ancestors."

Elijah was threatened because he had slaughtered all of Jezebel's prophets, as instructed to do by God. The whole of Israel had become divided, where those new "members" were not "neighbors of one another." Elijah was not told to be loving to that evil presence; and Jezebel and Ahab were not loving of Elijah.

An angel of the LORD came to him and told him, "Get up and eat, otherwise the journey will be too much for you."

Elijah was given spiritual bread and water, so he would not be hungry or thirsty until the evil presence had been ended.

We are at that same threshold now. We are exhausted because we are running for our lives, and we are without the nourishment of eternal bread from heaven.

"Whoever comes to me will never be hungry, and whoever believes in me will never be thirsty." That is the strength God sent to Elijah and it is the strength we are offered today through Christ.

Still, we must fully understand that when Jesus said, "Whoever comes to me" this means, "they shall all be taught by God" first – filled with the Holy Spirit.

Amen

# TWELFTH SUNDAY AFTER PENTECOST

# Proper 15

# YEAR B

**Relevant readings:**
1 Kings 2:10-12 and
   1 Kings 3:3-14
Psalm 111
   Proverbs 9:1-6
   Psalm 34:9-14
Ephesians 5:15-20
John 6:51-58

Robert Tippett

# Feeding on Christ through your inner child

Have you ever heard anyone mention "the child within" or the "inner child"?

Wikipedia has an article on the "Inner child," which begins by stating:

> "In popular psychology and analytical psychology, inner child is our childlike aspect. It includes all that we learned and experienced as children, before puberty. The inner child denotes a semi-independent entity subordinate to the waking conscious mind.
>
> The inner child is the best known lower third of a comprehensive model of the human psyche called the Three Selves."

This "modern" realization can be seen as very reminiscent of the Riddle of the Sphinx, which goes back millennia:

> "In Greek legend, the Sphinx devoured all travelers who could not answer the riddle it posed: "What is the creature that walks on four legs in the morning, two legs at noon and three in the evening?" The hero Oedipus gave the answer, "Man," causing the Sphinx's death."

The "creature" walking on four legs in the morning" is the child version of Man. We crawl on our hands and knees, unable to stand and walk. The child human is completely dependent on the protection and nourishment of adults – in particular the parents.

From the perspective of being on "all fours," a child looks up to those who stand before it. Thus, it learns first how its wants and

## After Pentecost Sermons: Proper 15, Year B

needs are dependent on superior beings.

As life unfolds, and the child grows to an ability to "stand on its own two feet," this dependency in superior beings is replaced by a preference for equal beings. It begins to shun recognition of superiority in others.

When the time comes that a prop is a necessary addition, by which standing on two feet is maintainedby a crutch or cane, there is a slight return to the childlike state. In a bent over or humbled position, the aged state of Man has to again look up to superior beings.

However, aged means a life of experience, which brings about wisdom. From a perspective of wisdom, Man can see God as the most superior aid to life.

These states of Man are the central theme of the readings this twelfth Sunday after Pentecost. Solomon was a child king. Paul wrote to "aged" Christians. Jesus spoke to free-standing Jews who saw him as an equal – not from heaven – and speaking crazy talk. Even Jesus' disciples' struggled to swallow what Jesus said.

The Galileans had each lost contact with their inner child. They heard Jesus speak through one-track ears, imagining his words in one-dimensional ways, as their life experience had programmed them to see.

It is that inner child that becomes repressed and suppressed as life goes on, because we learn that as children we get hurt, we cry, and we place our trust in those who give broken promises in return. We get laughed at and bullied to the point that a smiling, happy face turns to one sullen and wary.

Still, the inner child wants to express itself. The inner child wants to please others and wants to believe. The inner child loves to see smiling faces looking back at it and wants to please. The inner child longs to be dependent, nurtured, taught – and above all – loved.

But doubt is the damper that puts out that spark of trust.

In the reading today from First Kings, we read of David's death and Solomon's rise to the throne. Then, we read of Solomon's love of God and how God came to Solomon in a dream. In the exchange between Solomon and God, it is easy to overlook how Solomon said, "And now, O LORD my God, you have made your servant king in place of my father David, although I am only a little child."

We tend to see kings as adults, those who have been prepared for rule, which focuses on an ability to stand on two feet and keep the inner child safely hidden away.

However, Solomon was young and David had an older son, who would ordinarily have been the first in-line to the throne.

What is not read from First Kings, prior to reading, "David slept with his ancestors," is how David made arrangements for Solomon's succession, as well as how David gave instructions to young Solomon about what to do with all the enemies of Israel (within Israel), who would threaten Solomon's reign.

What is also not read, following us hearing, "So Solomon sat on the throne of his father David; and his kingdom was firmly established," prior to us reading about God visiting Solomon in a dream, is how young Solomon carried out all of his father's instructions.

**ALL** of those enemies of Israel were exterminated on Solomon's orders. Solomon looked up to his father **as a young child**, fully trusting David to teach him the right thing to do. Bathsheba, Solomon's mother (and something akin to "Queen Regent") reported to Solomon about his older brother (Adonijah), from another mother, having made a special request through her to pass on to Solomon.

Because Solomon believed in the righteousness of his father, he immediately saw through that request as an insult and threat. We do not read today how "King Solomon gave orders to Benaiah son of Jehoiada, and he struck down Adonijah and he died." That happened that very day Solomon heard his mother tell him of Adonijah's request.

Before that order was given, Solomon said, "May God deal with me, be it ever so severely, if Adonijah does not pay with his life for this request! And now, as surely as the Lord lives—he who has established me securely on the throne of my father David and has founded a dynasty for me as he promised—Adonijah shall be put to death today!"

Not only did God **not** deal severely with Solomon, God came to Solomon in a dream offering him the gift of anything he desired. Solomon was rewarded for his obedience – an obedience that was not clouded by intellect.

You see, Solomon did not have the mind of an adult when he obeyed his father's instructions. When God asked young Solomon to tell him what he desired, Solomon did not seek selfish things – like one would expect a child to want. Instead of "long life or riches" or for "the life of your enemies" the child king told God, "Give your servant therefore an understanding mind to govern your people, able to discern between good and evil."

That request came from a child who wanted to please his deceased father, while taking seriously the task of upholding his father's faith in God, as his own.

Years ago, when my son was about six years old, I took him to a theme amusement park. One of the rides was a Model T type car that moved within a concrete moat, with a steel rail down the center. It was impossible for the car to leave that path, but the steering was so poor that even the most careful driver would find himself banging from the left side of the moat wall to the right side, with the rail suddenly catching, sending the car jerking in the opposite direction.

When my son and I began the ride, after the attendant got us started, I told my son he could drive. Off we went … bouncing left, then right.

I was smiling and looked over at my son to see if he was also enjoying the bounding back and forth. Rather than finding him laughing and squealing, he was intently staring down the road, trying his best to steer the wheel and keep us on a straight path.

He was taking the responsibility of driving that car as seriously as he had seen me behind the wheel, driving the family car. He imitated what he viewed from his backseat car seat position. He undoubtedly wanted to please me by his taking the role of driver seriously. Seeing that warmed my heart and I'll never forget the look on his face as he watched the road and attempted to steer a car that could barely be steered.

This part of the personality always remains a part of us, even though life experiences cover it up and send it deep within our psyche. Still, this inner child is who God teaches and to whom Christ gives responsibility. Only the inner child can reach out for those rewards of guidance.

Therefore, when Paul wrote, "Do not be foolish, but understand what the will of the Lord is," it means to beware acting childish, rather than innocent. By following a stubborn adult mind, one that refuses to listen to the inner child's devotion to right versus wrong, to good versus evil, adults often lash out in subconsciously led irrational acts, which are foolish and childish.

# After Pentecost Sermons: Proper 15, Year B

The Christians of the early church had removed their build-up of "adult self" and found the core of their inner child, which allowed them to be "filled with the Spirit." They sang "psalms and hymns and spiritual songs among [them]selves, singing and making melody to the Lord in [their] hearts, giving thanks to God the Father at all times and for everything in the name of our Lord Jesus Christ."

They rejoiced as children. They danced and sang, unafraid of being seen like that … just as we saw David dance wildly before the ark, a few weeks back.

The Galileans to whom Jesus spoke, they could not fathom how they could ever "eat the flesh of the Son of Man and drink his blood." In that adult state of uncertainty, had they all been anointed the King of Israel following David's death, they would have refused to kill the enemies of the state. No one would order deaths without a personal hatred established!

As such, the adult Galileans would have all ended up dead and replaced as king. The threat would have been realized, rather than averted. As a result, none of them would have any life left in them … as Jesus said.

The inner child does not struggle with such instructions from heaven. The young mind has no concept of cannibalism. A young mind does not know how to tell good from evil, just as Adam and Eve had no such brain-power prior to them eating the fruit of the tree of Knowledge of such matters.

When Jesus says to eat his flesh and drink his blood … to the inner child of the faithful … they simply trust, believe, and act. There is no thought required. They react, becoming Jesus, by extension: being the flesh for acting upon his commands; and being excited and vitalized by the feeling of euphoria they receive from acting as loyal servants who love to please.

The reluctance of adults to allow the inner child to surface is why Jesus quoted Isaiah, saying, "And they will be taught by God." It is also why Jesus said, "Let the little children come to me, and do not hinder them, for the kingdom of heaven belongs to such as these." (Matthew 19:14) Jesus said that when adults were arguing over the legality of divorce … something of which children have no concept.

When old age sets in and adults still refuse to return to the child's stance of "all fours," many choose to rely more on material props. They seem almost upright as a show of safety in a world of cut-throats and thieves who take advantage of the elderly.

This is how we see the lessons of Jesus' parables focusing on adults waiting too long to regain their childlike faith in God, the Father – as told in the silo building rich man, the women without lamps filled with enough oil to last the night, the rich man who denied poor Lazarus, and the slave who wasted his opportunity by burying his talent.

There is a saying that pokes fun at how easy it is to steal from babies. In today's difficult economic times, adults with wily minds know the elderly have much more than candy worth stealing, and they prey on their age, because their wisdom makes them as trusting as little children.

The very old and very young see the love of sharing, but the majority who learn how life forces adults to stand or be run over, they grasp firmly onto that which they have fought hard to gain over the years, not thinking twice about how a business dealt that profits them costs others.

Thus, the Galileans in the synagogue hearing Jesus tell them to eat my flesh and drink my blood could not see themselves regularly preying on others for their livelihoods … eating their flesh and drinking their blood, like predators.

# After Pentecost Sermons: Proper 15, Year B

Are we not just like those who struggled to understand Jesus' words two thousand years ago?

Do we not laugh as we careen our way through the path of life, bouncing left and then right, rather than have a childlike mind that takes the responsibilities of life seriously?

When we pray to God we drop to our knees, as a step towards that inability to walk on our own two feet. We are automatically returning to that childlike stance, looking up to the Father. We place ourselves at the mercy of God, just as a child is dependent on the love and care of a parent.

As Christian adults seeking to follow Christ, we have to let our egos give way. We have to die intellectually and be reborn Spiritually. We have to stop holding onto props that keep us materially inclined.

We have to see ourselves as young servants to the Lord.

Amen

# THIRTEENTH SUNDAY AFTER PENTECOST

# Proper 16

# YEAR B

**Relevant readings:**
1 Kings 8:1-6; 10-11; 22-30; 41-43
Psalm 84
  Joshua 24:1-2; 14-18
  Psalm 34:15-22
Ephesians 6:10-20
John 6:56-69

After Pentecost Sermons: Proper 16, Year B

# Dedicating a new temple unto the Lord

My wife and I honeymooned in southern France. We visited Lyon, Avignon, Salon-de-Provence and Marseilles.

All along our stays we found huge cathedrals to visit. We saw the Basilica of Notre-Dame de Fourvière, which sits on a high ridge overlooking Lyon.

We toured the Cathedrale Notre-Dame des Doms, next to the Palace of the Pope in Avignon.

We walked up a high mountain ridge to visit the Basilique Notre-Dame de la Garde, which majestically overlooks the port city of Marseilles.

In every one of those grand buildings, we placed a euro in a machine, turned the handle and got a medallion that commemorated that "State monument."

You see, they were no longer functioning churches (for the most part), having become the property of the Republic of France, after the French Revolution. Today, they are primarily tourist attractions.

In Paul's letter to the Ephesians, he advised that the enemy was not "blood and flesh" but "the rulers" and "the authorities." As such, the enemies are the "spiritual forces of evil [taking over] the heavenly places," like ancient cathedrals and basilicas. The enemy to Christianity and to Christians (as heavenly bodies) is a "present darkness," which seeks to remove all sources of light.

Several years later, my wife and I accompanied her family on a guided tour of Italy, where we toured great basilicas and cathedrals that including Saint Peter's Basilica (the Vatican), the Pisa

Cathedral (Pisa), the Basilica of Saint Catherine of the Dominicans (Siena), the Cathedral of Saint Mary of the Flower (Florence), and Saint Mark's Basilica (Venice).

While those large buildings were still active as churches for the Roman Catholic Church, they were opened more as tourist attractions. Most were built between 1200 and 1700, with each taking many years to complete. All have intricate facades and are architectural marvels.

I imagine all had grand ceremonies that dedicated them to God, with some dignitary standing before a crowd of people orating, just as we read Solomon doing when the Ark of the Covenant was moved into the great Temple he had built in Jerusalem.

There are no tourists walking through Solomon's Temple today. There are no commemorative medallions that one can purchase, to take home and prove to neighbors, "I was there!"

That is because the Babylonians destroyed the Temple of Solomon. Again, a building's fate was decided by "the rulers" and "the authorities" who followed much later in history.

While the Persians would fund the building of a replica of Solomon's Temple – the Second Temple, the Temple that stood when Jesus walked the lands of Galilee and Judea – it too would be destroyed. That time it was by the Romans. They would act as the new "rulers" and "authorities" representing "darkness" and "spiritual forces of evil in heavenly places."

The "rulers" and "authorities" of Islam built the Dome of the Rock on the site believed to be where those temples in Jerusalem stood. At the time the Islamic Dome was built, Jerusalem was then part of a Caliphate of Arab Muslims (around 700 AD). Now, since the re-creation of the State of Israel in 1948, there is talk of rebuilding the Temple of Jerusalem a third time … meaning the destruction of an Islamic holy building.

After Pentecost Sermons: Proper 16, Year B

He who rules today is the new authority.

While that has as yet not occurred, the <u>thought</u> represents another example of "rulers" and "authorities," all of whom have little to do with Spiritual matters. It is an evil darkness that uses religion in ways that enslave and inflame the people.

In Solomon's dedication of his temple, he asked: "But will God indeed dwell on the earth?" He then added, "Even heaven and the highest heaven cannot contain [God], much less this house that I have built!"

We read that statement after we are told of the Ark of the Covenant being moved into its holy position, when "a cloud filled the house of the LORD, so that the priests could **not stand to minister** because of the cloud."

"The <u>priests</u> could not stand to minister" means the Levites had no role in the inner sanctum of the Holy of Holies. It means <u>no human can stand</u> and preach about how great God is and how much God means, while surrounded by the Spirit (cloud) of the LORD. It means <u>no mortal stands in the place of God</u>, as God's spokesman, as if speaking for the LORD's new building is valid reason for all to follow that mortal. When such a priest's lips move, it can only be to speak the words of the LORD, if they are indeed righteous.

Thus, Jesus was a mortal for thirty-plus years - but he became elevated higher as the Son of God when the dove of the Holy Spirit lit upon him and God said (in effect), "This mortal has proven himself worthy, so I am well pleased."

In David's psalm today, we heard recited,

> "Happy are they who dwell in your house! They will always be praising you. Happy are the people whose

strength is in you! Whose hearts are set on the pilgrim's way."

David wrote those lyrics when the Ark of the Covenant was still kept in a tent … in a tabernacle. Thus, the "house" of the LORD was not a building where people lived or worked … it was each **person** whose faith was kindled by the presence of the LORD in them … those whom were filled with the cloud of God's Spirit.

Thus, their hearts are set on the pilgrim's way because God fills them emotionally. The inner sanctum of the Temple of Solomon reflects the heart of faith. The heart is where the blood is pumped throughout the flesh – Spiritual blood eats away the flesh of doubt and pours out the blood of the pilgrims, who are followers of what is written. After proven devotion, they replace themselves with Jesus. They eat his flesh and drink in his blood.

You see, Jesus was the blueprint for the new Temple unto God. The Law was written into his heart, so God filled him with the Holy Spirit, like a cloud. However, as Solomon said, "Even heaven and the highest heaven cannot contain [God], much less this house that I have built!"

This means there is more of God's cloud to fill countless new temples - who were the Apostles and who we are expected to be built for such a holy dedication.

When this is realized, one can grasp the meaning of Paul's instruction, "Put on the whole armor of God, so that you may be able **to stand** against the wiles of the devil."

This means it is most important to see how each and every Christian has to see himself or herself as a temple unto the LORD. Once the Covenant is written upon our individual hearts and the cloud of God fills our total beings with His Holy Spirit, then we can become priests who cannot minister over ourselves.

## After Pentecost Sermons: Proper 16, Year B

We cease being in control of what directions our life can be pulled – influenced by outside "rulers" and "authorities." We become bodies through which God operates as our only King and Spiritual guide.

Thus, with God's presence we are able to be clothed in the armor that allows us to resist the outside temptations of a world ruled by Satan, with evil given authority. God clothes us with His strength so we "may be able to withstand" evil, so we can "stand firm" as Christians, as representative of truth and righteousness.

When Paul said, "Take the helmet of salvation," this is when we can assume the mind of Christ as our identity. That power of thought arms us with the "sword of the Spirit," which is an ability to defend the word of God against those who misuse it … who gain positions of rulership and authority falsely.

When we see ourselves as a building dedicated to the LORD, we can understand how Jesus told the Galileans in a synagogue of Capernaum: "Those who eat my flesh and drink my blood abide in me, and I in them."

To "eat" and "drink" is to "build" and "dedicate" a temple worthy of God's presence. It refers to the <u>actions</u> and <u>steps</u> that must be taken first – as priests who **stand** for the One God, the living Father – so those **actions** are building us into receptacles for the Lord. When completed and the Spirit moves into a position inside our inner sanctum, then God's Spirit has us stand down as servants to self. With God's presence within, the living Father grants us the ability to stand as God's Son.

When we hear how many of Jesus' disciples said, "This teaching is difficult; who can accept it?" they spoke as the followers of "rulers" and "authorities" that had taken over the Temple of Jerusalem after exile. Israel and Judah had fallen, and the imitation that rose to replace it was still preaching nothing that taught the Jews how to stand while dressed in the whole armor of God.

A Temple unto the LORD that stood as the presence of darkness was void of righteousness and truth. It was a shell built for rulers and authorities to use as a means of wealth and power. Thus, no one had ever said such a thing as "eat my flesh and drink my blood" before. None of the leaders had ever told their followers, "Be me! Lead!"

The same difficulty in accepting what Jesus had then said would be repeated when Jesus later said that he would tear down the Temple in Jerusalem – that magnificent jewel the disciples marveled over – and then rebuild it in three days. That was equally difficult teaching that was hard to accept, because no one could fathom how a body of flesh and blood could be a great Temple unto the LORD.

The reason for those who did not believe Jesus' words is they were not led by a light, but by darkness … meaning they served the devil's wiles.

Last week I spoke of how innocent little children know nothing, so intellect cannot cause them to doubt. If told to "eat the flesh of Jesus and to drink his blood," they will act like they are following the instructions of one they trust and revere. Adults know doubt, so they are less likely to believe so blindly, so innocently.

During this Ordinary Season, when all Christians should feel commissioned to go out and spread the Gospel so others will be led to receive the Holy Spirit of God, we should realize that Christ expects that we (those of us calling ourselves Christians) have the responsibility of becoming ordained into the priesthood, just like Paul was. Paul claimed he was "an ambassador in chains," which was much more than being a prisoner of the rulers and authorities of Rome. Paul's words mean he was enslaved to the LORD … happily.

# After Pentecost Sermons: Proper 16, Year B

We can only be apostolic ambassadors after we are clothed in the armor of God's Holy Spirit, which is the time when we hear an inner voice call us to minister. We stand before God as his servants, until the time he tells us to kneel and be "knighted" as His Son (regardless of one's mortal sex).

When that call is heard, we must see ourselves as the **building** that Solomon took years to make ready, before the Law was set deep within that body and God spread throughout that building from that heart-center, like a cloud.

We should all be on our knees in prayer, begging:

> "O LORD my God, heed the cry and the prayer that your servant prays today; that your eyes may be open night and day towards this body of flesh and blood, the being of whom you said, 'My name shall be there,' that you may heed the prayer that your servant prays towards this self."

May the LORD bless your supplications and may you wear the helmet of salvation for the rest of your life. Wear the chains of servitude as a smiling ambassador knowing your soul has already been freed, when you let God and Christ take over.

Amen

# FOURTEENTH SUNDAY AFTER PENTECOST

## Proper 17

## YEAR B

**Relevant readings:**
Song of Solomon 2:8-13
Psalm 45:1-10
    Deuteronomy 4:1-9
    Psalm 15
James 1:17-27
Mark 7:1-8; 14-15; 21-23

After Pentecost Sermons: Proper 17, Year B

# Look, there he stands behind our wall

When I was in college, I took a required psychology class that dealt with human growth and development. As adults, our past shapes our future; so, by better understanding the issues causing people to change and grow, that knowledge can be utilized to help people live up to their full potential.

As a classroom exercise, each student was asked to share some significant moment in their past where growth and development changed one's life course. One of my classmates told us about one such challenge in her life … a fairly recent epiphany.

She was born in America to Hindu (India) parents. She met a young man who also was born in America to immigrant parents (Pakistani), only he was raised Muslim. She explained such love was strictly forbidden.

Still, they fell in love and talked about marriage. My classmate said her parents would disown her if they knew she wanted to marry a Muslim; and, her boyfriend's parents would likewise reject him for marrying a Hindu woman. To add to this dilemma, the girl's parents announced to her they had arranged for her to marry a young Hindu man, whom she had never met. This new development meant the girl would seriously disgrace her parents by not fulfilling the bargain her father made with another Indian father. She faced more serious threats if she did that, especially rejecting an arranged Hindu marriage for a Muslim man.

The young woman in my class was in a dilemma of love. Keeping her heart hidden from her parents, she requested a meeting with the man she was arranged to marry. Her parents set up a meeting with her potential fiancée … something that was not commonly done, as it could be regarded as an insult. The girl said she was pleasantly surprised that the man was about the same age, good looking, and of similar mind.

My classmate told the class that she had decided to break up with her Muslim boyfriend and marry someone she had only met once, because she loved her parents and family. She said her parents had married without having ever met, and she was committed to making her new marriage work ... expecting love to come through the commitment each would make to the other.

While it may be difficult to see at first, the lessons of today's readings deal with the attractions and commitments of marriage, which includes having children and raising those children in an environment of faith. A serious commitment to marriage goes well beyond the physical attractions that relatively modern marriages have more commonly been built from.

As my classmate wept at times while she told her story, it should be realized that marriage is not always focused on feelings that make the rest of the world seem to disappear.

The Song of Solomon is considered by scholars to be love poems, with many rather sensual, read as expressions of the physical love between a man and a woman.

The love song read aloud today evokes images of passionate love, which I imagine mirrors the feelings my Hindu classmate felt for her Muslim boyfriend. Such burning emotions seem, initially, like those feelings will last forever, thus thoughts of marriage enter one's mind after the heart is ignited.

"Arise, my love, my fair one, and come away." Solomon wrote.

Now, I am not a scholar of Biblical writings, but reading this song of Solomon made me wonder, "How does a love song connect to James writing about the acts of faith and Jesus calling some Pharisees and scribes hypocrites over hand washing rituals?"

# After Pentecost Sermons: Proper 17, Year B

In fact, it should make all of us ask, "How do sensual songs of lovemaking find a place in the **Holy** Bible?"

Passionate love poems seem more fitting for the Kama Sutra or as waiting room reading material, before being called in as part of the Masters & Johnson sexual relationships research done in the 1950's.

Then, it dawned on me.

Solomon was not writing about his feelings of love with one or more of the over 700 wives and concubines he had. As a king, he did not need to woo any women into his arms. With so many lovers, it would make his words seem like he was a Casanova or playboy, pretending every woman was more exciting than the ones past.

Instead, Solomon was writing about the love between a believer – one of faith – and God. Solomon was writing about the most fulfilling relationship any human being could ever have. Solomon, like his father David, loved the LORD with all his heart.

In First Kings 3:3 we read: "Solomon showed his love for the Lord by walking according to the instructions given him by his father David."

That love is stated in his song today: "Look, he comes, leaping upon the mountains, bounding over the hills."

God came to Solomon in a dream. Can you imagine how heart-warming that was?

Can you envision the greatness of God coming to you, regardless of the obstacles that you face in your path of life?

"My beloved is like a gazelle or young stag. Look, there

he stands behind our wall, gazing in at our windows, looking through the lattice."

The plural pronoun says the two are one, "behind our wall," "at our windows." Can you feel God's presence in your heart, giving you an inner sense of grace (gazelle) and beauty (stag)? Can you see God within the boundaries of your body walls, a body that has become a temple unto God, with His Spirit piercing through the windows of your soul, looking through your skeletal framework longing for your heart?

Did you know a stag is a symbol for Christ, according to Medieval Heraldry? It stomps on snakes (evil).

A gazelle represents awareness, agility and speed.

I recommend you take the time to re-read all of the love poems in the Song of Solomon and see how the words are seducing you to fall in love with God. Solomon wants you to desire God's proposal and accept a union with Him … to be His bride … regardless of one's human gender.

If you can see how the words of Solomon's song are calling you to be God's lover, hear how Psalm 45 was David's song wooing us the same way:

> "My heart is stirring with a noble song, let me recite what I have fashioned for the king."

We have to feel our hearts pounding with the thought of having God choose to be one with us. We have to see how Christ is our king who we seek to wed.

When you feel the passion within your heart, then see how the Law of Moses becomes our "wedding vows."

In the alternate Old Testament reading selected for today – Prop-

# After Pentecost Sermons: Proper 17, Year B

er 17 of the Ordinary Time this year – is offered Deuteronomy, chapter 4. There we can see how Moses told the Israelites of the Law's marriage proposal:

> "You must neither add anything to what I command you nor take away anything from it." "You must observe them diligently," he said.

How different are those words that portray the seriousness of commitment with God from these words we so easily recognize:

> "Dearly beloved: We have come together in the presence of God to witness and bless the joining together of this man and this woman in Holy Matrimony."

> "Will **you** have this [Son of God] to be your husband; to live together in the covenant of marriage? Will you love him, comfort him, honor and keep him, in sickness and in health; and, forsaking all others, be faithful to him as long as you both shall live?"

While I skipped over some parts of a marriage ceremony, as stated in our Prayer Book, I only substituted "Son of God" for "this man." Marriage **IS** a Covenant before God; and, the greatest union one can experience is that where we join with Christ, all one with God.

From that marriage of one individual with Christ, all in attendance are asked, "Will all of you witnessing these **promises** do all in your power to uphold these two persons in their marriage?"

This means marriage is **not** only between one and Christ, but one's family and one's future members (children) with God. The commitment is made BECAUSE one has been dedicated to God at birth.

I can see why my classmate broke off her relationship with her boyfriend and chose to marry a stranger her parents selected for her. She was dedicated to her religion … not just by words of promise, but by a heartfelt commitment. Her parents prepared her for that epiphany, which changed the course of her human growth and development.

In James' epistle, we hear him state, "In fulfillment of his own purpose he gave us birth by the word of truth, so that we would become a kind of first fruits of his creatures."

Those "first fruits of his creatures" are Christians. We have a religion that is different than Judaism, because Christians are married to Jesus Christ … the Son of God.

Now, James is writing a letter that is not about his marriage to Christ, as much as he is writing a letter like one's grandmother or aunt would write words of advice, encouragement and warnings to a newlywed couple.

James wrote words of wisdommlike would a relative, saying, "Marriage is a work in progress. All married couples have peaks and valleys, but stay the course. Remember you vows."

James is known for stressing the value of **doing**, more than simply "being." James says faith is demonstrated in one's acts, while many are quick to assuage the shoulders of those who only have faith, as if saying, "It is okay. As long as you believe you are married to Christ, then you are."

That is the dilemma of "works versus faith," of which James is known.

James was primarily addressing the Jews, who were married to God but who had rejected the proposal from Jesus. Christians **acted** because they were filled with the Holy Spirit, becoming like new babies of Jesus. Jews did nothing of this sort. Instead, they were arrogant because God chose their ancestors.

# After Pentecost Sermons: Proper 17, Year B

Thus, James concluded, "If any think they are religious, and do not bridle their tongues but deceive their hearts, their religion is worthless."

Now, the word written in Greek that is translated as "bridle" is "*chalinagógeó*." It means, "To lead with a bridle, to curb, to restrain, to sway." The word "bridle" is used as a noun to describe the restraints placed around a horse's head, neck and mouth. The bridle is how one tames a horse and reins in its wildness, so that a horse may be broken of its wildness and become a dependable servant to a master.

When we are married to Christ, our heads also need to be controlled. In our vows we accept that condition of servitude ... happily.

But like some horses ... those who some might call "spirited" ... some Christians buck and resist that restraint and control. The Jews, then, are like wild horses ... unbridled ... thus James' conclusion:

> Without a bit across their tongues, they run wild with deceived hearts.

Had my classmate in that psychology course told us how she was going to run wild and free, hooking up with her Muslim boyfriend, knowing that both of them would be rejected from their families and friends, they too would have unbridled tongues, without religion. How they had been raised would then become "worthless." They would have been thrown to the wolves of the world, with no place to call home. Their hearts would have eventually been found to have deceived them.

This is how Jesus saw the Jews of the Temple, who came over to him just to point out how his band of commoners, those who were Jesus' disciples, acted like animals by not washing their hands before eating.

Jesus responded by telling those temple leaders, "Isaiah prophesied rightly about you hypocrites, as it is written: 'This people honors me with their lips, but their hearts are far from me.'"

When one is viewing today's readings through a "marriage-tinted lens," then what Isaiah prophesied can be heard as a charge of infidelity ... of Jews cheating on their husband (God). Isaiah, as was Jesus, was a witness to the marriage vows exchanged between the Israelites and God, but while the Jews who lost Judah and the Jews who came back to Judea all pretended to do "kissy face" with God – honoring God through rituals and covenants doing nothing more than lip service – their hearts lusted for other gods ... like power, position, wealth and influence.

Thus, Jesus continued the quote from Isaiah, saying, "In vain do they worship me, teaching human precepts as doctrines." The Jews, who lost Jerusalem, Judah and all Israel, just like the Jews who rewrote the covenant while in Babylon – they had all broken their vows.

"You must neither add anything to what I command you nor take anything away from it" meant nothing to those infidel brides. The slept with whatever god offered them advantages over others.

In today's news terms, Jesus would have found out that all the Pharisees and temple scribes had accounts on Ashley Madison's "discrete affairs" website, only to find it had been hacked by God, catching them red handed.

"You abandon the commitment of God and hold to human tradition," said Jesus to those who were spewing judgment on the innocent disciples of Jesus, as if their married name gave them the right to pretend to be God.

# After Pentecost Sermons: Proper 17, Year B

They had unbridled tongues. They were wild horses, running free on their own.

As far as marriage and infidelity are concerned, the Jews of the Second Temple were divorced from God. They just did not know their relationship with God had ended. They were in denial, while taking advantage of a past relationship, as long as God was not present to stop them ... like when Moses and Aaron, David and Solomon, and prophets like Samuel, Elijah and Isaiah had kept their ancestors in their place of subservience, being true agents of God.

The people of Judea and Galilee ... the common Jews ... they were not being properly prepared to become God's brides. None of them had ever witnessed true **Holy Matrimony** before ... they had only read the vows made by their ancestors to God, when Moses was the officiant.

Today, we are in the same condition of disregard as the vast majority of people proclaiming to be Christians have done little more than read the vows that the "first fruits of God's creatures" wrote (the New Testament), who were indeed married to Christ.

It is now time to fall deeply in love with God, with Christ. We **must** do more than give Christ "lip service," kissing him on the lips as Judas did, and only on Sunday mornings. When you let the wafer and wine pass your lips today, think of the words of Isaiah, which Jesus quoted to the Pharisees:

> "This people honors me with their lips."

Then ask, where is your heart concerning Christ? Is it far from him? Do you really love Christ with **all** your heart?

As you drive home after church today, will your heart pound for God and His Son? Will **ALL** your thoughts be only on Jesus, like they would be if you were infatuated with a new lover?

Robert Tippett

Will you read the Holy Bible while at home, as passionately as you would read love poems written especially for you?

Will you long and your heart ache for the days to pass quickly, so you get the opportunity to attend the soonest Bible Studies class, because you miss hearing, "The voice of my beloved!"

"Look, he comes ... like a gazelle ... " gazing in **NOW** at the windows.

&lt;point to the windows&gt;

   "Arise, my love, my fair one, and come away."

The proposal awaits your willingness to say, "I'm coming my Lord."

Your sincerity then awaits your commitment, through marriage, before witnesses.

Your commitment, just like that expressed by my classmate in that psychology class, requires an epiphany. Your own growth and development as a human being should desire a most spiritual relationship and commitment; but you have to decide, "Will I bridle my tongue?" or "Will I deceive my heart?"

Amen

# FIFTEENTH SUNDAY AFTER PENTECOST

## Proper 18

## YEAR B

**Relevant readings:**
Proverbs 22:1-2; 8-9;
 *and* 22-23
Psalm 125
  Isaiah 35:4-7
  Psalm 146
James 2:1-17
Mark 7:24-37

Robert Tippett

# Children and dogs at the table of the Lord

I am reminded today of my black cat Idi, who I wrote about a while back. I am reminded of Idi because of the reference to "dogs under the table eating the children's crumbs."

Idi was one of four cats we had, to go along with two dogs. I told how we fed the four cats in a line of bowls, but we fed the dogs in a separate place, away from the cats Still, like all adored pets, they all had a way of finding a place near the dinner table when it was time for us owners to eat.

One evening, my wife and I were entertaining another couple and we cooked six large, oven-fried chicken breasts. We served those along with other side-dishes. As the animals gathered around, one guest asked, "Do you feed your pets scraps off the table?"

Of course we did ... but not in front of company. So, we told them just to ignore the pets; and, they did.

During dinner, in the empty chair across from my chair, I saw a black pair of cat ears slowly appear rising above table level, soon to be followed by a pair of cat eyes. Idi had jumped into the empty chair there and was seeing how "the other half" dined.

Everyone saw him there, but I comforted everyone that he liked chicken, so he was just watching. Slowly, as we ate, Idi's full head rose above the table level; and, his head turned left and right, scanning everything that was going on.

When we were finished eating, my wife and I were clearing the table of plates and leftovers. Idi slowly raised his body above table level; and, as I was about to take some leftovers to the kitchen, I saw his little black paws gently rest against the edge of the table top.

When I came back to get the platter that had two leftover fried chicken breasts, there was only one there. Additionally, Idi was no longer at the table.

I asked my wife, "Did you take a chicken breast?" At the same time that she said "No," I heard growling from another room.

The chicken breasts were huge, but Idi had taken one in his mouth and then somehow run with it through the living room, down the stairs of the split foyer, to the front door landing. There, his impatience caused him to begin guarding his "catch" with a constant loud growl, as he began to rip into the meat with his teeth, while holding it securely with his claws.

Idi wasn't happy when I retrieved the partially gnawed chicken from his grasp; and, he was less happy when the same chicken (sans bones) was divided between the two dogs. Idi had already eaten his crumb from the table.

---

A theme found in today's readings deals with sharing. The first verse of the Proverb says, "A good name is to be chosen rather than great riches, and favor is better than silver or gold."

It goes on to say, "Those who are generous are blessed, for they **share** their bread with the poor."

Perhaps it was these two verses that led the beatnik generation to start seeing "bread" as "great riches"?

The other day I listened to a sound bite of Democratic presidential candidate Bernie Sanders – a self-declared Socialist, who caucuses with the Democrats in the Senate, as an "Independent."

He proposed a political revolution that would change America's economic system that protects large corporations. He said that change would benefit small business.

After the sound bite, the television channel I was watching flashed a clip of Bernie supporters on the street. One was a man; perhaps old enough to have been a beatnik in the early 1960's, banging slowly on a small drum, while "singing" the lyrics, "Vote for Bernie Sanders and **share** the wealth."

For some reason, I hear Bernie talking out of both sides of his mouth. One on side he was saying we need a government that is based on the religious morals of **sharing**; but on the other he was saying government must be rid of all connection to religion. While attractive to both the religious and the atheists, the message says, "Let Socialism be your religion and a Socialist government your god."

God did not send His Son to demand the world **share**. As such, Jesus was never a politician, never kneeling before a philosophy of his own making or that of another human being. Never was Jesus the son of a lesser god than YAHWEH.

Simply by wise Solomon writing, "The rich and the poor have this in common: the LORD is the maker of them all," wisdom recognizes that there will always be those with more and those with less. God created both for a reason. **Sharing** is then a purposeful option, one which determines where one's heart is, as known by God.

In a Socialist society, the State (run by people like Bernie Sanders) becomes the rich and the vast majority of the people become the poor. In that state, the people have little to **share** among themselves. All are dependent on the laws created by men ... to share the wealth.

In my home, where my wife and I have pets (all the children

have grown and left the nest), we are the <u>rich</u> and the pets are the <u>poor</u>. It is much like a Socialist society, since the pets do little **sharing**, with them more likely to fight like possessive children, if one attempts to use something that has been given to the other.

My pet Idi and his personal desire for more, shows how some people will take the risks that others are afraid to take, so more than what is normally **shared** can be obtained. In a Capitalistic system, pets like Idi represent a Middle Class that takes advantage of opportunities to take more.

But, I … like a Socialist dictator … took Idi's hard-earned wealth of fried chicken away from him; and, I gave what he had "earned" to the dogs … the ones who knew to show patience, because they were afraid of what would happen if they begged at the table. I shared the wealth ... but not like Idi wanted it shared.

Solomon said, "Do not rob the poor because they are poor," which means "do not take candy from babies" because babies cannot defend themselves and their possessions. It also means "the poor have nothing to take worth selling your soul for."

Snake oil salesmen prey upon the poor in a similar manner as does a highway man, who steals from whoever falls into his trap.

In the Gospel of Mark today, when we hear Jesus say to a Gentile woman of Syrophoenician origin, "Let the children be fed first, for it is not fair to take the children's food and throw it to the dogs," we have Jesus actually speaking out against a society that would "rob the poor because they are poor."

That society was one maintained by the Jews, which saw Gentiles as poor animals, unworthy of befriending. Yet, the poor people were who was a constant source of profit to be had by the rich (by comparison) Jews.

While the Gentile woman misheard what Jesus said, not understanding what he meant – due to Gentiles commonly being treated like the dogs of the land, by Jews – when she replied to Jesus, "Sir, even the dogs under the table eat the children's crumbs," she spoke from a position of poverty … yet she spoke with a firm tone of respect.

The Gentile woman called Jesus "Sir," a polite term for an adult male. The Greek word is "*Kyrie*," which can state "Sir," but also "Lord" and "Master." She saw Jesus as the one who sat at the most important position at the table – a Lord of "great riches," but also one "of good name" – with the Jews being "the children" of God, whom, Jesus served as his guests, family and children.

She admitted that she and her daughter with a demon within her, were but "dogs under the table" … waiting.

Except this dog … this Gentile woman … "**begged** [Jesus] to cast the demon out of her daughter." The dog was begging for a crumb to fall onto the floor sooner than later. She was like my cat Idi, taking a seat at the table, yet waiting for the opportunity to make a crumb fall his way … while still letting everyone finish eating, before taking what was left over.

When the woman admitted her recognition that the Jews were better off than she and that she knew her position as a common servant … one of the poor to be used by the rich … she avowed that she accepted this class status …

And when she did not grab at Jesus, knowing her place to stay at a distance, she instead pleaded for him to hear her request, which was more for her daughter than for herself. She was simply begging for a **prayer** to be sent to the God of the Jews, uttered by Jesus, for her daughter's sake.

Jesus saw her and her daughter as "the children that must be fed first." The Greek word translated as "fed" is *chortasthēnai*, a form of *chortazó*, meaning "to be satisfied" or "to be fattened." As "fattened," the implication is to take one who is thin and make one plumper – to share the wealth of plenty with the impoverished who have little.

Jesus had traveled to the region of Tyre and Sidon because the Jews in positions of influence in Jerusalem and Galilee were far from being <u>satisfied</u> with what Jesus was feeding them. They were too full of themselves to be "fattened" more. Thus, Jesus avoided the region of Galilee – the land of his hometown, Nazareth – probably because only dogs of persecution plotted there for his return home.

For that reason, it was not yet Jesus' time to throw himself to the dogs. That would come later … when he would be crucified. Meanwhile, the children of faith were fed Spiritual food in Syro-Phoenicia … and those children were Gentiles. Jesus told the woman, "For saying that, you may go – the demon has left your daughter."

Now James – the brother of Jesus – would become **THE** Christian Jew of the Jerusalem synagogues after Jesus' Ascension. The epistle of James is basically a proclamation telling all Jews that being born of faith was not enough. To James, the only measure of one's faith was each Jew's individual works, based on that faith.

In the part of that letter read today, we see James addressing why the Jews were indeed dogs – animals undeserving of a seat at the table of God – when they displayed "acts of favoritism." He wrote, "You take notice of one wearing the fine clothes," catering to the wealthy; but then, "to the poor you say, 'Stand there,' or 'Sit at my feet.'"

That, said James, "dishonored the poor" because "God chose the poor of the world to be rich in faith." To treat the poor as "dogs" and the rich as "kings," those who proclaim to be born of faith "show partiality," thus they "commit sin."

In that same vein, Christians are held to the same standards. Bernie Sanders is partial to tricking the poor into voting for his promises of wealth redistribution, when the only real redistribution of wealth will be away from the many and to the few ... the ones who would benefit from Bernie Sanders being president.

My cat Idi was likewise for food redistribution; but, Idi was ALWAYS hungry and would constantly be looking for more food to come his way.

Christians, like Jews and like Socialists, too often put more energy into creating ideas that benefit a world they would prefer ... while casting judgment on those whose ideas they do not like or whose "party" is different ... so James proposed the problem, "If a brother or sister is naked and lacks daily food (poor), and one of you says to them, 'Go in peace; keep warm and eat your fill,' and yet you do not supply their bodily needs, what is the good of that?"

If you want a Socialistic, income redistribution world – free fried chicken breasts in every pot – then stop selling that idea while you have income and chicken in your possession, with no plans to give any of yours away. What is the good of a plan that hopes someone else will take care of the poor for you, while your life remains comfortable and unchanged?

When you see how James would flatly tell the Jews of Jerusalem, "So faith by itself, if it has no works, is dead," you can see how no amount of faith in one's government can ever get one into heaven. The government of Jerusalem was the epicenter of a "dog-eat-dog" world, with plenty of ideas and laws, but little action of religious faith.

Thus, we can see how Jesus' touching the lives of two Gentiles of the region of Tyre is followed by his physically touching one outcast Jew. This order of sequence is fulfilling Jesus' words, "Let the children be fed first, for it is not fair to take the children's food and throw it to the dogs."

In the region of Decapolis, Jesus encountered Jews who brought him another "unclean" Jew to heal. They could not heal anyone themselves, because of their faith being so little. So, they were figurative "dogs."

It was time for Jesus to feed the dogs the leftovers.

Before you can fully grasp this physical touching Mark witnessed, you have to understand that any clean Jew who touched an unclean Jew – like was deemed the deaf and dumb Jew – one would have to be washed and officially cleansed by a priest, before being clean again. Because Jesus so often touched such Jews (or they touched him), scholars see that as Jesus not believing in the laws that forbid him from touching the deaf and blind, because touching them was against Mosaic Law.

I believe to seek such mental justification for Jesus' holiness, as the Son of God, blinds one from the power of God to heal those who came to Jesus BEFORE any physical touching ever took place. Their faith healed them just by coming to Jesus ("No one comes to the Father except through me." John 14:6b).

As such, Jesus had no need to physically touch the deaf and dumb man; certainly not twice. Both touches and the act of spitting are separately symbolic, relative to the state of being the Jewish faith had fallen – it had fallen to the dogs.

First, when Jesus "put his fingers in his ears," Jesus was preventing the man from hearing the negativity of what James would later call "favoritism." The man was treated verbally with insults and condemnations; but, Jesus blocked the man's ears from his being influenced by outside words. Instead, the man was enabled to hear the voice of God within, due to Jesus' touch.

Second, when Jesus "spat," he did not spit on his finger. Jesus symbolically cleared his mouth of the dust of travel, which was from the land deemed by Jews to be physically holy. Jesus also "spat" as a gesture to those who would condemn a man as being unfaithful, due to a physical imperfection. Jesus spat out the injustice of Jews seeing a deaf man as a sinner, while they sinned by doing nothing to help this "poor" man. Jesus "spat" at the inability of Jews to do the works of healing as priests of God.

Finally, when Jesus touched the man's tongue and said, "Be opened," Jesus was opening this one poor Jew's mouth to speaking the truth, which he heard spoken by his inner ear. The dog's mouth was opened to be fed by Spiritual food, which would be shared with many others. Jesus "opened" the man's heart and mind, after God had allowed him to hear and speak clearly, so he would become an Apostle who would care for others with infirmities.

The overall symbolism of this man's healing was that all Jews were welcomed to likewise be healed of their inabilities to hear the truth of Jesus' words and to speak clearly what the Holy Spirit would have them say, rather than keep on stammering when Jesus would ask them a question. The dogs of Judea, Decapolis and Galilee had ears, but could not hear; and, they had tongues, but could not speak the meaning of the word of God.

When Jesus ordered the witnesses, "Tell no one," this was so a rumor would not spread that Jesus healed the deaf and dumb man. God had healed him, after he came to Jesus with faith. They would say the man spoke the words Jesus put in his mouth, when Jesus opened his tongue to speak what God had him to say.

Jesus was not trying to have a world dependent on one man. Jesus was trying to open the world up to having faith in the One God – YAHWEH, so they could all eventually become another Jesus.

As successful as Jesus was two thousand years ago, we now have again gone to the dogs. We put our faith in political philosophies and blowhard politicians who say, "Vote for me!" for all the wrong reasons.

We need to become deaf to those lies and hear the voice of truth within.

We need to spit out all our endorsements of men and women towards whom we show favoritism, while they speak poorly of those who do not think like them.

We need to open our mouths without forethought and speak in the tongues of the Lord.

But neither God nor Christ is a Socialist, so no one is forced to **share** any "riches of faith." Everything is voluntary. It is the "honor system," where you honor God and Christ by receiving their willingness to **share** grace. Just as Jesus said, "The poor you will always have with you," the implication is there will always be those of wealth and riches … regardless of any plans our rulers devise.

Amen

# SIXTEENTH SUNDAY AFTER PENTECOST

## Proper 19

## YEAR B

**Relevant readings:**
Proverbs 1:20-33
Psalm 19
  *or* Wisdom of Solomon
  7:26-29 and 8:1
    Isaiah 50:4-9
    Psalm 116:1-8
James 3:1-12
Mark 8:27-38

After Pentecost Sermons: Proper 19, Year B

# How to be taught salvation

In astronomy there is a star cluster known as the Pleiades. According to Wikipedia: "The name of the Pleiades comes from Ancient Greek. It probably derives from "*plein*" ('to sail') because of the cluster's importance in delimiting the sailing season in the Mediterranean Sea: 'the season of navigation began with their helical rising'."

The captain of sea-going vessels would set their rudders based on this constellation.

It is the nearest star cluster and the one most visible to the naked eye, usually seen in the fall and winter night skies. Here is how it is seen magnified by a telescope.

I am reminded of this star cluster because of an old movie I once saw. One of the characters in the movie was pointing out the Pleiades to another character and explaining how looking directly at that group of seven stars (called "the Seven Sisters" in Greek mythology) makes them appear like a fuzzy spot in the night sky. However, by turning one's head so you could see them with peripheral vision (from the corner of one's eye), you can catch a glimpse of individual stars in that blurriness.

Of course, with a pair of binoculars or a telescope, each of the stars becomes crystal clear. Still, next time you are outside at night and see Orion's belt, look a little above and to the right for the Pleiades. See if you can make the blur become individual stars, when seen out of the corner of your eye.

The comparison I make to the readings today is this "fuzzy spot" effect is how Holy Scripture is seen at first. We get flashes of insight that allow us to see one or two of the hidden meanings, but it is difficult sometimes to maintain that clear focus, once we re-read the verses that the insight came from. Sometimes, looking directly at the words has a brain-numbing effect, with no clarity described other than what is readily visible ... a blur.

The flashes of insight that come when our eyes veer away are due to the whispers of God. We have to learn to listen to that inner voice.

The more we follow-up on the insights, and connect the dots – kinda like realizing how the Pleaides make up the shoulder of the Bull that is the constellation of Taurus – the more God sees our devotion and the more God reveals to us what true seekers need to have dawn upon them. Actively taking those steps on our own is what aids our learning process, more than simply remembering what someone told us to believe.

Such acts are like those told to us by James, when he said "faith ... without works, is death." As Christians, we should try to make contact with God, by showing God we want to understand. We must act to show God that we want to **DO** more.

When we prove that desire is when God places binoculars and telescopes into our minds, so we can see most clearly the meaning of God's intent. Those who possess such ability are Apostles, disciples who have been filled with the Holy Spirit.

The problem is the lack of people who are truly filled with the Holy Spirit ... on a permanent basis. Of this lack, I am not pointing a finger at the sheep in the pews (although they do mostly lack this Spirit), but at those who **TEACH** the meaning of Scripture. Therefore, I mean the professors of seminaries, the graduated priests of congregations, and those promoted through acts of favoritism of one kind or another – raised to the levels of bishops and popes of institutions.

The attitude these **TEACHERS** have (as what I have seen demonstrated) is that the "uneducated" people are too stupid or too lazy to be **TAUGHT** the deep meaning found in Scripture. Therefore, they THINK it is best to dumb down sermons. Instead of saying anything shocking or "boat rocking," they paint pretty pictures of love and bliss … that is, when they do not turn the pulpit into a political soapbox.

How many times have you heard a priest, preacher, pastor, minister or rabbi point at YOU and ask, "How long, O simple ones, will you be simple? How long will scoffers delight in their scoffing and fools hate knowledge?"

Everyone here should desire to be filled with the Holy Spirit and stop acting too simple to understand all that stuff, saying under your breath, "I'll leave the details up to the **TEACHER**"?

Do **YOU** realize **YOU** should demand more; and, do **YOU** realize that God and Christ EXPECT **YOU** to act on your own? Do not try to demand more from someone else – someone who thinks you are too simple to learn. Demand more of yourself!

Now, James wrote, "Not many of you should become **teachers** … for you know that we who teach will be judged with greater strictness."

The one who will judge the **TEACHERS** of Christianity is God. So, when James continued to say, "All of us make many mistakes," he was referring to those who were not filled with the Holy Spirit, so that only the truth could ever be **taught** … week in and week out ... by Apostles of Christ.

This means that when James then said, "Anyone who makes no mistakes in speaking is perfect, able to keep the whole body in check with a bridle," that "bridle" he spoke of is the Holy Spirit. So, the "perfect" speaker is Christ within one's mind.

There is no school that **TEACHES** how to be filled with the Holy Spirit. You do not choose which seminary to attend to become a saint. God does the choosing. Christ is the only **TEACHER**.

While there are ideas as to what Jesus intended Christians to be taught, ideas that many agree with (after centuries of debates and meditations), we find that much of the foundation stones of Christianity have been laid securely. However, much of what the various denominations of Christianity believe, which separates each from the others, creates a cloud of uncertainty around that which no one disagrees exists.

All agree Jesus was the Messiah, the Son of God, as well as a prophet on the order of Elijah and a high priest in the order of Melchizedek.

But, Christianity, like Judaism, has lots of questions surrounding those basic building blocks. The creation of sects and denominations is due to disagreements about this and that, with many answers guessed at, with some laws added that have questionable validities.

Thus, this nebulosity surrounding such a solid fact as Jesus, is like explaining how the Pleaides are a fuzzy ball of light in the night sky. Are the **teachers** properly telling us what is there by using holy binoculars and divine telescopes?

While there is truth, the incompleteness is a lack of truth. It is an imperfect way of **TEACHING** the true meaning of being

# After Pentecost Sermons: Proper 19, Year B

Christian.

In the words of James, who likened the failures of perfect **teaching** to being like the wildness and uncertainty of an unbridled tongue, where an untamed tongue becomes a "restless evil, full of deadly poison," James asked, "Does a spring pour forth from the same opening both fresh and brackish water?"

The answer, of course, is "No!" One is not speaking the truth at all times, when one is still not filled with the Holy Spirit, bringing God into one's heart and Christ into one's mind.

Last week we talked about needing to be engaged to Jesus, followed by each of us then being married to him, with God officiating that blessed union. We become one with Christ, so each of us can become the rebirth of Jesus.

Only when that happens can an individual have a <u>constant</u> flow of fresh, holy water **teach** us, so we can forever after speak in the tongues of Christ.

Still, prior to reaching that state of purity and perfection, there are spurts of freshness, followed by spurts of brackishness.

This is part of the learning experience. It is one's internship to Apostleship. It is the testing grounds of wisdom.

We who are on the path to being true Christians will always sputter in this way at first, with each episode of truth spurting forth proving to us the inner glory of the Lord.

We have an example of this in today's Gospel reading. The example is Peter.

When Jesus asked his disciples, "Who do the people say that I am," they gave a variety of answers. The people had the "fuzzy spot" view of Jesus.

Still, when Jesus then asked his disciples, "But who do you say I am," they were mute. They were just like "the people," as far as how well their brains could figure out who Jesus was. Even Peter did not know, because he had never before told the other disciples, "Jesus is the Messiah."

However, on this occasion, when Peter opened his mouth and answered Jesus by saying, "You are the Messiah," Peter was moved to sputter the truth. A spring of fresh, holy water flowed forth from his mouth.

Then, just as one might begin to feel that Peter was special, Peter then tried to rebuke Jesus for him saying he "must undergo great suffering," including death. When Jesus then "took Peter aside and said, "Get behind me, Satan!" we can see how Peter was then sputtering brackish water from that same mouth that sputtered the truth moments before.

Peter was not yet special … but he, like all the disciples who stayed with Jesus, was on the right path.

The crowd of people who tagged along behind Jesus was then called to attention, along with the disciples closest to him. Jesus announced, loudly, how seven points would be required to be contemplated, "If any want to become my followers."

1. Deny yourselves.

2. Take up your cross and follow me.

3. Those who want to save their life will lose it, and those who lose their life for my sake, and for the sake of the gospel, will save it.

4. What will it profit you to gain the whole world and forfeit you lives?

5. What can you give in return for your life?

6. Are you ashamed of Jesus and his words in this adulterous and sinful generation?

7. How can you justify Jesus not being ashamed of you when he comes in the glory of his Father with the holy angels?

Jesus was giving an assignment for all his students to do, as homework. Jesus was **TEACHING**.

But, for a **TEACHER** today to read those words of Jesus and then tell others that Jesus meant this:

Being a Christian means you believe Jesus died on the cross for your sins; and failure to believe that will cause your soul to roast in hell, when Jesus returns to take all the faithful to heaven.

Such sputtered words are like explaining the Pleaides are a fuzzy spot in space. The only truth in such a statement comes from understanding an inability to see clearly the depth of each star, such that the whole appears fuzzy. Likewise, such a "simple" explanation of what Jesus instructed means one has set one's "mind on human things."

What Jesus announced is as clear as are the seven individual stars in the Pleaides, when one is looking at a picture taken from the space telescope. Jesus stated what must take place if you are to be a constant spring of truth, as one filled with the Holy Spirit. You must open your eyes and understand what acts have to be taken, in order to follow Jesus … AS A REBORN JESUS:

1. You have to stop being **YOU** and deny yourself.

2. You have to raise your standard, as had Jesus, becoming a raised trellis upon which the true vine can be strung, keeping it from the ground and evil impurities.

3. You have to stop fearing mortal death and begin fearing the loss of God and heaven's reward, such that saving your soul is understood to mean letting your ego die, to be replaced by the mind of Christ. Otherwise, trying to save a mortal life, by refusing to **do** the acts attracting the Holy Spirit, means a death without the eternal reward of heaven.

4. You must realize how all of the troubles mortals face are physical burdens upon the body, which are lessened by Christ, while in the physical realm. So, desiring to remain on the physical plane, seeing all the sins of the world as valuable, will cause you to forfeit eternal Spiritual grace.

5. You cannot get something for nothing, such that faith without works is death, just as works of faith is life.

6. By not believing when Jesus repeatedly said to follow in his ways, you are ashamed to be seen as subservient to God, fearing the loss of an opportunity to please one's self through adulterous sins.

7. Being ashamed of Jesus means Jesus will not promote your salvation, such that God will not take up residence in your heart, nor will He marry you with Christ. Your rejection will keep you from becoming a holy Saint, who will live forever in Heaven after time in this realm is complete.

This that I have stated is only the surface features of each star of instruction. There is much more depth to explore in each point of light. It is important to realize that when Jesus said, "Comes in the glory of his Father with the holy angels," this is not directly prophesying the end of the world and the return of Christ.

After Pentecost Sermons: Proper 19, Year B

Thus, there is no reason to **TEACH** this lesson in the "fire and brimstone," "End Times" mode. While Jesus will return at the end of all life on earth, he "comes in the glory of his Father with the holy angels" every time one of his Apostles reaches a point of mortal death.

Still, more important to realize is how Jesus returns to bodily form in every Apostle who desires the "glory of the Father," from a heart-centered love. Thus, anyone who is ashamed of Jesus will never be filled with the Holy Spirit, never becoming a reborn Jesus.

What one should realize from contemplation of this instruction from Jesus is how any embarrassment one might feel from **BEING CHRISTIAN** and acting exactly as did Jesus keeps one from submitting completely to God. To come so close, yet then shy away, is then how the Proverb of Solomon brings out some truly prophetic points:

> "I will pour out my thoughts to you;
> I will make my words known to you."

You will also sputter the truth, as did Peter, while still just a disciple … just a plebe. You will know what the truth means. But, if you sputter the Holy Spirit and decide it is easier to play "simple" … then remember how God has said:

> "I also will laugh at your calamity;
> I will mock when panic strikes you."
> "Then [you] will call upon me, but I will not answer."

It is hard to find **TEACHERS** who will proclaim this lesson. This lesson does not sound beautiful or give a message that everyone will be forgiven for their sins … always … regardless of how sinful their lifestyle has become. This message – from the wisdom of Solomon's Proverbs – promotes fear.

Fearing God is a bitter pill to swallow. Such lessons, which are found throughout Scripture and not just seen for the first time this week, are difficult to **teach**. That makes it harder for a religious school, Protestant congregation, or Christian institution to keep tithing patrons in the pews, when they "rock the boat."

Still, Solomon prophesied:

> "Because they hated knowledge
>   And did not choose the fear of the LORD,"
> "they shall eat the fruit of their way
>   And be sated with their own devices."
> "waywardness kills the simple,
>   … the complacency of fools destroys them."

In our present times, when everyone here (probably) has a "smart phone," it is this technology that has taken a stranglehold on our faith. Priests will commonly use a smart phone like a teleprompter, to read a prepared sermon as if coming from their hearts … off the cuff. Bishops now take "selfies" with a congregation, as if God needs proof of one's presence in a church building.

We have become "sated with our own devices."

And, as Jesus said, we can see how little things have changed since those days when a holy temple could not hide the fact that human beings will always live in "an adulterous and sinful generation" … when not **TAUGHT** by God.

We need to be **TAUGHT** to hear what Jesus and Solomon were saying … because they were talking to us with bridled tongues.

Amen

# SEVENTEENTH SUNDAY AFTER PENTECOST

## Proper 20

## YEAR B

**Relevant readings:**
Proverbs 31:10-31
Psalm 1
    Wisdom of Solomon
      1:16; and 2:1;12-22
    *or* Jeremiah 11:18-20
    Psalm 54
James 3:13-18 and
  James 4:3; 7-8
Mark 9:30-37

Robert Tippett

# Father, Son and Holy Spirit equals Husband, wife and baby Jesus

A long, long time ago, when I was in the tenth grade, my homeroom was where the Home Economics class was taught. The room had kitchenware, range and oven, and even sewing machines in there; and, occasionally, before roll call, some female student would come in with a pleasantly smelling dish of food to place in the refrigerator in the room. Cooking and sewing were seen as skills well worth practicing.

I never signed up to take Home Ec, but I did spend two-thirds of my senior year taking Typing. Both Home Ec and Typing were seen as classes for girls. One other boy and I transferred from other classes to Typing at the beginning of the Winter quarter. We were the only males in a room filled with girls pecking away at manual typewriters. We sat at desks in the back of the room, so we would not be a distraction to all the girls who needed to seriously focus on learning to type.

Because we missed the first part of the year, we struggled to get up to speed (50 wpm, 0 mistakes). We constantly had our hands in the air, attracting the attention of the beautiful, young miniskirted teaching assistant, so she could come answer our questions about the "home position" and how many keystroke errors were allowed. It was more an effort of hormones than a desire to master typewriters.

Obviously, my thoughts of my past are of a by-gone era, of a time when education believed boys and girls were made differently and each would need special "education," based on gender. It was still a time when school systems believed that boys and girls would grow into gender-specific roles and responsibilities as adults. I took an extra year of Physical Education (P.E.) as an elective one year, and then Woodworking another ... both male dominated areas of interest. That was due to careers in coaching and carpentry were appropriate for adult men.

Today, we don't think that way. There are no Home Economics classes taught in high schools ... at least none that would only focus on soliciting female students. Typing is no longer a skill that only female secretaries need, as it is now absorbed into computer classes using keyboards. Unisex computer skills are taught as workplace and home activities that everyone needs to know.

The education of my youth was geared towards maintaining a heterosexual society, where boys grew up and married girls, with raising babies and supporting families the objective. A male-oriented military draft was in place when I was eighteen, where boys were turned to men ... while learning what war meant. Boys became men wearing suits and ties as they entered the workplace. Girls grew into women wearing skirts and aprons in a home, as the core of a family environment. Men worked to bring home the "bacon," while women worked raising the children and doing household chores.

I am sure, to some, that mindset sounds barbaric, biased, and prejudiced.

Now, we argue among ourselves over which ideals of society are greatest. Equality and Freedom are God-given Rights and protected by the U.S. Constitution. Who can then say that homosexual couples cannot be married? Who can typecast or pigeon-hole anyone into some blanket generalization, one that says what little boys and little girls should grow up to be or do?

Some preschools now promote boys playing with dolls and EZ Bake Ovens and girls playing with toy trucks and erector sets. Teachers in some elementary schools tell minds that are still blank slates, "You can choose what sex you want to be." Many others object loudly to all this change thrown into a world that is no long normal or typical.

Because of all the arguing today, Proverbs 31 reads like some old fart expressing an outdated fondness of what kind of woman would make his life go easy and smooth.

I am sure that some people (not only women) read how Solomon wrote, "A capable wife who can find?" and think (if not scream out), "I thought Lincoln freed all the slaves." Why wasn't Solomon countering that with "A capable husband?"

Such thoughts are doubts about Scripture … cracks in the armor of all Judeo-Christian beliefs. Today's reading makes the Islamic treatment of women – especially that which is most promoted by the media of the West – appear "barbaric, inhumane and cruel." Then, the same media defends the Right for Sharia Law to be applied in Christian nations, where everyone is FREE to be whatever they wish to be.

Everyone misses the point of Solomon's wisdom, which is: It did not come from Solomon's brain, but from the mind of God whispering songs for him to write down (such as this one about what a good wife's traits are). God was asking (through the wisdom God gave to Solomon), "A capable wife who can find?"

In Genesis, God married the Spiritual (God) with the Material (Earth). Earth became God's "capable wife." Therefore, all that is made of clay is wife material.

If you read this and think of being a wife as slavery, then open your hearts and realize God is calling **ALL** of us – males and females, boys and girls – to prove ourselves as worthy of being His good wife. We **should all desire** to be slaves for God.

The problem is very few think that way.

This message that we are all to be wives to God is the same message I mentioned in weeks past, in particular about the Songs of

Solomon. Those provocative verses are not simply sexual poems of lovemaking, although they project the love between a man and a woman ... which produces the love of children. However, the Songs of Solomon are ultimately Spiritual praises of one's love of God ... where males and females take on a feminine perspective, as a bride or wife-to-be.

Our hearts should pound with excitement about how special God makes us feel.

We **ALL** should be willing to do everything of servitude that God wants us to do. We should be happy slaves of God. Being FREED from that devotion is to be lost.

Because we have difficulty reading Solomon as if he were telling us the character traits of a good wife and see them as meaning what the devotion of a truly faithful believer is, we need to "get out of the box" and take a second look. When we can see how **ALL WE CHRISTIANS** must be God's wives ... when we can realize that ... then we should be able to hear James' epistle talking to us.

James asked, "Who is wise and understanding among you?" That is like asking, "Who knows they should be God's wife?"

James knew EVERYONE **not** filled with God's true Holy Spirit would be unable to understand any of the true wisdom of Scripture. Reading words written does not make one a master of interpretation, just as owning a manual typewriter does not make one an author of words of wisdom.

As far as our being at each other's throats over women's rights and gay rights, trying to beat one into submission, forcing one to believe like another does, James wrote, "Those conflicts and disputes among you, where do they come from?"

He asked, "Do they not come from your cravings that are at war within you?"

James hit the nail on the head when he said, "[When] you covet something and cannot obtain it, you engage in disputes and conflicts."

Is that not how we argue over the definition of marriage, gay rights, equal pay for women ... and on and on?

Is **not** the grass always greener on the other side of the fence, when you see others having something you do not have? Has it not become the entitlement system of government that makes everyone believe in equality, when God made human beings different on purpose?

Did the Jews **not** complain about having lost their land, because they believed it was entitled to them by God? (They forget the agreement was for as long as the Covenant was maintained.)

Do **not** politicians light those fires of rights and entitlement, so they seem greater than they really are? (When the same promises are always there to be promised again, because it is impossible for governments to give without taking.)

James' answer to this arguing was simple: "Submit yourselves to God. Draw near to God, and he will draw near to you."

You draw near to God by becoming engaged to Christ. You draw near to God by your submission to His embrace. God draws near to you when he marries your soul - when two become as one - and God sets up residence in each believer's heart ... permanently.

**YOU** become God's wife. God the **Father** becomes **your** husband. You completely submit yourself to Him.

**YOU** never become equal to God. **YOU** compliment God by

# After Pentecost Sermons: Proper 20, Year B

being living matter, from His living breath. **YOU** become One with God through the Holy Spirit.

Now, in the reading from the Gospel of Mark today, we see how the disciples were arguing among themselves as the group walked from Caesarea Philippi to Capernaum, in Galilee.

They "argued with one another [over] who was the greatest."

They argued from a position of not understanding the meaning of things and their fear of seeking the truth.

They lacked wisdom … which is how all arguments over religious philosophy begin.

We do not understand marriage and neither do we understand how human sexuality "shows one's good life, as works of gentleness born of wisdom." Likewise, we do not understand how to be a "capable wife" to God.

We argue because we are not filled with God's Holy Spirit … permanently. Oh sure, many of you can argue that you have felt the Holy Spirit before and dispute my saying you are not filled with the Holy Spirit.

"You want something and do not have it," is what James would say (and did write). So, here is how you need to realize the difference between being permanently married to God … being His wife … and "getting to second base on a date with God."

To put it in terms that old people should recognize … "second base" is half-way home, but not a score. Being on second base means no points have been registered yet, although you get credit for getting on base.

The disciples were on "second base" too, figuratively, "but they did not understand what [Jesus] was saying to them and were afraid to ask him."

When we read, "Jesus and his disciples went on from there," Jesus, Peter, James and John (of Zebedee) had returned from going up Mount Hermon. That was the "high mountain" where Jesus was transfigured before those three disciples. Mount Hermon is the tallest mountain in all of present-day Israel, overlooking the Damascus plain.

Then, Mark 9:14 states, "When they came [from the place of the Transfiguration] to the other disciples, they saw a large crowd around them and the teachers of the law arguing with them." They arrived to see the disciples who had been left behind arguing with local rabbis.

In Mark 9:14 – 29 (which we do not read this year), Mark stated that Jesus healed a boy possessed by an impure spirit. Before Jesus arrived, the disciples left behind had attempted to heal the boy, only to fail and then get into an argument about pretending to be something they were not … healers of impure spirit possession.

In Mark 9:28, after the healing was done by Jesus and he and his followers had gone inside a residence, we read how, "the disciples asked him privately, "Why couldn't we drive it [the impure spirit] out?"

In Mark 9:29, Jesus answered, "This kind can come out only by prayer," where the Greek word "*proseuchē*" means, "prayer (to God), a proper place for prayer (when a synagogue is absent), and earnestly (as in prayer)."

The intent of that answer said, "After you have learned **YOU** have no abilities to heal, then **YOU** realize how being married to God makes it possible for you to watch God heal on your behalf." It means a servant is only as strong as his or her Master allows. An impure spirit is too strong for a wife to order out of a host body. It could leave one body and possess the one acting as God, without God's approval. Evil spirits can only be removed by God, making serious prayer necessary for a wife of God, in order to call upon God for another's behalf.

The disciples were just like anyone who wants to be filled with the Holy Spirit. They were like everyone who can claim, "I have seen the Holy Spirit work through me!"

But, they, and others like them, were not quite there yet. None were yet at the point of crossing home plate.

The potential is there … just as a dater has the potential to make a deeper commitment to his or her date … but that potential only comes to fruition when the two say, "I do."

Therefore, the disciples were arguing among themselves about who was greatest, because Jesus had just told them for the second time, "I am going to be killed." Because Jesus had commissioned the twelve to heal in his name, they had been ordered to go and do marvelous things (such as healing and casting out demons). So, they were trying to figure out who would be the next leader … once Jesus was dead.

Because they were not yet permanently married to God, so they did not yet know how their future meant ALL of them would be equally great, with a commission to make many others equally great, showing believers how to be engaged to God and married by the powers of the Holy Spirit, they were at the stage of which James wrote.

James said, "You do not have, because you do not ask. You ask and do not receive, because you ask wrongly, in order to spend what you get on your pleasures."

It pleases some "Christians" to ask for equal pay, equal rights to have sex with whomever they please, as if they are the husband who will have God bless adulterous unions, as if God were submissive to them. But, it is wrong to ask for selfish things; and, it is wrong to think you know anything without deep prayer.

To stop the arguing among his followers, Mark said Jesus "sat down, called the twelve, and said to them, 'Whoever wants to be first must be last of all and servant of all.'"

Willing, loving slaves make the most capable wives for God.

Then Jesus used a child (a relative of the group's family) to symbolize everything. With a little child among them, Jesus said, "Whoever welcomes one such child in my name, welcomes me, and whoever welcomes me welcomes not me but the one who sent me."

That means: "If you welcome becoming a reborn child, one named Jesus, then you believe Jesus is truly the Messiah." That says you believe Jesus is the Son of God.

Still, it says, "If you believe Jesus is the Christ, then you marry the Father, who will take you as His wife. Together, within you will be created that reborn child named Jesus."

Jesus told them that he would be just another human being, if he had not married God and been filled with the Holy Spirit permanently. Jesus was a child bride, dedicated at birth; and, likewise, anyone who sought that child within could obtain it through being a capable wife to the Lord.

It is the same song, different verse. It is stated by Jesus repeatedly in many different metaphors and symbolic gestures found throughout the Gospels.

We each have to become Jesus reborn, so (as David sang) we can proclaim, "Happy are they who have not walked in the counsel of the wicked."

The wicked love to argue and dispute. They love to make everyone equal by the stroke of a man-made law, regardless of how many are treated unequally by such words.

The wicked loved to destroy the concept of marriage and traditional values, so that children are taught confusion before they reach puberty.

We no longer teach the values of a capable wife to young girls, nor teach young boys the responsibilities of becoming a quality husband. We see the beliefs of the past as being obsolete … like manual typewriters, spools of ribbon, correction fluid, band saws, radial arm saws and planers.

The ways of the world are **not** the ways that lead to Salvation; but, we have been given free will by God, so it is left up to us to choose the path we take.

Do we show a "good life where works are done with gentleness born of wisdom?"

Or, do we choose a path led by "bitter envy and selfish ambition in hearts, being boastful and false to the truth?"

While the more difficult path seeks wisdom from above, we find that purity, peace and gentleness lead to a willingness to yield to others, which makes us full of mercy and good fruits, without a trace of partiality or hypocrisy.

Still, we cannot force that path upon anyone else; and many will misunderstand that intent and use those words of wisdom as spears of persecution.

No one is filled with the Holy Spirit by faith alone; and no one can force work assignments into incapable hearts.

Robert Tippett

Amen

# EIGHTEENTH SUNDAY AFTER PENTECOST

## Proper 21

## YEAR B

**Relevant readings:**
Esther 7:1-10 and
  Esther 9:20-22
Psalm 124
   Numbers 11:4-6;
   10-16; 24-29
   Psalm 19:7-14
James 5:13-20
Mark 9:38-50

Robert Tippett

# Hey! You! Get off of my cloud!

In late 2006, I published my book *The Letters of Nostradamus*. The subtitle of that book is *Realizing a Prophecy of Jesus Christ*, which was not only a statement to the world that Nostradamus was a true prophet of the Lord; but, it was also a statement of what I had come to fully realize about Nostradamus, from understanding his letters.

After the book became available on Amazon.com, I began to join in discussions in the Amazon book blogs, as a way of promoting awareness of what I had found. I entered the realm of Christian Books and found it was an ongoing battleground between Christian believers and atheists.

The dialogues on the various "threads" (topics of discussion) were hostile. Insults of every kind flew openly and often. In a category that would lead one to think only Christians would share support with one another, in a friendly atmosphere, the title "Christian" attracted nonbelievers in droves.

It became obvious how better prepared the atheists were at insulting the Christians and how angry that made the Christians. The atheists had read more of the Holy Bible than most Christians and they used that knowledge to belittle how Christians could not put deep thoughts into their statements of faith.

I entered thinking the Christians would appreciate my support, but quickly found that the name Nostradamus made me the target of ridicule and insults from both atheists and Christians. It was easy for me to argue against the lack of logic that atheists and Christians alike put into their judgments about Nostradamus, as neither knew anything of value about him and no one was willing to learn.

# After Pentecost Sermons: Proper 21, Year B

I am reminded of those days by reading in Mark's Gospel, where he wrote, "John said to Jesus, 'Teacher, we saw someone casting out demons in your name and we tried to stop him.'"

I was attacked because I would dare to cast out the demons of ignorance about *The Prophecies* of Nostradamus, in the name of Jesus Christ.

One Christian woman in the Amazon forum, whose profile identified her as a Filipino, would use all-caps as an indication of her hatred of Nostradamus (and by default me) by her "screams" that repeatedly told me how Nostradamus was a false prophet of Satan. She basically told me I would roast in hell for trying to get anyone to believe that Nostradamus was a prophet of Jesus Christ.

Meanwhile, most of the atheists simply belittled me for believing in a charlatan, someone they thought had surely been disproved long before. They then would turn and attack the Filipino woman's use of Biblical quotes - the arrows she believed would slay all nonbelievers - as the tools of the ignorant.

After a couple of frustrating months of defending my views and logically pointing out the errors of others, I stopped entering that environment. I imagine the same antagonistic rhetoric is still battered about there. It was a hostile environment then, which constantly challenged one's beliefs of faith, and I doubt anything has changed. The war battles on. [**Update:** Those forums no longer exist.]

The only positive conclusion that can come from such storms of doubt is the realization that one's beliefs of faith must resist the mightiest of winds; but, those beliefs have their greatest strength in times of peace and calm.

Since then, I have experienced more hurtful frustrations from family and friends, business associates, seminarians and clergy, all who have seen my views as repulsive. The difference is they have mostly seen it as too "politically incorrect" to attack me openly ... usually because I married a saintly woman. Instead, they take the path of avoidance and silent rejection, much unlike the atheists and Christian Book Forum Christians.

Few of the people I knew before I rediscovered my faith in God and Christ, through my understanding of Nostradamus, have shown support towards me. Other than my wife, none have put their arm around me and asked me to tell them more. When I urge people to please tell me what they think, they scowl and say they think I am wrong. The worst hurt comes from my Christian "family" treating me exactly as John of Zebedee did to someone he saw "not following us." Anyone on a different path to the same place must be his enemy.

Fellow Christians see me as someone to stop, just as the disciples of Jesus admitted they "tried to stop him," the one who was casting out demons in the name of Jesus the teacher and miracle worker.

That emotion expressed by John is why there are many different Christian denominations in the world today, each secretly or openly attacking the others, because the others represent "someone not following us." The attitude is: If one is not with us, then one is against us.

The most dangerous Christians are actually **not** the ones that hurl biblical arrows, with spit spewing from their lips from anger and fervent hatred. Instead, the most dangerous are those who silently plot and refuse to debate. Their minds have been made up, and they are closed to any ideas not taught to them in Sunday School. In reality, they fear exposing their weaknesses, because their faith is too thin to defend.

In the readings today, we have an example of this type of person, one possessing the same poor spirit of weak faith. It is a universal spirit found in people who say they believe in God, or say they believe in something like a god, or who say they deny any existence beyond the physical realm. That example is Haman, the plotter of evil in the story of Esther.

According to Abarim.com, the name "Haman" implies "Certainty, Noise, or Thought Police." With a name like that, he symbolizes one who is <u>certain</u> his beliefs are the only ones of merit. Accordingly, Haman plotted to exterminate all the Jews who had been brought to Persia, after Cyrus the Great overran Babylonia and freed the Jews.

While not read today, Esther 3:13 states: "Dispatches were sent by couriers to all the king's provinces with the order to destroy, kill and annihilate all the Jews--young and old, women and children--on a single day, the thirteenth day of the twelfth month, the month of Adar, and to plunder their goods." This order was arranged by Haman, after he had convinced King Ahasuerus (Xerxes I) to give his approval.

Queen Esther was the wife of the king; but, it should be realized that King Ahasuerus had many wives, with all of them called "Queen." Esther was chosen as his queen after his wife Vashti refused to appear before the king and dance for him. Esther was one of many who "tried out," because the king demanded a new wife.

Esther was the niece of Mordecai and both were Jews living in Persia. King Ahasuerus did not know either Esther or Mordecai were Jews, as that fact did not matter to him. Loyalty and service were more important traits of character to the king.

The plot by Haman, which King Ahasuerus had approved, fell apart when the king was told the truth – that his respected queen and an honored servant were both Jews – AND that many innocent Jews were to be killed, simply because of Haman's biased belief. Haman had planned to impale Jews on a fifty-cubits high pole, built at his own house; but, it would be only Haman who would experience that fate.

This is how God's justice was served. Queen Esther and Mordecai were gentle, peace-loving sacrificial lambs. They did not plot anyone's death but the boomerang effect caused the one who did wish ill upon others to have that ill-will come back upon him.

This is why Jesus told John not to try to stop anyone from casting out demons in his name, even if there were those doing that who were not disciples of his.

While not stated clearly in the New Testament, EVERYONE Jesus healed, who he touched by his presence, who he told, "Go. Your faith has made you whole," THOSE were the first Apostles, who did not need to follow Jesus as disciples. They had already received the Holy Spirit and were acting as Jesus reborn, even as Jesus was still alive.

In reality, God is the only one who casts out demons; but, God only does that through those who welcome God into their hearts and receive the same mind of Christ, as Jesus had. Anyone who would cast out demons in the name of the Son of God would be risking his own life if it were not the truth.

Jesus not only told John to leave the man healing in his name alone, but he added, "Whoever gives you a cup of water to drink because you bear the name of Christ will by no means lose the reward." That means John was told to support the man casting out demons, by giving him emotional aids that kept the man doing what he was doing.

Jesus was saying, "We are all family, as those who are committed to serving the One God. Welcome him as your brother and show him the support of love he deserves."

In a world that can often feel as cold and unwelcoming as an

Amazon Book Forum, where there are only two sides - the one for and the one against - Jesus was promoting support for a stranger who meant no harm and served God in the name of His Son.

James, then, gave an indication of how one "gives a cup of water" to one who already professes to be filled with the Holy Spirit - in the name of Jesus Christ. James said, in effect, "You send a prayer to the one casting out demons. You sing songs of praise to God, rejoicing that another one has been found who serves Him. You send prayers of support, as an elder, for the one who is being healed of demon possession."

Obviously, Amazon.com will never be the place to go for such moderation in a real-world Christian Forum. Not many "cups of emotional support" can be found from atheists there. Places like that are like those streams of water James wrote of, which flow forth both fresh and brackish water.

In our zeal to defend our beliefs, we can easily act like John of Zebedee and the other disciples, saying, "We tried to stop him." That rejection can mean the use of condemnations, sent hurling through the air like poisoned Biblical arrows. Fighting evil with Scriptural one-liners always finds an atheist with multiple one-liners that seemingly contradict what was first said.

When Jesus said, "Whoever is not against us is for us," he meant there were already holy prophets spreading the good will of Jesus. More were to come in the future, from unexpected places and in unconventional characters. People condemned wrongfully for expressing the talents of the Holy Spirit would be heard. They would not have their voices silenced by ignorance.

Thus, Nostradamus has remained a name on the world's conscious mind for over four hundred fifty years. Had he not written the truth, his words would have dissolved into nothing long ago.

James wrote, "If any among you wanders from the truth and is brought back by another, you should know that whoever brings back a sinner from wandering will save the sinner's soul from death and cover a multitude of sins." It is then important to realize the books of the Holy Bible are the "truth" and wandering from that truth means an inability to discern that "truth," or reject the "truth" that is there.

Christians, those who wear quivers of memorized Biblical quotes, are armed so they can sling condemnations upon other Christians and foes alike. They represent the wanderers in our world. They know truth is there but they have wandered from the purpose of truth.

The atheists, the believers of other gods and those possessed by demons, are those who are lost, wandering far from the light of truth that Scripture brings. Those who carry the truth correctly will shine lights that attract the lost to them, bringing the lost into the proper light of truth so they can be found.

Jesus called those wanderings "stumbles." He then said anyone who keeps people lost and stumbling will be drowned in a great sea of misery. If you know the light of truth, you **MUST** make it available so others can find the path to truth.

Jesus then mentioned three body parts that causes wanderers to stumble: a **hand**; a **foot**; and an **eye**. You should see this as representing one's lack of lending a helping hand to others.

It means not holding out a **hand** to help others, or extending a **hand** of peace. It represents the steps one takes away from God. It shows how a **foot** can so easily be put on the throats of those in need; and, it states how a **foot** is used to kick at those seen as in our way. It represents an **eye** that only sees what one wants to see. It means a **vision** of only one path to righteousness and **blindness** to truths others see clearly.

# After Pentecost Sermons: Proper 21, Year B

When Jesus said, "Everyone will be salted with fire," he meant Christians will be preserved (as salt was used to cure meats and fish) through the Holy Spirit. One's drive to act will be the fire that burns the sacrificial lambs upon the altar before God. All God's servants will be prepared as spiritual food for others to consume ... spiritual food full of flavor and essential life-enhancing qualities.

To be preserved is good, but to never become a burnt offering before the LORD is to lose the flavor of **the reason** and **purpose** the Holy Spirit came into one in the first place. If one loses that gift, no other gift can replace it. All other spices fail to compare.

Thus, all Christians are called to "be at peace with one another."

We must support each other, as we must love one another. We must praise one another for sharing insights we did not have before. We must heal one another's wounds of persecution, through staying together as "elders of the church" who are filled with healing talents.

Queen Esther and Mordecai were Jews in a foreign land, both of whom respected the Persian kings for freeing their people from slavery to Babylon. They chose to go to Persia and serve the king, while also maintaining their covenant with God.

They had wandered but they refused to be forced to stumble. They learned of a plot to have all the Jews in Persia killed. That was not by accident. Instead, they found out because their faith in God allowed them to be enlighten by God, for the purpose of acting to prevent that end.

They did not likewise plot evil upon Haman. They did not hate all Persians because one Persian hated them. They prayed for favor from King Ahasuerus, whom Esther and Mordecai had served faithfully.

King Ahasuerus was not a Jew, meaning he did not <u>follow</u> their religious ways … but by siding with Esther and Mordecai he was not against them. He was for them.

The yearly Jewish holiday known as Purim was ordered by King Ahasuerus … a Persian. We read how Haman's plan for sorrow and mourning was turned into a holiday of gladness, when "sending gifts of food to one another and presents to the poor" would forever be remembered.

The "someone" John reported seeing casting out demons was probably someone affected by coming in contact with Jesus, who Jesus then sent out into the world, after their faith had healed their stumbling block.

John of Zebedee would be another "someone" who would be found no longer following Jesus, after Jesus had Ascended. John would be leading others who followed him, to likewise cast out demons in the name of Jesus Christ.

Nostradamus was yet another "someone" who the Holy Spirit fell upon, causing him to cast out the demons that were not yet endangering the world, but those to come. That future evil would be made possible by those whose masters always plague the wandering and stumbling minds of human beings.

My ears were allowed to hear that message cast by Nostradamus; and, because I listened and did not try to stop the voice of Nostradamus, I have been also shown the light of Scripture.

I, therefore, am just one more "someone" who is trying to cast out demons with truth and light, which has been given to me like food from heaven, intended to be shared with others, as presents to the poor.

Christianity represents a continual feast of Purim, where a second chance at life means to be reborn as Jesus.

Therefore, we must all realize this world is too big for any of us to control more of it than the small space we each take up. God is who we must serve, as individuals and as supportive collectives. Praise God and pray for God to use you properly.

As Jesus said, "Have salt in yourselves, and be at peace with one another."

After all, whoever is not against us is for us.

Amen

# NINETEENTH SUNDAY AFTER PENTECOST

## Proper 22

## YEAR B

**Relevant readings:**
Job 1:1, Job 2:1-10
Psalm 26
   Genesis 2:18-24
   Psalm 8
Hebrews 1:1-4 and
   Hebrews 2:5-12
Mark 10:2-16

After Pentecost Sermons: Proper 22, Year B

# Let the little children come to me

My mother raised me alone. I cannot remember ever having my father be part of my home life.

My parents were separated ... originally because my father was in the military and stationed in Germany. He met a woman while in the military, whom he preferred to be with more than my mother, his wife. So, he asked my mother for a divorce.

My mother refused to grant my father a divorce; but, because a legally separated couple no longer needed such permission after seven years apart, my parents were officially divorced when I was seven years old.

My mother received the news in the mail.

A while back, after my mother passed away and as I was going through all her belonging, my wife and I came across some letters my mother wrote.

The letters were not officially sent to anyone that I know of. They were more like loose pages in a diary. She lamented being a divorced woman; and, in one she cried out that she would have endured harsh beatings by my father's hands, if that would have kept the two married and together.

My mother never remarried; and, I now know that she did not believe in divorce ... because she did not want to be judged to be an adulterer. She did not want others to think she left her husband for another man.

I imagine today's Gospel reading from Mark (and that from Matthew 19) is where she developed that belief. That is how it sounds, when Jesus privately told his disciples, "Whoever divorces his wife and marries another commits adultery against her; and if she divorces her husband and marries another, she commits adultery."

This is where it becomes important to understand the difference between a couple developing "hardness of heart" ... desiring to find someone who will open their hearts again ... and someone like King Solomon, who had many wives, but no known divorces.

Last week we read from the Book of Esther, who was one of many queens to King Ahasuerus. While we did not read the part that said the king had not called upon Esther for over thirty days, we need to see how the king's heart had wandered onto other queens. Perhaps, the king's heart had sought someone newer or someone younger?

Still, King Ahasuerus had fond memories of Esther, who was still his queen. His soft heart towards her made it possible for him to grant her the wish that saved the lives of the Jews living in Persia.

There is no difference between a common man's lusts for physical pleasures and a king's. There is no difference between a woman's excitement from a man who sees her as desirable, regardless if that man be a handsome regular guy or a wealthy prince. All carnal desires, be them within normal humans or those born of privilege, are adulterous.

This goes to the root cause of the Greek word, "*moicheia*," and the Hebrew word "*naaph*," where both mean "adulterer." While the definition of both words is understood to mean (most likely) a man lying with another man's wife, one cannot miss the most basic intent.

One cannot commit "adultery" unless one is an "adult." Being "adult" means, "a person who has attained maturity; a grown up." That means one's sexual organs have matured and been activated.

It is the adult drive that compels two humans to have desires of the flesh. A couple cannot have children without having had adulterous contact. Thus, marriage is a result of one's adult lusts.

The sin of adultery is stated in Leviticus 20:10 as, "'If a man commits adultery with another man's wife--with the wife of his neighbor--both the adulterer and the adulteress are to be put to death."

By stating this sin as "**if** a man commits adultery with another man's wife," it can then be assumed that "adultery between a man and his wife" is not a sin. Further laws against sins of a sexual nature use the Hebrew word "*shakab*," meaning "to lie with," which implies a more temporary arrangement than the permanency of marriage. This difference would imply that "legal adultery" is an on-going relationship ... like "playing house," which includes all the sex and kids part ... agreed to be for good and for bad. Illegal adultery is like stealing, thus forbidden.

The most important things to know about marriage is it is foremost a relationship between a man and a woman, to produce offspring. Second, it is to raise those children in a stable environment that includes both natural parents (given neither parent dies).

Therefore, legal divorce, as allowed by Moses, assumes a child was never conceived. A "certificate of dismissal" is due to a man having committed himself to a barren woman, or a barren man is preventing a fertile woman from producing a child.

We can see how Abram and Sarai were together as a couple, attempting to get pregnant – committing the acts of adultery – but three times other high-ranking men attempted to take Sarai as their "queen," only to find out Abram and Sarai were an official "adult couple."

Because the two had no children together, Abram introduced Sarai as his father's daughter, which implied she was his sister and not his wife. She would today be called (one's father's) daughter-in-law. However, kings and pharaohs heard that, saw Sarai's beauty, and felt adulterous feeling about her.

Seeing this element of children, one can then hear Jesus quoting from Genesis, saying, "For this reason a man shall leave his father and mother and be joined to his wife, and then the two shall become one flesh," as pointing out how that is a two-step process.

   1. Grow up and get married to one of the opposite sex, for the purpose of being like father and mother.

   2. Have a baby (or many).

When two "become one flesh," one has entered the realm of genetics. This means every child born is "**married**" to the DNA of its father, joined (or "cleaved") together with the DNA of its mother. While husbands and wives separate after sex, and while they can legally divorce, they can only truly become "one flesh" through a child.

A man and a woman having adulterous relations with one another creates the right conditions – the proper ingredients made available together – but that by itself does not create a baby. God is the one who directs a sperm to enter the egg; and, God is the mastermind that turns that union into a developing embryo – a fetus – a newborn.

Thus, when Jesus said, "What God has joined together, let no one separate," that is minimally a directive against abortion. The child is a miracle of God. Jesus is the Son of God, the Messiah. Therefore, when Jesus told his disciples, "Let the children come to me; do not stop them; for it is to such as these that the kingdom of God belongs," the deeper meaning says, "Children are pure and without sin. Let all cleansed and reborn adults become children who replicate me in themselves. Do not stop them from God's hand transforming them who will be joined in my name; as the kingdom of God can only be reached via this marriage."

By seeing this, one can begin to understand the character that is Job. If you look closely, then you can see how Job was Jesus, well before Jesus was born.

To fully grasp that, one has to see how the epistle to the Hebrews says, "It was fitting that God … in bringing many children to glory, should make the pioneer of their salvation perfect through sufferings."

Job suffered, as did Jesus.

Thus, Paul wrote, "For the one who sanctified and those who are sanctified all have one Father. For this reason Jesus is not ashamed to call them brothers and sisters." That is like saying Job was essentially a brother to Jesus, just as Jesus is a brother to all subsequent male Apostles.

We sit now as brothers and sisters of humankind. We are called to be recognized as brothers and sisters of Christ, through the Apostleship of the Holy Spirit.

"God did not subject the coming world, about which we are speaking, to angels," wrote Paul to the Hebrew-speaking Jewish Christians.

"[God has] made them for a little while lower than the angels; [God has] crowned them with glory and honor, subjecting all things under their feet," wrote Paul, quoting David, from Psalm 8.

This means that just as God makes little babies to bless the adulterous unions of human males and females, God makes little baby Jesus reproductions from adult human males and females who **marry** God. **ALL** of those Apostles … just like Job and just like Jesus … were, are, and will always be higher than sinful mortals, but lower than the angels ... because they retain mortal bodies.

Thus, Job was one to whom Jesus would proclaim, "You are my brother. In the midst of the congregation I will praise you."

Jesus would praise Job, just as God praised Job to the *elohim*, which including Satan. He said, "There is no one like him on the earth, a blameless and upright man who fears God and turns away from evil. He still persists in his integrity, although you incited me against him, to destroy him for no reason."

To understand that last bit of praise, one has to see how Job was a brother to Adam. Thus, simply from Adam having been banished from a "higher than angels" status (in the heavenly realm of Eden), to one "but little lower than angels," as a mortal who faced eventual death, both Adam and Job were created by God. Job still maintained the integrity of being the Son of God; and Job continued that line of faith through the Holy Spirit.

Seeing how Apostles are born from the Holy Spirit, as a continuation of the lineage begun by Adam, through Abram, David, Job, Jesus, Paul and **ALL** brothers and sisters who are Apostles in Christ, one can then see how it was the marriage of a physical body to God that made those "babies" capable of being born.

Thus, the "wife" of Job was not a woman – like Eve after she fell for the serpent's trick – but the physical **body** that was Job. Remember, Eve was made from Adam's rib, where the Y-chromosome equates to Heaven and the X-chromosome to Earth. Adam's wife was XX, or fully material of Earth. Thus, the plan is for it always to be that a body of dust and clay (material elements) becomes the "wife" of God. For Job, that was his physical body; which, in turn, gave birth to the Holy Spirit Job, at the hand of God.

That means it was Job himself, as the **body** of matter that is completely opposite of the Spiritual realm, who spoke in Job's mind as Satan's influence, saying, "Curse God, and die." The "wife" of Job was his physical body voicing doubt, because of his physical sufferings.

That means when Job said to his "feminine side," his "earthly form," "You speak as any foolish woman would speak. Shall we receive the good at the hand of God, and not receive the bad?" Job was saying, "Get thee behind me Satan. Has my physical body not made vows with God?" Those vows included: for better or worse, for richer or poorer, in sickness and in health, till death does us part.

Interestingly, the name Job means, "Where is My Father" or "No Father" (according to some experts).

To grasp the symbolism of that name, one has to realize that Jesus' earthly father, Joseph, was in name only. The true Father of Jesus was God, just as was Adam's.

Regardless of whether or not Job had a human father in his life is moot. God was his Father, and only by one being born of God can one truly be "blameless and upright, one who fears God and turns away from evil."

Any lesser fathers cannot "make children for a little while lower than the angels."

In a way, the lack of a father in my life kept me from being raised by a mortal who would have been suffering from a hardened heart, one who could have blamed me for him being stuck with my mother – a woman he no longer loved.

My mother did not remarry but she married both of us to a church. She told me I would grow up and become a preacher. That made me be seen as a preacher boy.

I wanted to do that, when I was a child; but, once my body began to mature into adulthood, I divorced the church and became adulterous.

In many ways, I have been Job. In many ways, we all have been placed in positions of hardship, like Job faced … for no reason or no fault of our own.

Still, we cannot choose the righteous path alone. We need help. We need to become brothers and sisters of a lineage that is raised to the point of denying Satan's tests and temptations. We must be raised, just as Jesus instructed, "Pick up your cross and follow me."

Only the Holy Spirit of God can give us that strength. Only a test like that Job endured and like that Jesus spent forty days in the Wilderness passing can marry us to God and make that strength come forth.

We have to become divorced from our human roots and become reborn in subservient bodies joined with God, as the little children who have no adulterous lusts. We need to mesh our DNA with that of Jesus, becoming filled with the Holy Spirit and able to receive the kingdom of God as the reward for that commitment.

Amen

# TWENTIETH SUNDAY AFTER PENTECOST

# Proper 23

# YEAR B

**Relevant readings:**
Job 23:1-9; 16-17
Psalm 22:1-15
   Amos 5:6-7; 10-15
   Psalm 90:12-17
Hebrews 4:12-16
Mark 10:17-31

Robert Tippett

# Jokes about Heaven

I am reminded of a joke I heard a few years back. If I offend anyone by retelling it now ... perhaps you need to pay closer attention to the sermon that follows.

This is how the joke goes:

At the same moment, thousands of miles apart, a pope died in Vatican City, while a lawyer for a major film company died in Hollywood, California.

Both of their souls arrived at the gate of Heaven at the same time. Saint Peter was there to greet them.

Saint Peter greeted the pope and said, "Please, find this small hut as your place to settle." He then turned to the other man and said, "That shining mansion on that hill there is your new home."

After a few steps away, the pope turned and asked Saint Peter, "Brother Peter, excuse my asking, but why would I be placed in a hovel, while that soul gets such a grandiose arrangement?"

Saint Peter said, "Your excellency, Heaven has hundreds of ex-Apostles. However, this is the first Jewish lawyer to ever make it to Heaven."

&lt;pause for the laughter to die down&gt;

Now, before anyone walks off in anger or before anyone laughs so hard they might choke, let me say that this heavenly scenario will never take place.

In fact, a better way of truthfully presenting that joke – given my equal inability to see Roman Catholic popes as able to gain

# After Pentecost Sermons: Proper 23, Year B

access to Heaven, just as is any Jew who is not Christian cannot – let me change the characters to "a Pharisee and an Apostle."

That would take us back in time many centuries from now, when true Apostles were actually spreading Christianity to the world. But, alas, today's reading takes away all the humor of thinking any Pharisee could even get to the gate where Saint Peter awaits.

The closest the re-written joke could come to reality, based on today's Gospel reading, would be when a young man knelt before Jesus and asked him, "Good teacher, what must I do to inherit eternal life?"

End of joke there. Jesus had no punch line. He only spoke the truth; and sadly, the young man with many possessions "was shocked and went away grieving."

The funny thing (if you see irony as humorous) is Christians are no more likely to be guaranteed a space in Heaven (even a hovel) than was the rich young man. When (if ever) that dawns on Christians, those who think just like the young rich man, then they too will walk away in shock, leaving behind a trail of tears.

A better idea of what Heaven looks like to us mortals, who like to project our worldly existence as mirrored in Heaven, can be seen in *The Revelation* of John:

> "Then I heard every creature in heaven and on earth and under the earth and on the sea, and all that is in them, saying: "To him who sits on the throne and to the Lamb be praise and honor and glory and power, for ever and ever!"

Wake up people! Heaven is ALL about singing praises to God and Christ – here and there.

So, it is not easy to get to Heaven. You cannot get there by memorizing a few Biblical quotes or dropping a few bucks in the offering plate.

In fact, it is the Gospel truth that "for mortals it is impossible." To get to Heaven you have to do like Jesus said:

1. Know the Commandments.

2. Sell what you own, and give the money to the poor.

3. Follow Jesus.

The problems that come from that easy three-step instruction are three-fold.

First, Christians do not know there are six hundred thirteen commandments. The vast majority think there are only ten, with all other laws commanded by Moses to be only for Jews or so archaic they cannot be applied to these modern times.

Second, Christians think it is okay to only give ten percent of their yearly paycheck (not counting the IRA, 401k, investments and other capital gains, land holdings, houses, cars, livestock, slaves, and on and on) to a building called a church, run by employees of a religious denomination. Then, if they do give ten percent, they keep records of all charitable gifts and claim them as deductions on their income taxes.

Somehow they think that sidesteps "sell what you own."

And finally, Christians have come to think that "follow Jesus" means leave everything up to someone else to tell them what Jesus wants them to do. Thus, like sheep and cows move from one part of the pasture to another, because there is greener grass not yet grazed elsewhere, Christians will always love to hear sermons that tell them what they want to hear. They keep moving, looking for the one who tells them what they want to hear. They don't want to hear about being poor and loving that state of being.

The fact that so many jokes are made about Saint Peter at the Pearly Gates and about who will go there shows how little our society really cares about getting to Heaven. It shows why there has been such a decline in Christians over the years … and it shows why such a rise in atheism has occurred in response.

I was watching *Family Feud* on television the other night and one of the "fill in the blank" challenges posed (to 100 men) was, "Name something you hope Heaven has a lot of."

The first contestant answered, "Beer." That answer was on the board at number seven. The second contestant then answered, "Naked women," to which the host gave him a high five, saying, "Hell yeah." The number one answer then flipped over, stating, "Hot kinky chicks."

When that contest was over and they were flipping over all the remaining answers posted, number eight said, "Weed or doo-bage," meaning marijuana.

While that got laughs from the studio audience, the horrible truth is there are young Muslim men who are sacrificing their lives in a war against Christianity (and other nonbelievers of Islam). Young men are willing to blow themselves up, along with innocent victims, for the promise of seventy-something virgins waiting for them in Heaven.

Just in case you are missing the point here … Heaven is a place for souls. Souls are eternal. That means they have no need to reproduce. Thus, there is no sexuality, no intercourse, no desires of the flesh – no desires for physical-earthly pleasures at all there.

That includes beer and pot. There is no need to eat or drink or artificially get "high."

Sadly, in recent news, another mass shooting took place at a community college in Oregon. Today (as I write), news reports say the shooter considered himself as "not religious, not religious but spiritual" on an Internet dating site. Witnesses reported he asked his victims, "Are you a Christian?" A "Yes" answer got them shot in the head. A "No" answer, or no response at all, got them shot in the legs.

Also today, the Kentucky clerk who was jailed for not issuing marriage licenses to same-sex couples was reported to have received support – told to stand up for her values – by the pope, while he was visiting America. Now, with the pope safely back in Vatican City, "his people" say he never met privately with her and never gave her encouragement. After all, they said, he met privately with someone who was gay.

The butt of the joke in all this news (as I imagine many professional comedians have found it to be a steady source of joke material) **is** Christianity – at least as it is portrayed by Christians and non-Christians alike. The reason is people who call themselves Christians do not really know what being Christian means. That causes non-Christians to judge Christianity by observing people who are not truly acting Christian.

Christianity today – as a multidenominational hodgepodge of beliefs about right and wrong, good and evil – is lost. It has become the blind leading the blind, with Heaven not the goal.

That was basically what the disciples heard, which shocked them, when Jesus turned away the rich man and caused him to grieve.

"Who can be saved?" they asked. "Who can be assured of going to Heaven?" was the intent of that question.

Jesus answered, "For mortals it is impossible, but not for God;

# After Pentecost Sermons: Proper 23, Year B

for God all things are possible."

What do YOU think that means for YOU? Are YOU mortal or God? Is it "impossible" or "possible" for YOU to go to Heaven?

Before you answer those rhetorical questions, let me use Job, David and Jesus as our examples found this week, which shed light on just what it takes to say, "Yes. It is possible for me to go to Heaven."

Job, as we read last week, was afflicted by Satan, which was approved by God. God approved it because Job "was blameless and upright, one who feared God and turned away from evil."

Today, we read of a reply made by Job, which was to one of three friends who had come to visit Job. Since Job was covered in sores, he was seen as having sinned; but, he had done no sins. He was blameless and upright.

The three friends were the elders of the congregation that Job was part of ... if not their lead rabbi. As part of following the law, the three went to Job to plead for him to ask God to forgive his sins; but, Job had done no sins. He feared God, so he turned away from evil.

That is why we hear Job saying today, "Oh, that I knew where I might find [God], that I might come even to his dwelling! [Heaven] I would lay my case before him, and fill my mouth with arguments."

"I'm innocent, God!" Job would say.

As Jesus said, "For mortals it is impossible" to do everything required to get to Heaven. Job was a mortal; but, he was filled with the Holy Spirit, which made him blameless and upright, one who feared God and turned away from evil.

YOU cannot suffer the pain and persecutions of Job with a mortal plan in mind. Only the Holy Spirit can withstand that. Mere mortals would seek out the crutches and canes of material things, keeping them from achieving God's praise for Job.

David was filled with the Holy Spirit and became king. Then he broke the Commandments and suffered. His sores were internal, so no one could see them and banish him out of their sight.

His lament was, "My God, my God, why have you forsaken me?" which Jesus would quote as he died on a cross. That says how David felt just like Job … alone in his misery.

David cried out, just as the scene around Jesus' death would become a prophecy fulfilled, saying, "All who see me laugh me to scorn; they wag their heads, saying, 'He trusted in the LORD; let him deliver him; let him rescue him, if he delights in him." David's own guilt made him feel the Israelites saw him as a bad joke.

Job could have made the same lament as his friends blamed the blameless, rejecting his claims of having done no sins.

All three mortals (Job, David, and Jesus) were filled with God, so it was possible for them to withstand ALL that Satan could do to test their faith. Without that presence of God, they would have done like all mortals do, those who place trust in their brains to determine how much wealth they can keep from the poor and what sins are okay to commit, as long as they are hidden from view.

In the epistle to the Hebrews it is written, "Before [God] no creature is hidden, but all are naked and laid bare to the eyes of the one to whom we must render an account." That says your brain is no match for God or His Holy Spirit. To be filled with the Holy Spirit, you must submit your brain to God. YOU must marry your mortal body to God.

Paul then added, "We do not have a high priest who is unable to sympathize with our weaknesses, but we have one who in every respect has been tested as we are, yet without sin." That says all our sins can be wiped clean by Christ …

**BUT**, YOU cannot EVER sin again, once that cleaning … that Salvation … occurs. The marriage of YOUR body and brain to God produces the offspring that is Jesus, through the Mind of Christ. YOUR soul no longer serves the physical realm, as it must become totally prostrate before God and Christ.

This is why Jesus responded to the rich young man, after he made himself prostrate before the mortal Jesus, calling him, "Good Teacher." With that buttering up, Jesus then asked, "Why do you call me good? No one is good but God alone."

Jesus was not good without the presence of God in him AND Jesus' total submission to God.

The question then can be posed to the rich man, "Why are you **not** good with God?"

No one goes to Heaven but God, who has given freedom to all the souls filling dusty clay forms. Your soul must be rejoined with God. YOUR SOUL must marry God and make your bag of dirt tag along – but no earth ever forms in the Spiritual realm.

I often speak of the Big Brain Syndrome. That means we most often look at the stories of the Holy Bible and see ourselves as the "Good Teacher," and never as the flawed villains.

In today's Gospel reading, ALL OF US **ARE** that rich man who does not have God within. We do not allow God to **be** us because of material things and selfish reasoning.

ALL OF US **WANT AND EXPECT** to be told, "Yes, little one,

there is a place in Heaven saved for you."

And while that promise certainly is made, it requires a total commitment on every true Christian's part. We have to realize that when Jesus said, "Follow me," he did not mean walk behind me as a condemned mortal, moaning and groaning, while plotting what we deserve to possess ... even in Heaven.

Jesus meant, "**Be me**, after I show you what you can expect will come when you commit to God and become **me reborn**."

> "Let us therefore approach the throne of grace with boldness, so that we may receive mercy and find grace to help in time of need." (Hebrews 4:16)

Job, David, Paul, John (Mark) of Zebedee, and Jesus all faced times of need and God left them alone to die for their faith … with only the chord of the Holy Spirit within them. If you truly **NEED** Salvation, you must learn that it requires **much more** sacrifice than selling everything you own and giving the money to the poor.

You must begin to sing praises to the one seated on the throne of Heaven AND to the LAMB.

Otherwise, your religion is just another bad joke.

Amen

# TWENTY-FIRST SUNDAY AFTER PENTECOST

# Proper 24

# YEAR B

**Relevant readings:**
Job 38:1-7; 34-41
Psalm 104:1-9; 25; 37
Isaiah 53:4-12
Psalm 91:9-16
Hebrews 5:1-10
Mark 10:35-45

Robert Tippett

# Darkened counsel without knowledge

On March 30, 1981, a crazed lone gunman fired several gunshots, one of which struck President Ronald Reagan below his armpit, collapsing his lung. Ronald Reagan had only been in office sixty-nine days at that time.

In all the commotion following an American President being in intensive care for emergency surgery, the Secretary of State, Alexander Haig, held a press conference at the White House. During that event, he announced the news updates and said, "I am in control here."

In case you have forgotten your Political Science teachings, the chain of Presidential succession is: 1. President --> 2. Vice President --> 3. Speaker of the House --> 4. President pro tem of the Senate --> 5. Secretary of State.

The list goes up to a planned seventeen total, in case of a major disaster happening. Because Vice President George H. W. Bush was not dead, he was in line to succeed Reagan, had Reagan died in the hospital.

While Haig explained his words meant he was running the White House functions until the Vice President arrived, the mocking sarcasm that he immediately faced was akin to, "Who died and left you in charge?"

Haig responded to that criticism by saying, "I know the pecking order."

Of course, the sarcastic use of those words is based on the very true fact that when people die, then someone becomes responsible for tying up all the loose ends of the dead person's affairs. While presidents are so special the government has to plan ahead of time for deaths, officially stating who does what and when, normal people usually aren't that well at planning the future.

Raise your hand if you have ever had to deal with the Probate Court.

<look for raised hands>

My aunt died and left no children or husband to take over her estate. My cousin, who was the eldest child of my aunt's departed sister (whose husband was also deceased), was chosen to handle the probate requirements for her remaining siblings and their heirs. My aunt had ten siblings, but only she was without issue.

My cousin said she would never volunteer to take responsibility for handling such probate requirements again, because getting ten people – all scattered around the country and internationally – to sign legal papers and then mail them back to her was like trying to catch a litter of loose kittens and then get them all to stay put in an open shoe box.

While my cousin said "Never again," some people like being put in charge.

Remember the hall monitors in school or the ones told to take names if anyone talked when the teacher had to leave the classroom for a while? They always seemed to beam when given the role of tattletale.

Most people would prefer to just be left alone, without any added responsibility.

In the reading today from Job, we see God finally speaks to Job. It took God a while to make Himself known to Job … again. But once God spoke – in a way – God was asking Job, "When did I die and leave you in charge?"

By actually saying, "Who is this that darkens counsel by words without knowledge?" God was asking Job, "Who do you think you are to question me?"

In the words of Quick Draw McGraw, God said something like, "I'll do the thinning around here Job-a Louie."

Now Job had been a well-respected rabbi around town. While it isn't stated clearly to that effect, when God bragged on Job as being, "blameless and upright, one who feared God and turned away from evil," we have to be able to see how Job projected himself as a high priest of the best kind. Ordinary followers of the One God saw Job and knew he was righteous, without him having to go around telling people that.

However, when God allowed Satan to paint Job as a sinner, even though Job had done nothing wrong, Job withstood the physical pain better than he withstood the emotional pains of having lost the respect of others he once had enjoyed.

Last week, we read how Job cried out that if God would just come hear his complaints, then God (who Knows All) could confirm to everyone that Job had done no sins. Even if the pain of the sores remained, Job wanted God to at least tell everyone he had not sinned to be that way.

Now we hear God tell Job, "Gird up your loins like a man."

The esoteric meaning of "gird your loins" is "to surround yourself with strength." Here, it is important to realize that Job was male; but, we should not think that God would never tell a female Apostle the same thing. That is because being "like a man" is not a mortal gender thing. "Like a man" means "focus on the Y-factor of **Spirituality**." In Job's case it meant, "You have the Holy Spirit within you, so feel that power encircling you!"

Apostles all have their loins girded by God, the Father's Holy

Spirit, so they are "like Jesus." Jesus was a mortal male, but he was girded as "**THE man**" ... the Christ. The Son of Man.

Christians who find themselves bellyaching like Job can then expect God's voice to say to them, "Tighten up your waistband and be like Jesus."

That makes sense when we realize Paul wrote to the Hebrew-speaking Jews (Jews for Jesus), saying, "Christ did not glorify himself in becoming a high priest." That means Jesus did not walk around wearing high hats, carrying a grandiose crosier, with an entourage surrounding him that acted like a cross between Barack Obama Secret Service "red & blue light" escorts and Pope Francis in the Pope-mobile or his little black Fiat.

From this, one can get a real sense how Job was crying more for his lost ranking, as a high priest, than he was for his having been wrongly accused of having sinned – which he knew he had not.

When we read Paul quoting from two Psalms prophesying about Jesus, it is easy to miss David seeing those songs as relative to **his** relationship with God. God had said the same things to Job, in essence, because God bragged about him like a son and like a high priest:

> "You are my son, today I have become your Father." (Psalm 2:7)
>
> "You are a priest forever, according to the order of Melchizedek." (Psalm 110:4)

All Apostles – those truly filled with God's Holy Spirit – become Spiritual (Y-factor) more than worldly, thus, they are elevated as God's Son (as Jesus reborn). This is regardless of one's mortal gender, so Esther acted from Spiritual piety, not human wiles.

God is thus the true Father of those whom He has born as Jesus, taking His seat in His bride's heart (the X-factor mortal), begetting a new duplicate Apostle (Jesus reborn).

Once God enters into one's heart that eternal soul is rejoined with its eternal source, becoming the priest one was always intended to become ... forever. Thus, an Apostle assumes the duty of leading souls to the gateway of Eden, so they can become worthy of climbing the stairway to Heaven.

Once you see that Jesus did not "glorify himself in becoming a high priest," it is easier to understand why Jesus would ask James and John of Zebedee, "Are you able to drink the cup that I drink, or be baptized with the baptism that I am baptized with?" [Mark 10:38]

Although Jesus would forever make the passing of a cup at his last Passover Seder meal a repeated symbolic gesture in the Eucharist ceremonies in Christian churches; and, although Christian churches would forever make baptism by water [including Christening] another repeated symbolic gesture; AND, with those two "Sacraments," **symbolically** denoting <u>consecration</u>, <u>dedication</u> and <u>devotion</u> as **sacred** and **holy** ["Sacrament" coming from the Latin word *sacramentum*, rooted in *sacer*], the point Jesus made to James and John [Mark] was this:

**YOU** cannot drink the <u>blood of Christ</u> from a physical cup and **You** cannot be physically covered in <u>God's Holy Spirit</u> by bathing in the same water as Jesus of Nazareth.

You cannot be to the side – left or right – and feel Jesus Christ in your veins, knowing God is in your heart – as God was in Jesus of Nazareth – filling Jesus with the Holy Spirit and all the powers that presence of God brought him.

The fact that "the ten ... began to be angry with James and John" meant they all wanted to have special recognition, as they were all willing to do whatever Jesus told them to do ... including drinking from his cup and being baptized in the River Jordan [although that particular water Jesus stood in had long ago flowed downstream].

They all wanted [in the words of Paul's epistle to the Jews of Rome, who were Christians], "to be glorified as those closest to a Temple-born-like high priest," with all the special recognition that came with that.

They wanted what Job felt he had lost: **respect**. And, the disciples probably wanted some of the perks that came with that too.

The disciples still could not shake themselves out of their culturally bred minds, thinking how respect went hand-in-hand with one's personal wealth and power ... like that rich, young Pharisee had - the one Jesus had just sent away grieving. The disciples thought the Pharisee's wealth was due to God rewarding him for all the legal memorizing he had done AND they were okay with that.

We still cater to such views of outward appearances: Clothes make the man; Express your love with a diamond; and, the Face of success.

By being seated to the left and right of Jesus, James and John would be KNOWN as close associates of Jesus. Thus, they would be "glorified by association;" and that is what angered the other ten, as they were equally associated with Jesus of Nazareth.

For that reason, Jesus told his whole group of followers, "You **know** that among the Gentiles those whom they recognize as their rulers lord it over them, and their great ones are tyrants over them."

Can you hear Jesus speaking to us through those words? Are we not Gentiles, since we certainly are not Jews for Jesus, with few of us literate in Hebrew?

Robert Tippett

We Americans love to gaze out at the world and point out the tyrants – Saddam Hussain, Muammar Gaddafi, Bashar al-Assad, Vladimir Putin (to name a few past and present). However, we fail to look at ourselves and see how **many** within our present society would judge George W. Bush and Barack H. Obama the same way … with hatred … seen as tyrants.

The candidates lining up for the 2016 election, from both parties, are casting insults and condemnations on anyone who would dare keep him or her from being Top Lord. They make promises that sound like, "When I am **tyrant**, I will \_\_\_ …"

Fill in the blank, because it is like giving whoever wins a blank power check, signed by your vote.

We Americans **here** today … us Christians … love to see the principles of our nation as identifying the USA as being of Christian birth. We love to have the motto on our money "In God We Trust." We love that the Pledge of Allegiance says, "One nation under God." Those words defend our wealth and success as having been granted by Divine Providence, so we **believe** we are led by Christ to bring the world peace, security – and above all – Democracy.

We take great pride in our system that has largely become a two-party government – Democrats and Republicans. Although not shown by past presidential elections, we allow other parties to gather and elect candidates too. Bernie Sanders, for example, is a leader of the American Socialist Party.

Still, we divide all the parties into the left and the right. Those to the "far left" and "far right" are said to be "extreme," while those closer to center are "moderate."

In essence, we pretend our politicians sit beside Christ, as those who love the glory of speaking for Jesus:

"Jesus would have us tax the rich and give to the poor!" say those on the left side of Christ.

"Jesus would have us protect the middle class so they can become rich and give jobs to the poor!" say those on the right side of Christ.

"Jesus would have us provide free health care for women through Planned Parenthood!" say those on the left side.

"Jesus would have us cease funding all organizations that provide abortions as a business!" say those on the right side.

"Jesus would have us stand by and allow the people of other nations to rebel against tyranny!" say the left.

"Jesus would have us send our military in to protect the poor downtrodden of foreign tyrants!" say the right.

Can you see how both sides of American politics represent typical "lording over" philosophies – **US vs. THEM** [just like the disciples of Jesus became divided when two tried to gain more authority than the ten]?

Is this not our Gentile nature showing?

If America were to ever be a Christian nation, it would become a nation of three hundred-million human beings **ALL** filled with the Holy Spirit. **ALL** Americans would then be Apostles girding their loins like Y-factor men, with no time for anyone to volunteer to play government. We would be changed to a Royal Christian Theocracy. Christ would be our King and we his Knights and Ladies.

Most likely, if a miracle like that ever happened, some well-armed foreign tyrant would try to take advantage of our nation.

All the peace and love here would project as a seeming lack of concern about international matters. Some might try to invade us, only to find out how the power of God protects us.

God would lead those against us to their own defeats, by their own weapons. Through their own self-defeats, perhaps they would see the power of true Christianity and willingly convert, so true Christians could teach them the truth. True Christian Theocracies could then spread around the whole planet.

Unfortunately, **IF** we became a nation where there were only 100-million true Christians (a third of the population), without a majority to take control of the whole, everything would be like it already is. The same false leaders who seek our votes today, those parading as possessing Christian values, they would drop much of that pretense and cater more to the majority. Promises would be made to Christians, much like promises are made to illegal immigrants now ... to gain a majority of an important "voting bloc" of citizens.

In the end, the same human beings would rise to lord over us – making the United States of America a reflection of the Gentile way Israel and Judah had become, under their corrupted rulers.

Just as God-fearing Jews were persecuted by the likes of Ahab, his queen Jezebel, and Hezekiah (*et al*), we would face more Constitutional challenges and new laws supported by the Supreme Court, forcing Christian Americans to modify their moral standards or forfeit their rights as citizens. They would, in essence, kill all the priests, sending the high priests hiding in caves, calling out for the Lord's help.

After all, true Christians are meant to be servants, not rulers. We would be forced to speak out against all injustices, as did Jesus; but, we would all be expected to be punished because of our faith. That would mean never running for political office ... as if that would ever cure the evil disease politics is.

Thus, "whoever wishes to be first among us must be the slave of all." A truly Christian government would be one where a name was randomly picked from a name pool, with the "winner" publicly apologizing for having to take on such a demeaning role. Still, that leadership would make the government a slave for the people, rather than the way it is now.

Jesus then continued, saying, "For the Son of Man **came not to be served** but to serve, and to give his life a ransom for many."

The Greek word translated as "ransom" is "*lytron*." It means, "as an offering of expiation or atonement." Its truest meaning in the context says Jesus came as payment to free slaves … the many who will always find themselves the slaves of governments and religions.

**YOU** become the same slave, when the Son of Man becomes **you**. **YOU** become one of the many Jesus has freed, those who have received the gift of **his** life … when you sacrifice of yourself and allow God's Holy Spirit to transform **you** with the Mind of Christ.

That can only happen when you stop trying to sit on the side of Jesus, pretending to have all the glory, all the piety of one who associates with Christ … on Sundays … some Sundays.

One who then uses that pretense to support political agendas the rest of the week, for the satisfaction of a sense of self-righteousness, at the expense of others who believe they sit on the opposite side of Christ.

**You** must become a reborn Jesus, twenty-four hours a day, three hundred sixty-five days a year, eternally drinking from the same cup of sacred vitality, forever immersed in the same baptism of the Holy Spirit.

Anything less is just business as usual ... darkened counsel without knowledge.

Amen

# TWENTY-SECOND SUNDAY AFTER PENTECOST

# Proper 25

# YEAR B

**Relevant readings:**
Job 42:1-6; 10-17
Psalm 34:1-8; 19-22
Jeremiah 31:7-9
Psalm 126
Hebrews 7:23-28
Mark 10:46-52

Robert Tippett

# He always lives to make intercession

A couple of weeks back we had to put yellow cones around the bus stop because of the trail of tears caused by the reckoning that it is impossible for a mortal to get to heaven ... especially a rich mortal.

Today the same limitations apply, but at least there can be some solace found in reading how Job had his latter days blessed by the LORD ... in what would amount to great wealth and comfort.

In terms of Zen Meditation, one could say Job reached Nirvana, as long as one knows that state is defined as, "A transcendent state in which there is neither suffering, desire, nor sense of self, and the subject is released from the effects of karma and the cycle of death and rebirth. It represents the final goal."

Job reached his goal ... but his goal was NOT to find wealth and comfort. That was a residual effect of his state.

The problem so many have today is trying to reach a goal of wealth and comfort before ever attempting to reach a goal of a transcendent state ... the state of Spirituality ... the state of self-sacrifice to God. The parable of the rich man who wanted to fill one more silo with grain before dedicating the rest of his life to God tells how upside down that rationale is. God called the rich man, upon his death, a "fool."

There is a saying for Zen meditators that goes: "As soon as you THINK you have reached Nirvana, you have already lost that state." There can be no sense of self in a state where the goal is to be removed from self.

Material things only distract one from one's spiritual being.

# After Pentecost Sermons: Proper 25, Year B

Now the last verse we read in Job today says, "And Job died, old and full of days." We learn he was one hundred forty years of age when he died.

Raise your hand if you know a relative who lived to be one hundred forty ... or if you expect to live that long.

<look for raised hands>

With the retirement age now somewhere between sixty-six and seventy-two, it would seem your silo would have to be full to the brim, in order to live off it for what would amount to another lifetime beyond retirement ... if you were blessed by God and lived to be one hundred forty.

I know there are people who doubt how Old Testament people – especially those in Genesis – lived so long. Some relate it to calendars that were lunar based, such that a "year" was not 365.25 days, but much less.

In my studies of Nostradamus' work, *The Prophecies*, his letter to King Henry II of France explains the lineage of Adam, up until Jesus. In listing those great ages after Noah, Nostradamus wrote, "*les dons estoyent Solaires*," which says, "the ones given are Solar ones." The meaning says a "year," as stated in the books of the Holy Bible, was based on the Sun's return to the same position in the sky – a year later. He then added no times listed in the Bible were lunar related.

Now I am not asking anyone to believe Nostradamus; but, because I believe Nostradamus was a true prophet, I believe all the books of the Holy Bible were written by true prophets. Therefore, I believe Nostradamus and the Biblical authors ALL knew that a Solar year was how ages were calculated.

This means Job lived to be one hundred forty Solar years of age

AND Adam lived to be nine hundred thirty Solar years of age. Because we do not see normal mortals live to such lengths simply means Job and Adam were not "normal mortals."

Job was much closer to the genetics of Adam – whose birth came by the hand of God in Eden – so he and his children had life spans more like immortals, than mortals. After the Great Flood, there was more interbreeding with mere mortals; but still, Abraham, Sarah, and Job lived much longer than we do today. They were closer to God than we are.

Jesus came to give us such closeness but instead of a "long full life" on earth, with lots of sheep, goats, oxen and camels, Jesus is offering us eternal life. That "long full life" comes by having God within our hearts and Christ in our minds.

Rather than a reward of long mortal lives, Jesus seeks those seeking spiritual longevity. Paul (in his epistle to the Hebrew-speaking Jews of Rome) wrote about this, saying, "[Jesus] is able for all time to save those who approach God **through him**, since [Jesus] **always lives** to make intercession for them."

Jesus **IS** our intercessor, which means it is most important to understand what intersession means.

Raise your hand if you have heard of "intercessory prayer."

<look for raised hands>

"Intercessory prayer" is understood to mean, "the act of praying to God for others."

If you noticed, God gave Job a long full life with lots of stuff **AFTER** we read, "Job … prayed for his friends."

Job had a lot of stuff before God let Satan strip it all away from him. After Job realized he was indeed sinning, and he repented

# After Pentecost Sermons: Proper 25, Year B

AND then prayed for his friends, then God gave Job much more than he had prior.

That reward came once Job became the intercessor for many people; and although the mortal named Jesus had not yet walked the face of the earth then, the Christ Mind, from God, through the Holy Spirit, made Job a living, breathing, replication of Jesus … as a representation of the intercessor who always lives.

That makes Paul truthful when he wrote the words "always lives," as "**always**" represents that which is eternal - past, present, and future.

Now when you see how Job was an intercessor and you believe Jesus is THE intercessor, then you see how their prayers for their friends were MORE than just having a list of people to pray for and trusting God would answer those prayers.

The example today of Jesus and Bartimaeus shows that Jesus was not praying for anyone in particular. He did not tell his disciples, "Be on the lookout for some blind guy named Bartimaeus. He is on my prayer list."

Jesus walked amid the people, so his prayers were for God to **USE** him as the answer to the prayers of others to God. Bartimaeus was praying to God for God's help.

When Bartimaeus got the attention of Jesus and Jesus called for him to come, Jesus asked Bartimaeus, "What do you want me to do for you?"

Bartimaeus' answer was, "Let me see again."

In the words that Jesus spoke to the Pharisees about their blindness – "Do you have eyes but fail to see" – the same could have been said of Bartimaeus. He had been able to see, but at some time sin clouded his vision and he became shunned as a sinner

... reduced to begging.

We have to see the parallel of Bartimaeus and Job. In Job's case, his "blindness" was his inability to "see" the presence of God within him. When God finally answered Job's prayers for help, Job said, "I had heard of you by the hearing of my ear, but now my eye sees you; therefore I despise myself."

Bartimaeus had heard of Jesus of Nazareth being in the crowd that walked past him on the Jericho road. He cried out, "Jesus, Son of David, have mercy on me!"

Bartimaeus' name means "Son of Timaeus." Timaeus (depending on what vowels are read between the consonants) either means "Highly Prized" and "Of Honor" or "Unclean One," "Uncleanness." This makes Bartimaeus a "Son of Job," who was both honored as blameless and upright, but unclean once Satan cursed him with sores.

That "Son of Job" was calling out to Jesus as the "Son of David," as the "Beloved Son," recreating the story of Job that is read today.

When we read Job crying out, "I have uttered what I did not understand, things too wonderful for me, which I did not know," he was realizing God had always been with him, but his selfishness blinded him from that understanding.

Likewise, when Bartimaeus told Jesus he wanted to see again, Jesus said, "Go; your faith has made you well." Jesus did not give Bartimaeus faith in God, as it was already there.

Faith led Bartimaeus to cry out for God's help, just like Job's faith caused him to beg God for mercy.

That faith is where the true intercessor lies – within one's heart, causing one to pray for help, so one can help others.

# After Pentecost Sermons: Proper 25, Year B

Now that Jesus has left the world as a physical being, Jesus remains always to intercede in our lives through prayer. Our faith leads us to talk to Jesus.

As Job said, "Hear, and I will speak; I will question you, and you will declare to me." That was what Job heard God tell him.

We must listen through prayer, not speak and question God. We must hear the questions God places in our minds; and we must answer those questions.

We have to become the new version of Jesus. We do that by despising ourselves. We do that by repenting in the dust and ashes of our own egos.

Until our eye is opened to see the light of Christ, we are blind beggars by the side of the road, going nowhere. We crouch so that Satan waits at our doorsteps to tempt us to sin.

We must become the intercessor – the answer to the prayers of others – by becoming Jesus … going out in public and being accessible to those who are seeking God's help.

We have to understand how Bartimaeus immediately regained his sight because of his faith and he then followed Jesus in the same way that we must follow Jesus.

Bartimaeus did not walk the Jericho Road behind Jesus as a sideshow – and example for Jesus to point to, saying, "Look there and see how powerful I am. I healed a blind beggar. Show the people how well you can see Bartimaeus!"

No. Bartimaeus became a model of Jesus and became an intercessor of God, walking a different path where he would be led to find others were praying for God's help.

Robert Tippett

We are not to be priests who offer sacrifices day after day, first for our own sins, and then for those of other people – as would one who seeks to retain one's self as an outer reminder of faith ... as did the Pharisees and Temple priests.

We must suffer like Job and Bartimaeus, but retain our faith in God, always listening for when He will whisper, "Call upon Jesus, Son of David. Your sins will then be washed clean and you will be full of days as Jesus reborn."

We must be quiet examples of Jesus of Nazareth, listening for someone to call for us, so we can ask them, "What do you want me to do for you?"

Amen

# TWENTY-THIRD SUNDAY AFTER PENTECOST

# All Saints [Souls] Day - Proper 26

# YEAR B

**Relevant readings:**
Wisdom of Solomon 3:1-9
 *or* Isaiah 25:6-9
Psalm 24
Revelation 21:1-6a
John 11:32-44

Robert Tippett

# Everyone made or set apart as holy

Today is All Saints Day, also known as All Hallows. Today it is on a Sunday, because Halloween fell on a Saturday. That means All Saints is ordinarily only celebrated by a handful of women during Vespers service in a Catholic church the evening before. That is then followed by a lite crowd on November 1st, usually mid-week, when busy people are busily working. However, the nearest Sunday most frequently becomes a combo-day for All Saints and All Souls, since November 2 is All Souls Day.

All Saints or All Hallows is today.

All Souls Day (aka Faithful Souls Day) is tomorrow.

Election Day is Tuesday.

<pause>

Raise your hand if you attended Vespers somewhere last evening.

<look for raised hands>

Raise your hand if you passed out candy to Trick or Treaters last night.

<look for raised hands>

Raise your hand if you plan to vote Tuesday.

<look for raised hands>

According to the Wikipedia article on "All Saints Day," they report the possibility that the day is recognized because of an ancient Roman observation of malevolent and restless spirits –

# After Pentecost Sermons: Proper 26, Year B

which is more in-line with Halloween.

I imagine after such a frightful day of recognition, one would need time to reflect on why the whole world has not been overtaken by malevolent and restless spirits.

The addition of All Souls Day (or the Commemoration of All Faithful Departed) should be understood that there is a difference between a Saint and a Faithful Soul ... just as those two differ from malevolent and restless spirits.

The readings set aside for All Souls Day are different than those read today, which is why today's lessons are focused on what makes a Saint be distinguished from a Faithful Soul and why God has a need for Saints on earth.

In regard to this sense of mission for Saints, it becomes important to realize that the Eastern Orthodox Church routinely recognizes All Saints Day the Sunday after Pentecost. That becomes a direct link between Sainthood beginning after the Holy Spirit entered Jesus' disciples, forever changing them into apostolic Saints.

That change turned Faithful Souls into Saintly Servants; and, the root word that we English-speaking Americans read as "Saint" is "*Sancio*," the Latin infinitive meaning, "to consecrate , hallow, make inviolable, confirm, ratify, decree," with "*Sanctus*" being the particle bearing the meaning, "consecrated, holy, sacred; pure, virtuous." Thus, a Saint is consecrated by God as holy.

The word "hallow" means (as a verb) "To make or set apart as holy," or (as an archaic noun), "A holy person or saint."

It is, therefore, impossible to be a Saint or to be Hallow without God's presence allowing for that piety.

The first Saints were those listed in the canon (or list) of holy people in the Holy Bible. Of course, the Roman Catholic Church has since come up with a method for canonizing "confessors" – those who claimed to have the powers of faith, which were then publicly confirmed.

If one looks up the list of Roman Catholic popes, the first thirty-five popes were Saints. There were forty-eight in the first fifty, then fifty-two in the first fifty-four (Saint Felix IV was the 54th-pope, dying in 530 A.D.), but then only seventy by the time the first one hundred had served (Valentine served only forty days as number one hundred, in 827 A.D.). If you notice a trend, there is one, being less and less frequently were popes deemed Saints as time passed.

By the time the one hundred fiftieth Roman Catholic pope was named (Benedict IX, serving 252 days between 1047 and 1048), only three more had been added, raising the total to seventy-three Saints out of one hundred fifty total. By the time the last pope of the 19th century had served (Leo XIII, who served over twenty-five years, ending in 1903), two hundred fifty-six popes had been named and the number of saintly popes had only risen to seventy-seven, although several had been Beatified, or named a "Servant of God." That means the canonization process had begun for some, but then stopped after all documented witnesses to miracles had passed away and sainthood could no longer be confirmed.

While a chart graphing the frequency of Saintly popes would accurately reflect the rapid spread of Christianity over the first 500 years after Christ Ascended, where there were certainly many common Saints from which Saintly popes were then chosen, the decrease in Saintly popes does not mean Saints ceased being around.

Crusades and Inquisitions obviously played a role in Saints ceasing to be commonly found around Europe, as the Church of Rome focused on consolidating its hold on how religion would be taught to the people. That began what today is a misunderstanding of why All Saints Day would follow the Day of Pentecost.

The Day of Pentecost – to Christians – represents when Christ Jesus was reborn into faithful souls of God, through God's Holy Spirit. Because *"Sanctus"* means "Holy," that presence is what transforms one into a Saint.

From the reading in the Wisdom of Solomon, it clearly states, "The souls of the **righteous** are in the hand of God."

From that beginning, the season following the Day of Pentecost is termed "Ordinary Time," which does not mean "normal" or "usual," but "Ordained." From the Day of Pentecost ALL APOSTLES become SAINTS, as Jesus reincarnated and reanimated within other human beings. Thus, Saints are Ordained to serve God just as Jesus did. Jesus the mortal - the Son of Man - was an earthly Saint.

That becomes an awareness that allows us to see "**ALL** Saints Day" **not** as recognition of all the past humans who were saintly – having works of art depict them with halos over their heads – BUT that THE CHURCH of CHRIST – CHRISTIANITY – is and can only be ONE CHURCH that is made up TOTALLY of Saints … **ALL** Saints recognizes that EVERY true Christian is a Saint, filled with God's Holy Spirit, acting as a reborn Jesus, with the Mind of the Christ.

Of course, there should also be faithful souls surrounding those Saints, who seek to also be Saints. Thus, Solomon wrote, "Having been disciplined a little, they will receive great good, because God tested them and found them worthy of himself; like gold in the furnace he tried them, and like a sacrificial burnt offering he accepted them."

It is important to realize that gold ore is largely rock with bits of gold. The testing by fire removes all the worthless, leaving the 99.9% pure.

Such proving and testing is the necessary step towards transforming a mortal from a follower to a believer, from a believer to a disciple, and from a disciple to an Apostle – given the gifts of the Holy Spirit as the measurement of sainthood.

Therefore, David sang out the questions, "Who can ascend the hill of the LORD? And who can stand in his holy place?"

He then answered by singing, "Those who have clean hands and a pure heart, who have not sworn themselves to falsehood, nor sworn by what is a fraud."

When you sit alone and think about it … meditate on it … pray to God to understand it … a CHURCH can only fulfill its purpose to God and Christ by being **ALL** IN. A chain is only as strong as its weakest link. For the true Church of Christ, the weakest link is a disciple with no intent to become an Apostle - a Judas - a falsehood version of a faithful soul.

The world is already filled with evil, under the masterful influence of Satan, such that the only way to counter the ways of the world is to be completely committed to the ways of the spiritual – as Holy, as Saints.

Saints must become the beacons of light that attract both evil (the tests of fire) and the lost souls searching for light and truth. You cannot defeat evil through weakness of any kind, where "weakness" is defined as "human frailty." You cannot bring salvation to others who cannot see the miracle of your presence holding the Holy Spirit of God. They cannot see that by your proclamations but only by your actions without explanation.

We live in very challenging times (historically) because we have less Saints and more evil present. We then read from the end of *The Revelation* of John, when he saw the future that comes. John said, "I saw a new heaven and a new earth; for the first heaven and the first earth had passed away, and the sea was no more."

John was shown death, where the symbolism of "the sea" is emotional – where the great depths of ocean waters reflect the subconscious state and our deepest feelings for that which cannot be physically sensed … only spiritually and faithfully known.

Such deep faith "was no more" in this future told of by John.

Likewise, "the first heaven and the first earth" will cease to exist … as we know it today. When read through the filter of sainthood, one should be able to see how we separate the spiritual from the material and see that as the norm. Heaven and earth are two separate places, although Saints represent a convergence - the Trinity - where each Saint becomes "the Son."

We think people are born, they live and they die, which is the end of the earthly days and the beginning of the heavenly days. We think all souls go to heaven.

Solomon wrote, "In the eyes of the foolish [the souls of the righteous] seemed to have died, and their departure was thought to be a disaster, and their going from us to be their destruction: but they are at peace." We see mortal death as the ripping off of one's bodily sin, freeing a pure soul to find endless peace.

We see a very famous scene that reflects that vision of Solomon in the Gospel of John today. Jesus returns to Bethany to find family, friends and neighbors all weeping over the death of Lazarus. They could not fathom that he was "at peace."

"Jesus wept," we read, but Jesus is the Saint in this picture. Jesus is not some ordinary crybaby who is not fully aware of just how "at peace" Lazarus is. Jesus shed tears because he asked his closest follower – Mary Magdalene – "Did I not tell you that if you believed, you would see the glory of God?"

Mary Magdalene was a Faithful Soul through belief, but the human side of Jesus was moved to tears because being a trustworthy follower and believer was not enough for her to "see the glory of God."

You see that grace ONLY when God fills your heart and your eyes are opened as a Saint.

There is more to this story than Jesus being a showman, when "he cried with a loud voice, "Lazarus, come out!" Lazarus rising again was not some 'dog and pony show.'

Lazarus was dead; the end of his earth time had come. The physics of decomposition had already set in – "already there is stench because he has been dead four days."

However, the Lazarus that came out at Jesus' command was a reborn Lazarus – Lazarus the Saint.

Jesus said, "Unbind him and let him go," because what bound Lazarus was the death wrappings of an earthly existence. Lazarus was "let go" to serve God, through the approval of Christ, filled with the Holy Spirit. Lazarus reborn represented, as John wrote in *The Revelation*, "See, the home of God is among mortals … for the first things have passed away."

I recommend you contemplate that after your bus drops you off at your intended destination, as it is important to see how Lazarus transformed from a Faithful Soul – like All Souls who are drawn to the One God [YAHWEH] are – to being a Saint.

While we must believe the event happened precisely as detailed by John, we must also be filled with the inspiration to see beyond the normal and usual. We must be able to see how Lazarus was brought back to the earthly plane as a saintly soul ... through **REINCARNATION**.

I want to tell you a little story from my life as an end to this sermon, as food for thought.

I believe in reincarnation; but, I believe that reincarnation is taught in the books of the Holy Bible, often and in ways that require the inner voice to point that out to one. I believe Jesus was the reincarnation of Adam - as the "Son of Man" bears that meaning.

I have learned that the Cathar people – pious people of France in the Twelfth century – Gnostic Christians - believed that reincarnation was the failure of a soul to release from the material binds surrounding a faithful soul, so it could become a Saint. Failure to become a Saint thus denied one access to heaven, meaning the next option was to return a soul to mortal existence ... to try again.

I have long <u>felt</u> that I had lived before ... well before I knew anything about reincarnation from study. My "sea" of emotion made me **feel** that past beyond material record.

I am naturally drawn to the metaphysical, which is defined as the relationship between Mind and Matter, where the roots of Spirituality lie hidden in the first earth and first heaven realms.

I have studied metaphysical topics, such as astrology and the Tarot, and I have practiced those arts as an aid to others ... with good response. Yet, I have found it quite difficult to use those gifts of interpretation on myself.

I have to seek others to help me heal my wounds; and, often I do that through looking for signs, many of which come from unsolicited comments made in my presence. I feel they are intended for me hear, as a guide to where I can seek deeper understanding.

That is how I am.

I once lived near a major city where there was such a large population there was a sizable number of metaphysical 'enthusiasts.' That number made it profitable enough for an organized monthly promotion, which was advertised as a "Psychic Fair."

I never attempted to become a featured "sample," at this Smorgasbord of psychics, Tarot readers, and palmists, which included one astrologer, an "aura photographer," and various crystal and aroma vendors. I attended to listen for signs for myself. Still, I did not attend this every month, although I attended several times.

Now, I am not telling this story as a testimonial about "Psychic Fairs" or seeking "spiritual advisement" from people charging money for "readings." As the Latin saying goes ["*Caveat emptor*"], "Let the buyer beware."

I only use this background as the setting for how I received a needed message from God … one that I am still learning to understand … more and more.

The Psychic Fair was always in a large hotel, taking up the space of two meeting rooms, opened as one. The "readers" were lined along three walls, with the registration desk at the front door. Admission was $15 (to cover the overhead of the facilities), but one could purchase fifteen minute time slots with specific readers, for ten dollars. Above the registrars was 'the big board' that listed the readers along the top, and the time slots along the left. The event opened at noon and lasted until six, with each reader given an hour off for lunch.

Most times the readers were the 'usual suspects,' being the regulars who appeared each month. Since the regulars tended to draw crowds, their twenty slots could fill up quickly, causing many patrons to be lined up before the doors opened.

I always arrived late and my twenty bucks for two readings often had me waiting and hour to get one reading, with a couple of hours to fill afterwards, before my second reading. Again, I did not take anything too seriously; and, I always tried to not give any indications of what a reader might think I wanted to hear them tell me.

One day I looked up on the big board and saw the category listed for one reader as "Past Life." I had never encountered a past life reader before, and it was a new addition in the big board's category separations. That unfamiliarity probably was why she had few takers, with many slots still open. So, I paid ten dollars for the experience. I only had to wait until the next quarter-hour ticked off to get the reading.

The reader was a young woman, perhaps only twenty-one years of age. She asked me to shuffle a very large, thick deck of cards, and then cut the deck. After I did that, she flipped over a card that depicted a Chinese Emperor.

We both looked at the card and then at each other, with a pregnant pause of anticipation and hesitation. Then, the woman picked up a large hard cover book and began flipping through the pages until she found the one explaining the Chinese Emperor card.

Just as an aside, let me point out that one did not expect a paid sampling of a "professional" psychic reading to include "on the job training," with the "How to" manual being read as part of one's fifteen minutes.

Already slightly upset over the book being read to me, I interjected, "I do not have any feelings about having been Chinese in a past life."

To the contrary, I had told several close friends in my life about my feeling of having been German and French before. It was part of the strong feelings I had about past lives, but not something I shared commonly. I certainly had said nothing to that effect to this strange young woman.

After I interjected, she said, "Oh, no. You weren't Chinese. Your soul last left the earth plane when this emperor was installed in 1932." She then said, "You were German military in your past life, highly decorated and honored."

She caught me completely off-guard with the German comment, which I had felt and expressed to my close friends. I felt my fascination to World War history was related to having served on the German side. I had taken German in high school and college because of that affinity.

Then she hesitated and added, "You did not <u>need</u> to come back. You came back willingly."

"What does that mean?" I asked.

"You came back to find love." she said.

My time was up. This little novice of a girl blew me away with her reading. I have not forgotten that one reading, whereas I only have slight memories of most others ... insignificant readings.

What she said made so much sense to a man in his mid-life crisis, in search of female companionship ... physical love.

Then, after a few years led me to being able to understand Nostradamus, I was in search of a passion quest ... mental love.

Then, after a few more years led me to being able to understand Scripture, I was in love with God and Christ ... spiritual love.

Now, after a few more years of seeking to please God, I feel as if I have failed him because no one hears me. I see I am in love with being in love with God ... selfish love ... like we just realized was Job's limitation.

From here on out, I need to become like Lazarus, dead but risen, unbound of all the earthly wrappings that prepare one for death and blind one from seeing the ways earthly things make us stray from heaven. I need to be let go so I can find the love of the Holy Spirit helping others, as one with my soul ... sacrificial love.

We are here not as Saints, but as Faithful Souls. However, we all have either volunteered to come back to help God, evident because we are here today, gathered; or, we are running away from God motionlessly, faithfully rejecting to sacrifice ourselves before others.

The call is for Faithful Souls to become sacrifices - as Lazarus was sacrificed - because we need to find the love of Sainthood upon us.

We need to understand how Jesus speaks to us, saying, "Did I not tell you that if you believed, you would see the glory of God?"

We need to become a part of a real Church, one that truly is All Saints.

Amen

# TWENTY-FOURTH SUNDAY AFTER PENTECOST

## Proper 27

## YEAR B

**Relevant readings:**
Ruth 3:1-5 and
 Ruth 4:13-17
Psalm 127
 1 Kings 17:8-16
 Psalm 146
Hebrews 9:24-28
Mark 12:38-44

After Pentecost Sermons: Proper 27, Year B

# Houses made by the hand of God are constructed with flesh and bones

In an interview recently, presidential candidate Dr. Ben Carson was asked about his tax plan to help America and Americans. He said it would be similar to <u>tithing</u>, where everyone would be expected to pay the same percentage of their income and earnings.

The common perception of tithing to a Christian church is ten percent. That figure is based on the laws of the Israelites [Old Testament law], where landowners were required to give ten percent of their crops and livestock to the temple/tabernacle. However, according to an Internet search about where the ten percent figure came from, "Got Questions.org" gave this answer that expanded that percentage:

> "Old Testament Law required multiple tithes—one for the Levites, one for the use of the temple and the feasts, and one for the poor of the land—which would have pushed the total to around 23.3 percent."

Dr. Carson's plan [and all other candidates that would change the tax rate from the present 10% - 39.6% range, based on income brackets] would call for fifteen percent, which would be added to the tithing people pay to their churches. Since he has not yet been elected, it remains to be seen if one might be able to deduct the amount of religious and charitable donations from the income used to calculate a national tax.

I guess one way to ease all the headaches that are associated with taxes and monetary responsibilities is to take a deep breath, count to ten, and then say the word "Stewardship."

"Stewardship" is a word that sounds like a kinder and gentler way of reminding people about a financial responsibility.

Robert Tippett

"Stewardship" can be defined as "The state, quality or condition of one who manages another's property, finances, or other affairs." As Americans, we manage the property of America, so we justify paying taxes.

As Episcopalian Christians, we manage the property of the Episcopal Church [not to be confused with the United Episcopal Church of North America], which is specific to one property managed locally. Therefore, the churches make sure we get a card to turn in that pledges financial support, based on loyalty and a faith commitment.

We can even extend the "Stewardship" responsibility to each person's family. In that case, each of us bears the burden of managing the property of one's family.

What happens then, when there are so many mouths and hands in one family that the responsibility of paying twenty-six percent Income Tax (joint return), added to Social Security withholdings, state and local taxes (ad valorem, school & property), health care mandates, licensing fees, the monthly costs for public utilities (allowing the cell phones and computers for every family member to work), tax on gasoline, sales tax … tax, tax, tax, etc. … Where does one begin to calculate a ten percent voluntary tithing to one's church?

What if there is nothing left after taxes?

How does one respond to the hourly pleas for charitable donations seen on television … for our wounded soldiers, for our crippled children, for starving babies all over the world, for natural disaster victims all over the world … even for the poor in Israel who cannot even afford a box of Passover food?

This is where the Gospel reading from Mark has been used as a "Stewardship Campaign" reminder, by most (if not all) denominations of Christianity. It paints Jesus as saying, "put in everything she had, all she had to live on," for the purpose of casting guilt on congregations to give more than what feels safe.

Unfortunately, that is not the message. There is nothing material that Jesus demanded from any of God's children.

I have remembered previously, some time back, about a steward of a large church who led a Lectionary Class I regularly attended. One of the readings discussed one Sunday was from the Book of the Acts of the Apostles, where a man and a woman sold possessions to give to the church - Ananais and Sapphira. Instead of turning over all the profits, they decided to keep twenty percent for themselves.

When Peter realized that – a revelation told to him by the Holy Spirit, not by the rumor mill – Peter confronted the couple, one at a time. They both instantly fell dead.

They "gave up the ghost" because neither was ever asked to give anything to the All Saints Church Peter and the other Apostles were building. They passed out zero tithing pledge cards. They lied to God about being All In, when they were only eighty percent in. Because they died, the deeper meaning is they were not allowed to go and live eternally in heaven, as All Saints get to do.

I asked the steward, as he was shuffling off to his preferred seat in the nave prior to the main service: "Whatever happened to that "All-in church?"

He replied, "That didn't work out too well," and then scurried off.

That steward was (and I imagine still is) a lawyer, making lots of money. He gives more to that church than most, because he can afford to do so.

He is like a Pharisee, which was the unstated class of donors Jesus watched "putting money into the treasury ... in large sums," "out of their abundance."

The sad reality is this: Jesus never said anyone has to be a Christian. Being Christian is **a way of living**, not a club one joins and pays dues to.

Jesus never approved any percentage of wealth that anyone had to pay-donate-tithe, in order to go to heaven. You either are Christian or you are not. It is much like being pregnant, but there is no device that one can buy and use, to show to others and say, "See! I told you I was filled with the Holy Spirit."

Christianity boils down to one of two options: Christian or Non-Christian. Non-Christians are EVERYONE who is **NOT** ALL-IN, as far as following the laws of Moses and the teachings of Jesus of Nazareth are concerned.

That includes those of other religions, who serve other gods and lesser prophets. That includes all secular Americans, who serve philosophies and forked-tongued politicians. That includes the modern-day equivalents of Pharisees, who justify holiness based on amount of U.S. dollars pledged, not on a total commitment to God, through Christ.

The constant problem Christians face is so many want to believe it is okay to keep a little something (or a lot of something, based on just how wealthy one is) for one's self. That simply is not allowed.

If you recall a couple of weeks back, we read how Jesus told his disciples, "It is easier for a camel to go through the eye of a needle than for someone who is rich to enter the kingdom of God." (Mark 10:25) Same song, different verse.

After Pentecost Sermons: Proper 27, Year B

In the Acts reading, where Ananias and Sapphira "gave up the ghost" for thinking it was okay to keep a little for themselves, the same message applies. It means Jesus never said you have to give anything at all. He certainly never said to the crowd at the treasury, "Hey guys! Go back home and bring back more and be like the old widow lady there."

You can be Jewish and give like Jesus saw the crowd giving to the temple. You can be Roman and "give unto Caesar what is Caesar's." You can be like an American billionaire and buy politicians so you can pretend to be some god's gift to humanity. You can be a billionaire and make a big deal about having pledged to give away all your money … to some social justice organization … after you die

But, none of that makes anyone Christian.

From the perspective of one suffering from Big Brain Syndrome, one can read the lessons today as if one was a male disciple of Jesus, hearing him point out all the flaws of others. One can say, "I give to the church out of love, just as I give to my family and charities because I care about others." However, excuses that over-use the "I' word are often blinding.

The point is how often one fails to see one's self as part of the **crowd** in today's Gospel reading, as one of those "who are those contributing to the treasury."

One is also blinded to seeing any comparison to the <u>widow woman</u> who is impoverished. The story of Ruth is only thought to be for the church ladies, with nothing whatsoever to do with big burly, bread-winning male Christians.

Why can't people see a poor widow as Jesus pointing out a model character that leads Christians to truly becoming Christian?

If anyone who is a regular at this bus stop has a brain at all, one can recall how I have said the love poem of Solomon are about a **longing for God** in one's heart. The "good wife" is each of us – male and female – because God wants us as **His brides**. The character Esther reflected our role as the **wife of God** to help save others.

Today, we are **ALL** named Ruth, regardless of our gender; and, we are **ALL** widowed Gentiles, led by some inner voice to follow the path that takes us to the One God of the children of Israel.

We are nothing but Gentiles or widows without hope, grasping a few laws we memorized in our hands, saving a few morsels of Bible studies for ourselves … like the widow woman Elijah commanded to give him bread and drink, when famine had left her with only one last meal. She was waiting for death to come to her and her son, so she could be free of this world.

We lose hope if we do not follow the instructions of Naomi and marry God, as she told Ruth – a Gentile widow – how to be a "good wife." We ALL need to know the commitment that Ruth had, so that each of us can hold our newborn selves to God's source of nourishment in our bosom … each a new born Jesus.

In the Psalm of David, numbered 127, we sing, "Unless the LORD builds the house, their labor is in vain."

In the epistle to the Hebrews, we read, "Christ did not enter a sanctuary made by human hands."

**THINK ABOUT THAT!!!**

God is not in the business of hammering nails into boards, nor does the hand of God reach down as a cloud and slap mortar on bricks. No bell tower was ever placed on top of a building personally by YAHWEH.

While we read today that Jesus was "teaching in the temple," in reality Jesus spoke what God told him to teach, because Jesus had the Mind of Christ within him.  **Christ** was one with the body of Jesus of Nazareth, so that the human form of Jesus (carrying the Holy Spirit) entered into the Temple of Jerusalem ... a physical building, made by the hand of men.  Still, that building was not a **sanctuary** of God.

**WHAT DOES GOD BUILD?**

**WHERE DOES CHRIST SIT ON A THRONE, AT THE RIGHT HAND OF GOD?**

I assure you there is no physical address that answers those questions.

God builds us, after our daddies and mommies leave the physical supplies for human-building in the hands of God.  God puts each of us together and then fills that "building" with the breath of life ... as a soul extended from God.

**ALL** human beings since the Creation have been made by God ... in His image ... but simply being made by God does not make one a holy institution of God.

Jesus is the example of holiness.  He is the model to which all human beings seeking salvation must become **AND** that means becoming a widow to the material trapping of the world and positioning you to be married to God.  Your only option is to be reborn **AS A HOUSE BUILT BY THE LORD THAT IS NOT IN VAIN**.

From that marriage one then receives the Mind of Christ, from God ... as a wedding gift.  Thus, "Christ did not enter a sanctuary made by human hands."  Christ entered a body housing the Holy Spirit, from the hand of God.

The marriage of one to God means total submission of the self to God, as a wife pledges to her husband. The pledge is then reciprocated. That union then produces new life, which is one's self being transformed into a reborn Jesus. We are to be called *Obed* [meaning "Servant"] and held to the bosom of God's love for nourishment.

In order to feel confident of this message that repeats throughout the New Testament story of Christ and his Apostles, I ask you to re-read Hebrews 9:24-29. Do this slowlyl and, do that after prayer and meditation. Ask Christ to open your eyes to see the truth that is written.

Focus on verse 26, which says, "Christ would have had to suffer many times since the creation of the world; but he has appeared once for all at the culmination of the ages to do away with sin by the sacrifice of himself."

See if you can see yourself in that statement, as **one** part of the "**all** at the culmination of the ages," **one** of those who have and will continue to come **after Jesus sacrificed** himself.

Then, see if you can see **yourself** as the intent, "to do away with sin by sacrifice of **himself**."

The Greek word translated as "himself" is "*autou*," from "*autos*." The word can mean, "himself," but also "herself, or itself." The emphasis is more as a pronoun of "**self**." It reflects being "the same."

Knowing that, can you hear a voice leading you to realize that Jesus gave up his own "self" identity "to do away with sin," by that "**self-sacrifice**." Can you hear the call to make **the same** sacrifice as Jesus, by becoming Jesus reborn?

See if you can glimpse how Jesus died to cleanse us of sin by being the model that is repeated again and again, by us dying in

**self**, being **reborn** as Jesus.

Following the lesson of All Saints last Sunday, where the true Church of Christ only has members who are All-In, you have to realize that you are built by God to house Him in your heart.

However, **you** hold the deed to that building and it is up to you to decide what percent of yourself you let Christ control. Anything less than one hundred percent means you choose you being you, over you **becoming Jesus**.

The jar with meal and the jug with oil, which was all the widow woman Elijah found had … it never emptied, due to faith. Likewise, one can assume the widow woman who placed three copper coins into the Temple treasury forever found three more pennies when needed to make a tithing installment.

Faith in God will not let one down; and, the promise of eternal reward is much greater than anything this world has to offer.

Please … keep that in mind.

Amen

# TWENTY-FIFTH SUNDAY AFTER PENTECOST

## Proper 28

## YEAR B

**Relevant readings:**
1 Samuel 1:4-20
1 Samuel 2:1-10
Daniel 12:1-3
Psalm 16
Hebrews 10:11-25
Mark 13:1-8

After Pentecost Sermons: Proper 28, Year B

# Praying for rebirth

In Hebrew, the word "*El*" means, "God." We see that parts of many names in the Old Testament including that word, such as "Isra-**el**." That name is said to mean "Persistence of **God**" or "**God** Strives." Another is Immanu-**el** – where the meaning is "**God** (is) With Us.

Today, we read from the first book of Samu-**el**, which is named for a great prophet of Israel, prior to it becoming a nation with kings.

The name "Samu-**el**" means "Heard of **God**," where the reading states Hannah proclaiming she named her miracle son Samu-**el** because, "I have asked him of the LORD."

"**God** Heard" Hannah, so she named her son Samu-**el** as a statement of truth.

Still, the name Samu-**el** can be translated so it says, "Name of **God**," where the person named has a "Godly Name." In that way, Hannah blessed the LORD by naming her gift from God as being possible ONLY because he came in the "Name of God," to whom she prayed.

Samu-**el** was then like Jesus, in the sense that both were miracle babies, both were born to serve **God**, and both heard the voice of God speaking to them.

What is missed from this focus on the result of prayer is the character Hannah, the one who prayed. Hannah is a name meaning, "Graciousness" or "Gratuitous Gift." The definition of "graciousness" (in a Christian context) is, "Merciful or compassionate."

In this next-to-last week of the Ordinary season, where the practice of apostleship has now stretched twenty-five weeks, with a large portion of the lessons pointing a laser beam at an Apostle being the "wife of God," Hannah reminds Christians of their need to be "Merciful" and "Compassionate."

Then we see Hannah as a reflection of **OUR NEED** to feel barren, simply because we have not brought forth the "Name of God" from within our bodies, look at the "other wife" in this story of Hannah praying for a son – Samu-**el** – **God** Heard.

The "other wife" is Peninnah, whose name means, "Coral" or "Pearl." The other wife represents those who commit to God, but then see themselves as valuable because of that relationship. Together, they form a strong, protective reef, but one underwater and dangerous. As pearls, they are valuable; but, only when found, as they too are enclosed in a protective covering. They bear children, but they do not bear their souls in the "Name of God."

Peninnah represents typical people who call themselves "Christian." For that commitment … going to church, reading the Bible, and raising their kids in the same manner as they were raised … God rewards them.

Standard Christians earn a "single portion," as that which has already been sacrificed – Jesus of Nazareth. A "single portion" is like a smiley face sticker on a grade school project.

Hannah then represents the people who are truly "Christian," for they put forth a greater level of commitment to Christ AND God – deserving a "double portion." They not only believe in Jesus as the Christ,;they **sacrifice** like Jesus did, becoming a reborn Jesus.

From this view, we should see God as our husband, just as Hannah's husband asked her, "Why is your heart sad? Am I not

# After Pentecost Sermons: Proper 28, Year B

more to you than ten sons?"

A true Apostle of Christ is sad by **not** being the One Son of God. With God in one's heart, sadness is not having reborn that one son – Samu-**el** – he who comes in the Name of God, from God having Heard our heart's prayer.

Of course, by not having yet become the reincarnation of Jesus, one looks to typical Christians for support, only to have them act as "rivals," who "provoke severely." Jealousy has them ask, "Who are you to think there is more to being Christian than simply believing in Jesus as Christ?"

Christians like that give Christianity a bad sense of faith, which causes more and more people who feel deeply there is supposed to be more that simply the same old same old: no one allowed to question, with no one having answers.

They weep and stop taking communion, just as "Hannah wept and would not eat." Still, true Christians never stop talking to God.

The high priest Eli, who would later raise Samuel as a prophet, saw Hannah and thought she was faking her devotion, which truly came from being filled with the Holy Spirit. Eli had been around a long time and knew some things. He knew that many do fake devotion in a place of worship, for others to take notice. As a prophet and priest, Eli was going by the book that says the first judgment is, "Stop it! You're drunk on wine."

The Apostles heard that same rejection on the Day of Pentecost, when they were moved by the Holy Spirit at 9:00 AM. It was no different when Hannah heard Eli write off her lips moving as if she had gotten high on the beauty of a building.

Eli treated Hannah as if she were overdoing her emotional feelings for the ceremonial passing out of wafers and wine.

Have you ever heard a fellow Christian say how moved they are by the Sacramental Eucharist? Have you heard them swear they are filled with the Holy Spirit simply because of the moment at the altar, inside a church building?

Eli – a true prophet himself – would talk to them just as he accused Hannah of <u>pretending</u> to be spiritually uplifted.

You do not get filled with the Holy Spirit by simple presence in a building of sacred acts. That is pretense.

Read the prayer of Hannah again and see if you can be so committed to truthfully say, "My heart exults in the LORD, my strength is exalted in my God." If you can, then you do not need a sanctuary setting to feel that way.

A few weeks back, I pointed out how being married to God means you leave this bus stop and **long** for Christ, **pine** for him as your husband. You cannot stop the longing, to the point that you **pour over** the meaning in the books of the Holy Bible when away from church, and then **cannot wait to share** that meaning with others.

Does your heart truly "rejoice greatly and become jubilant in the LORD?" Does it truly "jump triumphantly" in your chest, as **DEEP LOVE** for the LORD … with or without crackers and wine?

It can be that way … if you do what is required … and receive an earned "double portion" of <u>sacrifice</u>.

Now, by seeing ourselves as Hannah, who is praying to bring about the rebirth of Jesus – who sacrificed so we could see the same need to sacrifice our egos [a double sacrifice] – we can see how we also should be praying to bring about the rebirth of Samu-**el**. We must pray to be transformed into one who is sent in the Name of **God**.

That transformation then makes us represent God. We become dedicated servants, just as Hannah dedicated Samu-**el** to service, under Eli. We stop being who we were and begin being who God plans us to be.

As such, we – like Jesus – also sit at the right hand of God, because God is <u>within</u> our being – not external to us. This is what Paul meant, as he wrote to the Hebrew-speaking Jews of Rome, when he said, "[Jesus] sat down at the right hand of God."

We **ARE** a temple unto the LORD, with His throne being in our hearts.

Paul then went on to write, "For by a single offering he had perfected for all time those who are sacrificed" … those who are sacrificed because of the single offering … those who sacrifice like Jesus, so they will become Jesus reborn.

Paul then quoted Jeremiah 31:33, "This is the covenant I will make with [the people of Israel] after [that time]," declares the LORD. "I will put my law in their minds and write it on their hearts. I will be their God, and they will be my people."

That is the meaning of Hannah, as the wife dedicated to God. It is why Jeremiah wrote the promise, "Where there is forgiveness of sins, there is <u>no longer</u> any offering for sin."

One sacrifice means no more sacrifices; but, **YOU** are that one sacrifice, BECAUSE Jesus died to show everyone you can only stop sinning by having the laws written on your heart and Christ in your mind … just like Jesus.

This brings us to the Gospel reading from Mark, where the focus seems to change and turn to stone and mortal temples.

Robert Tippett

You are the only temple unto the LORD that matters. God molded your development in your mother's womb, so you are the house built by God. Upon your heart and mind must the laws of God be written.

That covenant is only obtained through marriage … a deep commitment of subservience, based wholly on LOVE.

Once again, we sing the same song, different verse.

Christ must become the cornerstone of **YOU**. That will transform you into an Apostle, filled with God's Holy Spirit. What looks like **YOU** and what goes by **YOUR** name is really Jesus, due to the love of God and the Mind of Christ.

**YOU** must realize that "not one stone [of **YOU**] will be left here upon another; all will be thrown down." **YOU** will cease being **YOU** and **YOU** will be rebuilt as a Temple of the LORD.

When the disciples were with Jesus later, they asked him, "Why will this be?" Jesus said, "Beware that no one leads you astray."

Imagine yourself asking, "What's wrong with me as I am? Why do I need to be destroyed and then rebuilt?"

It is because your big brain gets bedazzled by great size and beautiful things, just like the "single portion" disciples were.

Jesus then warned, "Many will come in my name and say, "I am he!"

You will be fooled, no matter how smart your big brain is. You will fall for fancy suits, ornate buildings and preachers that tell you "Do nothing at all! I come to tell you Jesus died so you just need to put a little offering in the plate."

After millennia of big bad wolves taking advantage of the

religion called Christianity, leading people away from praying to be Samu-**el**, whose Name of **God** was Jesus, people stopped being true Apostles. A Roman Church built huge cathedrals and anointed high priests and national leaders as God-sent. The consequence was the world has been led so far astray that "war and rumors of wars" have long been upon us.

As it always will be in times of darkness, we should heed the words of Jesus warning, "Nation will rise against nation, and kingdom against kingdom."

"There will be earthquakes in various places."

"There will be famines."

Now, seeing that vision of the future of the world, see **YOURSELF** as the focus of those words. Can you see your "single portion" religion as drawing lines in the dirt, condemning politicians of "the other side," hearing threats upon your almighty authority over your own family and place of origin as reasons to war?

Is your position on earth crumbling and quaking?

Are you hungry for the way religion used to soothe the world … rather than inflame it?

 "This is but the beginning of the birth pangs," said Jesus. **YOU** need to be reborn, become a second sacrifice and receive a double portion. Otherwise, the "Pearl" that is this worldly version of **YOU** will be all there is of value. No mercy or compassion towards eternal reward can be expected, if you hold your light inside an oyster.

Next Sunday is Christ the King Sunday. It will end the Pentecost Season and end the liturgical year, B. Advent will follow … a new beginning of the cycles becomes Year C. Cycles that never cease, because people will always be called to STOP – LISTEN – HEED.

Year after year you come and sit in a pew, listening to men and women telling you, "Do what I say, because I speak for Jesus Christ!"

Year after year they tell you, "Do not worry. Ignore the rumors and natural upheavals surrounding you. We are saved."

It is time to tear down the old and let Christ become your cornerstone, as God rebuilds you into who you were intended to be – His Son … regardless of your gender.

To reach that point, **YOU** have to become engaged to God and pass the tests of sincerity. You have earned a single share of Jesus' sacrifice already; but, you lack the deep love of total commitment and personal <u>sacrifice of self</u> to God.

You have to decide if you are Hannah or "the other wife," Peninnah. You have to earn the right to add "*El*" to your name.

Amen

# LAST SUNDAY AFTER PENTECOST

# Christ the King Sunday

# YEAR B

**Relevant readings:**
2 Samuel 23:1-7
Psalm 132:1-19
   Daniel 7:9-10; 13-14
   Psalm 93
Revelation 1:4b-8
John 18:33-37

Robert Tippett

# Long live Christ the King!

Today is the last Sunday of the Ordinary after Pentecost season. Next week we begin the Advent season, when we read stories that prophesy the coming of Jesus … which we then address during Christmas.

Just as life is a cycle, the Christian calendar passes through seasons … periods of growth and development. We begin a new cycle with the Advent of Christ and we close that cycle with the last Sunday of Pentecost, which is also called Christ the King Sunday.

The cycles appear to be the same, repeating the same themes from a slightly different set of eyes … different prophets prophesying, different authors of important Epistles, and different Gospel perspectives on the life of Jesus Christ. However, there is a difference worth recognizing.

The Year A lectionary is followed by that of Year B, which is then followed by the readings of Year C. The differences symbolize the transitions of life, which parallel the stages of faith development.

As humans we are born, we live, and then we die – or as the Sphinx riddled: We walk on four legs in the morning, two legs in the day, and three legs in the evening. Human life is the same, with differences.

As Christians, we follow this same repeating model in the sense that we learn, then we mimic what we learned and then we own the lessons taught us. That normal progression then reflects upon the experiences of life that take belief to true faith. You can only have ownership through having proved something's worth and applied that worth to one's belief system.

# After Pentecost Sermons: Christ the King, Proper 29, Year B

Because **we** are not the focus of faith … God is … the cycle continues. We are supposed to be part of a spread, like the arms of a hurricane sweeping out from the eye, only as a gentle force - not destructive. As such, Christianity grows because there is the force of those who are truly faithful, who move forth to teach the beginning learners.

We are all expected to grow in our faith, just as children are expected to grow into mature adulthood.

Life goes on the same, with slight differences.

That brings us to the aspect of Christ the King, which is recognized on the last Sunday of Pentecost … when the death of a cycle is upon us. We need to understand "Christ the King" in order to continue the cycles of Christianity.

As Americans we have no firsthand experience of living under a king. To us, a king is **like** a president. To other Westerners, a king is **like** a prime minister or chancellor. To those in Eastern lands, a king is **like** a political party or supreme religious leader.

I remember when Jerry Seinfeld was being interviewed about the wedding of Prince William and Kate Middleton. He was asked about who the possible successor to Queen Elizabeth's throne would be. He quipped, "Who are these royal people? Who made them royal? Who gave them the right to be rulers?"

This attitude mistakes a king for one who is elected … as one who is chosen due to popularity … as one who is known to be the strongest or richest. To many people like Jerry Seinfeld, a "king" is one who has the majority backing of the people (or the most powerful segment of the people).

We can even see how this attitude was present when Jesus of Nazareth was being tried in Jerusalem, when asked by Pilate,

Robert Tippett

"Are you the King of the Jews?"

Pilate was doing his "stand-up comic" routine, when he asked Jesus (tongue in cheek), "I am not a Jew, am I?"

Just as Jerry Seinfeld could not understand what made the kings and queens of England be those simply by birth - because "He was not British, was he?" - Pilate asked Jesus if he was a king; because, if so, he best have the votes and support of a lot of Jews. Otherwise, Caesar's followers would destroy Jesus and his army of supporters.

Pilate was asking Jesus, "Who are you to make people think you are royal? Who touched you with a sword and made you the highest ruler? Who gave you the right to rule over people who want you dead?"

Now, Pilate was a Roman provincial governor of Judea, the "fifth perfect" there, serving under Emperor Tiberius. Thus, he was like all of us here (and even Jerry Seinfeld), in the fact that he was not a king. Still, Pilate did not want to kill Jesus and then find out he had stirred a hornet's nest by doing so. He had to test the claims of others by directly asking Jesus, because a true king would never deny his royal birth status.

He saw a king as **not** an ordinary kind of guy, **not** of common birth and origin. We are like that too, when we hear the word "king." As such, none of us here would ever seriously present ourselves as royalty, deserving of special attention and respect. For Christians, that would be an insult to God ... and no one wants to be struck by lightning.

When we rationalize that almost innate sense of commonality we all share that means we hear the words "Christ the King" and think, "That means I am a subject of Christ as a Christian and Jesus is the king who all Christians serve."

After Pentecost Sermons: Christ the King, Proper 29, Year B

Unfortunately, thoughts like that are misplaced and wrong.

We become Pilate in the Gospel reading, by making the same common error he made. The Big Brain Syndrome strikes yet again.

The wrong comes from seeing Jesus as an entity that is impossible for us to **EVER** aspire to be. We immediately shy away from being Jesus, even though we like to pretend we are Christian flies on the wall, watching the scene unfold. As those professing our faith in Jesus Christ, we would **NEVER** pretend to be the governor, Pilate; but we are forever rooting for Jesus to convince Pilate that he is indeed a king, only in heaven.

<in tiny, buzzing "fly" voice> "Pppppleeeeeease Pppppilaaaate, beeeeeelieeeeve Jeeeeeesuuuus" we cry out like the little voice in "*The Fly*" - Vincent Price or Jeff Goldblum versions.

But, Jesus **is** just like US, as a human being, mortal and made of all the cells of death that common people AND rulers all have. But, Jesus was filled with the Holy Spirit of God, thus his mind was filled with the arm of God that is **the Christ**.

Jesus was **not** the Christ ... **not** the Messiah ... per se ... as much as **the Christ** appeared in the form of Jesus. Jesus spoke the words of God, the Father, not the concepts, philosophies and ideas of the common man named Jesus, born in Bethlehem, raised in Nazareth, the son of a woman named Mary.

If you remember the movie *The Exorcist*, the priest called out the spirit who was possessing the girl played by Linda Blair - named Regan. When the demon spoke, it was not speaking the mind of the girl; it was speaking the mind of the possessing spirit.

While exactly opposite - such that Jesus was not possessed against his will, but born into a body with a holy soul completely welcoming the Spirit of Christ to inhabit him - just like the girl

Regan in *The Exorcist*, Jesus did not respond to Pilate when asked questions.

**The Christ** spirit spoke through Jesus. "My kingdom is not from here," said the Messiah of God.

That answer spoke the truth; but Pilate heard "here" and thought "Judea." He did not think "here" meant the earthly ... a concept exceeding the lands and territories controlled by the Roman Empire. Pilate had no idea that "not from here" meant "not from the material-physical realm," implying the speaker was from the eternal-spiritual.

Pilate could not fathom that because Jesus stood before him as a human being of common presence. Given the opportunity to place ourselves into that scene, where we would be the one before Pilate, we too would project the same frailties and weaknesses of a humbled human form. No one would ever see us as of royal birth.

Still, when we hear John write in *The Revelation*, "Grace to you and peace from him who is and who was and who is to come, and from the seven spirits who are before the throne, and from Jesus Christ, the faithful witness, the firstborn of the dead, and the ruler of the kings of the earth," we hear "Jesus Christ" and think, "Jesus is **THE ONLY** Christ."

Jesus is the earthly Son of God, as the descendant of Adam. **The Christ** is the spiritual presence within the body of Jesus, as the presence of God through the Holy Spirit. God is the totality of all that has been created, as the Father of all in heaven and on earth. The Trinity is when the Spiritual (God) is joined with the Material (Son), by the hand of God (the Holy Spirit).

That model means Jesus was the Christ host, just as the disciples would become duplications of the Father-**Son**-Christ Spirit union. That model means the Apostles became reborn to be just as

After Pentecost Sermons: Christ the King, Proper 29, Year B

Jesus ministered in his life. That model means we are also called (regardless of our mortal gender) to fill that position as **Son of God**.

We must feel the same emotion for God as did David, when he asked, "Is not my house like this with God?"

Our "house," as I addressed a couple of Sundays back, is our "bodies," as "ourselves" being temples unto the LORD.

We must then feel the emotion of the words, "[God] has made me an everlasting covenant, ordered in all things and secure."

The alternative is the realization that "the godless are all thorns that are thrown away; for they cannot be picked up with the hand; to touch them one uses an iron bar of the shaft of a spear."

When you sense that presence of godless thorns and know that the same godlessness would soon be wrapped around the head of Jesus, mocking him as an earthly king, you can then see why John quoted Daniel 7:13, saying, "Look! He is coming with the clouds."

That means the Holy Spirit of Christ is coming; but, he cannot be seen because he is hidden by clouds … obscured, unseen … as a Spirit.

Still, "Every eye will see him," which means all who are filled with the Holy Spirit will have human eyes that can see the truth.

As for Pilate and the godless, who are "those who pierced [Jesus]," rather than listen to the holy words Jesus spoke, "on his account all the tribes of the earth will wail."

"So it is to be." Either you become the **SON OF GOD**, connecting the circuit of the Trinity, continuing the cycles of faith, or you become "the godless," by not being linked to God.

We are called to be knighted as the Son, so we have been recognized as allegiant servants to Christ the King.  <u>We are called</u> to play the role of Jesus before Pilate.

We are called to sing, just as David wrote in Psalm 132:

> "Let your priests be clothed with righteousness; let your faithful people sing with joy."

We must all be priests of common origin, who have learned from our mistakes, who have become compliant from memorizing external laws set before us, but who have matured to have **ownership** of God's ways.

When we recognize Christ the King has a kingdom that controls all of our physical being, from within, then we will be clothed with righteousness.  Then the laws of God will be written on our hearts and our mind, through the Holy Spirit of Christ.

Long live Christ the King!

Amen

# Ordinary after Pentecost Sermons

# Year C

# FIRST SUNDAY AFTER PENTECOST

## Trinity Sunday

## YEAR C

**Relevant readings:**
Proverbs 8:1-4, 22-31
Psalm 8
  *or* Canticle 13
    (*or* Canticle 2)
Romans 5:1-5
John 16:12-15

After Pentecost Sermons: Trinity Sunday, Year C

# It is Ordinary Time once again!

This is the first Sunday after an apostle's "Ordination Ceremony." Today the newly "ordained" begin their true calling.

To be "ordained" means one has been: "Invested with ministerial or priestly authority; or conferred with holy orders; or decreed by virtue of higher authority."

A priest comes out of a program that is a worldly approval of that investment, conference, and decree. However, ordination following successful seminary study does not reflect that a school feeding graduates to a religious organization can ordain apostles.

No Church has the power to give the Holy Spirit to anyone. Therefore, apostles are not employed by the will of churches. No church advertises a job opening for just anyone to volunteer to fill.

Churches can only play a role in discerning the call of a priest, such that a "calling" is defined as "An inner urge or a strong impulse, especially one believed to be divinely inspired." The key words in that definition are "inner" and "divine."

The discernment of a candidate for ordination is to determine if the Holy Spirit is **within** one. Discernment can also determine if one simply wishes to be associated with a church because he or she thinks being within a building of worship places one with the divine.

There is a difference, which should be obvious.

In addition, it should be realized that only those who are filled with the Holy Spirit can truly discern what candidates for ordination are filled with the Holy Spirit. Therefore, the discernment process should not take long because "it takes one to know one."

In the readings today, these issues of ordination are brought forth. The proverb asks, "Does not wisdom call, and does not understanding raise her voice?" Paul wrote to the Christians of Rome saying, "We have peace with God through our Lord Jesus Christ, through whom we have obtained access to this grace in which we stand." And Jesus told his would-be apostles, "When the Spirit of truth comes, he will guide you into all the truth."

Wisdom, understanding, peace, grace, and truth are all words describing the same thing – the Holy Spirit. That presence of God within one's being **IS** the ordination to priesthood, as a true Christian sent to assist in the transform of others into true Christians.

Now, in the psalm we read aloud today – Psalm 8 – verse two sang to us, "Out of the mouths of infants and children your majesty is praised above the heavens." This too is a condition of the Holy Spirit's presence.

Still, more than seeing this as a miracle of children speaking in the tongues of the Lord, it is a statement of how us grizzled **old** adults ... far more advanced in <u>intelligence</u> than a baby or a toddler who barely speaks a language everyone understands ... **will become <u>like infants and children</u>** when we are filled with the Holy Spirit.

The Big Brain Syndrome we all possess will be healed and we will stop <u>thinking</u> we know some stuff, so that out of our <u>newborn</u> mouths will come wisdom and understanding never experienced or learned before.

If you have not been ordained by Christ to serve God, you have not yet allowed God to place his **grace** upon you – where "grace" means his <u>favor</u> or <u>kindness</u>, as a **gift** of his Spirit. If your inner child has not yet returned to the forefront of your being, the Lord's grace is still missing.

We cannot hear wisdom's call when we <u>think</u> we must learn how to be righteous. We cannot fathom the meaning of Scripture until our brain's humming becomes quiet enough to hear understanding's voice become raised.

Psalm 8 hits the nail on the head as to why Jesus called his disciples "little children." John wrote the Greek word "*teknia*," which is plural for "little children," but the use of "children" to adults implies a deep love for someone, as endearment.

That deep love figuratively stated is the inner child, where the soul lies. The soul is God's breath placed within flesh, bones, and blood – matter – giving life to that which symbolically is death. While the physical goes through many changed states over a lifetime, the soul is forever young.

The quest of our religion is to release our souls so they praise the majesty of God, from a source that comes from "above the heavens." Higher than the most distant galaxy detected by the Big Brained Hubble telescope – so high it is undetectable in any state of astrophysics – there is the throne of our Lord.

God calls to us from a metaphysical realm, where the abstract of "higher" is not limited to looking up. "Higher than the heavens" is <u>within</u>, where one's soul must invite God to come. That invitation is welcomed by God … desired by God.

Solomon's proverb says God's call of wisdom raises the voice that says, "To you, O people, I call, and my cry is to all that live." When we read "all that live" that is a freed soul that is no longer trapped within a material body … a body of death. "All that live" are those who have been saved and thus understand through the wisdom of the Holy Spirit.

One who hears that calling is then placed into a most holy discernment process ... one that is well beyond what any seminary can teach. Paul tells us what that process is.

Paul wrote, "We are <u>justified by faith</u>, we have <u>peace</u> with God through our Lord Jesus Christ." He then went on to add: "We also boast in our <u>sufferings</u>, knowing that suffering produces <u>endurance</u>, and endurance produces <u>character</u>, and character produces <u>hope</u>."

The word "justified" actually means, "to be made righteous." In printing terminology, "justified" means centering, so there is an equal margin on the left and the right. That meaning can then also be applied to "being made righteous by faith," where one becomes "centered" because of one's beliefs remaining within the boundaries of God's Law.

Our "faith" is therefore a belief in God and an understanding of the Law of Moses, to a degree that one diligently abides within the structure of that Law. Rather than 'hanging out' at the perimeters of the Law, where the Law becomes representative of city walls and tall towers that oversee the forbidden turf outside those boundaries, allowing one to see what one misses by obeying laws, one is "centered" or "justified" by adhering to a **lifestyle** that is based firmly on belief that following God's will is an absolute **must do**. One is then always within the boundaries of the law, even when confronted by sin's presence.

Of course, purposefully going outside the Law makes one a sinner – by definition – so "justified by faith" means a brain-led first step - to serve God by not sinning. To know sin is to know the **grace** of redemption from sin.

For Paul and the Christians of Rome, who were predominately Jewish, that first step meant, in essence: "Since we have all been devout Jews who <u>religiously</u> stayed within the boundaries of the laws of Moses, we have **acted** righteously, by Law.

# After Pentecost Sermons: Trinity Sunday, Year C

For us Gentiles, who know nothing of the Jewish ways, having only whispers of knowledge of what laws define what a sin is for a Jew, we have made the Ten Commandments our Law. A good first step towards acts of righteousness is then to follow those laws that we have chiseled in Christian stone.

Like a toddler who first finds its legs and acts by standing and taking steps, the parent stays near to protect the child from a fall. Still, the parent must let the child learn to walk by walking on its own. Therefore, once one has taken the steps that display righteousness by faith, then "we have peace with God through our Lord Jesus Christ."

The "peace of the Lord" is a "peace of mind," where the original root word in Greek, "*eirō*," means "to join, tie together in a whole." We are joined in our acts by the confidence of the Holy Spirit. Our **acts of faith** have won us a union "**with** God, through our Lord Jesus Christ." God brings us peace of mind.

From that <u>stance</u> of calm, where our little baby minds have nothing to add, which would confuse our thoughts and bring forth misconceptions about sins and righteousness if it tried to think, we can then "boast in our hope of sharing the glory of God." This is why God is **with** us – to share him with others. God's presence makes an apostle "boast," which means holding one's head high with God-given confidence, to proclaim **hope** is available for all of faith.

This boasting so others can find hope leads to persecution – "Who are you that makes you better than me?" is the initial and immediate response.

People who claim to have **faith** <u>react</u> with disbelief. They want to pick up stones to hurl at one proclaiming loudly … boastfully … "Listen to me! I have the Lord with me!"

We saw that last week when we remembered the day of Pentecost, when the immediate reaction by the crowd of pilgrims was to call the apostles drunks … filled with the spirits of new wine at 9 AM.

Still, the apostles were not deterred, as they had endurance. Each apostle gave more testimony of understanding, spoken by the Holy Spirit, through their mouths having tongues like fire. The Words of the Lord were burning hot and had to come out.

Peter's explanation of their ability having been prophesied by Joel gave them character … that of a respected prophet of Israel.

From that ability to see Peter and his apostolic companions in the light of prophets of the Lord, the people's hearts and minds were opened. They saw and heard the product of their words … words they all knew as devout Jews, but never knew like this before. Therefore, **hope** appeared before them like ripe fruit on a vine … wisdom ready to be picked.

Here … behold the fruit of the Word is ripe and sweet … so pick it as your own and savor the meaning as only possible through the power of God.

The ordination of three thousand apostles took place that day, as they grasped that hope and saw the acts of their faith had been seen as righteousness, worthy of the peace of the Lord, through belief in the Lord Jesus Christ.

They heard wisdom's call and <u>understanding</u> was raised within them. They heard God's cry being to all who seek eternal life through the Advocate of Jesus Christ. They heeded that calling and were ordained.

Those Jewish pilgrims found out what Peter and his Galilean partners had found out. They all found out what you too can find out. That is stated in what Jesus said to his disciples [paraphrased]: "When the Holy Spirit of truth comes, you will not

## After Pentecost Sermons: Trinity Sunday, Year C

speak your own thoughts, but those that you hear coming from within your heart; so you will speak what the Holy Spirit declares - whatever that will be coming to you."

Whatever it will be that comes out of a new apostle's mouth, you can count on it being for the benefit of others of faith to hear.

Faith alone is not enough, because faith without understanding serves God as a house of cards … a castle built on sand. Faith requires the peace of the Lord, through our Savior Jesus Christ, as the grace that empowers us to stand before any and all, boasting of the power and glory of God Almighty.

Amen

# SECOND SUNDAY AFTER PENTECOST

## Proper 4

## YEAR C

**Relevant readings:**
1 Kings 18:20-39
Psalm 96
   1 Kings 8:22-23 and 41-43
   Psalm 96:1-9
Galatians 1:1-12
Luke 7:1-10

After Pentecost Sermons: Proper 4, Year C

# What is a Christian's name?

We are now at the second Sunday after Pentecost, so the ordained are getting settled into their ministries. The lessons of this week shed light on the challenges an apostle faces, after speaking the truth to others has begun.

It is not to be assumed that Elijah, David, Solomon [for alternate Old Testament readers], Paul or Jesus were newbies as ordained priests for the One God [YAHWEH], as their devotion was always tested for weakness. The apostle knows this will always be the element of persecution that has been promised.

Still, persecution does not always come as a direct threat to one's being. Often, a new apostle will face the "Consuela effect" [named after the maid on *Family Guy*].

People claiming faith act like they understand what an apostle says, then they go about doing what they had been doing before.

Call that the, "That's Nice ... I Clean Now" type of persecution.

Another way that new apostles can find a low level of rejection is when so-called Christians receive the message an apostle gives; but, then (because the apostle is new and unknown) they become easily persuaded to follow someone else, who offers a different message. This is regardless of how amazed they were at the truth spoken by the apostle.

Call that the "Oh, I forgot all about you" effect.

Of course, the primary form of rejection of an apostle comes when a person professing faith sees the apostle's message as a threat to the stability of the way things have always been, so plots and schemes are whispered behind an apostle's back, which are not favorable to the apostle's well-being.

Call that the "Watch Your Back" form of persecution.

That was what Elijah faced as he and one hundred priests of the One God were all who were left in the Northern Kingdom, after Ahab and Jezebel plotted to kill them all. A man named Obadiah had helped those hundred stay alive, hiding them in two caves. Elijah left that safety and sought out Obadiah and told him to arrange a meeting between him and the four hundred fifty priests of Baal that Ahab had advising him.

The persecutors were to be directly confronted via a "my God against your gods" contest. The meeting was arranged on Mount Carmel.

It was like a "Cook-off for God" challenge placed upon the persecutors. Elijah presented a simple task for four hundred fifty priests to cumulatively have their god Baal do: ignite dry wood under a grill, with fresh meat waiting to be cooked up.

They could not do that. Elijah mocked their gods while they cried out feverishly to get Baal to come down from heaven and set the wood ablaze.

In reality, "*ba'al*" means "the lord," and there were many gods who the Assyrians and Phoenicians [non-Israelites] worshiped, such that Ba'al Hammon and Ba'al Zebub were only two names commonly worshipped.

Later, the "*ba'al*" title would be left off, so the god worshipped would just go by one name. One of those worshiped then (and still a huge lord followed today) is Mammon, who probably was originally called Ba'al Mammon – the Lord of Wealth.

Elijah and the other priests of Israel who had been hidden in caves by Obadiah served One God who had no name. We see that today when Jews speak of "G-d," not even pretending to say they can give a name to one who cannot be named. God told Moses to tell the Israelites in Egypt he was to be "I Am Who I Am," the closest translation of YHWH.

YHWH is not a good god's name, such as the "Lord of Money" is or the "Lord of Grain," the "Lord of Spring Rain," or the "Lord of Fertility." Jezebel had married Ahab and introduced the concept of a specific god for a specific need, rather than one overall god.

The Egyptians had a similar polytheistic belief system, until one pharaoh [Akhenaten, as Amenhotep IV] said, "We are only going to worship one god – the god Ra – the Sun god."

When Akhenaten died, his "one god" ideology fell out of favor and his name was wiped from the records, returning Egypt to worship of multiple gods, each with a specific talent.

Elijah might have teased the four hundred fifty priests of Ba'al to "Call upon Ba'al Barbeque to light your grill!"

This lack of a need to divide One God into many lesser functions is a major lesson that newly ordained apostles learn. That is what Paul warned the newly ordained of the churches in Galatia about.

When Paul asked them, "Am I now seeking human approval, or God's approval? Or am I trying to please people?" he was telling them he was not the Lord of the Gospel, such that one should put a statue of Paul on the mantel and pull it down whenever one wanted to pray to Jesus Christ.

That is why Paul said, "If I were still pleasing people, I would not be a servant of Christ." Paul, as a name, was insignificant. No apostle of Christ … no servant of the One God … can be anything more than the messenger of the word of God.

Anyone who was traveling through Galatia, stopping at one of the newly organized Christian churches, either spoke as a nameless entity speaking for God and Christ, or they came promoting themselves or another who claimed to be the Messiah of the Jews.

Paul made it clear not to listen to those **named** fellows, when he wrote, "the gospel that was proclaimed by me is not of human origin; for I did not receive it from a human source, nor was I taught it, but I received it through a revelation of Jesus Christ."

**Only** the Mind of Christ speaks through an apostle, as the voice of YAHWEH.

That included Jesus, the Son of Man, born of a woman … who was human like we all are … all sons and daughters of God as human beings. But, no words spoken by apostles [of any gender] come from a human origin, such that no sect of religious philosophy has figured out what Paul and/or Jesus [or Elijah, David, or Solomon] meant.

**Only** when the Mind of Christ has replaced the human brain can **ALL** understanding take place.

Thus, in the Gospel reading, when a messenger is sent by the nameless Roman Centurion, requesting that Jesus heal his ill slave, who did good works and was a worthy human being, the Centurion displayed great faith in the **God** of Jesus … more than great faith in the human being named Jesus.

The Roman Centurion knew he was in a position of power, a position that was and could always be filled in the future by capable leaders of soldiers. Any one proven as capable would then give orders and those orders would be acted upon quickly by servants to that master.

# After Pentecost Sermons: Proper 4, Year C

Jesus was seen by the Roman Centurion as nameless, as the one people talked about was simply a human being with close access to a powerful God. When Jesus gave orders, they too were acted upon quickly, but not because of a command given by the only person who could ever give commands. Those healing powers came because of a prayer sent to a most powerful God, just as a Centurion would send a request to his superior, in order to receive authority to act.

Thus, the Roman Centurion held great faith in the <u>truth</u> that was told by witnesses of a human being who worked miracles for God on earth. He believed Jesus would help others who were good people and also helped others.

Now, what is seen (but not seen) is how Jesus responded to the message of faith sent to him by an unnamed Roman commander, as a prayer for his slave, who was a good man, loved by many.

Jesus, we are told by Luke, "heard this [and] was amazed at [the message sent by a **Gentile** Centurion], and turning to the crowd [of Jews] that followed [Jesus], he said, "I tell you, not even in Israel have I found such faith." We are not told that Jesus **did** anything to heal the good slave. He only spoke those words as an apostle of the One God.

What is missed completely is Jesus was not in a land named <u>Israel</u>. The land named Israel was the name of the nation David and Solomon ruled, and it was the name of the Northern Kingdom, in which Elijah served. Jesus had lived his entire life in the Roman kingdom named Judea [under Herod the Great], later divided into the provinces of Galilee, Perea, Decapolis and Judea. Jesus never lived in a land named Israel.

That means Jesus spoke the word of God, such that God saw that land as Israel. Jesus spoke nothing to heal the slave because God's remarks instantly filled the good slave with the healing power of God's Holy Spirit.

It might even be that the slave was the one who influenced the Roman Centurion to become a Christian … as an apostle of God and Christ … who made it possible for an angel of the Lord to contact that Centurion, telling him to send messengers to bring the apostle Simon, called Peter, to him.

That Roman Centurion was then named Cornelius.

The point of this week's lessons for newly ordained apostles is that all apostles of Christ have the value of zero. Thus, through the law of arithmetic, $0 + \infty = \infty$. Any other value added to the infinite everything of God leaves only that value: $1 + \infty = 1 - \infty = 0$. Trying to retain the value of self (1) acts to negate the addition of God ($\infty$).

Thus, Elijah prayed: "O Lord, God of Abraham, Isaac, and Israel, let it be known this day that you are God in Israel, that I am your servant, and that I have done all these things at your bidding. Answer me, O Lord, answer me, so that this people may know that you, O Lord, are God, and that you have turned their hearts back."

That is why Paul introduced himself as, "Paul an apostle-- sent neither by human commission nor from human authorities, but through Jesus Christ and God the Father."

It is why the Roman Centurion prayed, "Lord, do not trouble yourself, for I am not worthy to have you come under my roof; therefore I did not presume to come to you."

It is why David sang the praises:

> "Ascribe to the Lord, you families of the peoples; ascribe to the Lord honor and power.
>
> Ascribe to the Lord the honor due his Name; bring offer-

> ings and come into his courts.
>
> Worship the Lord in the beauty of holiness; let the whole earth tremble before him.
>
> Tell it out among the nations: "The Lord is King! he has made the world so firm that it cannot be moved; he will judge the peoples with equity."

Perhaps we can see why Luke wrote that Jesus "was amazed" that no Jew had shown him "such faith" as that the Roman Centurion had shown.

Perhaps we can see how Paul was "astonished" that those proclaiming to be Christians, because they had been allowed to see the truth of the Holy Spirit, would then be "quickly deserting the one who called [them] in the grace of Christ."

We are no different than the Jews of the Northern Kingdom, who thought worshiping Ba'al was okay, even though Elijah asked them, "How long will you go limping with two different opinions?"

They did not know that Jesus would come and say, "You cannot serve two masters."

We read that but we cannot see how serving the 'Lord of a Weekly Paycheck' makes us limp along to the bank to deposit the check, when we know we cheated people in order to survive. We do not serve two masters … we serve **many** masters: I-phones, computers, automobiles, houses, and vacations at Disney World, on and on and on.

We call ourselves Christians when we are not filled with the Holy Spirit to the point that we recognize our value of zero. We have to have zero **ego** value to be Christians. We have to be servants of God – not self – to be Christian.

If any of you have watched the HBO series *Game of Thrones*, then you know that series certainly is not a place to seek religious guidance. Still, I was reminded of a storyline in that show, where a young Stark family daughter had sought out the temple of "the god of many faces" as a place of refuge. She sought spiritual powers to kill her enemies.

In her experiences inside the temple she was stripped of her ego, in a brainwashing kind of way. She was repeatedly asked the question, "What is a girl's name?" She <u>learned</u> never to answer with the name she had been known by, before entering the temple. She learned to answer, "A girl has no name."

If you look closely, you can see just how well that reflects the loss of ego that God and Christ require of an apostle – the likes of Elijah, Paul and Jesus.

The concept of "a girl," which is that of all who classify as "girl," is impossible to give a specific value to, such as one proper name. It would be egotistical to say that all girls are named the same as one girl. Thus "a girl has no name." A girl is simply a girl.

When one applies this to the question, "What is a Christian's name?" the tendency is to blurt out one's own name. "I am a Christian" is not the same as saying "YHWH Christian." It places "I" at the center of all that is Christian.

To see "YHWH Christian" as meaning, "A Christian has no name," by stating that "I Am Who I Am Christian," only God is of value. As such, all Christians are God speaking through human beings whose name is of no value.

To put this in words that Forest Gump's momma might have said: "A Christian is as a Christian does."

## After Pentecost Sermons: Proper 4, Year C

No **one** human being can claim exclusive rights to Christianity, just as the Stark girl could not claim exclusive rights to being a girl.

Paul said it perfectly, speaking from the Holy Spirit's guidance: "I did not receive it from a human source, nor was I taught it, but I received it through a revelation of Jesus Christ."

A Christian has no name that alone is representative as valuable, because only God has value that is everlasting.

Amen

# THIRD SUNDAY AFTER PENTECOST

## Proper 5

## YEAR C

**Relevant readings:**
1 Kings 17:8-16 (17-24)
Psalm 146
  1 Kings 17:17-24
  Psalm 30
Galatians 1:11-24
Luke 7:11-17

After Pentecost Sermons: Proper 5, Year C

# The miracle of life or the miracle of eternal life?

On this third Sunday after Pentecost when the new lives of the Spiritually ordained have gone out into the world to spread the gospel of Christ we see the same stories told last Sunday are continued this Sunday.

Continuation is a theme of ordination. Ordination is not a "one-shot wonder," given to a "one trick pony."

After Elijah won the cook-off contest with the priests of Ba'al, we see him again today – although in a "flashback" in time, to right before that contest came about. Today we see when Elijah came to know that the whole power of God was at his disposal. That firsthand knowledge of heavenly support - up close and personal - gave Elijah the confidence he would need to call out the priests of Ahab and Jezebel.

Last Sunday we also read about the beginning of Paul's letter to the Christian churches that he had formed in Galatia [Turkey]. Those converts had been sending signals that their faith was wavering, as others had been telling them to follow different so-called Messiahs. Paul called those false prophets, who would speak opposite of what the Holy Spirit said, liars; and Paul warned the Galatians how they should not be tricked into believing liars. The Holy Spirit only speaks the whole truth and nothing but the truth.

Today, Paul's letter continues to tell of his own experience with the Holy Spirit upon him, and how he did not seek out people who would follow him because of his prior (Saul's) reputation. Paul never used the sway of "I" as reason to convince the Galatians to believe in him. Instead, Paul told them he sought out Gentiles first, so they could know God through Christ, as strangers who knew little to nothing about a promised savior that would be sent to the Jews.

Last Sunday we read about how Jesus found the faith of a Roman Centurion amazing, so the Jewish slave of that Centurion was healed from an illness ... *in abstentia* ... from afar. Today we read how Jesus moved from Capernaum to a town called Na-in, where he felt compassion for a widow woman whose son had died. Jesus commanded the young man to rise and he was resurrected.

All of these stories are closely connected because they demonstrate how being filled with the Holy Spirit, as an APOSTLE of Jesus Christ, servant to God, is not some one-time thing you can tell people happened to you ... once ... a long time ago.

These stories tell of <u>continued</u> faith and <u>growing</u> service to the Lord.

Being ordained, as seen in these Ordinary Time lessons, means a lifestyle **change**, where the stories of God's glory keep on coming ... and never stop. Ordination means you stop "riding the pines" [church pews or aluminium bus stop benches] as a part-time "player" and take up a full-time leadership role.

Ordinary Time is when apostles are born and when they start being available for those in need ... daily and regularly. Going to church a couple of hours each week is not qualification for being ordained by God and Christ. A real "priest to the One God" constantly seeks people to hear him or her speak the word of God.

The Gospel reading from Luke today points directly to this willingly accepted responsibility taken on by a typical person of faith.

It is so easy to be a Christian bystander and not a true Christian. All of the churches left in Paul's wake in Galatia were not simply small gatherings of Jews and Gentiles who signed a document stating, "I will believe Jesus of Nazareth is the Messiah, because Paul said so."

The people left behind by Paul were filled with the Holy Spirit, because Paul came into their midst and spoke the Word of God in their presence. That voice fell upon hearts that believed, in people who feared God and onto humans who did good works. Those Galatians became changed by the Holy Spirit ... not by some passing fancy or fad.

This means a true church is a gathering of two or more people who have been reborn as Jesus Christ, coming together to share insights from the Holy Spirit and to encourage each other to **keep the faith**.

All of Paul's epistles were directed towards this goal – to encourage true Christians to withstand the persecution that is about and to remember how the power of God is available to them through Christ within. Paul taught how to be "Christ Strong."

When one has a personal relationship with God and Christ – as those who are resurrections of Jesus, filled with the same Holy Spirit – one cannot stand off and persecute one's self, by saying, "I could never be Jesus. I could never be as committed as Paul. I could never be as holy as Elijah. I could never sing high praises to the Lord, like David."

Being filled with the Holy Spirit is not about **being you**! There is no "I" in apostle.

It is about sacrificing your ego for God and letting the Holy Spirit make **your body** be a kingdom of His holiness.

The evidence of this is found in the words of Luke, when Jesus said to the dead son of a widow in Na-in, "Young man, rise!" We are then told how the people surrounding his resurrection remarked, "A great prophet has risen among us!" and "God has looked favorably on his people!"

That "great prophet **risen**" was the **son of the widow**, because "The dead man sat up and began to **speak**." He spoke from the Holy Spirit, just like Jesus did; but that young man who had been resurrected became the spiritual leader of a new Christian presence in Na-in. He became (although not named as such) a "great prophet risen" in the same way an apostle is born.

Of course, Jesus of Nazareth was also an apostle of Christ, thus a great prophet making his lone appearance in Na-in that day … according to the scriptures. God had looked favorably upon Na-in by sending Jesus to find compassion for a widow woman whose son had died.

Still, there is duality in those statements, so that favor was sent **through** the Holy Spirit in the risen young man AND Jesus's visit. And, in case you might struggle with that "double meaning," look closer at the Luke writing, where he said, "The dead man sat up and began to speak."

The Greek word for "speak" is "*lalein*," which also means "proclaim." The young man sat up and began proclaiming … but what was there for him to say?

Look now at what Paul wrote in his letter to the Galatians, where he said, "The gospel that was proclaimed by me is not of human origin … but I received it through a revelation of Jesus Christ." That revelation caused Paul to **proclaim the gospel**. Therefore, the risen young man proclaimed the same truth as Jesus and Paul.

Now, we adults have all been to funerals, vigils and wakes, so we understand what death is and the permanence of loss that death means. Knowing that, I want you now to imagine yourself being **<u>DEAD</u>** for a moment.

# After Pentecost Sermons: Proper 5, Year C

<pause>

Envision your body as no longer being able to physically respond to your soul's directions. Imagine you hovering above your corpse, looking down at your body, seeing it on a bier at a wake as your friends and family pay their last respects.

Your body is about to begin the procession to be interred while your soul watches ... knowing death has separated your soul and body. **But**, then some voice says, "Rise!" – AND then you instantly come back to life.

Your soul is eternal and has witnessed that vision of death many times (through reincarnation), so it is not hard to imagine that scene of death now ... where the soul lifts out of a lifeless and <u>useless</u> body.

However, in all of one's many incarnations (unless you have come back now on a **special assignment from God**) your soul has yet to realize how beautiful spending **eternity** with God will be. We visit God between death and a planned new life on earth, agreeing each time that we **must** do better ... in the next life. Challenges are accepted and we promise God we will achieve the goal He has set for us. Thus we are reborn <u>a first time</u> over and over again ... yet forever failing to be reborn a second time within one mortal lifetime.

We all **know guilt** from our inabilities to make the complete sacrifice that is required to be reborn a second time - to be born a mortal, then die of ego so we can be reborn as a vehicle for God and Christ.

But think about the readings today ... and ponder the impact of rebirth from a "near death experience" (NDE). They are not uncommon, although not routine. Recently, a book came out about a doctor dying and returning to life, explaining his experiences in-between here and there.

<pause>

Would an awakening from death by the voice of Jesus Christ telling one's soul to return to life in an old body … would that experience soon be forgotten?  Would you come back thinking how special you are to God?  Would you come back with a sense of urgency to serve God and tell others we should not fear death … if we have lived a reborn life for God?

<pause>

Would you **not** sit up and **speak** of having "seen the light in the tunnel," which is not of human origin?  Would you **not** explain that you had personally witnessed a **real** experience that was not some final synapses in the big brain firing off?  Would you **not** point out the truth that all the machines your body had been hooked up to had said your brain was **<u>DEAD</u>**?

Would such an event – your **<u>RESURRECTION</u>** – not make you go out and **proclaim** the gospel as revealed by Jesus Christ, through the Holy Spirit … just like Paul did?

Saul <u>died</u> so Paul could be reborn.

Or would you be like Consuela on *Family Guy* and be unable to understand the language of resurrection, simply saying, "That's nice.  I go back to doing the things that lead to death again"?

<pause>

Why not believe that the young man in Na-in did the same … or Lazarus, when Jesus called him to "Come out!" in Bethany?

What about the ill slave to the Centurion that we read about last week?  Do you think he just had a chest cold that caused the

Centurion to send a messenger to Jesus to save a good man? That slave probably (although not directly stated) **died** before the messenger reached Jesus, but news of the Centurion's faith caused the slave to be <u>revived from death</u>.

Today we read about the young son of the widow resurrected by Elijah. I imagine that young boy also knew full well what God had done for his soul, knowing the prayer of Elijah to God had resurrected him.

Paul said his experience of seeing the Spirit of Jesus (when his name changed from Saul to Paul) was so powerful that he immediately spent three years preaching the meaning of Holy Scripture to Arabs, in Arabia and Damascus (Syria).

Paul did not seek out "those who were already apostles before" he was an apostle … to make sure he hadn't dreamed everything and maybe he should just keep going as he had … "business as usual." The message of **change** was <u>so clear</u> that he immediately became ordained and sought people to minister.

Saul **<u>DIED</u>** and Paul's soul heard the revelation of Jesus Christ saying, "Rise!" so Paul got up and began speaking the gospel. Paul was exactly the same as the young son of the widow in Na-in, and the young son of a widow in Zarephath.

Paul told the Galatians, "Then I went into the regions of Syria and Cilicia [which is in southeastern Turkey, bordering Syria], and I was still unknown by sight to the churches of Judea that are in Christ; they only heard it said, "The one who formerly was persecuting us is now proclaiming the faith he once tried to destroy." And they glorified God because of me."

Listen to those words and tell me if you heard any fear of Paul in those churches of Judea that were in Christ. Paul encountered true Christians when he went – unrecognizable – into a those churches filled with Jews for Jesus. Were those Jewish

Christians trembling in their sandals, worrying that Saul and his Jewish lawyer buddies might show up at any moment and try to destroy them?

No. There was no fear of any man in them. After all ... what could they do to hurt them/ Kill them? They had no fear of death by man.

It was like how the people of Na-in were, when we hear Luke write, "Fear seized all of them; and they glorified God." That means they suddenly began to fear God ... not persecution ... not death. They glorified God by praising the power of God that had come upon them. The became witnesses to the power of the Holy Spirit, so they glorified God by only showing fear of losing his love and protection.

They did not fear the miracle that a dead young man had just sat up and began preaching the truth to them. They feared God and only God, which means they stopped fearing stupid worldly matters.

No more would they pull out excuses for not fearing God, saying things like:

> "I'm afraid I might not be able to buy groceries, if I don't increase the price of my wares or services to people who need them most."

> "I'm afraid I might not be able to pay my cell phone bill, if I take a day off work to spread the truth about God."

> "I'm afraid people might stop inviting me to their parties or helping my business, if I always try to talk about my having been given a new life by God."

<pause>

# After Pentecost Sermons: Proper 5, Year C

Fear is natural.

Jesus felt fear at Gethsemane. He cried as he prayed to God. He admitted, "The spirit is willing but the flesh is weak."

Elijah also feared, when the widow woman, whom he had been sent to live with, had her young son die. She asked Elijah, "What have you against me, O man of God? You have come to me to bring my sin to remembrance, and to cause the death of my son!"

Elijah was beside himself with fear. He did not know what to do. He just reacted to the fear.

Elijah took the dead boy's body upstairs to his room and laid it on his bed.

We then read that "he stretched himself upon the child three times." That means Elijah's rapidly beating heart was placed upon the boy's still heart three times. Three, of course, being a holy number – representative of the Trinity. So, Elijah placed his heart on the dead boy's heart once for the Father, twice for the Son, and thrice for the Holy Spirit.

Then, Elijah cried out, "O Lord my God, let this child's life come into him again." The Lord answered another prayer. The boy was **revived**. He was born again to life ... by the Holy Spirit.

The widow woman said to Elijah, "Now I know that you are a man of God, and that the word of the Lord in your mouth is truth." Still, Elijah knew he had been used by God, as no one could repeat those steps and bring another dead boy back to life. Elijah worked no miracle ... he simply sat up and **spoke the Word of God**. That was Faith, as a man of God, and Holy Spirit, with the truth of the Lord in his mouth, extending a miracle of God onto another. Elijah feared God ... thinking he had failed God by doing something that caused the child to die.

That fear of God caused the Holy Spirit to overtake Elijah, so he acted as he did.

<pause>

Do you think that experience forever affected the widow woman and her son?

Elijah had made just a little bit of meal and a little bit of oil last for many days, feeding her whole household and himself … certainly a miracle … much like Jesus fed a multitude with five loaves and two fish; but do you think that miracle made as great an impact on the widow woman and her young son as did Elijah speaking to God and God returning life to her dead son?

A widow woman's son represented the future to her. Without her son, she had no reason to live. She was more lost without the hope of her son than she had been from a facing certain death from famine, having only one last meal left. The widow woman did not fear death, as she prepared for her and her son to die as good servants of the Lord. The resurrection of her son returned hope to her life.

God gave both widow women in today's stories **hope**, seen as the fruit of faith received in the glory of the Father. Being given a sustained reason for life is a wondrous feeling … more than that of being kept from death by worldly staples provided by heaven.

Minor miracles happen all the time … and many of us give full credit to God and Christ when they happen to us or those we know. But, has the miracle of resurrection made you change your lifestyle?

Are you a full-time servant to God and Christ?

Are you a man or woman of God with the truth of the Lord in

your mouth?

Do you fear only God and glorify him through your faith and devotion, shown by your acts and words?

Do people hear you speak and say, "God has looked favorably on us by this great prophet"?

<pause>

That is what Ordinary Time is about. For mortals, it is ordinary to fear death; but for true Christians, those resurrected with the word of truth upon them to speak, Ordinary Time means a fear of God, so one glorifies God by becoming an apostle. **Now** becomes the most important time to rise and speak.

> "Praise the Lord, O my soul!"

> "I will praise the Lord as long as I live."

> "I will sing praises to my God while I have my being."

Amen

# FOURTH SUNDAY AFTER PENTECOST

# Proper 6

# YEAR C

**Relevant readings:**
1 Kings 21:1-21
Psalm 5:1-8
   2 Samuel 11:26-27 and
     2 Samuel 12:10,13-15
   Psalm 32
Galatians 2:15-21
Luke 7:36-8:3

After Pentecost Sermons: Proper 6, Year C

# When dining with Pharisees, try the teardrops foot washing

Soon after making the move here, I began exploring Dish Network. There are lots of free movies available, for the first three months at least. I watched one named *Campaign*, starring Will Farrell. It was about the sin of politics and it made fun of the politicians that use empty promises to excite a populace to vote them into office.

Without spoiling the whole movie for anyone who might want to watch it, a candidate was created to challenge a John Edwards like incumbent. The new man was cut from God-fearing cloth, and his sins would be deemed the least heinous of all possible sins. However, he fell for the lust of power – winning at all costs – which is the trap of politics.

The good man candidate came clean of his sins in a last minute commercial, actually confessing the worst things he had done in his life. He told the audience that he had entered politics to help his local district; but, he said he had failed to live up to that original intention. However, he promised, if elected, to live up to that high standard as a representative of the people.

That was a movie. Now back to reality.

We just do not see that level of honesty in politics. Instead, we see how schemers take advantage of the honest. Those initial attempts by people who enter that arena that might actually be trying to do good ... well, that hasn't happened in the last two hundred years.

Rulers are more like Ahab and Jezebel, plotting to have someone who is against them killed – using the system that is at their disposal. It is also reflected in rulers that are more like David, plotting to have someone killed who might hold him back from his true desires and lusts – using the same self-serving system.

Rulers like that change the rules, making sure they are in their favor once in power. The common people pay with their lives, so the rich can get richer.

The difference between then and now is Ahab had a priest of the LORD that was above the Law. His name was Elijah.

We know Elijah was the priest to the One God, because we read about him going up against four hundred fifty priests for Ba'al in the reading two Sundays ago. Last week, Elijah raised the widow woman's son from being dead. This week, Elijah is telling Ahab that Ahab will pay dearly for his sins – he will die.

In the same place the dogs licked up the blood of Naboth, whose life he caused to end by stoning, so too would the dogs lick up the blood of Ahab.

That is the Law – an eye for an eye, a tooth for a tooth – a life for a life.

Do the crime, do the time. Blindfolded justice plays no favorites.

In the Gospel reading from Luke, we find a woman who has gone outside of the limits of the law. She has sinned and she recognizes her past mistakes. As penance, she works as a servant for the Pharisee named Simon; but, for all she does, she gets no respect.

Once a sinner, always a sinner; at least in the eyes of those who police the limits of the law. It is as if she has a criminal record that can never be expunged.

Jesus had been invited to eat with Simon and some of his pious friends (presumably also Pharisees). The woman comes to Jesus when he sits and bathes Jesus' feet with her tears, dries them with her hair, and continues to kiss his feet afterwards.

Simon chides Jesus for letting a sinner touch him, causing Jesus to ask the question about two people in debt, both unable to repay what they owe. If both are forgiven their debts, with one owing ten times more than the other, then who will love the forgiving creditor more?

Simon answered correctly – the one who had more debt forgiven will love the forgiving creditor more. Thus, one with more sins in their past, with more to be forgiven, will love the forgiver more.

This caused Simon and friends to murmur, "Who does he think he is that he can forgive sins?"

Jesus answered, "I am not forgiving sins. God forgives this woman because of her faith, such that she believes she must repay her debt in this life."

The woman servant had done the crimes, and she was willing to do the time necessary to be justified (or absolved, meaning free of blame). Jesus told her that her time was served and she could go in peace.

The woman who had sinned died that day. The woman who would follow Jesus and sin no more was born that day.

This is what Paul said to the Galatians, in his letter that we read today. We read how he asked, "But if, in our efforts to be justified in Christ, we ourselves have been found to be sinners, is Christ a servant of sin?"

Paul was saying that there is no yo-yoing back and forth between sin and absolution. You don't get freed to go in peace if you then go out and sin again.

This means that absolution – the remission of sins – forgiveness of sins – comes not from without, but from within.

In essence, the penalty for sin is death. Like Ahab, a sinner can act like the law allows one to sin and deny all need for absolution. In those cases, people die without God.

David wrote in Psalm 5, "God does not take pleasure in wickedness" and "evil cannot dwell with God." God destroys liars and abhors the bloodthirsty and deceitful. God "hates all those who work wickedness."

If you die – if you leave this life – without having paid the price for the crimes committed, then don't call on God from the deathbed.

It is much better to die like Paul and the woman servant of Simon the Pharisee. You leave the old self behind. You stand aside and let Christ run your life. As Paul wrote, "For through the law I died to the law, so that I may live to God. … it is Christ who lives in me. … the life I now live in the flesh I live by faith in the Son of God."

That is the commercial we all need to run on television. We need to announce to the populace that we realize the traps we have fallen into, from getting caught up in the game of life, where the law allows us to sin first, pay later.

We have to promise not to ever sin again, meaning the law no longer is a boundary we lean up against and look beyond … peering towards an outside world … seeming to be prisoners to our own desires and lusts. That self must die to be with God.

Amen

# FIFTH SUNDAY AFTER PENTECOST

## Proper 7

## YEAR C

**Relevant readings:**
1 Kings 19:1-15
Psalm 42 and 43
Isaiah 65:1-9
Psalm 22:18-27
Galatians 3:23-29
Luke 8:26-39

**Dying with dignity doesn't always happen as planned**

Robert Tippett

I am reminded today from the readings of a scene from the movie *Little Big Man*. Dustin Hoffman played the role of Jack Crabb, who had learned the ways of the Indians after his parents were massacred by a Pawnee raid. Chief Dan George played the role of Old Lodge Skins, the Cheyenne tribal leader who raised Jack. Jack Crabb was born a white child, raised by red men, then captured by a U.S. Calvary raid where he renounced the Indian ways. As a young adult back with white people he spent time in various occupations, including being a muleskinner for Colonel George Armstrong Custer.

The setting for the scene I remembered was after Jack had returned to the Cheyenne, after Custer had been killed at Little Bighorn - Custer's Last Stand. The chief decided it was time to go to the hill of the Indian Burial, in full chief regalia; so, he could die with dignity. Jack accompanied his adopted father and watched as the chief lay down on the hill in the spot where he would await death. The chief offered his spirit to the Great Spirit, laid down on the grass, facing the sky. Closing his eyes he said, "Today is a good day to die." Then, the chief cited how the magic of the moment was right for dying.

Jack Crabb patiently sits with the chief as he lays there motionless. Several hours pass by. Then, dark clouds roll in and rain slowly began to fall. Some drops landed on the chief's face. The chief opened one eye and asked, "Am I dead yet?" Jack Crabb tells the chief he is still alive.

The chief says, "Sometimes the magic works, and sometimes it doesn't." He got up and returned to being a living chief.

The same can be said for Elijah, when he asked God to end his life. The ways of life had changed. He said "Enough. I am no better than my ancestors," those who gave their lives trying to keep Israel from falling prey to evil rulers and foreign priests.

# After Pentecost Sermons: Proper 7, Year C

Elijah then had a death sentence on his head, and rather than die by the sword of one of Ahab and Jezebel's soldiers, he would rather God take his life in a dignified fashion.

Sometimes that works, sometimes that doesn't.

The readings today focus on the pressures we all feel, where we think we are up against a wall – between a rock and a hard place – left with few or no options.

God asked Elijah, "What are you doing here?"

He starts to unload all those pressures. He says, "I have tried very hard to stop the evil the Israelites have been doing – forsaking your covenant – throwing down your altars – killing your prophets – with me the last on that list who is left alive."

Elijah was like David, who wrote in Psalm 42:

> "My soul is heavy ... why do I go so heavily while the enemy oppresses me?
>
> While my bones are being broken my enemies mock me to my face."

The man of Gerasenes, named Legion, similarly expressed fears when that demonic leader shouted out loudly to Jesus, "What have you to do with me! I beg you, do not torment me."

Then, the demons within the Legion's dominion begged Jesus, "Do not order us back to the abyss. Let us enter into that large herd of swine."

The demons were allowed to enter into the swine, but the herd ran and jumped into the Sea of Galilee, drowning. The locals asked Jesus to leave because they were seized with great fear.

Even the man who no longer had demons inside him begged Jesus to take him with him, and not leave him behind.

The whole theme is focused on people being afraid of the challenges before them. Afraid of living when someone is looking to kill you, to break your bones, to mock you. Afraid of dying and going to the abyss. Afraid of being left behind.

Been there, done that.

Who hasn't?

We run away. We pray to God for help. We are at the end of the rope, at our wit's end.

I'm also reminded of a documentary I saw, called *The Conscientious Objector*. It was a documentary about a man named Desmond Doss, who was a conscientious objector to killing, even at a time of war.

He was like the Andy Griffith character in *No Time for Sergeants*, in that he was a simple country boy drafted to serve his country. He was also like the Andy Griffith character, Sheriff Taylor of Mayberry, in that he was one who stood for the law without using a gun. However, Desmond Doss was a real patriot, who served his country at a time of war – World War II – refusing to ever take up a weapon.

The fact that Americans were at war, serving their country fighting, meant he wanted to also serve his country by helping in any way he could ... without touching a firearm.

Because of his faith, Desmond Doss was belittled. Like in *No Time for Sergeants*, he got latrine duty and KP (kitchen patrol) more than anyone else. The non-coms and the commissioned officers overseeing him tried to break him – tried to force him to take up a weapon; but, he refused, regardless of the punishment placed upon him. The orders came down from the top; he had the right to object because of his religious beliefs.

Desmond Doss was assigned to the medical detachment for the 307th infantry. He was sent to the Pacific Theater – to Okinawa. He refused to wear a sidearm, which was a standard precaution for medics. His actions on Okinawa were heroic. His platoon refused to make assaults until Desmond had read his Bible (a daily routine) and prayed for their safety.

Desmond Doss risked his life repeatedly, retrieving wounded soldiers and dragging them out of the line of fire and lowering them by a harness devise he created, to a place where they could receive treatment. He was wounded; and, he treated his own wounds, rather than call for help and assistance. After nightfall, he was reached by stretcher bearers and taken to safety.

Desmond Doss is one of very few conscientious objectors to be honored with the Congressional Medal of Honor. He was presented this award by President Harry Truman.

Desmond Doss was stationed on Okinawa for twenty-three days, in 1945. He did not do what he did because he was brave and unafraid. He simply feared God more than he feared a Drill Sergeant or a Captain who might threaten him. He feared God more than a Japanese machine gun's bullets. Desmond Doss did what he did because God protected him so he could do it.

He was like Elijah in his faith; so, after Elijah heard a great wind splitting mountains and beating rocks into pieces, he knew that was **not** the LORD. After Elijah heard an earthquake, he knew that was **not** the LORD. After Elijah heard a fire, he knew that was **not** the LORD. Desmond Doss, like Elijah, knew God was present when he heard silence.

God told them both, "Go" and "return" and they did, no longer frightened by the sounds of danger. Instead, they were comforted in the sounds of serenity.

The man Jesus healed of demonic possession, we are told, had been seized many times by the loud sounds in his head, so frightening "he had broken his chains and shackles and been driven by madness into the wilds." Without the demons inside him, he was comforted by the silence of God's presence.

In Paul's letter to the Galatians, he tells us how the Law is like being bound by chains and shackles. Before Christ came, we had to be put in a prison and guarded by the law. The law becomes that fence that keeps us within its boundary, screaming at us, "This is the limit!" Meanwhile, outside the fence is all the noise saying, "Come sin! It's just a little beyond the law's boundaries." The temptation drives us wild, so we break the chains and shackles and run amok.

But, we know Christ, so we feel guilt. We have been baptized as Christians. We wrap our faces in the mantle of Christ, to keep us from being distracted by the ways of the world. Still, the demons keep on calling out our names.

They beg, "Please don't order us back into the abyss, where you can no longer hear our temptations."

Jesus came to free us of the law's prison and guardianship. That can only happen when we hear the silence of the LORD.

We have to become conscientious objectors to sin of all kinds, unwilling to break under the pressure. To do that we have to die a figurative death. We have to say, "Today is a good day to die in a way that dignifies the LORD."

Then, "Go, return to where you came through the wilderness," with the peace of the LORD with you.

# After Pentecost Sermons: Proper 7, Year C

Amen

# SIXTH SUNDAY AFTER PENTECOST

## Proper 8

## YEAR C

**Relevant readings:**
2 Kings 2:1-2, 6-14
Psalm 77:1-2, 11-20
　1 Kings 19:15-16, 19-21
　Psalm 16
Galatians 5:1, 13-25
Luke 9:51-62

After Pentecost Sermons: Proper 8, Year C

# Before you can walk on God's carpet, you have to remove your dirty shoes

It is an Asian custom to remove one's shoes before entering a home. There are various reasons why this is deemed a good practice, but the primary reason is a home's floors remain clean when one does not track the outside filth and grime onto carpeted, wood, and tiled flooring.

I remember watching a *60 Minutes* episode back in 1968, where they visited Joe Namath's "bachelor pad" in New York City. They made a point of showing the white-haired llama skin carpet he had, back when shag carpet was in vogue. They made a point of telling how Joe had a "no shoes" rule. He explained how expensive the carpet was and how hard it was to keep it clean. Therefore, to keep it white, no street dust was allowed inside. The shoes came off at the door, and only clean socked feet came inside.

While Joe Namath came to that realization either by accident, or by the carpet installers telling him it was his responsibility if the carpet got dirty, Joe adopted an Eastern custom. If you wanted to visit Joe, and if you felt it was a privilege to walk upon his white llama-skin carpet, you had to follow that "no dirt allowed" rule.

Us Westerners often think that is a good idea; but, we give up on making it a custom by the time we have children that are constantly running inside, then outside, always forgetting to wipe their shoes clean, much less take them off. Anyone with inside-outside dogs also know how hard it is to control a wet dog with muddy paws. We give up on that plan fairly quickly.

The key to a plan becoming a custom is dedication; and, dedication is the theme strongly weaved through the readings today. We have the dedication of Elisha to follow Elijah. We have the dedication of the disciples to follow Jesus. And, we have the dedication told by Paul, of Christians to follow the Holy Spirit.

Custom means you stick to a plan that knows both right and wrong, from experience; and, the plan calls for doing the right thing.

In all the readings, we find how dedication means compliance through hard work. This hard work is symbolized by the plow. It is symbolized by journeys that leave this world behind. There is no looking back once you commit to the custom. Once your hand takes hold of that plow you are expected to maintain the works.

In other words, you have to always take your shoes off before walking on Joe Namath's white llama-hair carpet. Just one time not being compliant and WHAM! The carpet gets dirty. Once dirty, might as well let everyone walk on it with their dirty shoes. It has been soiled. The inside has become the outside.

Another reason Asian people always take their shoes off before entering someone's home is respect. You have to have respect for your neighbor's home, the same as you respect your own home. If you want to maintain a clean house, respect your neighbor as if they too have the same desire.

Cleanliness being next to godliness is a good rule to live by, but, just because someone else does not live by that rule does not mean you are free to let go of your rules and be disrespectful. You respect others by not changing your ways. Treat others with the same respect you want in return.

It could be possible to mistake Elisha's respect as being disrespect. In the Second Kings reading, he is told by his elder, "Stay here," twice. Both times he seems to have had a stubborn streak, perhaps even showing selfishness, by refusing to do as he was told.

We read how he said, "As the LORD lives, and as you yourself live, I will not leave you."

That is respect for the LORD, respect for Elijah, and the self-respect Elisha has for his dedication to God.

We see how this is respect, because Elijah offers to do a favor for Elisha after the two cross the Jordan River.

Then, once Elijah has told Elisha his gift will be granted by God if he sees his ascension, it could seem that Elisha is once again showing disrespect by tearing his clothes in two. He even goes so far as question, "Where is the LORD, the God of Elijah?"

But Elisha would be rewarded by God. His respectful dedication meant he was given him a double share of Elijah's spirit.

In the optional reading from First Kings, we see Elisha seemingly disrespecting Elijah by returning to the oxen, after leaving them to follow Elijah. Elijah had told him to keep following him and asked why he would "go back again." However, Elisha did respect Elisha by acting as a priest, sacrificing his father's oxen and preparing a feast for the people.

The plow attached to yoked oxen was an instrument dedicated to earthly gains. By the plow, the soil was tilled for planting seeds and the seeds produced a bountiful harvest. Elisha destroyed the instrument requiring physical labor and beasts of burden, the plowshare.

That implement was designed for earthly rewards. The fruits of those labors enslaved one to a dedication to working the earth. He transformed the yoke into the tools necessary for producing spiritual rewards and he shared them with the people. That was an act of respectfulness.

Robert Tippett

In Paul's letter to the Galatians, he tells them of the fruits of the Spirit. He names a few as, "love, joy, peace, patience, kindness, generosity, faithfulness, gentleness, and self-control." He said, "There is no law against such things." This means there is no limit that determines you have loved too much, you have been too patient, or you have exceeded your legal amount of kindness.

Respect is one of these fruits.

The fruits of the Holy Spirit that Paul named come naturally, once one has become free of the yoke of slavery, represented by the plow. To till the land is hard work. When one's life depends on the fruits of one's labors, one is enslaved to producing those fruits. When one's livelihood depends on one toiling to produce material rewards, one is enslaved to that labor.

Call it white collar, blue collar, red neck, or black tie, the team we drive makes no difference. The yoke of slavery is in this earthly realm, not a spiritual one.

Paul tells us what happens when we wear that yoke of slavery. We bite and devour one another, so that others are trying to consume us. They consume us by keeping us focused on the physical and material, not the spiritual. They take our hearts and minds off heaven and throw them down so they become prey to "fornication, impurity, licentiousness, idolatry, sorcery, enmities, strife, jealousy, anger, quarrels, dissensions, factions, envy, drunkenness, carousing, and things like these." The list goes on and on.

Christ frees us of that focus.

Still, freedom does not come without a price. With freedom from slavery comes a different kind of yoke that must be worn, and different kind of plow we must labor behind. It is not something we can stop doing, and it shouldn't be something we want to stop doing. Paul named all those wonderful fruits that come from this yoke, from this plow, making the labor of freedom a labor of love (among other things). That labor is a plan that we must make a custom, something we always practice.

Paul tells us we must become slaves to one another, through love. We must have ownership of a labor of love and see passion and desire through fellowship, helping our neighbors, sharing our time with those closest to us ... those who are like us.

If not, as Paul warns, we misuse our freedom as Christians and see an opportunity for self-indulgence. We snip at others and avoid them. We come up with excuses.

While traveling to Jerusalem with his disciples, one said, "I will follow you wherever you go." He did not realize that would be a 24/7 task. Jesus told another disciple, "Follow me," but that disciple had to bury his father. Jesus told him that a follower of Jesus only seeks the living, so that by the time they die they will have been saved. A third disciple volunteered he would follow, but after he went home to say his goodbyes. Jesus told him there was no going back, once one has been filled with the Holy Spirit and made able to call down fire from heaven on people who don't receive that spirit.

When you make a commitment to be dedicated to Christ, to follow his path in life, and to receive the Holy Spirit when the time has come for him to Ascend in a whirlwind, then you will be fit for the kingdom of God. Anything less than love, joy, peace, etcetera ... having a lack of respect for the blessing that the Holy Spirit's gift means ... and you are too grounded to take off in a chariot of fire. You become too busy to find the whirlwind.

Imagine how nice a carpet God keeps in Heaven. You have to wipe the sin off down here before crossing that threshold.

Amen

# SEVENTH SUNDAY AFTER PENTECOST

## Proper 9

## YEAR C

**Relevant readings:**
2 Kings 5:1-14
Psalm 30
   Isaiah 66:10-14
   Psalm 66:1-8
Galatians 6:1-16
Luke 10:1-11, 16-20

After Pentecost Sermons: Proper 9, Year C

# Every Gentile has to bathe sometime

Three weeks ago, Paul told the Galatians, "We are not Gentile sinners." Today, we meet Naaman, who can be seen as an example of a "Gentile sinner."

Naaman was a commander of the army for the king of Aram.

Aram was the Hebrew word describing what we know today as Syria. The word means "high" or "elevated," which describes Syria as the land north of Israel. However, it is rooted in a word that makes it also mean "citadel," which is a fortress in a commanding position near a city. Thus, the king of Aram was the leader of a strong nation.

The Assyrians would overrun and destroy the Northern Kingdom, about one hundred fifty years after the Elisha and Naaman story took place. So, they can be seen as on a rise in power.

Every Gentile has its day.

Naaman was a great man in high favor with the king of Aram. We are told this is because the LORD had given victory to Naaman's troops. Despite Naaman being a "mighty warrior," he suffered from leprosy. Leprosy can be read as a noticeable skin deformity, such as cysts and boils on his hands and face. They would have appeared on the visible parts of his body, those not covered by clothes and armor. This means, for all his greatness Naaman was one ugly dude. He did not look great.

It has to be understood that the Jews of Jesus' time made those who were "impure" outcasts, such as those possessed by evil spirits, those who were deaf and/or blind, and those who had obvious skin lesions. They were seen as not being in good standing with the LORD. The rationale was their sins had brought that curse upon them.

Now, let's take a moment to look at what we know about Naaman. He is a Gentile, because he is not one of the children of Israel. Yet, he is a great warrior who the LORD of Israel had led to victory. The LORD of Israel rules over Gentiles, just as He rules over Jews, but Gentiles do not recognize that.

That lack of recognition can then be seen as explaining why Paul would say, "We Jews are not Gentile sinners." Sin can then be seen as a symptom of disrespect of God. Thus, Jews are capable of likewise being sinners by their acts disrespecting their God.

So, Naaman was something of an enigma. The LORD had blessed him with greatness as a warrior, but had cursed him with leprosy as a sinner. Naaman's leprosy can then be seen as a sign of his not giving the LORD of Israel credit for his victory (rather than punishment for being a Gentile).

Naaman probably did not know he was doing anything wrong. He probably gave some Ba'al credit for his victories as a warrior, just not the One God. He probably knew his leprosy was an obvious drawback to his greatness, something that kept him from winning lots of friends and influencing lots of strangers; but it seems he was able to accept the good with the bad, as the cost of doing business.

We read that it was a young girl who had been captive from the land of Israel that told Naaman of a prophet in Samaria could cure him of his leprosy. A captive Israelite shows that all was not fully well between the Northern Kingdom and Syria. Probably some border clash led to her being captive.

The use of "Samaria" references the capitol of the Northern Kingdom, where the king of Israel would have lived, along with his prophets. The girl believed in the prophet Elisha and in the LORD of Israel, regardless of her captivity and servitude to a

Gentile sinner. She wanted to help cure him of his obvious sin.

In the reading from Paul today we hear him say, "If you sow to your own flesh, you will reap corruption from the flesh." He went on to write, "Whenever we have an opportunity, let us work for the good of all, and especially for those of the family of faith."

Even though Paul wrote that letter to the Galatians nearly a thousand years after the story of Naaman and Elisha, that captive Israelite girl was a reflection of that sense of goodwill. She recognized and lived what Paul would later explain. She recognized that Naaman had reaped a corruption from the flesh, based on what he had sown in his life. Still, his leprosy could be cured through faith in the LORD.

She also knew, as Paul wrote, "All must test their own work; then that work, rather than their neighbor's work, will become a cause for pride." If only Naaman would carry his own load to Israel and ask for guidance from the prophet Elisha, he could realize a skin of which he would be proud.

Thus, as Paul wrote, "Those who are taught the word must share in all good things with their teacher." Elisha would be the teacher, and Naaman would be the one taught the word.

This teacher-student relationship is then found in the Gospel reading from Luke, as the commission of the seventy-two. Jesus sent disciples out with the "authority to tread on snakes and scorpions, and over all the power of the enemy," such that they were protected from harm.

The captive Israelite slave girl was likewise in a dangerous position, recommending her master go into a hostile nation seeking help. However, she was safe in her recommendation to Naaman to go see the prophet of Israel, as no threat of harm would come to him..

Remember, Aram and Israel were not on the best of terms, due to border clashes. Neither was at a point of strength to overtake the other, so they lived as neighboring wolf packs. The girl was recommending that Naaman go out like a lamb into the midst of wolves. He lowered his risks by taking with him all kinds of booty as an offering for the King of Israel. Naaman took ten talents of silver, six thousand shekels of gold, and ten sets of garments. He came like a lamb of peace, bearing gifts.

The wealth of the king of Aram was seen as an insult. It was perceived as, "What? Are you trying to pick a quarrel with me by trying to bribe our LORD to cleanse you of your sins?" This is why Jesus told the seventy-two, "Carry no purse, no bag, no sandals; and greet no one on the road." He was instructing them to go meekly to where no one knows them and announce, "the kingdom of God has come near." Naaman was instead announcing, "The kingdom of Aram has come near." That was insulting to the king of Israel.

However, Elisha head the words of Naaman as would a disciple of Jesus. A Gentile full of sin had come near the kingdom of God, like a lamb in the midst of wolves. Elisha heard the words of Naaman as would Paul, an Apostle of Christ hearing one wanted to carry his own load, to test his own works and to bear his own burdens.

Elisha eased the anger of the king of Israel and then said (paraphrasing), "Have him come by my place. If it is the LORD he wants, then I will tell him where to go to be near the kingdom of God."

We know the ending of the story. Naaman's flesh was restored like the flesh of a young boy. He was cleansed of his sin. In the words of Paul, "A new creation is everything!" And Naaman was a new creation to the LORD of Israel.

# After Pentecost Sermons: Proper 9, Year C

Naaman listened and acted as instructed, albeit with some coaxing from his servants. Jesus told his disciples, "Whoever listens to you listens to me, and whoever rejects you rejects me, and whoever rejects me rejects the one who sent me." Naaman did not reject the word of the one who sent Elisha, who is the same one who sent Jesus.

One can imagine that Naaman was filled with joy when he was cleansed of sin. The seventy-two returned with joy reporting how demons submitted to the name of Jesus. Paul said, "May I never boast of anything except the cross of our Lord Jesus Christ, by which the world has been crucified to me, and I to the world."

Boast of a new creation! Rejoice that a name has been written in heaven! Be joyful that sins have been cleansed!

What we might miss in the Naaman story is the aspect of him having to bathe seven times in the River Jordan. Think about the number seven for a moment.

How many days are there in a week? Seven, right? What if that meant bathe every day of the week in the Lord of Israel, the river of the Holy Spirit?

Maybe that is why Paul wrote, "Let us not grow weary in doing what is right, for we will reap at harvest-time, if we do not give up." Jesus said, "The harvest is plentiful," there are lots of sinners out there. "But the laborers are few," meaning too many do not do the works necessary, from faith. All one has to do is keep a daily regimen, and "Go on your way." "Peace to this house!" Peace and mercy upon those who follow the rule of Christ.

Peace be with you.

Amen

# EIGHTH SUNDAY AFTER PENTECOST

# Proper 10

# YEAR C

**Relevant readings:**
Amos 7:7-17
Psalm 82
  Deuteronomy 30:9-14
  Psalm 25:1-9
Colossians 1:1-14
Luke 10:25-37

After Pentecost Sermons: Proper 10, Year C

# The language of agreements isn't always clear

The checking account I recently closed was one I had held for some time. I opened it way back in 2005, when I first moved here. When I moved to the seminary location to establish residency, the same bank had a branch there. That made it easy to keep using the same bank account.

Still, that always confused the teller when I made a deposit. She would always ask, "Did you open this account in this state?" I got used to telling them as soon as I saw them look at the check and start keying in numbers, "I opened the account in another state."

When we came back to this state, to this new location, we found there is a local branch for that same bank. So, I could still use the account without changing; but, for a while I had to keep myself from wanting to tell the teller that I opened the account in this state. I would confuse them when I offered that unnecessary information.

There is something to be said about having a relationship with a bank. Like with all business relationships, we are comforted to believe there is a level of trustworthiness, as well as friendliness. Regardless of how much business we generate for some company, we all want to be recognized as respected, simply for doing business with them. They should make the customers feel welcomed.

After nine years with the bank that I used for various accounts, I felt the need to change banks.

I opened the account in 2005 because that bank honored people of my age by allowing them to have free checking. I was over fifty, so that got me a break. In the agreement paperwork that I signed, there was obviously some small print that said, "Free checking as long as we do not want to charge a service fee." Because they offered free checking for people over fifty, I opened (over time) three other checking accounts, mostly for transfers to accounts opened for my wife and children. All had the same small print.

In 2011, when the financial collapse was in full swing, the bank began taking out $8 every month, from each account. They had sent me e-mails giving me advance warning that they were changing the agreement that said "free checking."

When the bank actually began to take my money simply because I had checking accounts, I went to the bank to personally ask the bank manager what advantage a "50-plus" checking account had. That conversation did not go over very well. The bank manager was not friendly, and I felt a trust had been broken. Still, I went to them to open a new account after my mother died.

I had a life insurance check to place in a saving account. Since savings accounts were not paying much interest, I was told I could get more interest for that money if I put all the money in a money market account. The small print, as stated by the bank representative, said "As long as I did not need the money any time soon."

It was my fault for not listening closely, but the friendliness of the bank representative (not the manager) was enough for me to sign an agreement with small print I did not read. For each of four months, I received about $4 interest on the money in that account - about $16 total. Then, I had to withdraw some of the money to pay some bills. My account balance dropped below the minimum I needed to have in the account. As punishment, I learned I was then earning seven cents of interest per month, instead of $4. On top of that, I was being charged a $25 fee for them holding my money, because my money was less than the

# After Pentecost Sermons: Proper 10, Year C

sizable minimum they required for an interest rate that paid $4 a month. I had to bite the bullet and pay the price. I had signed an agreement.

I am sure we all have some stories like that to tell. I hear people complain about how breaking their phone agreements, before the agreed contract period is completed, can be quite costly. The I.R.S. also has a reputation of being hard on people who forget the agreement we have with the Federal government, at income tax time. The point is that our society is built upon laws, such that we know breaking an agreement or getting out of a contract will be costly.

The readings today reflect the root source of our agreement with God, as American Christians. We are part of a society that stands by laws from moral values, based on our Christian beliefs. The news of recent times has been a reflection of attacks of that belief system, carried out by non-Christians. There have been stories about Ten Commandments monuments being forcibly removed from state-owned property because not everyone in the state is of a religion that links to that history.

Those ten commandments in stone were an agreement between the children of Israel and God. In the Book of Deuteronomy, Moses brings down the Ten Commandments, along with a book of decrees, and tells the Israelites, "Surely, this commandment that God is commanding is not too hard for you."

Moses told them that two stone tablets, along with the book of laws, was a physical presence in their midst. That presence would bring "the word very near to you; it is in your mouth and in your heart for you to observe." Seeing a reminder in the lawn outside a courthouse is meant to have the same purpose.

It is, as long as you memorize the large print and the small print, which devoted Jews do.

Robert Tippett

Two weeks ago, we read how Paul said Jesus freed us from the Law, such that it all came down to loving your neighbor as you would love yourself. That meant, if you are filled with the Holy Spirit, then you never come close to breaking any of the agreements the people of Israel made with God, certainly none of the Ten Commandments.

Today we read how God told Amos to go tell the people of Israel the service fee is coming, and it is going to be huge. In the gentlest terms, Amos said the king will die by the sword and the country will go into exile, away from its land. That would be like the email notice or the statement that says, "What you thought you had is now less."

If you are surprised and decide to go in to talk to the manager about this new change, then you hear Amos get real specific and personal. The changes are due to a failure to be reminded of the agreement. You dropped below the minimum requirement. In the fine print it says, "No prostitution. No turning your back to God; and, No worshiping of false idols. The penalty is your land sold out from under you; you die in unclean lands; and, you will be exiled, away from this land."

You signed the agreement, and those are the terms. Did you forget them? Did you delete the email?

In the Gospel of Luke, we have a lawyer inquiring about the clause about eternal life in heaven. Jesus asked the lawyer if he had read the agreement documents. The lawyer said he had. He knew the part about loving your neighbor as yourself; but, he wanted to clear up some of the small print. He asked, "Could you detail what a neighbor is, please."

Jesus told the parable of the Good Samaritan. In that make-believe story, the first passerby was a priest, meaning one who had the role in the Temple to sacrifice animals to God. The second passerby was a Levite, meaning one who had the role in the

# After Pentecost Sermons: Proper 10, Year C

Temple to hand the priest the sacrificing tools and a wet towel. The Samaritan was symbolic of someone who was either of Assyrian descent, or one of the children of Israel who had married someone who was not of Jewish descent. Either way, he had impure DNA within him, so he was a Gentile as far as the priest and Levite were concerned..

Jesus asked the lawyer to decide who of the three was the most likely to be considered a "neighbor." The lawyer answered correctly – the Samaritan – the mix breed.

That was not something spelled out in the Laws of Moses. Just like how a financial crisis could alter the way free checking accounts are administered, causing them to go the way of the dinosaurs, the errors of the children of Israel (the Northern Kingdom) sent them scattering to the four corners of the earth. It was time to find a new bank. It was time to make a new agreement. This means a new agreement that was to be drawn up in Christ.

A "neighbor" used to be anyone who lived close enough to walk to Jerusalem (from Judah) or Samaria (from Israel) three times a year, to partake of the grilled meat the priests and their aides were cooking up. The Jews who wandered back into Jerusalem, under foreign rule, they redefined "neighbor" as one who maintained the old agreement, with any lost Samaritans no longer part of the equation. However, Jesus was explaining to the lawyer (a Pharisee), "neighbor" includes Samaritans. If one classified as a Gentile is a "neighbor," then everyone following the laws of the One God can be considered a "neighbor."

It is hard to write down every exception to the rule. In the parable, the man who was beaten and robbed and left for dead did not personally know the Samaritan who came to his aid. He just came by at the right time. The man who was left with the innkeeper might have been unconscious when the Samaritan treated his wounds and carried him in the inn, over his shoulder from the back of his animal. The man might have recovered and gone on his way before the Samaritan would return to settle any debt still owed. Thus, a neighbor does not need to be spelled out in writing. It is beyond the letter of the law. God is the only record keeper.

Paul's letter to the Colossians was written from his prison cell in Rome. Paul never visited Colossae; but, he had passed the Holy Spirit onto Epaphras, who had spread the Holy Spirit in Colossae. Epaphras had gone to Rome to aid Paul and he told Paul about the church he left behind. Paul wrote the Colossians to tell them to keep the agreement with Christ, so they would always have love in the Spirit.

Without knowing the people of Colossae, Paul wrote, "We have not ceased praying for you and asking that you may be filled with the knowledge of God's will in all spiritual wisdom and understanding." He said keep the faith without everything being written on paper. Let it be in your mouth and written in your hearts.

Moses said that too, remember?

The caveat is Christ, who advocates the Holy Spirit be the law within us. Paul reminded the Colossians, "so you may lead lives worthy of the Lord, fully pleasing to him, as you bear fruit in every good work and as you grow in the knowledge of God, you will have spiritual wisdom and understanding" of what is right and what is wrong.

As long as you maintain that minimum balance – follow the Laws – and because you go well beyond the minimum – model Christ - you will never pay a service fee – be lost in darkness - and you will always be reaping the benefits – earn eternal life.

Amen

# NINTH SUNDAY AFTER PENTECOST

# Proper 11

# YEAR C

**Relevant readings:**
Amos 8:1-12
Psalm 52
  Genesis 18:1-10
  Psalm 15
Colossians 1:15-28
Luke 10:38-42

Robert Tippett

# The machinery of life is busy, busy, busy

My favorite author is Kurt Vonnegut. He had a way of summing up life simply, while grasping the way life is ... satirically.

While I like all of Vonnegut's novels, I have a fondness for his 1963 book, *Cat's Cradle*. In that book he introduced several terms, which can be found on the Wikipedia article about the book.

One is "busy, busy, busy." This is defined as words whispered by a fictitious religious sect [Bokononists] when "they think how complicated and unpredictable the machinery of life really is."

In the reading today from the Book of Amos we can sum up how God saw the people of Israel. They were "busy, busy, busy."

In that reading, God shouts at the people of Israel, saying (through Amos), "Be silent!"

You remember a few weeks back when Elijah was in a mountain cave, trembling, and God told him to go outside as he was going to be passing by? God was in the silence, not the noise of business.

In the optional reading from Genesis today, we see how Abraham got "busy" when the LORD appeared to him as a trinity of men passing by. Abraham begged them to stay and he went to work getting himself, Sarah, and his servant working on preparing the three men something filling.

In the Gospel reading today, Luke tells the story of Martha and Mary and the time Jesus was welcomed into Martha's home. Martha became "busy, busy, busy," because she wanted to make

After Pentecost Sermons: Proper 11, Year C

everything perfect for such an esteemed visitor. Mary sat in silence and listened.

The complication of the machinery of life (busy, busy, busy) is pointed out by Jesus, when he tells Martha, "You are worried and distracted by many things."

Jesus said, "There is need of only one thing."

Paul explained how Jesus is that one thing, which is the "better part, which will not be taken from" ... anyone who stops being "busy, busy, busy."

We have to sit at the LORD's feet and listen to what Jesus said and what the other lessons of the Holy Bible say.

Paul said, "I became [a servant to the church of Christ] according to God's commission."

This means he sat at the feet of Christ and listened. For that dedication he was rewarded with the Holy Spirit.

Paul said he was given that gift so others could be helped. That help comes by making the word of God fully known. What we think we know is not complete. There is a mystery element hidden, which is only revealed to those who have the Holy Spirit within them. It is revealed to those who live holy lives. That which is hidden is revealed to the saints.

Paul went on to basically give a job description of a Saint.

He said they proclaim Jesus as the Messiah. They warn EVERYONE who is "busy, busy, busy" to sit and listen. Then, they teach EVERYONE in all wisdom. This is so other Saints will be born through that wisdom, with EVERYONE mature in Christ.

The word that has been translated as "mature" is the Greek word "*teleios*" (τέλειος). It can also translate to say, "complete [in Christ]," "perfect [in Christ]," or "more perfect [in Christ]." The word can likewise state, "brought to its end, finished," "wanting nothing necessary to completeness," and "consummate human integrity and virtue."

The translation as "mature" is actually more relative to the fact that Paul was writing to male Colossians, who were "full grown adults of full age." The concept of perfection comes from age. "Aged to perfection," like a fine wine or cheese.

Have you seen the commercial on television for Cheez-it crackers? There is a man in the white lab coat who has a checklist for maturity and a hoop of cheese tries to act mature to get recognized for having that distinction. The cheese hoop is found to still be in need of more aging, because it does sophmoric things.

Being "mature in Christ" is the difference between Martha and Mary. It is the difference between someone who is "busy, busy, busy" and someone who sits and listens. It is the difference between someone pretending to be aged to perfection, when really being childish.

In the Amos reading, God showed Amos "a basket of summer fruit." This is a statement of the "first fruits," which in ancient Israel were the sacrificial gifts brought up to the altar during the festival of *Shavuot*. There were seven: wheat, barley, grapes in the form of wine, olives in the form of oil, pomegranates, dates, and figs. They represented the fruits grow in Israel.

The first fruits are picked in the Spring. The summer fruit are those picked later in the season, after the blessing of the first fruits on the Day of Pentecost. The metaphor is relative to the people of Israel, who were blessed by Yahweh. However, Amos described some of them as unripened and immature, thus sour and bitter, Some were seen as over-ripened, thus mushy and putrid.

# After Pentecost Sermons: Proper 11, Year C

The fruit of Christ are seen in Martha, Mary, and Paul. Martha still needed to overcome the distractions and worries of being a fruit still on the branch. Mary was a fruit picked at the right time for it to ripen in the basket ... to age to perfection. Paul was the seed planted in the ground, growing to the maturity of a tree, yielding new fruit.

The people of ancient Israel lost their focus. They became distracted and worried, meaning they turned their backs to God and got lost. Martha was lost for a while, but she had someone call her back to the light. Paul had been spoiled fruit, as Saul; but his seed was planted in good soil by Jesus Christ, so Paul grew to becomes a beacon to those in the body of Christ, a Christian church.

But, walking towards the light is not easy, because of all the distractions and worries ... all the "busy, busy, busy" of a complicated and unpredictable machinery of life. Paul said, "You were once estranged and hostile in mind, doing evil deeds." Paul had been there, done that. So, he knew just how hard it seems to be to stop trying to do it all and just stop and listen.

Paul said, "I am now rejoicing in my sufferings for your sake."

That says he suffered for stopping and listening. He felt pains because he sat at the feet of Christ and paid attention. However, the reward of fruits ... like the Colossians ... made it all worthwhile. He celebrated their efforts as a growing church of Christ, like a day of feast for the First Fruits. The faithful were blessed, as commanded by God, to become His first good fruits of the vine of Jesus Christ..

Unfortunately, those people of Israel who God had Amos speak to hadn't live up to their end of the bargain and became scattered like weed spores in the wind. Neither had the Jews of Judea nor the outcast living in Assyria lived up to their ancestor's agreement with Yahweh. They all became too "busy, busy, busy" to listen.

Using another term from Vonnegut in *Cat's Cradle*, they became "granfalloons." They became a group of people who imagined they had a connection that did not really exist. In Vonnegut's book, the narrator used the example of "Hoosiers," where Hoosiers are understood to be people from Indiana that have no true spiritual destiny in common. In reality, all they share in common is a name.

God's gift to mankind is the freedom to choose to live like you want. You can be a Christian in name, easily distracted and often worried. Or, you can be truly connected to God, through the Holy Spirit.

If you take the time to mature in Christ ... to know the perfection of God's wisdom ... to sit at the feet of Christ and listen ... then those gains will not be taken from you. You will be more.

You will bear fruit in Christ.

Amen

# TENTH SUNDAY AFTER PENTECOST

# Proper 12

# YEAR C

**Relevant readings:**
Hosea 1:2-10
Psalm 85
 Genesis 18:20-32
 Psalm 138
Colossians 2:6-19
Luke 11:1-13

Robert Tippett

# Funny names created through philosophy and empty deceit

What's in a name?

I'm sure you remember the Johnny Cash song "A Boy Named Sue." A boy with a girl's name. That was a made up scenario; and, because of that, it was humorous. A boy named Sue ... ridiculous.

Would you think it was funny if you had to grow up with a name your parents thought was unique, but all your classmates and friends thought was just odd?

Some parents don't want their child to be named like all the others being born, those with the popular names of the day. Some parents like to think up a name that has unique meaning that only they know. Some parents take delight in giving a name that is not found in a baby names book.

How do you think you would feel every time you had to fill out an employment application, and under "name," you had to write ...

Moon Unit?
Diva Muffin?
Sailor Lee?
Moxie Crimefighter?
Lark Song?
Banjo?
Audio Science?
Jermajesty?
Seven Sirius?

How about "Lé-Mongello" ... which is Lemon Jell-O as one

After Pentecost Sermons: Proper 12, Year C

word?

All of these are real names given to children by movie stars and singer-musicians. So (hopefully), those children will never have to seek work and fill out an application.

Still, do you think some of those children will have their names changed, after they become adults?

The reading from Hosea tells us about some horrendous baby names:

The name Gomer, the prostitute Hosea was told to take as a wife, comes from the Hebrew verb "*gamar*." The basic meaning is 'to complete, finish,' but it can also be used to indicate a sudden stop or termination.

God told Hosea to marry a woman by this name, to symbolize the sudden termination of the relationship He had with the Children of Israel. The living God had been their heavenly father, but the children had grown up and decided not to maintain the time share agreement their forefathers had signed off on.

The name Jezreel means 'God sows'

Jezreel is the name of a valley in Israel and the name Hosea was told to give to his first son with Gomer. Jezreel was the fertile land God gave to the children of Israel, symbolic of how they could bear other children to the living God. It symbolized where God let his children grow strong and be protected. The first son of Hosea would symbolize that God had sewn a marriage between his prophet and a nation that chose to sleep with many other prophets.

The name Jehu consists of two elements:

    1) *Jah*, which in turn is an abbreviated form of the name

of the Lord: YHWH.

2) The nominative pronoun *hu'*, meaning he, she or it. Thus, the king of Israel bore the name meaning 'the LORD is he,"

But, Jehu was not living up to that name; or perhaps, Jehu though he was God and could do no wrong?

The name Lo-Ruhamah consists of two parts.

1) The first part is the word *lo*, meaning, "no or without."

2) The second part comes from the root *raham*, meaning to love deeply or have mercy.

This means the second son of Hosea and Gomer was named 'No mercy,' which was symbolic of an Israel that had turned away from God, shunning His compassion. It sought 'no mercy' from the One God.

The name Lo-Ammi means "not my people."

The name of the third son of Hosea symbolized the people of Israel were no longer children ... they had grown up. They had the right of free will ... to choose not to have the One God in their lives anymore. They chose "not" to be God's people.

All of these names have meaning and that meaning says, "The children of the living God" had broken their agreement to serve the LORD.

It can seem like God disowned the Children of Israel.

However, they would be overrun by the Assyrians - by bow, sword, war, horses, and horsemen - because of their own failures. God knew that would be the outcome ... without His protection.

# After Pentecost Sermons: Proper 12, Year C

The people of Israel would be scattered around the globe, like the sand of the sea, neither measured or numbered … as yearly census' by nations do. God knew that would be the outcome … without His protection.

God didn't disown the people of Israel. We know that because He would later send His Son to save them. That would be later, after they had some time to learn a few life lessons.

By the way, the name Jesus is the Greek transliteration of either the name Joshua or its shortened form Jesuha. It means "YHWH Will Save."

The Gospel reading from Luke is continuing this Father – Child relationship theme.

We begin by the disciples asking Jesus to teach them to pray. Jesus is often called "rabbi," meaning teacher; and, a father's role is to teach his sons. Jesus teaches the disciples the Lord's Prayer.

After Jesus had told his symbolic children how to pray, he asks, "Who would not give a child what he asked for?" He had just done that.

Jesus said, "Ask and it will be given. Search and you will find. Knock and the door will be opened" … to all children asking God to be led correctly.

Those of us with children know what it is like walking through the grocery store or Walmart.

They love to say, "Momma, buy me this. Momma, buy me that."

Jesus told the parable of the friend coming by after bedtime, saying, "Friend, gimme this."

Robert Tippett

"Go away!," he was told. "No!," is what we keep telling our children.

The last time I was in Walmart, on the way to the garden center I walked down the aisle where the toy super heroes are sold. Each way, to and from, I passed a different child standing there marveling at action figures on display. I could see their eyes and I could read each of their minds. Both wished he could have one of those toys. They each had a pure and natural desire for something new, something to play with.

Children thirst for outlets for their imaginative minds. They each probably went to petition momma for a super hero action figure.

Persistence ….

As a Rolling Stones song says,

> "You can't always get what you want,
> but …
> if you try …
> sometimes …
> you just might find …
> you get what you need."

God is our heavenly father. He listens to our prayers. He leads us to find what we need. He puts doors before us, more than the super hero toys we lust for. When we stop crying over an imagined loss and actually open one of those doors, then we not only get what we asked for, we get it in ways we never ever imagined was possible.

Just as Jesus taught his disciples the lessons they needed to know, and after he ascended to his Father's house, the disciples became fathers.

They grew up and had children of their own. Their children

were the first members of the first Christian churches. Those "fathers" taught their children about Jesus and the way to God, through the Holy Spirit.

They weren't blood relatives, like the sons of Hosea and Gomer, but they were family. Families in Christ. Fathers and sons ... bishops and priests ... shepherds and flock ... all related by the blood of Christ, the Holy Spirit.

Paul never knew the man Jesus; but, he knew the Spirit of Jesus and became an Apostle. Paul also became a father to the children of the churches he founded.

By the way, the name Paul means "small, humble." He changed it to that. His name had been Saul, which means "asked for."

Paul never met any of the Colossians personally but he wrote a letter to them. He wrote the letter because Paul had fathered Epaphras (his name, in Greek, means "foamy"), who in turn had fathered the church in Colossae. Paul then wrote to the Colossians more like a grandfather sending a card to his grandchildren.

Some of us are grandparents. Hopefully, many of us have wonderful memories of our times spent with loving grandparents. There seems to be a generation gap that makes grandparents and grandbabies a good fit. Parents are often busy raising a family, especially if there are several children and/or if both parents work. Grandparents often have a little more time on their hands, and can help their children by babysitting. I don't have any yet but I delight in the thought of grandchildren.

Paul said to the Colossian grandbabies, "See to it that no one takes you captive through philosophy and empty deceit."

The call of the adult world can spoil the child inside us. Our inner child is always wanting to get out; but, it is kept captive by adult mentality. Paul warned his grandchildren: Don't let yourself get caught in an adult world that forces you to turn away from God.

Paul then said, "Do not let anyone disqualify you, insisting on self-abasement, puffed up without cause by a human way of thinking."

Grandfatherly advice: The best laid plans of mice and men ... so often they go awry.

Paul said, "You were dead in sins" until "God made you alive."

He said we are a "growth that is from God." We are born of God, as God's children ... not God's adults. Adults have free will to do as we wish ... like Jehu ... grown to act like "he is Lord."

Jesus said, "Know how to give good gifts to your children" so "the heavenly Father will give the Holy Spirit to those who ask."

The Holy Spirit keeps us children ... the children of God ... in the family of Christ.

As long as we remain in the family and ask Our Father for help, then listen for His wisdom ... our names will be written in Heaven.

And God likes our names ... no matter how funny they may be.

Amen

# ELEVENTH SUNDAY AFTER PENTECOST

# Proper 13

# YEAR C

**Relevant readings:**
Hosea 11:1-11
Psalm 107:1-9; 43
   Ecclesiastes 1:2, 12-14
    & Ecclesiastes 2:18-23
Psalm 49:1-11
Colossians 3:1-11
Luke 12:13-21

Robert Tippett

# Whisper campaigns that miss the original point

There is a game played that some call "Telephone." It is also known as "operator," "grapevine," "whisper down the alley," "gossip," "secret message," and "pass the message," among still others. Perhaps you have played this game?

It begins with a message whispered to the first person in a chain of people, with each person instructed to pass the message on to the next person, by whispering. The message can only be spoken once by each who passes it on. The last person who receives the message then announces the message aloud to the whole group. That is when the laughter begins, because the announced message is nothing like the original message.

The point of the game is to show how "confusion" and "incomprehensibility" make people try to understand something that is not easily understood. Everyone is told it is important to listen to the message and pass it on word-for-word. But multiple words blend together as whispers, with one not able to clarify by questioning. The words heard seem to need corrections, not fitting with the thoughts projected by the other words heard. Following the directions, however, means one has to pass along what one thinks one heard.

Confusion abounds simply because people are told to play the game as instructed. The message is a secret, which means you cannot let on that you know it ... until the time comes for the secret to be revealed publicly.

Has anyone played that game? (Look for hands or nods)

If that game had been played by the Apostles before Jesus died and before the Day of Pentecost came, can you imagine how the

# After Pentecost Sermons: Proper 13, Year C

original messages Jesus whispered would have been confused and laughable?

If Jesus first whispered, "Love your neighbor as yourself," then the twelfth disciples could have announced, "I believe he said to loathe your neighbor if he doesn't do what you like."

Fortunately, when the Holy Spirit is the whispering source, mistakes like that **do not** happen.

The readings today are very clear in the message: "Do not get caught up in going after earthly goals, because the heavenly goal is the only one that matters."

Messages like that are passed around in Christian circles. Biblical quotes are frequently tied up in a nice box with a bow on top, always made to look pretty when presented. Then Bible quotes can be freely given away as gifts. However, they never seem to be the message gift that people want to receive.

Many of the Jesus messages are received, but not a good fit. They're not applicable to the latest styles. They're, the wrong colors or something … but we nod and say "Thank you." Then we put the gift in a closet … to re-gift later. We often put the message back in the box and hide it away, wishing it was something we could actually use, more than a thought that mattered.

Sometimes it's the thought behind the gift that counts more, so people will secretly … occasionally … go look at the gift and imagine, "What if this could be right for me?"

If someone were to ask us, "What was the unspoken message accompanying the gift?" we might reflect for a moment. If we feel an answer come to mind vividly, then we see how perfectly something initially unwanted, unasked for, was intended just for us.

When that dawning makes perfect sense, then we are able to remember it. We get the point right on, word-for-word. We are then capable of passing on the message of Christ, without mistake. We **want** to pass on that message as true Christians.

It might be hard to pick up on this when reading Scripture, but we have a relationship with God and Christ that is like a Father-child relationship. Everything written in the Holy Bible is a Sunday school lesson. We are being taught to memorize the stories, to recognize them, and even to know what the meaning of the lessons is.

A good child pays attention. "Listen to the message. Repeat the message."

"I know it! I heard it word-for-word!" the child says.

Living it is something else. That requires growing up, gaining some experience and acquiring some wisdom. Letting everything we have been taught as children come to life ... click (light bulb turned on) ... is like a light coming on.

Aaaaaahhhh haaaaaah. A moment of understanding. A remaining lifetime for wearing and displaying the gift received.

In the reading from Hosea, we see the life of the child of God ... Israel. Israel memorized all the Scriptures and then put in some mental exercised for fun and games ... but their learning never matured. They learned every rule of Moses; then they broke everyone of them. They acted with sin while still calling to the Most High, as though knowing the message kept them privileged.

Paul gives us a long list of things that the child, Israel, probably did, which led the people to serve an Assyrian king instead of God. Those failures can be summed up as them falling prey to the vanities of the flesh and vanities of the mind. We want to use others as our possessions.

# After Pentecost Sermons: Proper 13, Year C

People are made gifts to ourselves, to make us feel good. We want to display our emotions towards others, in order to establish our dominance in this world. It is a right and joyful thing to have our way be THE WAY.

Everything boils down to being selfish.

Paul said, "Do not lie to each other."

In short, this means stop being an egocentric child. Grow up! Be a new self in Christ. **Live** the lessons you have memorized.

Jesus was asked about an issue one follower had about the inheritance rules, such that the eldest got everything and all the younger male siblings depended on the eldest brother's generosity. Sometimes the gifts of inheritance are not so balanced and evenly divided.

Jesus called the man, "Friend," because Jesus knew we all need earthly rewards to some degree, just to maintain life on this earth. Someone asking a question for clarity is a friend, not an enemy. The question was a just concern, because the rules require a society that actually cares for its neighbors and family. Friends share so everyone's needs are met.

The message Jesus then whispered into the ears of those listening was, "Don't get caught putting off for tomorrow what should be done today."

In the parable, the wealthy land owner started thinking (a deadly thing to do, sometimes). He thought:

"I might not always be as fortunate as I am now. To ensure I will always be fortunate, I will build a super-sized storage bin for my grain. I will hoard my plenty so I will be prosperous until the day I die."

Supposedly, maintenance of wealth ... enough to live comfortably on until death ... would allow him the ability to share more with others later. Otherwise, he might mismanage that grain and give it all away before he died, causing himself to die a poor man. In other words, "I need to have more than enough before I can give more away" was his mantra of altruism.

God said to that rationale, "You fool!"

"The **End Times**, in your case, is tonight. You were selfish to the end."

Sometimes, as children of God, we see money as the new grain of life.

I remember from my youth how it seemed the Christmas season began when the Sears "wish book" came in the mail. I would tear the brown paper wrapping off and turn to the toy section, immediately making a list of EVERYTHING I wanted ... not having any real concept of money. I wanted this. I wanted that. I wanted just about everything in between this and that. The costs for all that I wanted were prohibitive; but, I did not know that because I was a child.

How many of us have grown up with that mental concept as a cornerstone of adult life ... a life when so many playthings are available ... for money?

The costs run up. They can become prohibitive; still ... some people go into deep debt just so they can have this, so they can have that, and so they can have everything in between. At an adult age, people like that are acting like children. They know the message of Christ, but they have not grown to live it.

Paul wrote a lot of letters, as we can see. He was the bishop to several churches, where **all** the members were truly filled with the Holy Spirit. He wrote letters as a way of helping his fellow Christians stay "mature in Christ."

Those letters were gift messages, sent to those to whom the letters were addressed **and** to those who still read them today. They are gift messages that keep on giving ... but are they gift messages we understand? Do we truly understand what they whisper?

Christians are those who have grown beyond the child they once were, when they first heard a whispered message that came in the form of a colorful cartoon-like Bible story. Adult Christians - those who have "matured in Christ" - live the lessons that have been passed on to them. They then pass on the messages of wisdom to their children ... both in their words spoken and their deeds demonstrated.

You see, in a society so filled with financial worry, with people divided into groups - the haves and the have-nots, with one group always trying to stay on top and the other group always trying to keep from drowning - the message about helping your neighbor is not about giving money to strangers.

Christianity is like a support group, where your neighbors are other Christians.

It is like a support group for addicts - like AA - but I am not talking about alcoholism, drug habits, sexual binds, or any of the evils that come to mind when you hear the word "addiction." In the most basic sense, an addiction is about selfishness, one's addiction to "me first." To addicts, others do not matter. Addiction is more than a love of material things. Therefore, all addicts are like sinners, with the recovery program representing whispers about how to be saved from yourself, with the help of sponsors (like Paul) who the weak can lean on, in a neighborly way.

We have all been there, done that, and our sins are known; so we feel guilt every time we fall back into our selfish behavior. To keep going back to a state of guilt is vain. We need one another's strength to remain adults, much more than we need some stranger to give us a hundred dollars … which will disappear like last night's dream.

A church that I attended several times in the past had me meet a man who was a high-ranking member of that church. He told us in a Sunday school for adults' class about an "all-in church." That was how the first churches of Christ were. Members of that Church did not put a check in the plate, but totally supported one another. You had to be "all-in," so the Apostles and new Christian disciples could devote their lives to living meagerly and spreading the Gospel. They were "all-in" so that others would be filled with the Holy Spirit.

That church thrived and spread exponentially.

I asked the man one day, "What happened to that "all-in" church?"

As he rushed off like the white rabbit in Alice in Wonderland, he looked back and said, "That didn't work out too well, did it?"

\<buzzer sound\> Wrong answer!

\<whisper into microphone\> "Do not get caught up in going after earthly goals, because the heavenly goal is the only one that matters."

Pass that along.

Amen

# TWELFTH SUNDAY AFTER PENTECOST

## Proper 14

## YEAR C

**Relevant readings:**
Isaiah 1:1, 10-20
Psalm 50:1-8, 23-24
Genesis 15:1-6
Psalm 33:12-22
Hebrews 11:1-3, 8-16
Luke 12:32-40

Robert Tippett

# And God said, "I'll do the thinnin around here Baba Louie!"

The Egyptians used to prepare their dead pharaohs for an afterlife, which included an embalming process known as mummification.

In this process, they removed all the internal organs and mummified them as well in separate containers. They believed that when the body reached the other side it would need those parts to be reassembled – to be born anew, whole again.

One thing the Egyptians did not bother mummifying was the brain. They threw that in the trash.

Moral of that story: You don't need a brain in the afterlife, because it only gets in the way during this life.

They (whoever they are) say we only use 10% of the brain's power – CONSCIOUSLY.

We would be in trouble if we had to THINK about making our lungs take in oxygen, THINK about making our heart muscle beat, THINK about taking the images our eyes are receiving right now and processing them from upside down to right side up, while also THINKING about the meaning of these words your eyes are reading.

Perhaps that's why our teachers in elementary school wouldn't let us chew gum in class?

Making our mouth chew gum could be too much to consciously THINK about, should the teacher suddenly ask us to answer a question in class. We could choke on that gum by shifting our thought to THINK of something other than chewing. Add to that being instructed to walk to the blackboard in math class and …. danger abounds.

So, you can see why the Egyptians would throw the brain away rather than preserve it for future use. The brain, for all its power and abilities, limits us. The afterlife is heaven, when our souls enter a place of unlimited possibilities, which defy our brain's concept of physics and rationale. So, a brain would only be processing doubt, like the robot in television show *Lost in Space*.

"That does not compute, Will Robinson."

Let's just say that Peter actually walked on water during the storm on the Sea of Galilee. He did that until he starting THINKING - consciously and/or subconsciously - "I can't do this."

"Oh ye of little faith" can be amended to add, "and heavy brains."

In the reading from Isaiah, we see how Isaiah prophesied the truth that would unfold during the reigns of the four kings of Judah, all to whom he would serve as Temple prophet.

King Uzziah would defeat the Edomites by being the first to employ a mercenary army, rented from the Northern Kingdom. Uzziah took a liking to some of the idols the Edomite people worshipped. When Isaiah wrote, "incense is an abomination to me," that was a prophecy of Uzziah taking incense into the Temple of Jerusalem, causing Uzziah to be stricken with leprosy. From that point on, Uzziah would be forced to be a king in exile, unable to interact with the people of Judah.

His brother, Jotham, would become co-ruler of Judah until Uzziah would die about twenty years later.

Under Jotham, Isaiah and Micah were co-workers in the Temple of Jerusalem. At the same time, Amos and Hosea (who we have read of over the past weeks) also served as prophets in Israel. Jotham, while he did ease some of the ways of Uzziah, he did not completely remove the idolatry allowed by his brother.

The practice escalated, so that by the time Ahaz became King of Judah, Isaiah prophesied of his rule, writing "your hands are full of blood."

Ahaz sacrificed his son on an idolatrous alter he had erected in the Temple.

King Hezekiah was the ruler who was in place by the time the Assyrians first invaded Judah and held a siege of Jerusalem. Hezekiah removed all of the idol worship and returned the people's eyes, temporarily, to the LORD. Thus, Isaiah's voice changed in his prophetic writing. His focus changed to state what it took to have the graces of God:

> "If you are willing and obedient, you shall eat the good of the land; but if you refuse and rebel, you shall be devoured by the sword."

Understanding the times of Judah, when everything was rapidly going down the tubes, Isaiah was regularly telling them what not to do and what to, in order to enjoy the favors of God. We can now look back from a position of hind-sight and ask, "What were they THINKING!?!?"

That brain again. It gets us in trouble. It even makes us THINK we would have acted differently ... we would have listened to Isaiah and changed everything.

The letter to the Hebrews was authored by Paul, although that authorship is questioned. There are brainy people – scholars – who will say, "You don't know that Paul wrote that letter! The Greek is different!"

# After Pentecost Sermons: Proper 14, Year C

Well, I have FAITH that Paul is the author, although someone other than Paul might have taken dictation for him, while Paul was in prison.

Paul wrote, "Faith is the assurance of things hoped for." He added that faith comes from a "conviction of things not seen."

Therefore, one cannot see Paul's name on the letter to the Hebrews of Rome; but one is assured "of things hoped for." Have FAITH that Paul wrote the letter to the Hebrews. Don't hope that.

This states that "Faith" is different than "Hope."

I can hope the homeless person I give a dollar to will use the dollar to stop being homeless … rather than use it to buy some alcoholic beverage. I can hope that my prayers to God will be answered exactly as I request …

> "Please Lord, send me money to pay my car note."

I hope I don't have to learn a lesson about how I don't need a car.

I can hope the lottery ticket that I drive to Louisiana to buy will at least win me back the cost of the gas to drive to Louisiana AND the price of the lottery ticket.

However, hope comes with an understanding that odds are at play. Hope knows there is a chance that my hope will not be rewarded, depending on the percentages in or against my favor.

Faith, on the other hand, "is the assurance of things hoped for," such that Faith is a sure thing that one wants, but is not presently in hand.

The brain calculates hope, but Faith cannot THINK. Faith … IS.

In the letter to the Hebrews the example of Abraham's faith is given. Abraham was told he would receive an inheritance from God but he would have to go to find it at an unknown place.

What are the chances he would get there without a map? With hope, not very good. With Faith, it was assured he would go to the right place.

Abraham was one hundred years old; Sarah was ninety. That was when their Faith was rewarded with the "power of procreation." By being too old ... AND barren ... hope said the odds for receiving the power of procreation would be "as good as dead." Zilch. Zero chance of having a baby at that age and in that state of being.

But through Faith, "descendants were born." "As many as the stars of heaven and as the innumerable grains of sand by the seashore."

Abraham never saw an earthly realization of his inheritance, "but from a distance they saw and greeted" that reward, due to Faith.

You see, Abraham acted as though he had no brain. He acted because he had a heart. The descendants of Abraham, Isaac, and Jacob went to Egypt, the land where they threw brains in the trash after death.

Paul said, "If they had been THINKING of the land that they had left behind, they would have had opportunity (a word of chance) to return." However, because they had a "desire" for a better country, a heavenly one, the Israelites followed their hearts.

In the Gospel of Luke, we hear Jesus say, "For where your treasure is, there your heart will be also."

If you let your brain calculate opportunity and chance, then you

## After Pentecost Sermons: Proper 14, Year C

will be able to find an earthly reward. Your faith will be put into the power of intellectual procreation, which means your hopes and dreams can be materialized.

But, at what cost?

Jesus said, "Make purses for yourselves that do not wear out, where no thief comes near and no moths destroy." The best laid plans of mice and men often go astray. No assurances when you lean on a brain. Only hope.

Jesus told the parable of the slave being dressed for action and keeping a lamp lit for when the master returns. He said, "You must be ready, for the Son of Man is coming at an unexpected hour."

Your brain will not be able to project that time.

The lamp is in the heart, and the Egyptians had a special vase in which they mummified a heart. That was because the afterlife, just like this life, requires a heart.

The brain, on the other hand ….

Amen

# THIRTEENTH SUNDAY AFTER PENTECOST

## Proper 15

## YEAR C

**Relevant readings:**
Isaiah 5:1-7
Psalm 80:1-2, 8-18
Jeremiah 23:23-29
Psalm 82
Hebrews 11:29-12:2
Luke 12:49-56

After Pentecost Sermons: Proper 15, Year C

# A Good Vineyard Keeps You from Having to Drink the Bad Water

We went on a bus tour of Italy back in 2008. While in Venice, we learned that the first artesian wells were designed there. Their incorporating sand and limestone with groundwater created pressurized water, which was continuously available as a fountain, with water that was also purified by the sand and limestone.

In the rest of Europe, where such water purification technology hadn't been gained yet, the water source was mostly on the surface, from streams and ponds. Because those sources also were the places where people bathed their bodies and clothes, as well as where they deposited their sewage, the water became too polluted to be drinkable, especially the further downstream one lived.

One of the solutions for having bad drinking water was to make wines. Distillation was a way to remove any impurities that fell in the rain and absorbed by grapevines. That is why so many wines come from regions of France, Italy, Spain and Germany.

On that bus tour, while driving through the Apennines Mountains of northern Italy, we were taken to a winery. The hillsides were covered with domesticated grapes, in all directions for as far as the eye could see. It was very scenic to look at that vista. The villa that was the mansion for the family that owned the vineyard was available for weddings; and, they even had a chapel for wedding ceremonies, with a local priest ready to officiate.

Inside the winery, we saw the process for making wine. The places for the vats, where the wine aged, was kept very cool. While we were in Italy, it was suffering through a record-breaking heat wave. The place where the wine aged was a place to be physically renewed ... a welcome refuge from the heat. From the aging vats, the winery tour guide led us to the store, where they provided a wine tasting and made bottles of that vineyard's wine available for sale. As the bus driver was about to pull off and leave, we had to shout for him to wait, as one of our party had gone into the rows of grapevines to take a picture.

The rows and rows of grapevines, up close, was not where the tour had taken us; but, the pure vastness of the vineyard was attractive. There was beauty in the dry, almost gray ground, the support posts, the thick, bark-covered vines running up the posts and green leaves flowing with tendrils along wires connecting the posts. Row after row of the same ... like a pattern. It made me wonder how many people it would take to harvest all the grapes that were grown there each year.

When I read the Isaiah passage, and Psalm 80, my mind went to that visit to an Italian vineyard. My thoughts also went to Sewanee, up on the mountain while at seminary, because there is also a winery in Monteagle, Tennessee. It is on a much smaller scale and we never took a tour there; but, I could see all the maintenance that went into producing good, drinkable wine.

Isaiah stated the facts of a good winery:

> It was on a fertile hill. It was dug and cleared of stones. In the holes were planted choice vines. There was a watchtower in the middle, so all the surroundings could be seen. A wine vat was constructed for aging the fruit's juice.

Isaiah then told of a vineyard not kept properly. It yielded "wild grapes."

Wild grapes are to be understood as coming from plants that have tendrils and produce something that looks like grapes, but are not. They usually grow high in trees, not being easily accessible. While having a purple color – the sign of ripeness in a good grape – they are very sour. Some wild grapes are even poisonous.

Even though there are people who know how to tell the differences and how they can turn wild grapes into a variety of wines, we must understand the focus put a yield of wild grapes as being a failure. For all the work put into creating a vineyard of choice vines, to yield wild grapes means continued vineyard maintenance was not done.

The metaphor is how God's children are the grapes of choice vines. God planted His vineyard in Israel.

David wrote the lyrics that told of that vineyard:

> You have brought a vine out of Egypt
> You have prepared the ground for it
> It took root and filled the land
> The mountains were covered by its shadow
> You stretched out its tendrils to the Sea
> And its branches to the river

David also said:

> O God of hosts, look down from heaven; behold and tend this vine, preserve what your right hand has planted.

This preservation comes by tending the vines. Keeping them free of wild and domesticated animals, free from briers and thorns, and free of pretender vines that would turn choice vines into dead branches, turning the yield into wild grapes.

In the reading from the Book of Hebrews, it is easy to see that "Faith" is how one tends to God's vineyard. Faith allowed the Red Sea to part so the choice vine could cross from Egypt to the Promised Land. The walls of Jericho can be seen as the cultivation of the land for a proper vineyard and winery, and that clearance came by Faith.

Just as the vineyards of Italy were the product of generations of people in that area of the Italian mountains, continuously tending to the vines, through good years and bad years, we read how the vineyard of Israel was tended by the judges, prophets, and kings, "through Faith."

All of the stories of the Old Testament are examples of how those times of acts, as Faith demonstrated through earthly miracles, while commendable they only yielded temporary results. The dead branches must be cut away and thrown into a fire, just as we must "lay aside every weight and the sin that clings so closely."

Until we reach the promised reward of heaven, life is a race of endurance. We endure through acts of Faith. The promised reward is being made perfect, and Jesus is "the pioneer and perfecter of our Faith." Jesus is how we get the strength to maintain the vineyard, year after year, through years of good seasons and poor seasons.

This perfection brought on by Jesus is why he says, according to Luke, "I came to bring fire to the earth."

David wrote in Psalm 80, "They burn it with fire like rubbish."

Jesus said, "How I wish (that fire) were already kindled." He saw all the dead branches yielding wild grapes, as those calling themselves choice vines.

Jesus asked, "Do you think that I have come to bring peace to the earth?" He then answered his question by saying, "No." Instead, he said he came to bring "division." "From now on five in one household will be divided, three against two and two against three; they will be divided."

Think about what Jesus is saying, when the vineyard metaphor is maintained.

The Temple of Jerusalem was the watchtower in the midst of Israel, the vineyard planted by God; but, the people left it up to God to tend to the vines. Israel had been divided by those who wanted to take back the land that had been cleared and cultivated. It was divided by the wild boars and the wild ox and the wild sheep. The good grapes were mixed with sour grapes, having become wild grapes. Just as Gideon, Barak, Sampson, Jephthah, David, Samuel, and other prophets had been sent to clear away the dead branches and burn them in a fire, Jesus had come to do the same thing.

The division is then said to be within the family. The family is the Church. The family is the owner of a vineyard of God.

Jesus would send out disciples to divide the family. They would ask, "Who believes Jesus is the Messiah? Who does not believe? Who has Faith enough to act and clear the dead branches so the good grapes will grow and the choice vine will continue to spread?"

Some Jewish synagogues became Christian churches, while some remained Jewish synagogues. Christian churches have since divided, as well. We are of the Episcopalian vineyard; but, there are vineyards surrounding the hills of many different castles, where the family names are: Methodist, Baptist, Presbyterian, Roman Catholic, Assembly of God, Church of the Latter Day Saints, Greek Orthodox, etc., etc. Christian vines are cultivated, rows upon rows, over the hills of the world.

Each of those houses is further divided as a subset of a sect.

Imagine when a child of one Faith marries another child of a different Faith. Do the two Faiths unite and prune the dead branches together, attempting to return the vineyard to one owner

- producing nothing but good grapes? Or, do they become one against the other, arguing over what kind of grape is the one God prefers? Isn't that an act that tries to destroy the other's vineyard? Is that not how "wild grapes" spread?

This is nothing new. Ever since God took choice vine from Egypt, it has been an exercise of endurance, just to keep the yield good. As often as the wind blows, seeds of all kinds will take root, including weeds and bad seeds, those of vines yielding wild grapes. Faith tends to the vineyard so that at any given time – the present time – the grape is good. Collectively, we act continuously from Faith, always toiling against a never-ending challenge; but, the ultimate reward is not the vineyard. It is the produce the vineyard yields.

When Jesus called out the hypocrites, he was referring to the Pharisees, those who tended to the vineyard of Israel, which was then under Roman ownership. Jesus said, in essence, "You know the signs of a good harvest – the rain and the heat – from which you can gauge how profitable the wine will be." Jesus then asked them, in essence, "If you know what conditions make for valuable wine, then how can you not see the good gardener, who comes to maintain the vineyard for the production of the best grapes possible, when he stands before you?"

Working a vineyard is a full-time job. The constant gardener has to be the owner. While it is much less work just to wait until harvest time, and then hire the lowest paid workers to reap what comes naturally – whatever the result – a few bad years in a row can mean the owner loses the vineyard.

When the vineyard has "gone to seed" and it stops producing good produce, it has to be burned clear of the bad, before a new owner can replant choice vine.

Amen

# FOURTEENTH SUNDAY AFTER PENTECOST

## Proper 16

## YEAR C

**Relevant readings:**
Jeremiah 1:4-10
Psalm 71:1-6
　　Isaiah 58:9b-14
　　　Psalm 103:1-8
Hebrews 12:18-29
Luke 13:10-17

Robert Tippett

# Your financial security is not because God has spoken through the profits

In a little while we will recite the Nicene Creed. Near the end of that affirmation of faith we will each individually state, in essence, "I believe God has spoken through the prophets."

(Pause)

Today, we have a reading from Jeremiah, who is recognized as one of the "major prophets" of Judah. That distinction can be seen by the recognition he gets from Judaism, Christianity, and even Islam. All three religions now believe God spoke through Jeremiah.

The problem for Jeremiah was Judaism (or whatever they called their religion back then) did not believe that when Jeremiah was alive.

Jeremiah was deemed a "false prophet" and thrown into a cistern, where he sank into the mud. When he didn't drown, they left him there, with intent was to let him just starve him to death; but, before that could happen, he was rescued by a Cushite (an African – Ethiopian). Once rescued, he was jailed.

After Jerusalem fell to the Babylonians, Jeremiah was freed. King Nebuchadnezzar ordered that Jeremiah be treated with respect.

If you recall a few weeks back, when we celebrated the Feast of St. Stephen, we read in Luke how Jesus said Jerusalem was "the city that kills the prophets and stones those sent to her." Jeremiah was one of whom Jesus was referring.

When we say we believe God has spoken through the prophets,

we have to remember that Jesus was a prophet too. We can assume Stephen was a prophet as well, because we read from the Book of the Acts of the Apostles that the synagogue of the Freedmen stood up and argued with Stephen. We then read:

> "But they could not withstand the wisdom and the Spirit with which he spoke."

When one has the "wisdom and the Spirit," one is speaking for God, thus a prophet; and, Jesus certainly had that.

It is presumed that Paul wrote the letter to the Hebrews of Rome while he was imprisoned there. He, too, was speaking for God as one filled with the Holy Spirit. Paul was a prophet, thus we believe God spoke through him.

So, when we state that we have faith that God speaks through the prophets, we can understand that everything we read each Sunday is the word of God, written by human beings through whom God spoke. We believe God spoke through Jeremiah, King David, Paul (or whoever wrote the letter to the Hebrews), and Jesus.

Through Jeremiah, God said:

> "Before I formed you in the womb I knew you,
> And before you were born I consecrated you;
> I appointed you a prophet to the nations."

While God said that to Jeremiah, would it not apply to any and all prophets of God?

God then said through Jeremiah:

> "You shall speak whatever I command you,
> Do not be afraid of them."

The same can be said of David, of Paul, and certainly of Jesus. God knew they would all serve Him ... before they were born God knew ... before they were adults God knew ... before some even knew they would be God's prophets God knew.

In David's Psalm 71, he wrote:

> "I have been sustained by you ever since I was born;
> From my mother's womb you have been my strength."

Scholars of David have said he would often stay up nights, with his harp in the candlelight, waiting for the words of God to flow through him in song. It would have been so much easier for a king to get a good night's sleep and let court musicians write songs for him to approve, rather than stay awake writing emotional songs - of lamentation or praise. But, when the voice of God is whispering in your ear, who can ignore that? When God speaks, prophets listen.

In Luke, we find Jesus teaching on the Sabbath, in one of the synagogues of Jerusalem. When one reads between the lines, so to speak, we can imagine how Jesus taught like a prophet. He was inspiring those who listened ... speaking with wisdom and the Spirit. Jesus was not simply reading the Torah and asking questions, such as, "What do you think about that?"

We can assume that Jesus quoting Torah was welcomed. We see that when we read in Luke, "the entire crowd rejoiced at the wonderful things Jesus was doing." That describes his teaching as much as anything, even when we find Jesus also healing a woman on that Sabbath.

The healing of the woman took less than a minute, as far as the reading goes. Luke said, "When Jesus saw her, bent over and unable to stand up straight, he called over to her and said, "Woman, you are set free from your ailment."

# After Pentecost Sermons: Proper 16, Year C

Think about that.

Jesus was teaching and he stopped in mid-thought to heal a lame woman. One could assume she was keeping others from hearing him; but, it is more probable that Jesus wanted her to be able to hear his words spoken with wisdom and spirit about the lesson. He called over to her because he could see she was impeded and her condition kept her from hearing prophecy interpreted. As long as she was in pain, she could not benefit from the lesson and neither could those near her. Jesus saw that, so he then laid hands on her and immediately she was healed.

I imagine Jesus then continued teaching, "Now ... as I was saying ...."

The leader of the synagogue found reason to criticize Jesus for his healing on the day of rest. Jesus called that criticism hypocritical. After all, isn't teaching in a synagogue on the Sabbath technically working? Wasn't being a prophet of God on a Sabbath one of the wonderful things Jesus was doing, which was recognized by the crowd who listened to him? Healing a woman on a Sabbath was just as natural as teaching, and those who were critical of God's work being done on God's day ... they were put to shame.

You see, when Jesus was prophesying, some of what the old prophets had written wasn't then recognized as being about Jesus. They recognized that Jeremiah was right ... after all he warned about came true ... a verified prediction; but, they did not then realize how Ezekiel and Isaiah had written about the coming of Jesus, who was in their midst. So, teaching in a synagogue on the Sabbath was a good chance for God to speak through Jesus, enlightening the hearts and minds of devout believers in God ... to receive His messages through Jesus.

Jesus would be doing more of this type of "hind sighted" prophesying on the road to Emmaus, when (in an unrecognizable form after the Resurrection) he amazed two listeners, whose eyes were opened and their hearts lifted. All of the Apostles, once they were filled with the Holy Spirit, explained Biblical prophecy like this too.

Prophets are always expected to be clearly pointing to things in the future, so we can test them for accuracy. But Paul explained how the Holy Spirit not only leads one to prophesy; it also leads one to explain prophecy, as well as heal by a laying on of hands. So, prophets do other things, besides seeing the future. They follow God's lead, through the Holy Spirit.

In the Hebrews reading, we read Paul tell his fellow Christian Jews, "You have not come to something that can be touched." Paul counseled others filled with the Holy Spirit, who had come to that epiphany WITHOUT a blazing fire, WITHOUT darkness, WITHOUT gloom, WITHOUT a tempest, and WITHOUT the sound of a trumpet. The first Christians were NOT hearing "a voice whose words made the hearers beg that not another word be spoken to them." They would interpret the words of prophets … telling the Good News to welcoming ears.

Could the same words written by Paul be just as easily read as if he was prophesying a coming time when all those things mentioned … all that was <u>not</u> something believers would have to deal with then … would sometime in the future come to pass?

Read them again … don't the words of Paul sound a little like the prophecy of John … and of his flow of words from God found in *The Revelation*?

John is another recognized prophet, thus we believe God spoke through him …

Perhaps … however … we believe without completely understanding everything written?

## After Pentecost Sermons: Proper 16, Year C

We believe through faith ... even though you read *The Revelation* of John ... or Daniel ... or Isaiah ... or Ezekiel ... or Hosea ... or Jeremiah ... and we find we have come to something that cannot yet be touched by our understanding.

As Jeremiah said, "Then the LORD put out his hand and touched my mouth; and the LORD said to me, "Now I have put my words in your mouth."

We believe that.

(pause)

Do we believe God stopped speaking through prophets?

(pause)

Are we all so filled with intelligence ... not necessarily the wisdom and the Spirit of the Holy Spirit, but that of science, history, and technology, medical breakthroughs ... and books written by smart men and women who we let guide our decisions - that knowledge influences us to think that we don't need to believe in modern, contemporary prophets? Did God stop speaking to prophets when John wrote *The Revelation*?

Since the deaths of the Apostles - roughly around 100 A.D. - there have not been many new books written that have been given canon status. The ones written that we read from each Sunday, they took about three hundred years to gather up and be read by holy men, who then had to determine which ones came from God's inspired writers and which ones were less holy. We trust those judges were inspired by God (as prophets) to know such things, but who has judged since then?

Who judges divinely inspired people now?

Today, we hear the title "prophet" tossed around fairly liberally.

We hear stock market analysts called prophets. We see inventors and innovators, those well ahead of the times, all called prophets. A prediction, based on percentages and chance, is now associated with a prophecy. That becomes man-made predictions, not the word of God.

The History Channel has produced numerous shows announcing many "modern" personalities as "prophets," due to some uncanny accuracy that appears noteworthy.

By "modern," I mean since the Renaissance.

How often do we not call those "false prophets," because some are not recognized as Christians, or because none have written works judged to be accepted as holy?

Didn't Paul tell the Hebrew people of Rome to be glad they were NOT hearing a voice whose words made them beg that not another word be spoken?

It used to be said in television commercials, "When E.F. Hutton talks, people listen." As popular as that advertising campaign was, it trained us to listen to the false prophets of Wall Street. We learned to trust financial advisors and beg to hear their words about the future ... never begging them to stop.

Jeremiah was deemed a "false prophet" who the Judeans begged to stop prophesying what the people did not want to hear. They tried to kill him ... but he lived and was proved right. He wasn't a false prophet.

Jesus suffered a worse fate, as did Paul, Stephen, and most of the Apostles.

John wrote *The Revelation* in captivity, on the island of Patmos, with that book taking three hundred fifty years to be added to the Holy Bible.

People want to hear more when the speaker is painting pictures of success and profitability. However, start talking about, "a blazing fire, and darkness, and gloom," and people start yelling, "Shut up!"

The key is, as God told Jeremiah … "Do not be afraid of them, for I am with you to deliver you."

The message may not be one the crowd wants to hear. The miracles may not be recognized as truly holy until much later. Or they may be criticized because they were done on the wrong day, and not judged as worthy according to the agendas of groups.

But, the repeated pattern has long been to kill the messenger and ignore the message.

Our faith is to believe God **HAS** spoken through the prophets. Between the lines we can equally assume: He **IS** speaking through prophets, and He **WILL AGAIN** speak through prophets, just as we believe Christ **has** died, Christ **is** risen, and Christ **will come** again. If once, then always.

God always says the same thing through ALL His prophets, with the only differences being based on the times surrounding an individual prophet; but, Jeremiah's times reflected Jesus' times, and Jesus' times reflected John's times, and John's times reflect our times. The truth is true at all times.

Because of that, when God whispers in your ear regularly, you can listen to all the pretenders, just like you can listen to men telling fish tales and children telling fibs.

No harm, no foul. "Sticks and stones may break my bones, but pretend words of prophecy never hurts … when listening to them."

When God is with you, He will expose all the lies through wisdom with the Spirit.

If you are blessed to understand a prophecy, you will be amazed. You will be just like the people in the synagogue on that Sabbath when Jesus taught. Once you know the truth, then ... tag, you're it. You are also a prophet.

Let everyone know not to believe a lie ... let everyone know the truth ... and why. Expose false prophets from the position of inspired truth. Do not run from them from fear, cursing their words as you flee.

"Do not be afraid" means walking with that whisper of God in your ear. We should always welcome news from God, which can come from the lips of those brought to us, specifically because God wants us to hear it. Respond through Faith.

The last thing we want to do is refuse to listen to what God wants us to hear.

The next to last thing we want to do is not pass along to others what God wants all of us to understand.

Amen

# FIFTEENTH SUNDAY AFTER PENTECOST

## Proper 17

## YEAR C

**Relevant readings:**
Jeremiah 2:4-13
Psalm 81:1, 10-16
  Sirach 10:12-18
   *or* Proverbs 25:6-7
  Psalm 112
Hebrews 13:1-8, 15-16
Luke 14:1, 7-14

Robert Tippett

# Try not to step in the pride pit.  It is hell getting that stuff off.

It has been said that it is a male characteristic to not ask for directions, which always shows up when lost while driving in strange surroundings.  It seems as if it is a sign of weakness to pull into a gas station, stop the car, get out, go up to someone and ask, "Where am I and how do I get to where I want to go?"

Perhaps this is a sense of pride and to ask for direction is an admission of having done wrong.  Who can say?

If you are familiar with the Wisdom of Sirach, it is written, "Pride was not created for human beings."  Sirach even says, "The beginnings of human pride is to forsake the LORD."

That passage is an alternate reading for today, in the Revised Common Lectionary, and, human pride fits into today's theme.

As a child, when I was growing up there were cartoons on television for entertainment.  I would watch them after school but the real time for some serious cartooning was Saturday morning.  Maybe you were like me and had your favorite cartoons?

I loved to watch the Hannah-Barbera cartoon "Quick Draw McGraw," where the main character was a horse, who was an Old West sheriff.  He had a sidekick named Baba Louie, who was a Mexican burro.  In every episode Quick Draw would say, "I'll do the thinnin around here Baba Louie."  The comedy came from Quick Draw being luckier than smart, as his "thinnin" usually got him in more trouble.

Another cartoon I liked was called "Tooter Turtle," which featured a dimwitted turtle named Tooter, who was always dreaming up how he could be someone better than he was – like a knight, a gunslinger, a highway patrolman, a deep sea diver, etc. To be such a hero figure, Tooter would visit Mr. Wizard, who was something like an alligator wearing a wizard cone hat and a robe. With the wave of his magic wand, Mr. Wizard would transform Tooter Turtle into what he dreamed he wanted to be. Of course, Tooter always got in way over his head and ended up calling out for help. His call, "Mister Wizard!" brought him back home to reality. Mr. Wizard would advise Tooter, "Be just what you is, not what you is not."

Both of those cartoon showed how pride is a negative aspect of humanity. It is a form of self-destructive vanity, where we think we are better than others, or even ourselves. Quick Draw took pride in his cunning and intelligence. Tooter Turtle took pride in his dreams of self-grandeur.

In Jeremiah, today we read how the people of Judah were forsaking the LORD through human pride. They "went after worthless things ... and became worthless themselves."

What God was not hearing from his people was, "God help us!" They did not call out in desperation, "Where is the LORD?" Their pride kept them from realizing they were in danger.

Even the priests of the Temple of Jerusalem had forsaken the LORD through human pride. They advised the rulers of Judah; and in turn the people were assured by their leader that it was okay to keep off course and steer the ship into the unseen rocks ahead. They did not yell out, "Where is the LORD to save us?"

No. Instead, they told little sidekicks like Jeremiah, "I'll do the thinning around here!"

Long before Israel was divided into two kingdoms, David ruled over the children of God. For as much as he tried to stay connected to the LORD, the people invariably did as they wished.

Robert Tippett

In Psalm 81 we read the David lament the voice of God saying, "My people did not hear my voice, and Israel will not obey me. So I gave them over to the stubbornness of their hearts, to follow their own devices."

David then lamented, "Oh, that my people would listen to me! that Israel would walk in my ways."

That is the lesson today ... walk in the ways of the LORD. In the Book of Hebrews, Paul lists some of those "ways."

Paul wrote of: Mutual love; hospitality to strangers; remembering those who have been imprisoned and/or tortured for their beliefs and faith; holding marriage honorable – monogamous and fruitful; worshiping God, not money and things; and, being content with what you have.

Paul said, if we can live in those ways, we can say with confidence, "The Lord is my helper; I will not be afraid." We will not need to shout out, "Where is the LORD?" This is because we know Christ and he dwells in our hearts, as that "fountain of living water" from God. By living in the ways of Jesus, we take delight in those ways. Those ways call for sacrifices that are pleasing to God.

In the Gospel reading today, we see Jesus going to a luncheon held by the leader of the Pharisees of Jerusalem. It was held on the Sabbath; so, it must have been much Episcopalians regularly go to the Sunday buffet after church these days. Jesus had been invited so he could be inspected for his piety to Jewish Law.

This makes it important to understand the setting. The Pharisees of Jerusalem were the political, social, and philosophical judges of Jewish Law, as far as those outside the walls of the Temple who worshiped Yahweh were concerned. In a sense, being a Pharisee was like being a member of an American political party, who regularly met with others of like allegiance, to plot and plan the future.

The word "Pharisee" comes from the Hebrew word "*parush*," meaning "set apart." The capitalization is then a pronouncement indicating a "Separatist," or one who believed the Jews were different from Gentiles and should be kept separated for purist reasons. That made a Pharisee a higher ranking Jew, but also a different philosophical platform than Sadducees and certainly opposed to the Romans and other Gentiles.

To some degree, it is like those who have political beliefs and a position of wealth, which demands recognition. That ego is stroked by others of similar political beliefs, where there is the boldness that comes from safety in numbers. Imagine a Democratic fundraiser, where the minimum cost is $1,000 per plate; but, once the luncheon begins (with perhaps nothing more than a hot-dog and chips being served on a paper plate) the checkbook is expected to come out and a little extra "offering" is going to be what determines "just how Democratic" one is.

Jesus saw how the Pharisees were not living in the ways of the LORD. They jockeyed for positions of honor, with the host leader of them at the head of the table. Their positioning was an indication of self-importance – of pride within the ranks of a group.

Jesus told them how petty this was; as there was no heavenly reward from hosting "round-robin" luncheons, where each would repay the others in kind. Over time, all would eventually sit at the head position of a table. For all their self-importance, as judges of who are the ones most obedient to the Jewish Law, they were equally humbled by not walking in the ways of the LORD themselves.

When their ultimate times would come … when they would think they had earned a position of honor and go to take that seat of judgment before God … they would be told, "Sorry. That seat is taken. You have to move to a lower position."

If they were truly wanting to live in the ways of the LORD and help others live that way too, then they would throw feasts for those who could never repay them ... the poor; the crippled; the lame; the blind ... those who need help the most.

You see, Jesus told a parable that all of the Pharisees recognized, as it comes directly from a Proverb of Solomon. It reads:

> "Do not put yourself forward in the king's presence or stand in the place of the great; for it is better to be told, "Come up here," than to be put lower in the presence of a noble."

It is pride that makes one start thinking one knows where to sit, due to all the things one has done to earn extra credits and special recognition. But, as they say about Zen Meditation ... when you start thinking you are in Nirvana, you are not.

When your pride is showing, you are blind to your need to throw some humility over it.

> "For the sake of your Son Jesus Christ, have mercy on us and forgive us; that we may delight in your will, and walk in your ways, to the glory of your name."

Amen

# SIXTEENTH SUNDAY AFTER PENTECOST

## Proper 18

## YEAR C

**Relevant readings:**
Jeremiah 18:1-11
Psalm 139:1-5; 12-17
    Deuteronomy 30:15-20
    Psalm 1
Philemon 1-21
Luke 14:25-33

Robert Tippett

# Jesus was not a scapegoat

In a dictionary, the word "atonement" is found defined as "Amends or reparations made for an injury or wrong." This is specifically defined, relative to Christianity, as meaning, "The reconciliation of God and human brought about by the redemptive life and death of Jesus."

Nothing is said about the connection between "atonement" and the Jewish people's most holy day each year, Yom Kippur. In Hebrew that translates to say "day to atone," more commonly known as The Day of Atonement.

This day is preceded by the Days of Awe, when Jewish persons try to amend their individual behaviors and seek forgiveness for their wrongdoings against God and against other human beings.

The Jews, on the Day of Atonement, set aside the evening for public and private petitions, as well as confessions of guilt. At the end of Yom Kippur, one hopes that one has been forgiven by God.

Rather than one day a year, Episcopalians each week recite a Confession:

> "We have not loved you with our whole heart; and we have not loved our neighbors as ourselves. We are truly sorry and we humbly repent."

One of the ceremonies done on the Day of Atonement was to symbolically place the sins of the people on a goat and cast it out into the desert. That was begun during the Exodus and continued until the days of the temples in Jerusalem. It was called the goat for Azazel (meaning, "who God strengthens"); but, we know it as a "scapegoat."

# After Pentecost Sermons: Proper 18, Year C

In a way, the readings for today all recognize how flawed the children of God will be - all verions, then and now.

We see God telling Jeremiah that they are like clay, which can be good or bad. Pottery made with flaws cannot properly work as needed. The determination is up to the potter to decide if it can be reworked, to remove the flaw. If not, then it is not strong enough to be tested by fire in the kiln.

In David's psalm, we see how we are woven from the depths of the earth, with nothing hidden and all known by God ... both sinful thoughts and well intentions.

In Paul's letter to Philemon, the head of the church of Colossae, its shortcomings were to be corrected by the return of Onesimus. He should be welcomed as a beloved brother, just as Paul himself would be welcomed back. Both Paul and Onesimus were 'good pottery,' molded as duplicates of Jesus Christ, thus without flaws.

In the Gospel of Luke, Jesus recognizes there are those who can be his disciples. He made that clear by stating who cannot be his disciples. Flawed followers would not be able to handle the purpose that would mean learning from him and becoming a model of the master.

All of these readings are offerings for atonement, in varying ways of presentation. A warning from God says, "Atone or else evil will befall you!"

The song of David sings, "Always seek atonement because God knows everything about you, and God's hand can forgive your flaws."

The letter from Paul is stern, saying, "I command you to accept atonement because sin will not be acceptable."

The message from Christ is, "Atonement can only be wholehearted, or else it will not be granted."

Who here has not seen some action-drama movie where the hero is forced to make a decision that he or she hadn't planned on, while chasing down a villain?

They turn a corner and come face to face with evil, who has found a hostage to barter with. The hero always hears the ultimatum: "Put down the gun or I'll shoot your _____." (fill in the blank – wife, girlfriend, child, father, mother, favorite pet, etc.)

The hero **always** gives in and drops the gun.

Why?

Would dropping the gun suddenly be an act of atonement for having chased someone with a gun, as if doing what the bad guy wants will solve anything? Is the hero expected to let the table be turned, as an act of humility intended to help the villian stop being evil? If the guy is evil, why wouldn't he or she then shoot the hostage and the unarmed hero? If the hero will drop the gun because of a threat against someone else, why not run in without a gun in the first place? Then when he hears, "Drop it!" he can say, "Oh I don't need a gun. Drop yours."

Jesus said, "Whoever comes to me and does not hate even life itself cannot be my disciple." He was making a loud statement that life on earth is an obligation of service to the LORD, more than it is a reward from God. Hating life means wishing for death. Death can be our release to Heaven …

But, that is only a viable goal as long as we have atoned for our past … as long as we are good clay that has been fired in the kiln.

# After Pentecost Sermons: Proper 18, Year C

Certainly, when one has atoned for past sins, one is not running around with guns trying to shoot people who are also running around with guns trying to shoot people. Innocent people, like wives, children, mothers, fathers, and favorite pets are always put at risk then. And while our mundane lives will rarely be the stuff from which action-dramas are formed in Hollywood, an invisible enemy will be always be lurking nearby. An evil villain is constantly trying hard to compromise our ways, to force us to sacrifice a commitment to God.

We will find our faith extorted by evil. Evil - which comes in many pleasing forms, yet all flawed - will test our worth.

Invariably, some personal attachment in this world will be held hostage in exchange for that commitment Christians make to walk in the ways of the LORD. We will be forced to choose between that commitment and the possibility of sacrificing someone or something loved in this life that we have here on earth.

Our personal ties to those we love seem so real because we can use all of our five senses to know them. In contrast, we cannot know God or Christ in such physical ways. Our faith is for things hoped for, which cannot be seen.

The ways of the LORD are what our faith is based on. We hope our lives will always go just as we hope and pray they will go; but, too often we have to recalculate what we thought worked. We have to rework the clay of our individual faith. Sometimes that means totally changing what we had been, starting over from scratch.

The word in Luke that translates to say "hate" is the Greek word "*miseo*." Reading that translation makes it seems as if Jesus was requiring a disciple to "hate" his family. However, the word, in this context should be read as stating "to love less," such that all are loved. That means whoever loves Jesus less than his family cannot be his disciple. Jesus must be loved more than family, just as one must love God with all one's heart and with all one's soul.

Jesus then said, "Whoever does not carry the cross and follow me cannot be my disciple." Knowing what we know ... where we have read the ending of Luke's book and seen the end of Jesus' life on 'the ole rugged cross' ... it is difficult to not read that statement and think of that cross. We think that Jesus was telling listeners they had to be willing to be crucified ... to give up their lives in an agonizing public death ... in order to be a disciple of Christ.

Well, while that will often be found to be the case for the Apostles, Jesus did not go quite that far in this context. Just aas he didn't say to "hate," he didn't say being crucified was a requirement to be his disciple.

The Greek word that does translate as "cross" is "*stauros*." A Roman cross was shaped more like a 'T', but not everything shaped like a 'T', or even a 't,' was meant to infer a form of Roman execution. The basic meaning for the word "*stauros*" was "to hold something up straight." Hence, a Roman crucifixion would hold a human body up straight (relatively speaking) for public display.

Regardless of that use of a cross at the end of Jesus' life (realizing crucifixion was not an element of the Gospels prior to that final Passover), the most common use for such a "cross" was in a vineyard. It was the post set into the ground, and along the top of the 'T' a cross beam was set, which was for the weight of fruitful vines to be supported. In that way, the weight of the vine would not cause everything to fall to the ground. The cross needed to be upright, not bent over.

This means Jesus was saying, in effect, "Whoever does not maintain the cross of support, to remain upright and follow my path

# After Pentecost Sermons: Proper 18, Year C

(as a good vine), cannot be my disciple."

Being upright and following Christ may lead to persecution and death, but one has to be willing to accept such attacks to be a disciple of Christ. Therefore, "Whoever comes to me and does not love, even life itself, less than me cannot be my disciple."

Being upright is a way of the LORD that is required.

The final requirement stated by Jesus is in line with the message God sent to the people of Israel, as evil people not following the ways of the LORD. Jesus said, "None of you can become my disciples if you do not give up all of your possessions."

When they coined the phrase, "You can't take it with you," the point was to admit recognition that one loses all material things when one dies. If one is upright and walking in the ways of the Lord, thus good clay and atoned of past sins, reworked to be strong disciples of Christ, then the cross of death is a possibility before death would come naturally. Either way, you will reach a point in time when you cannot take things with you to the other side, to Heaven.

When that day comes, you cannot be a disciple of Christ if you think losing things is reason for being sad.

The children of Israel did not have the luxury of that clarification given by Jesus, when Jeremiah was giving them warnings about being flawed pottery. Although history believes the Jews were actively practicing recognition of Yom Kippur in the temples of Jerusalem then, perhaps they though placing the sins of the people on the back of a goat and sending it out into the desert would allow them to continue having their cake and eating it too.

Keep in mind that a goat does not usually stand upright, and it has no mental abilities to understand symbolism and metaphor. Thus, Jesus was speaking to those who were the descendants of

Jews who had been blown like chafe in the wind to the four corners of the world. All the sins of their lives had been placed on their backs and they were forced to leave. Those scapegoats who found their way back to Judea and were there at the same time as Jesus of Nazareth, they had returned to repeat the same mistakes.

Simply wandering around lost does nothing for redemption.

Thus, we are each a potter with our lives. Our clay must be molded to fit the ways of the LORD. The cross we bear is how we are tested by God, so we adjust ourselves through repentance, based on knowing the ways of Christ to follow. If we cannot stand up straight and face the LORD, then we have something to hide.

We must always rework the clay so that it is ready and able to be placed in the oven and be fired. If we are not upright, the heat will shatter us to pieces and we will not be disciples of Christ. We will be incapable of following the commandments, decrees, and ordinances of the LORD our God.

We do not have the luxury of a scapegoat. We do not have the luxury of a Hollywood script writer who will make us wily sharpshooters, whose gun never runs out of bullets, while our enemies are always the worst shots imaginable.

We pack our own sins on our backs, so that only by becoming Jesus reborn will be for our sins to be lifted away.

When our end comes, it will not be about self-glory, from having saved the girl or having won the big prize. It will be about knowing we were good enough to be disciples of Jesus, good enough to be Apostles.

Amen

# SEVENTEENTH SUNDAY AFTER PENTECOST

## Proper 19

## YEAR C

**Relevant readings:**
Jeremiah 4:11-12, 22-28
Psalm 14
    Exodus 32:7-14
    Psalm 51:1-11
1 Timothy 1:12-17
Luke 15:1-10

Robert Tippett

# We have met the enemy and he is us

The readings today bring about a need to understand the duality of everything. There are two sides that need to be considered. In general, we understand the warning of Jeremiah, the prayer of Paul, and the parables of Jesus from an Us and Them perspective.

The central theme for today – the golden thread connecting the readings – is Sin. The Judeans were sinners. Timothy was a sinner; and, Jesus welcomed sinners.

As Christians, WE see all the errors of THOSE times. That is the Us and Them duality of which I speak.

In the sayings "walk a mile in my shoes" and "when the shoe is on the other foot" the aspect of two sides is understood and one is always more able to see sin in others, while one's own sins are ignored.

From the US perspective, we can sit back – 2,700 to 2,800 years from the times of Israel and Judah – and say, "How stupid they were!" Jeremiah wrote how God told him to write, "Now it is I who speak in judgment … for my people are foolish … they are stupid children."

We read a perspective of God and accept it as our own – "Yeah! Stupid children!"

From that holy perspective, where we recognize Jesus as Christ speaking for God, we see the Pharisees the same as we saw the children of Judah – "Fools! You are stupid for rejecting Jesus!"

When we do actually walk a mile in someone else's shoes or when the shoe does actually get on the other foot, the part we so

# After Pentecost Sermons: Proper 19, Year C

often forget to consider is this: We are flawed human beings.

We do not have the luxury of pretending we are gods.

The Pharisees are always among us, as we are the Pharisees of our age.

We have the opportunity to live like Jesus, but as the saying goes, "When opportunity knocks we still have to get up to answer the door." This means we are only a few missed opportunities from being exactly like the Judeans of Jeremiah's time.

In the cartoon strip *Pogo*, the famous quote was coined, "We have met the enemy and he is us."

The tendency is always to see the enemy as THEM, not US. The shock always comes when one realizes, "I am my own worst enemy." The mind has a way of defending against such reality – the technical name for that defense is DENIAL.

Addicts use this once they are addicted to a way of life that even they – if they could see someone else acting like they themselves were – would deem wrong ... sinful. As such, the Pharisees and the Judeans were addicted to a sense of piety. They were addicted to the power that piety brought them. They thought only others were filled with sin and it was their role to purge the sinners from the midst of the people.

In the prayer by Paul, we find one who gives thanks for having been saved from sin. Paul stated he had been a sinner, where he had persecuted those who he saw as sinners; and , he had had acted violently in those persecutions.

One can imagine Paul as one who honored the Pharisees, if he himself was not one. When he said he had been a blasphemer, one can imagine he condemned others ... calling others sinners in the eyes of the self-praised righteous. Paul stoned them. He sinned by doing that in the name of God. He was admitting to his own actions as a sinner, for playing the role of god on earth.

In Paul's letter to Timothy, he confessed to having acted ignorantly in unbelief, because – like the people of Judah – he did not know God. Saul had no understanding of goodness. Saul was a stupid child of a Jewish mother and a Greek father. When Paul wrote, "Christ Jesus came into the world to save sinners," he was restating the Gospel reading; but, Paul said he himself was the foremost sinner.

The word "foremost" comes from the Greek word "*protos*," which can translate as, "first, in time and order of importance, chief, principal, and most important." That usage is such that the intent says there are no other sinners ahead of Paul. This is not a statement of how much sin Paul committed, as it is instead a statement of how important it was for Paul to admit to himself that he was a sinner, before he went pointing the finger at someone else.

They say the first step for an addict's recovery is admitting that a problem does indeed exist. Recovery begins when an addict realizes the root cause of his or her problem is self-centered. Paul admitted he was the sinner he needed to be concerned about, not the sins of others.

In the Gospel, the Pharisees grumbled about Jesus welcoming all the sinners, who were seen specifically as the disliked tax collectors. Jesus overheard the complaints and told two parables. Each focused on something being lost and then searched for until found. The recovery of the lost object was reason for celebration.

The first parable told to the Pharisees was about being a Good Shepherd, which meant leaving the flock to search for one lost sheep. The second parable was about a woman who had lost one silver coin from the ten she had in total. The two can be seen as saying the same thing but there is a difference in the loss of a living creature and the loss of a valuable material.

To find the living creature – the lost sheep – the shepherd was required to leave ninety-nine sheep unattended in the pasture, while he went off looking for the one hundredth sheep. The pasture can be seen as the church, where there is safety in numbers and where the flock protects each other while the master is away.

This is why the Apostles wrote letters to the heads of different churches. They had left their flocks behind, in search of lost sheep – those who did not yet know the Gospel, who did not yet have the influence of the Holy Spirit within them.

Jesus told this parable to ask the Pharisees, "Why are you not tending to the flock of Jews that come to you for shepherding, instead of scaring them off in fear?"

The woman who had lost one of ten silver coins (ten percent of her wealth) must be seen as not selfishly hoarding material things; but, instead, she supports a ministry of disciples – whether it is the Temple and its tithes (10%) or the "all-in" church of Jesus. She seeks hard for the lost coin so that others will not suffer from her loss. The ministry of the LORD is sustained through such material sacrifices and such urgency of dedication.

Jesus told this parable to ask the Pharisees, "Why are you asking poor women to give more of their possessions, which they gladly do, when you give a lesser percentage and expect more of God in return?"

What were the people of Judea getting from their priests and rabbis? As lost as they always were, always thirsting for someone to come save them and show them the way, one would think they needed someone to tell them - step by step - how to stop being sinners.

The point of one sinner repenting and being brought back to God is the true work of a priest, of one dedicated to the LORD. This was something none of the Pharisees were doing. It serves no purpose to point out the flaws of others, if you do not seek out the aspect of yourself that is lost and return it to the fold. If you cannot lead by example ... if you cannot explain - like Paul and the other Apostles of the Epistles - how to let the Holy Spirit save you, then is that not the blind leading the blind? Isn't that what was going on 2,700 - 2,800 years ago? Isn't that still going on today?

The purpose of the children of Israel, those of David's House of Israel and those of Jeremiah's Judah and Jerusalem, was to serve the LORD. They were meant to seek out the sinners and return them to the sheep pen. They were chosen to be God's priests. They failed in that regard.

God told Jeremiah, "I will not make a full end. I have spoken, I have purposed; I have not relented nor will I turn back." - There is purpose and need, so they will always be some flicker of hope left burning.

David's song sings, "The LORD looks down upon us all, to see if there is any who is wise, if there is one who seeks after God." - Those are the hope for the people, for all who are lost.

Paul says the answer is yes, to the question, "Who seeks after God?" There is Christ Jesus who seeks after God. - We receive the mind of Christ through the Holy Spirit.

And, when the sinner's eyes are opened by Christ and the foremost sinner is seen for who he or she really is, another will be forgiven and allowed back to the pasture ... to also seek God and tend the flock.

Amen

# EIGHTEENTH SUNDAY AFTER PENTECOST

## Proper 20

## YEAR C

**Relevant readings:**
Jeremiah 8:18-9:1
Psalm 79:1-9
Amos 8:4-7
Psalm 113
1 Timothy 2:1-7
Luke 16:1-13

Robert Tippett

# This week's simpleton-hero is: Navin R. Johnson

For anyone who is familiar with the Steve Martin movie *The Jerk*, you know it is a rags-to-riches, then riches-to-rags, and then finally a rags-to-riches again story. In the riches-to-rags part, when Navin R. Johnson (the main character) has lost everything, finding himself poor once again, he says while sobbing, "I don't care. I don't need anything ... except this ... and this here ... and this too ... and this."

The scene is a classic because it is very funny ... and it is very true, because we can all identify with that scene. We just might choose different things to keep with us, if we were being sent on the our way to the poor house.

In order to live in a material world we must have material things. It is more than a desire for things. There is a **need** for certain things.

An American psychologist, named Abraham Maslow, is known for creating what he termed a "hierarchy of needs." It is a theory of human motivation.

Maslow theorized that one's mental health was predicated on the fulfillment of certain innate human needs, necessarily being met in an order of priority. Some are more important for one's mental state to be stabilized, with others naturally being sought as additions, once one's state of being is stable. One's base needs are those most urgent for sustained life; and, once those have been met a quest for higher needs begins. As each new level is met, more needs motivate one to be happier about one's life. The ultimate realization is the need Maslow called "self-actualization."

Happiness can be found on the base level ... and on all levels ...

After Pentecost Sermons: Proper 20, Year C

but, in order to be happy, one needs to have some level of stability ... some sense that things are not so bad ... as long as I have this ... and this here ... and this too ... and this.

In a way, Navin R. Johnson realized he did need some things ... especially since he was going to be poor again. Because he had been poor before, he thought he knew what was too important to lose. As a wealthy man, Navin had learned about needs he never knew before, when he was a happy poor boy.

Maslow built a five-tiered pyramid with the base needs, those on the lowest level, called the physiological needs. Basically, those included: air to breathe, food to eat, water to drink, sleep to recouperate, and some sense of social equilibrium [not being the only one of your kind].

From these base needs being met, one then naturally seeks safety, through clothing for dangerous elements, support from family, a sense of morality, decent health, property [things needed], and for those rightfully obtaining things – employment.

With the physical needs level met, one then seeks love and a sense of belonging, through friendships, family of one's own, and the intimacy with one that makes adding to family possible.

Once one gets to that third level, esteem is sought. This is self-esteem, confidence, achievement, a respect of others and the respect by others.

The highest level – self-actualization – comes with a sense of personal morality, creativity, spontaneity, a lack of prejudice, and acceptance of facts.

In the story of Navin R. Johnson, you can see how he went from a "poor boy" to being self-actualized. He reached all of the five levels in one way or another and he did so without even knowing who Abraham Maslow was.

In many ways, Maslow's hierarchy of needs would be something way over the head of a simpleton like Navin. That theory can be seen as some common sense being mixed with some complexity to make it seem difficult. Simple people don't think that deeply about things; and, part of the beauty of a simpleton-hero story is that good things happen to good people, simply because they don't dwell for long on the bad things.

When one looks at the climb to reach self-actualization, we all are naturally drawn to the needs Maslow named, regardless of our intellectual acumen. However, there is not a fixed path to take.

In a way, one can see there are two movable ladders that assist us in finding our personal way to the top. In reference to the Gospel reading today, you could say Jesus was telling us that one ladder to self-actualization serves God, while the other ladder serves wealth.

Self-actualization does not depend on one's reaching a higher-class level, such that the pinnacle comes with being recognized by Fortune magazine as a member of the billionaire club. You can be poor and reach self-actualization. Still, self-actualization can be attained through the development of a self-serving morality, shrewdness, quick thinking, a willingness to do business with whoever helps you most, and an ability to use facts to one's advantage. In that case, self-actualization could be associated closely with a plethora of worldly comforts.

The question becomes, which ladder to self-actualization dose one climb?

What master does one serve?

One can imagine that the temples of Israel and Judah, in Samaria and Jerusalem, during both the times of Jeremiah and Jesus, struggled to use the ladder that served God. When one reads the words of Psalm 79, we see how David (probably young David, before he was king) was well aware that there were those around who always waited to knock the ladder serving God down and hide it.

There were always the enemies of good surrounding servants like David, who knew that to climb the ladder serving wealth meant God would suspend His protection for the Israelites, leaving Jerusalem open for ruin. In that sense, the heathen are often the business partners of dishonest managers.

We have all heard that it is the LOVE of money that is the root of all evil …

One often gets corrected with that scripture lesson, after one has made the mistake of saying, "Money is the root of all evil."

LOVE of money is clearly serving a master of wealth. Money, by itself, is just another necessity in the world. People secretly loving money often deny a fondness for things of the material realm. That makes them feel safer to quote the Holy Bible as a support of their hidden desires.

Money is no different than coats. Both are material things. We can like a coat, even say we love the look and feel of a coat; but, that love isn't true LOVE.

We pay money to buy coats. We can only wear one coat at a time, so to have many coats is like having a savings account at the bank. If we see someone without a coat … and it is coat weather … we can AFFORD to GIVE someone one of our extra coats … Or, we could take that person to the outlet mall and spend money on a coat just for him or her. Same thing … if you serve God, then you share. If you serve wealth, then you let people go without coats … remembering that a coat would be classified as one of Maslow's security needs.

In the movie *The Jerk*, Navin R. Johnson was honest. In his business, he made the perfect product ... something many people could use ... a want ... a need. Navin made little rubber rings that went on glasses frames, so the frames wouldn't slide down one's nose. A packet cost $1.43 (or something like that) and Navin guaranteed them for life. Navin became rich meeting the needs of others ... but he went bankrupt because people wanted their money back, once his product was found in some way to be dangerous. That news stopped all future sales, causing refund requests to pour in. The people said, "Live up to the guarantee, wealthy Navin!"

Navin individually wrote checks to everyone who asked for their money back ... $1.43 at a time ... until all his money was gone.

He was a man of his word.

Had Navin been a dishonest manager, he would have ignored all those requests and hid all the money he made in offshore shelters, planning for such things as recalls and refunds. Or, he could have only dealt with the Walmarts, ignoring the individual purchasers; dealing only with those fat cats who bought the biggest blocks of his product. He could call them in to review their outstanding debt, then make a compromise deal on how much he would give the buyers back ... something in return for bad merchandise. That way, both sides profit, so a dishonest manager could keep something for himself.

That was what Jesus was saying the dishonest manager was doing, before he got fired by the rich man. He was giving the buyers credits for their debts, the profits from which he had already embezzled a portion. With the buyers happy to get anything for nothing, the dishonest manager would be able to do business with the same buyers again, once he found another rich man to work for. His rich employer even said that was shrewd dealing, and commended his dishonesty for having handled adversity in that way. That is a sign that his rich employer got rich from taking advantage of the poor ... something more easily done by purposefully hiring a dishonest manager.

In the movie *The Jerk*, Navin R. Johnson was rewarded for his honesty and for having a mind too simple to be shrewd, unable to purposefully cheat people. His family, who he had sent money to while he was wealthy, they had invested that money wisely. When they saw their windfall, after Navin was no longer wealthy, the family saw it was time to share their wealth with Navin. Goodness prevailed and those who supported one another all benefited. It wasn't heaven ... and it was only a movie ... but it was a "feel-good" ending.

In reality, there are few Navin R. Johnsons in the business world. There are many, many, many more successful entrepreneurs who serve wealth, than there are those who serve God and are rich men and women. In fact, to accommodate those who serve wealth, there has been a rise in a branch of morality that helps ease the pains of guilt from lusting for self-actualization through wealth. It preaches Jesus wants people to be materially rich, so the rich can use their wealth to get into Heaven.

That is a slippery ladder to climb.

I went once to a church that preachs that message EVERY Sunday. It falls in line with the false shepherd warnings of Jesus. Thus, the parable today is focused on the Pharisees, who were bad shepherds to poor people. It was to their eavesdropping ears that Jesus told his disciples, "You cannot serve two masters, God and wealth."

Verses 14 and 15 of Luke 16 say, "The Pharisees, who loved money, heard all this and were sneering at Jesus. [Jesus] said to them, "You are the ones who justify yourselves in the eyes of others, but God knows your hearts. What people value highly is detestable in God's sight."

Jesus was saying, "You cannot preach wealth to the poor (by demonstrating wealth and implying an association with righteous reward), then sit back as rich men while the poor people cry, "Is the LORD not in the shepherds of Zion?"

Paul wrote to those early Christians, many of whom were Gentiles. It was they who were of heathen origin but who had been shown the light through apostles like Paul and Timothy. Paul said to those seeking salvation, "come to the knowledge of the truth."

The truth is that there is only one living God ... not two, or three, or many. There is the mediator who gave himself in ransom for us all – Christ Jesus. Christ was truth in human form ... the model for all other human forms to match. Jesus died a rich man, through his wealth was not counted in coins bearing the likeness of Caesar. Jesus was self-actualized. He was happy because he sacrificed all that was excessive in the material realm ... for a much higher reward.

All of the apostles taught the Gentiles they welcomed how to find "faith in truth." Truth is honesty. Had the apostles been dishonest managers of the master's property way back when, then we would not be here talking about this today.

Thank God they told the truth, which can be attested.

Amen

# NINETEENTH SUNDAY AFTER PENTECOST

## Proper 21

## YEAR C

**Relevant readings:**
Jeremiah 32:1-3, 6-15
Psalm 91:1-6, 14-16
Amos 6:1, 4-7
Psalm 146
1 Timothy 6:6-19
Luke 16:19-31

Robert Tippett

# Please, sir, might I have one more crumb?

In today's readings we heard a series of names: Zedekiah, Nebuchadnezzar, Hanamel, Shallum, Anathoth, Baruch, Neriah, Mehseiah, and Lazarus. To most of us, we hear these names and it is like when the parents speak in a Charlie Brown television special:

"Wah, wah, wah, wah."

Adult talk is beyond the grasp of children, so it seems more like noise than words that can be understood. Ignoring it means much less instruction to follow.

To turn this sermon into a lesson in Hebrew and a class in how names have meanings, would take more time than a twelve-minute – 1300 word sermon will allow. Therefore, I will only tell you the meaning of one name … that of Lazarus.

We all recognize the name Lazarus as he was the brother of Martha. We also remember how he fell sick and died, while Jesus was away. They put Lazarus' body in a tomb; but, upon his return, Jesus raised Lazarus from the dead.

"Lazarus, come out!" is what Jesus ordered. And, Lazarus did just that.

When you plug in the Hebrew meaning of the word, "*lazarus*," Jesus actually said, "God will help, come out!"

The word "*lazarus*" means, "God will help, "God is my help," or "Whom God helps."

With that lesson taught, look at how the parable told by Jesus is symbolic of the paradox of those living beings who help themselves (but not others) and those who cannot help themselves (but serve others). One goes to Hades. The other, the one "God will help," he goes to Heaven.

As a parallel to Lazarus, Jeremiah was not much different. Jeremiah was a prophet of the LORD who was thrown in a cistern to drown, but God helped him survive. Earthquakes cracked the walls of the cistern so the water drained out. Jeremiah just got stuck in the mud that was left behind. So, like the character named Lazarus in Jesus' parable (a story not always intended to be a factual recount of a past event), Jeremiah lay at the gate of the king's palace as an unwanted presence that King Zedekiah (one who dressed in purple, of the finest linen) ignored.

In a metaphorical way, Jeremiah was seen by the King Zedekiah as though he was "covered with sores," simply because every time the king heard Jeremiah speak, it was to tell the king how sinful he was and how painful the fall of Jerusalem was going to be.

Ouch!

Those were sore topics to the king, especially when the Babylonians occupied Judah and held siege over Jerusalem at the time of this part of Jeremiah's book. Only the dogs of Jerusalem would lick Jeremiah's wounds, as a prisoner who longed for rulers and leaders to drop one crumb of interest his way. He longed for those rulers to ask him to have the LORD tell them how to get out of the mess they were in.

Instead, mindless followers of orders would bring Jeremiah a bowl of gruel, some moldy bread, and a cup of sour wine. Figuratively, that was the dog licking his open sores.

The deaths of King Zedekiah and Jeremiah eventually did come, thus paralleling the story Jesus told the meeting of Lazarus (the one Whom God helped) and the "rich man" who did nothing to help the poor man. The last king of Judah was Jeremiah's "rich man." In death, the rich man/king saw someone he recognized, as Zedekiah would recognize his servant, the prophet Jeremiah. He called to him to serve him still … to moisten his finger in water and cool the king's tongue.

If only King Zedekiah had asked that of Jeremiah before Jerusalem fell. If only the heated tongue had not condemned Jeremiah and brought about the stiff neck of stubbornness. After justice had been served, Zedekiah's good times were over and Jeremiah's hard times on earth brought him heavenly reward. A chasm kept the two from doing more than see one another, maybe wave and point.

So, it becomes possible to see how Jesus was telling a story that had already been lived out and was one that was worthy of mentioning as a parable. That is because … as the saying goes, "History repeats."

The aspect of five more brothers of the "rich man" remaining to repeat the offenses of their lost relative means the story continues. Five more important, rich men needed to be warned not to lead the people poorly, or they too would suffer the same fate. Perhaps, generally speaking, more rich men would become the Pharisees of Roman-controlled Jerusalem, who, like their "rich man" descendant (Zedekiah), would be living lives that would not honor the LORD, while ignoring the poor.

No matter what the number is, the same result will always come to be … if you do not live by the Law of Moses and you do not listen and obey the prophets of the LORD, then there is a place that is not heavenly awaiting.

In this parable today, we pick up reading at verse nineteen, in chapter sixteen of the Book of Luke. Today's part is a continuation of the appearance of Jesus, where just before Jesus had told

# After Pentecost Sermons: Proper 21, Year C

the parable of the bad manager. We read that a couple of weeks ago. In that parable's verses, Luke wrote about how the Pharisees grumbled about Jesus hanging out with sinners - tax collectors. He even dined with them!

So the same audience can be assumed for this similar parable of the rich man and Lazarus – the one God will help. The same ears are meant to overhear this parable, as the Pharisees and Temple Priests are the ones robed in the finest purple linen. They are the rich man, each of them, and Luke said as much.

The Pharisees, just like King Zedekiah, represent the ones who say they believe in God and the Law,. They are the ones who give God the credit for making them become wealthy; but, they are the ones who in reality do the least, as far as demonstrating faith in God. They accuse others of sins, often causing the poor increased pain and suffering, when not ignoring the lame and ill.

While it isn't expressly stated by Jesus, Paul did a good job of pointing out how little the "rich man" does not share with others. Not only do they not share, they cheat, they steal, they connive against others, and they commit all kinds of evil in order to make sure they retain wealth and the power over others. They desire riches more than God's presence within them. Perhaps, their greatest evil is flaunting their wealth before the poor, while claiming God has made them rich, thinking that as a sign of their greater faith.

The reality is, as Paul pointed out, the Pharisees suffer from a love of money, which is the root cause of much evil. A couple of weeks ago we read how Paul confessed to having been a terrible sinner. He had acted as a god (blasphemy), persecuting others for their beliefs, doing so violently (he stoned the accused to death). During those days, Paul was named Saul; and, he most likely voted to keep the Pharisees in office, if he was not a card-carrying member of the Pharisees Party himself. But, Paul had to have a conversion … an epiphany … in order to give up his love of money.

The love of money being the root of all evil is a repeating theme in the Holy Bible.

While everyone recognizes that, it would seem that the "rich men" Jesus told parables about no longer go to churches today.

What priest or pastor would dare preach a sermon about today's Gospel reading without stepping on the toes of one or more of the largest contributors?

Jesus was talking about the Jewish Temple and the Pharisees … right? Not Christians. After all, didn't Paul stay on the road raising money to keep the new Christian Church alive?

Not exactly.

The message about being rich often comes across just like the names we read today in Jeremiah. The themes of being rich, ignoring the poor, and doing evil for the love of money.   all that can come across like, "wah, wah, wah, wah."

Just like a child being told the dangers of crossing the street alone, or the safety of cleaning one's room, they prefer to ignore being told what they don't want to do. It's time to tune out.

"Nah nah nah nah … I'm not listening."

After all, can't we all say things like:

> "I'm sure you are talking about someone else, because there are plenty of other people with money, much more money than I have."

> "I work hard for my money and I'm not about to help some lazy people who are only looking for handouts."

# After Pentecost Sermons: Proper 21, Year C

> "I give many dollars each year to charities, including this church ... and I have the income tax records that prove what I claimed as charitable deductions."

It is a hard topic to talk about, because we all know the world stops spinning if someone doesn't pay the rotation bill.

We are all "covered in the sores" of not having enough money, even if some have past money woes have healed ... maybe even no longer visible. Still, our wants make it seem many other economic shortfalls are still oozing and festering.

The sad thing about a parable like the one today, where the rich are clearly told to stop being selfish BEFORE IT IS TOO LATE, is this:

The poor always hear this message and they always believe it applies to them. The poor are so used to being poor, they will always try to give what little they have left, just to keep from losing Heaven. It is their only hope, all they have left, what they do not want to lose.

They know the rich ignore them. They have been taught by the Pharisees that they are poor because they cannot make themselves rich. Perhaps, if they could have just a little more faith?

"Please, sir, could you show me how to put **more** faith on my plate?"

Lazarus ... the man whose name means, "God will help" ... "longed to satisfy his hunger with what fell from the rich man's table."

The Greek word written is "*epithumeo*," which means, "to set the heart upon, i.e. long for, covet, desire, lust after." As the translation says "longed," know that the verb "longed" means "earnest, heartfelt desire, especially for something beyond reach"

So, Jesus said the one Who God will help (Lazarus) had an, "Earnest, heartfelt desire for a morsel … for a crumb … to satisfy hunger pangs." That is a powerful word, as it paints a picture of how so many poor people lay at the gate of some "get rich" scheme, longing to somehow get something from the table of some icon of wealth. We all have urges to eat – hunger – which is a need that must be met, or we die of starvation. The symbolism of longing to satisfy hunger for what falls from the table of the rich is where we all come into this story.

We are all Lazarus. "God will help" those who suffer from the negligence of the rich. If you work at Walmart, or McDonald's, barely getting by, working from paycheck to paycheck, while the heirs of Sam Walton and Ray Kroc live like royalty, totally oblivious of your meager existence, you will be helped spiritually.

However, we are all the "rich man" just the same. Everyone here has more than enough to meet one's needs. By that, I do not want to know how much you have in your retirement fund, your inheritance account, your land holdings, or your investment portfolio. Some may have great material wealth, while some may be materially comfortable, and some may be "just getting by, but no complaints." Some may only be rich in faith and life in general, happy to go share in fellowship at their church.

Because we are all rich in a way unique to each of us we must remember what Paul said. "As for those who in this present age are rich … do not be haughty, or set your hopes on the uncertainty of riches, but rather on God who richly provides us with everything for our enjoyment."

"Enjoyment" is based on contentment. Like the song goes, "Don't worry, be happy." Be happy with what you have, and if you can help others, if you can share so those who are without can also be happy, do so.

# After Pentecost Sermons: Proper 21, Year C

Paul went on to say, "We are to do good, to be rich in good works, generous, and ready to share."

Over the past three years, I have had reason to travel quite frequently. When one travels, one always finds a need to refill the car with fuel. I have lost count of how many times I have been approached at gas stations, by seemingly ordinary people who, "Ran out of money and gas, and have a long way still to go." They always ask, "Can you spare something … anything?"

To be honest, I rarely have money in my wallet or pocket, simply because I have become adept at debit card usage. When I have had a few coins in my pocket, I have given that away. At times, I have explained, "I have no cash."

I do not believe these people are being honest about their need for cash, or about how anyone could go on a road trip expecting their fuel costs to be cared for by begging. However, one time I was approached by someone with a different request.

While holding the pump in the car's fuel hole, I was approached by a man who immediately saw I was not giving away money, but he explained, "I don't want money. I wanted to know if you could buy me a sandwich inside the store?"

I said, "Sorry," and he apologized and walked away.

It was a little cold outside, and the wind was blowing, and I began to think, "Buy the man a sandwich." When I finished filling up, even though I had paid at the pump, I walked over to the man who was standing outside the store as if looking for someone else to pull into the station. All I did was show him my debit card and nod, and he smiled broadly and opened the door to the store.

He began happily leading me to a place where they had bottled juices and pointed to the one he wanted. I told him to get it. Then, instead of a sandwich, he chose a pack of cheese crackers. I asked if there was anything else and he said, "no." The total came to about $3.50. The Indian fellow who worked there gave me a look like I wasn't the first to fall for this man's request; but, I paid, the man thanked me and I left.

As I was getting on the Interstate, it dawned on me that the man was probably putting the juice and the crackers back on the shelf, trading them in for a quart of beer. I hoped that was not the case, as I wanted to help someone who seemed down on his luck. Inside, I felt good even if I had been "tricked."

The point of today's parable is more about how many times we totally ignore all the requests for money, simply because we know most of them are scams or tricks to get our money. Jesus himself said, "There will always be poor," and "There are too many poor for me to help them all." The point is not how many dollars we give to charity or how much spare change we hand out the window to the beggar on the street corner. It is more about not being hardened to giving of ourselves.

It is more important to be there for our children, making their lives develop in positive ways, than it is to be a slave to work, when the result of those toils are much more than one needs to support a family. It is not up to anyone to tell you how much to give and in what manner you must help others. It is up to you and your heartfelt desire.

Sometimes, seeing someone at a restaurant short the waiter on the tip, or overhearing the waitress complain about times being tight, it might be a good time to put a couple of extra dollars into your tip … then just leave without saying anything.

Amen

# TWENTIETH SUNDAY AFTER PENTECOST

## Proper 22

## YEAR C

**Relevant readings:**
Lamentations 1:1-6
Lamentations 3:19-26
 *or* Psalm 137
   Habakkuk 1:1-4 &
   Habakkuk 2:1-4
  Psalm 37:1-10
  2 Timothy 1:1-14
  Luke 17:5-10

# Free! Faith pills ... take one!

In Matthew's eighth chapter we are all familiar with the fear the disciples had when a storm came upon them while fishing on the Sea of Galilee. Jesus walked upon the turbulent waters, causing Peter to attempt to try and do the same feat. He began to sink, until Jesus saved him and all were in the boat. At that time, we read in verse 26, Jesus asking, "Why are you afraid, you men of little faith?" Then the verse goes on to say, "Then he got up and rebuked the winds and the sea, and it became perfectly calm."

In the Greek text to that verse, the word "*ogliopistos*" is translated as "of little faith." That is a combined word, with "*oglios*" meaning "of uncertain affinity; puny (in extent, degree, number, duration or value), as well as briefly, almost, a little, short, small, a while." It is then combined with "*pistis*," meaning "persuasion, i.e.: credence; moral conviction (of religious truth, or the truthfulness of God or a religious teacher), especially reliance upon Christ for salvation; by extension, the system of religious truth itself: - assurance, belief, believe, faith, fidelity." The yield of the one combine word is meaning that states, "incredulous, i.e.: lacking confidence (in Christ), or: - of little faith."

In today's reading from Luke, we find the apostles saying "*prostithemi pistis*," which means, "place additionally, add again, give more, proceed further, or increase" "assurance, belief, faith." As we read, "Increase our faith."

When you compare the Matthew passage with this one in Luke, it becomes clearer that the mustard seed analogy means, "What faith!?!?"

After you tag-alongs have been with me for a couple of years, "If you had faith the size of a mustard seed ...." Or, "oh ye of such little faith, if only you had one iota of faith, you could actually say, "Hit me again with some of that faith, brother Jesus."

When you see this, it is easier to see how Jeremiah lamented [I believe Jeremiah wrote the Lamentations] the fall of Jerusalem, the forced exile, the lost respect, much more than the lost land, all because of a lack of faith. Jeremiah gift wrapped faith for the kings of Judah – "Just take one warning from God and believe each day, and all your troubles will be washed away."

"Oh ye of little faith."

Paul wrote to Timothy [I believe Paul actually wrote the letters to Timothy] telling him to keep the faith. He said, "Do not be embarrassed by your faith. We have been emboldened by the power of the Holy Spirit, which has been granted to us by Christ Jesus. Please do not lose that faith, even if it means some pain and suffering."

Jesus told his disciples, "If you had just an itty bitty bit of faith, you could work miracles. See that huge mulberry tree over there? With just a smidgen of faith you could tell it to take a hike, and it would say, "How far would you like me to hike, sir?"

Of course, a grain of faith does not a god make. God works miracles through tiny openings of faith in us. Give God an inch, and He can take a world. God works miracles when just a sliver of faith welcomes Him in.

In the "response" to Lamentations 1, we read from Lamentations 3. In that response for Judah and Jerusalem having been lost to Babylon, we find Jeremiah reminding us that is no reason to lose faith. We can find faith through loss.

Jeremiah wrote, "My soul is bowed down within me," which means our brains reject what our souls know. Repentance is not something best thought about. It is something best felt emotionally.

From the heart we can scream out to the brain, saying, "Remember there is hope!"

"Steadfast love of the LORD never ceases; his mercies never come to an end; they are new every morning; great is the LORD's faithfulness."

Our portions of faithfulness come from the LORD ... even if it only a small amount, similar in size to a mustard seed. The main point of the Gospel reading from Luke is not how to increase faith ... no, it is why do you want faith?

Certainly, the people of Jerusalem thought they had faith in God. The thought they were safe or they would have changed. With their enemies all around them ... with Jerusalem under siege by the Babylonian forces, they must have thought they still had God on their side.

They had faith ... faith in themselves being the master of God, with God their slave.

<horn or buzzer sound> Wrong answer!

Jesus told the disciples another parable about the master and the slave, where he put them in the position of master, asking, "Who among you would welcome a hard-working slave to the table?" Then, before they could answer, Jesus said, "Would you not rather order the slave to do more work; and then, after everything was done for the master, the slave would be allowed to eat and rest too?"

That was the way the people of Jerusalem thought when Jeremiah was warning them to stop doing wrong and listen.

That was the way the people of Jerusalem thought when Jesus was speaking: So Pharisees and Sadducees could overhear his in-

After Pentecost Sermons: Proper 22, Year C

structions to some disciples, who (at least) wanted to know more.

Imagine, if you will, that **IS** the way of the people in Jerusalem today (as well as in Washington, D.C., and London, Paris, Rome, all presumably Christian nations.) when we re-tell the scripture passages about faith.

Everyone thinks he or she has faith. Raise your hand if you do not think you have faith.

Who here is afraid because of what is going on in Syria? In Kenya? Across North Africa over the past two years? In Iran? In North Korea? In Russia? In China?

Who here can order the leaders of all those land to go jump in the ocean … and it will be done?

Oh ye of little faith.

We are not immune.

We are the slaves to God. Our works of faith will have God tell us, "Come here at once and sit at the table." However, if there is more work still to be done … should God tell us, "Go to Washington D.C. and feed the minds of the leaders, so they will be warned of an end (should they not change), before you rest and get a bite to eat," … who would not also do this work?

One of faith does works of faith, as Paul did. He suffered, but he kept the faith. One of faith does works and does not expect to be glad-handed and placed on a hero's pedestal and thanked like being greeted by Sean Hannity … "You're a great American."

Being a slave to God is a thankless position, as far as the way others without faith see slaves of any kind. Only God gives recognition, but God's recognition is usually in Heaven … not here.

So, to demand, "Increase our faith!" One has to first receive the spirit. Then learn from a master ... learn from the teachings of Christ ... and Paul ... whose words come from the Holy Spirit, from God.

Once you do have faith, willingly offer yourself as a slave who seeks no thanks for the work that must be done. Enter into slavery ... to the right master.

Amen

# TWENTY-FIRST SUNDAY AFTER PENTECOST

## Proper 23

## YEAR C

**Relevant readings:**
Jeremiah 29:1, 4-7
Psalm 66:1-11
  2 Kings 5:1-3, 7-15
  Psalm 111
2 Timothy 2:8-15
Luke 17:11-19

Robert Tippett

# Can we afford to play god?

In the readings today, we find Jeremiah instructing the exiled Jews to pray for the welfare of Babylon, because their welfare depended on God's blessings upon the land where His faithful lived.

Then, we find Paul in exile, of sorts, imprisoned and bound with chains, but praying to Timothy to see the blessing that his words were free ... to be placed on paper and leave that confined space. The welfare of the churches to which Paul wrote was blessed by God, through the prayers of His faithful servant.

Then, we find Jesus healing a group of ten lepers, instructing them to go present themselves to the priests so they can be inspected and allowed back inside with the normal people. Their states of exile, as sinners with physical maladies, had been removed; but, in this process, only one leper came back to thank Jesus. That one was one of those lowest of the low Israelites, a Samaritan. Because of his faith maintained, even in exile, and because of his faith causing him to act with praise **before** he could return to be normal again, he was given welfare.

The definition of "welfare" is "Health, happiness, and good fortune; well-being." It also means, "Prosperity." Still, it means, "Financial and other aid provided, especially by the government, to people in need." Combine a few definitions and you come up with "Health aid provided to people in need."

In the news these days has been talk of a government shutdown, largely due to efforts to defund the Affordable Care Act, which is said to be not affordable. This is a topic that has touched many emotional nerve-endings, causing uproars - against those who want it defunded and against those who see insurmountable debt as a necessary evil. All the uproar is because the act is based on giving welfare to those who cannot afford welfare.

To sum that up another way – the lepers of our society, those who cannot afford to have the pains of their lesions, sores, and deformities lessened by the doctors and hospitals that demand guarantees of payment up front, they want Jesus to meet them along the road to Washington, D.C. and say, "Go and show yourselves to the government officials so that as you go, you will be given welfare."

The only problem with this is we have removed God from the mix. There is no faith in God that will make healthcare affordable.

There is only faith in a form of idol worship, where we bow our heads and pray to the government for help.

> "Help us, oh government, to find welfare."

> "Help us, oh government, to find the way to afford welfare."

> "Help us, oh government, to keep from shutting down and stopping the services we have become dependent upon."

> "Help us, oh government, to not go bankrupt from national debt and end up being like third-world nations, full of misery."

As much as our government loves the idea of playing god, and as much as people of all political-party persuasions love to have faith in one-sided government, the end result will always be just like what happened to every nation in Biblical times ... those who worshipped some Ba'al.

That result is still valid today. Nothing of truth ever happens. Only self-healing problems ever get fixed. The rich always get richer, the poor always get poorer, and the lepers are always still left on the outside of the temple, wishing they could get in.

If this were truly a Christian nation ... meaning a democracy truly existed ... where the vast **majority** ruled as Christians (said to be over seventy percent of 350-million total) ... **AND** that **majority** actually demanded their representatives run the government as Christians ... knowing Jesus Christ would have great disdain for any government that would be used as a means for a minority of governors to profit by means of corruption and greed ... then the words of Paul to Timothy could actually guide our views on healthcare.

In the letter to Timothy, Paul wrote: "If we have died of something we could not afford preventing, and if we were all that time dying with Jesus Christ, then we know we will live with Jesus Christ in our hearts, regardless of what afflictions we suffer."

We know that, "If we endure through all the suffering, then we will also run our government with God as the ultimate motivator, knowing that to save a day of life on earth is to prevent a day one could be in Heaven."

We above all realize that, "If we **deny** Jesus Christ as the one who we must honor in all our actions, personal and public, then Jesus Christ will leave us alone to make our own beds to sleep in. If we choose to pretend we have control over our own lives, which we do whenever we allow our governors to act as gods, we can only expect miracles from flawed minds."

Instead of watching the media present politicians ... live or broadcast by some means ...

Those who quarrel noisily, or angrily, and who bicker to win or obtain a point through argument (the definition of "wrangling") ...

# After Pentecost Sermons: Proper 23, Year C

Those who use words that do no good, but only ruin those who listen to them (the words of Paul) ...

Then, we should act as Christians ... by paying them no attention.

We should present ourselves to others as ones who are approved by God. We do this openly, to prove we do not feel ashamed by presenting ourselves as dedicated to God, through Jesus Christ (more words of Paul).

But, then, sadly, we are not a Christian nation.

And thus, we need to realize the meanings of the readings this week – as every week. We need to see ourselves in every aspect of the readings.

As such, we are exiles in a foreign land. The United States of America is a land of Natives and Immigrants. While we are natives, we are foreigners, just as were the Jews who were born in exile in Babylon. Because we are strangers in our own land (a nation separated from its immigrant religion), at any time, we can be the persecuted (as foreign Christians) and the persecutors (as established Christians).

For every stone we throw it always hits us – like a boomerang - regardless of how much collateral damage we inflict in that process.

Therefore, if you want welfare for yourself, then pray for the land where God has sent you as an exile, as an immigrant, as a homeland. Regardless of how long you have lived here, pray for America - the land of our captivity. No matter how many children you have raised in this place, no matter how interbred with the populace you have become - pray for America.

Pray to the LORD on behalf of the United States of America ...

Pray so that **IT** – more than a part of its people or only a few of its sects – **as a whole** can find welfare ... welfare in its truest meaning, as a grace from God through **faith**.

We need to see ourselves as the authors of the psalms. As such, we need to be joyful in God. We must sing the glory of his Name. We should sing the glory of his praise.

We must all understand the works of God and how wonderful he is in his love toward all people, regardless of their state of existence. We must see the beauty of having our faith tested and proved, tried just as is silver, understanding that God has brought us into this snare for a reason. God is who has laid heavy burdens upon our backs, such as addiction to anger and being plagued by economic demands, so we might realize when we have become godless.

Just as God sent his people into to exile in Babylon, he has sent us to here, now, with a purpose we should celebrate, whether or not we know why. We must pray for our land to be blessed by God, because those who remain true to Christ are imprisoned here.

We need to see ourselves as prisoners in chains, as slaves to lesser masters than God, in all phases of life. Because all life is interconnected, we cannot move others by will, lest others willingly move us.

We must also see ourselves as freedmen and women, quite capable of ruling over a nation that consists of, in totality, a citizenry of ONE - oneself and only oneself. Each of us is an island nation for Christ and God, each of us the President and Congress presiding over our welfare and actions. As such, we should realize we have the freedom to worship Jesus Christ and God all we want, at our pleasure and leisure, because our ability to worship is beyond a legal right.

# After Pentecost Sermons: Proper 23, Year C

Our love in our hearts and our thoughts in our minds are always beyond any legislative restrictions, because legislative restrictions only apply in external places. We must see the beauty in the ugliness that surrounds us, as God and Christ are sights for sore eyes. We must realize that no temporary respite to our earthly woes is worth the sacrifice of one iota of heavenly reward, as promised by God, as the price of faith and acts in support of that faith.

No political-speak, no double-talk, no talking points, no hidden agendas will ever best what we know is right and what is truth, says the LORD.

We need to see ourselves as those approaching Jesus on the road to Jerusalem and not only as those who follow Jesus. Therefore, we are lepers in need of help, as well as witnesses to the fearless dedication to God that Jesus displayed.

Just as we needed to see ourselves a couple of weeks ago as Lazarus, full of sores at the gate of the rich man, we also needed to play the role of the rich man, capable of recognizing Lazarus or ignoring him. We had to realize just how covered with lesions and sores we are, due to our inadequacies of faith. We must realize it is us who needs to be healed because it requires being like Jesus Christ to work miracles.

When we walk in faith we will be cleaned of our leprosy. This means that we bring on leprosy because of a lack of a faith ... a failure made by any individual unwilling to walk as Christ and God commands one to walk.

We give thanks to God when God gives us what we want ... sometimes.

But how often do we run to show ourselves off to others, forgetting to give thanks first?

How many of us give thanks when we still have leprosy and have not yet been cleaned?

Those who do give thanks first they may go on their way knowing their faith has made them well.

That is a God-given state of welfare that will never go bankrupt.

Amen

# TWENTY-SECOND SUNDAY AFTER PENTECOST

## Proper 24

## YEAR C

**Relevant readings:**
Jeremiah 31:27-34
Psalm 119:97-104
　Genesis 32:22-31
　Psalm 121
2 Timothy 3:14-4:5
Luke 18:1-8

Robert Tippett

# The separation of the Law from states overseen by unjust judges

On July 4, 1776 a group of representatives from thirteen colonies got together in Philadelphia, Pennsylvania and signed the Declaration of Independence. Religiously oppressed and economically over-taxed foreign nationals were separated from English domination. The supreme laws that guide the United States of America were written into the Constitution, created on September 17, 1787 and ratified on June 21, 1788.

As stated in Article 6 of the Constitution, in reference to the debts of the new nation and its abilities to make treaties and "Engagements," all elected officials must swear an "Oath or Affirmation," to support the Constitution. However, no religious test shall ever be required as a qualification to any office or public trust under the United States.

On December 15, 1791, the Bill of Rights went into effect. That bill presented Ten Amendments to the U.S. Constitution. The First Amendment states, "Congress shall make no law respecting an establishment of religion, or prohibiting the free exercise thereof;" … etcetera, etcetera.

Thomas Jefferson wrote of this Amendment, referring to it as "a wall of separation between church and State." This has since been regarded, through legal decisions made by the Supreme Court of the United States, as an intended distance in the relationship between organized religion and the nation state.

The background setting was the European relationships between the Nation Church [either Roman Catholic or Anglican, led by a figurehead of Divine Guidance] and the Nation Government [led by a royal figure of Divine Birth]. The people of the European nations were thus restricted in power and voice.

# After Pentecost Sermons: Proper 24, Year C

Discontent with the European concept spawned a trend of Revolution. There were bloody affairs that resulted in either divorce [the colonies' legal disunion from Britain] or death [the French Revolution's murder of royalty, usurping power]. In a sense, the United States of America was much like a divorcee to the crown of England; and France became a widow to its crown.

A "widow" is defined as, "A woman whose spouse has died and who has not remarried."

In a way, the philosophy of "separation of church and State" symbolized the death of the parent State (England) when the United States of America was created. Dead was the marriage between Christ (Church) and King (State), leaving a "Widow State" here, where the vast majority of colonists were Christians. Suddenly, those early Americans were no longer married to the Church of England.

This means we, collectively as Americans, are represented by the "widow" of today's parable reading. Keep that in mind.

Along this line of the widow who was always complaining to a judge, let me tell you about a man named Roy Moore.

Roy Moore was a judge for the State of Alabama. He was best known for his time serving as the Chief Justice for the Alabama Supreme Court.

Shortly after he was sworn in to that office, in January 2001, Roy Moore commissioned a 5,280 pound granite monument to the Ten Commandments. He had it placed in the central rotunda of the state judicial building. The monument was covered in quotes from the Declaration of Independence, the national anthem, quotes from various founding fathers, and the first Ten Commandments received by Moses, from God, as stated in the Book of Exodus.

The monument was dedicated on August 1, 2001.

On October 30, 2001, a lawsuit was filed to have the monument removed.

On November 18, 2002, a federal U.S. District Judge declared that the monument violated the "Establishment Clause" of the First Amendment to the U.S. Constitution, and was thereby unconstitutional.

On July 1, 2003, that court's decision was upheld; and on August 27, 2003 the monument was moved to a non-public side room in the judicial building.

In this path of removal, Chief Justice Roy Moore refused to comply with the orders of other courts; and, he was suspended, pending an inquiry of his ethics.

On November 13, 2003, the panel found Moore had violated the Alabama Canons of Judicial Ethics and he was immediately removed from his position.

One could say that a divorce between religion [in particular Christianity] and the government of the United States of America was final on that day of removal, although this "widow" went kicking and screaming ... and then came back to complain some more.

The reading from Jeremiah today focuses again on the exile of the Jews in Babylon. God had watched Judah and Israel "pluck up and break down, overthrow, destroy, and bring evil" upon their Nation States. They would die for their sins and "the teeth of everyone who eats sour grapes shall be set on edge."

If you remember back several weeks ago, we read about the good vine and the wild grapes. Those who eat sour grapes are those who have strayed from the good vine. Their teeth are on edge because they are angry about the way their lives are going.

No one knows right from wrong any more. The people get lost in the shuffle. It used to be right believing one way, but all of a sudden that way becomes the wrong way. It is confusion that gets nations overrun and its people scattered and captive.

"Do we honor our government over our God?" the people ask. The State says, "Yes." It has judged it to be so.

The lesson of Jeremiah is that God said He was the husband to Israel [both houses], but they divorced God by breaking His Covenant and no longer teaching it through such things as National monuments and Constitutional laws.

The good news of Jeremiah, when applied to our present, is that God will not forsake us, although we still have to pay the price of sin. God will use our self-caused misery to lead us back to Him, so that we will be more obedient believers. When hard lessons have been written on the hearts of the children of suffering, they tend to learn better.

God will forgive those who continue maintaining the Covenant, with minor alterations made – such as Him saying, "You can no longer live where I promised you could live. Now, you have to go out into the world and serve me."

The message of Psalm 119 says it all when it begins, "Oh, how I love your law!"

Love is an emotion of the heart, which means the Law is written within ... in our hearts, not out heads (where philosophy lurks). Paul wrote to Timothy telling him, "All scripture is inspired by God," and those "sacred writings are able to instruct for salvation through faith in Christ Jesus." The written word teaches, but the inner voice enlightens us to understand everything to the point of going out and acting from faith.

Paul encouraged Timothy to "be persistent whether the time is favorable or unfavorable." Through Paul's words, we are told to "convince" and "rebuke," "with the utmost patience in teaching."

Paul warned, "For the time is coming when people will not put up with sound doctrine, but having itching ears, they will accumulate for themselves teachers to suit their own desires, and will turn away from listening to the truth and wander away to myths."

Can you imagine that? It is not hard, is it?

Our government celebrates ineptitude. Sound doctrine is not written so complexly that plain folk cannot understand it. It should not be written so that individuals must pray for guidance understanding the specifics. Sound doctrine does not need lawyers to explain the meaning of the words or bog the legal system down with lawsuits of insincere origin.

Itching ears means people are tired of hearing the same ole same ole. Tell me something new and exciting. Tell me a new craze that can be incorporated into the way we do business. Don't tell us about regulations. How about some de-regulating?

Seeking those who teach to suit the needs of those paying the teachers means the education system will be tainted by the philosophies that lead one away from their religion, to acceptance … to ignorance … to complacency. This allows unjust judges to rise over the populace, setting a path to ruin for everyone.

The trend has long been to take us away from the truth … much longer that the United States has been in existence.

In fact, the United States can be seen as a result of being led away from the truth and wandering upon the notion that "All Men are created equal, endowed by their Creator with certain unalienable Rights, that among these are Life, Liberty, and the pursuit of Happiness" ... through Governments instituted by Men.

While the Declaration of Independence also says, "whenever any Form of Government becomes destructive to the Ends [of allowing Life, Liberty, and the pursuit of Happiness], it is the Right of the People to alter or abolish, and to institute a new Government."

Try that today and find out just how much a myth that is ... as it is forbidden by law.

We have wandered into areas that cause us to forget what the cornerstone of our written law is.

It is not the Ten Amendments [now 27], but the Ten Commandments.

As a reflection of this wandering, on November 6, 2012 Roy Moore was re-elected as Alabama Chief Justice.

If he was deemed unethical to hold that post before, how could he be redeemed? Did he recant his religious beliefs?

Regardless of the reasons, one has to wonder if this is an example of the widow crying out for justice. The widow is Roy Moore, who has never given up his political desires in Alabama. Was his re-election a sign of God's reward for his patience?

Or, was it a case of the system saying, "Though I have no fear of God and no respect for anyone, yet because this Roy Moore keeps bothering me, I will grant him re-election, so that he may not wear me out by continually trying to get on a ballot."?

Amen

# TWENTY-THIRD SUNDAY AFTER PENTECOST

# Proper 25

# YEAR C

**Relevant readings:**
Joel 2:23-32
Psalm 65
    Sirach 35:12-17
      *or* Jeremiah 14:7-10; 19-22
    Psalm 84:1-6
    2 Timothy 4:6-8, 16-18
    Luke 18:9-14

After Pentecost Sermons: Proper 25, Year C

# When do we believe God last spoke through a prophet?

In the Nicene Creed or the Apostles' Creed, which we recite each week, we all avow that God has spoken through the prophets.

In the breakdown of that creed, as our profession of faith, the first part states our belief in God. The second part states out belief in Christ; and, the third part states our belief in the Holy Spirit.

Thus, we state, "We believe in the Holy Spirit … who proceeds from the Father and the Son, with whom [the Holy Spirit] is worshipped and glorified."

This means we believe that the Holy Spirit has spoken through the prophets. We believe the prophets speak for the Father and the Son, through the Holy Spirit.

From the Holy Spirit having been within other human beings – Christianity began with the Apostles of Christ and spread outward – we believe in one holy catholic [in the lower-case meaning universal] and apostolic [meaning those having the same characteristics as the Apostles, having received the Holy Spirit] Church. "Church" with a capital "C" means an organized body that continuously promotes the spread of Christianity.

We are here today because we believe in One Assembly - One Gathering - One Congregation - One *Ekklesia* - One Church of people dedicated to Christ. Thus, we believe that ordinary people have been filled with the Holy Spirit over the past two millennia, in growing numbers.

There is no longer any school for prophets, designed for those who were born of a lineage of prophets. That ceased with the fall of Israel and Judah. Christian seminaries, therefore, are not schools for prophets.

In the words of Joel, we believe people who prophesy have the spirit of God poured out upon their flesh. In the words of Paul, prophets of that nature have influenced others to continue the flow of faith, by allowing themselves to pour out as a libation, the wine of God and Christ, through the Holy Spirit.

It is important to realize that our profession of faith maintains this belief.

We exist as a denominational church [the Episcopal / Anglican Church], which is only a part of the grander Church that is the whole body of faithful who are dedicated to the One God. As Episcopalians, in particular, we are part of a universal Church that believes in the One God, which also believes in the holiness of Jesus as the Christ ... the promised Messiah to the Israelites.

The commonality of our belief then links the universal Church of Christ to all denominations, such that we all seek to be Apostles, as "one Apostolic Church." As Apostles, we should be promoting individual holiness through having received the Holy Spirit into each one of our hearts. That presence means we can be guided in our actions and encourage those who are still seeking this state.

People have been reciting this statement of faith, in one version or another, since the First Council of Constantinople in 381.

In 397 AD, at the Council of Carthage, the *Book of the Revelation* was accepted as a faithful example of God speaking through a prophet named John.

In 419 AD, *The Apocalypse* [its Greek title] was added into the canon. It is a book that prophesies, presumably by the Apostle John – the Beloved – while he was in exile at Patmos.

After Pentecost Sermons: Proper 25, Year C

The *Book of the Apocalypse* is not part of the Divine Liturgy of the Eastern Orthodox Church.

It was said by Martin Luther to be "neither apostolic nor prophetic." He said that in the 16th century.

In short, despite statements of faith, we often place mind over heart. Instead, we believe we have the right to deny prophecy, before we believe God has spoken through people who some "church officials" do not recognize as "legal tender."

We believe in the axiom, shoot first, ask questions later.

We believe it is safer to kill the messenger, than it is to open the gates and welcome a Trojan horse.

We nail those who think they are Christ to the cross almost every day, in a never ending play where we raise our hands and scream out, "Please! Let me play a Pharisee, a high temple priest, or one of the Roman guards whipping Jesus!"

After all, Jesus was a prophet; and, we know full well those are best served OVER THERE, not here. We do not welcome prophets among us normal folk. Since we are where Jesus lives - his hometown within our hearts - we will have no prophets other than him here.

Is that faith or doubt?

Is that playing Master or servant?

Will God be the one to enlighten us about false prophets? Or, will scholars have that distinction?

We read so much about "false prophets" that we often find it is easy to be confused and misled. I imagine Peter was confused after Jesus was arrested. He found it best to deny Jesus and then hide behind a locked door, more than have the courage - inner fortitude - to stand by Jesus with the women and relatives.

Sometimes we are like Peter, without realizing it.

Joel is called a "minor prophet," one of twelve at the end of the Old Testament. The designation of "minor" must be realized as being relative to the length of the prophecy written and not to the validity of the prophecy. Thus, we believe Joel was a prophet through which the Holy Spirit spoke the word of God and Christ.

Joel wrote the words of the LORD, saying, "Then afterward I will pour out my spirit upon all flesh."

He then said, "your sons and daughters shall prophesy, your old men will dream dreams, and your young men shall see visions. Even on the male and female slaves, in those days, I will pour out my spirit."

That sounds like a lot of ordinary people will become prophets. The prophets God told Joel about would not be born as the children of prophets, as all the schools of prophets will have ceased being. Instead, they will be people like Amos - a self-proclaimed sheep herder and sycamore fig farmer. Several of the "minor prophets" can be seen as fitting this description prophesied by Joel.

So, we believe Joel, who Peter quoted to Jewish pilgrims entering Jerusalem for the Festival of Weeks, which begins on the Day of Pentecost - "the Fiftieth Day."

Many heard them "speaking in foreign tongues" and thought the disciples were drunk at 9:00 AM on the Day of Pentecost.

"No, no!", said Peter. "We're not drunk. We are filled with the Holy Spirit, like Joel said would happen."

# After Pentecost Sermons: Proper 25, Year C

It is so easy to not believe. It is so easy to **not** be filled with the Holy Spirit. It takes faith to listen to someone you think is speaking drunken foolishness and then be converted to belief in Christ by what is being said. That is because it comes from the Holy Spirit and is Truth.

Paul summed up what being filled with the Holy Spirit means. He said It means being able to say, before one's time on earth ends, "I have fought the good fight, I have finished the race, I have kept the faith." The reward for having received the Holy Spirit and having then poured it out to others - as a libation of fine wine - is a reserved crown of righteousness.

In the Gospel reading for today, we read of Jesus telling the parable of the Pharisee and the tax collector (or Publican). We read the conclusion stated by Jesus, "For all who exalt themselves will be humbled, and all who humble themselves will be exalted."

It all seems simple enough – live a humble life and go to heaven – but is life ever that simple?

How easy is it to be humble? We need to look at this selected Gospel reading through the lens of the Joel passage. We need to see the words with a tint from Paul's letter to Timothy.

As is the case with all of Jesus' parables, we are not innocent bystanders - lambs hearing a story about someone else. We are both of these characters, in some way or another. We are the Pharisee and we are the tax collector. We are more justified in some things and we are less justified in other things. We are humble but we also see ourselves as exalted, as Christians.

With that understood, look at our beliefs again, in respect to the statement that says, "We believe God has spoken through the prophets, via the Holy Spirit."

Neither the Pharisee, nor the tax collector was a vehicle for the Word of God. Neither was a prophet filled with the Holy Spirit.

They were both people who believed they were the children of the One God, with expectations placed upon them, in order to receive special recognition as God's Chosen Ones. One expectation was that they should go to the synagogue or Temple on the Sabbath, for the purpose of praying to God for forgiveness. In a sense, they were forced by Law to humble themselves.

We continue this tradition in our reciting of the Confession of Sins. We recognize that sin can manifest through thought, word, and/or deed, measured by acts done and those not done. We state we are truly sorry and we repent from a humbled position of guilt.

In the parable today, one prayed from a perspective of self-righteousness. The other prayed from a perspective of self-dishonor. One was blind to his own sins. One was afraid of his desire for goodness, because being good would mean losing everything he had.

Neither saw himself truthfully, thus neither welcomed in the Holy Spirit.

Paul wrote in his letter to Timothy, "the Lord stood by me and gave me strength."

When the Holy Spirit manifests itself within us, we cease to be the most important person in our lives. We sin by ignoring our thoughts telling us to do good acts, instead acting in ways we know are wrong.

When the Holy Spirit is within us – when it is welcomed by us to be within us – when we receive the spirit of Christ and allow the LORD to pour out his spirit upon **our** flesh – then we are truly righteous. From that position of strength, we are rescued from the lion's mouth and rescued from every evil attack.

To receive the spirit, we must recognize how easily sin devours us. We must recognize the shame that was felt by the tax collector – the shame of not having the Holy Spirit within us – when we profess to have that faith.

In Greek, the word that translates as "justified" is rooted in the verb that means, "to be deemed righteous," "to defend the cause of," or "to be vindicated." Therefore, the tax collector, by emotionally admitting his sins before God and asking for forgiveness, was more righteous than was the one who thought he already was righteous, and happy he was not someone obviously filled with evil, like the tax collector.

More righteous is better than not righteous,;but more righteous is not the same as righteous.

In the prophecy that so many love to avoid believing – *The Revelation* of John – that book begins with the spirit of Christ telling John, "Write a letter and send it to the seven churches."

That was an instruction to send a message, via the Holy Spirit, to the branches of the one universal and apostolic Church, of which the Episcopal Church is a part. As such, John wrote *The Revelation* to us, as members of a Christian church.

Do we believe a letter many have never fully read? Do we believe a letter most do not fully understand? Some say the seven churches were nothing more than long since vanished outposts established by the early Apostles, not relevant since the Muslims took control of Turkey.

Is any prophecy ever that literal that it cannot be metaphorically naming our churches today, using some ancient names?

Robert Tippett

In that letter, John was told to write about how each church did some good things, but each church also did evil deeds.

Each of the seven churches had sins they were in denial about. It is just as Luke prefaced today's Gospel, "Jesus told this parable to some who trusted in themselves that they were righteous and regarded others with contempt."

Do you think the Pharisee in the temple had a clue that he had some flaws he was blind to and unable to see? Do you think guilt was running through his brain as he thanked God for his wonderful life?

Have you ever heard a priest speak about the Pharisee, as a reflection of himself or herself, saying "I must admit. I am a sinner just like the Pharisee, because I believe my degree from seminary makes me closer to God than all you penny-pinchers"?

The message of the letter that the Holy Spirit dictated to John said, in a paraphrase, "God does not want to hear your prayers about how good you are. Let Him hear some emotional confessions and promises to do better."

The publican was closer to doing that than the Pharisee, even though he knew he was not about to stop collecting taxes.

God then added, "Let me see the evil deeds ceased. To do that you will need my Son's Advocate to make you strong enough to stop sinning."

Do that. Then the promise made by God is there will be a crown of righteousness waiting for you in heaven.

You can believe that.

Amen

# TWENTY-FOURTH SUNDAY AFTER PENTECOST

## All Saints Day [2 days removed] - Proper 26

## YEAR C

**Relevant readings:**
Habakkuk 1:1-4; 2:1-4
Psalm 119:137-144
Isaiah 1:10-18
Psalm 32:1-8
2 Thessalonians 1:1-4; 11-12
Luke 19:1-10

Robert Tippett

# The meaning of altar calls

I remember when I was a child going to a big tent revival meeting held at the Fairgrounds. I remember the large area the tent covered, with sawdust on the ground and many wooden folding chairs set up in rows. They all arched around the big stage. I remember watching people being called to come be healed. They lined up a ramp on the right side of the stage, one at a time walking onto the stage to be touched by the preacher. Some were walking freely, some used crutches and some were pushed in wheelchairs.

It was a week-long revival and my mother took me more than one night. I never was taken to the State Fair there, so being in the same place was memorable to me. However, the thing I remember the most about going to that big tent revival meeting was the fried apple pies the vendors sold outside the big tent.

I was probably only eight years old. All my friends and schoolmates would talk about going to the State Fair, which was held at the Fairgrounds; but, I never got to go to one of those. Still, there was a circus-like atmosphere surrounding the revival meeting, because the setting was the same as for the fair.

From the parking lot to the big tent, everyone had to walk past the neon lights of the vendor buildings that were always there ... in the open-air pavilion. I imagine that was where the ring-toss, coin flip, and cotton candy stands were calling out to the people passing by along the path leading to the circus tents and the fair rides. It had to have been just like it was going to the revival meeting.

The last stand going in and the first one coming out was where they sold the fried pies.

# After Pentecost Sermons: Proper 26, Year C

I don't think I have ever found a fried apple pie that has tasted as good as the ones my mother bought me after the big tent revival meeting at the fairgrounds. The revival lasted several nights, and each night we went I got a pie as we were walking back to the car. Mmmmmmm.

That was the early sixties. I don't remember exactly when. I do not even remember who the main speaker at the revival meeting was; but, I imagine he was advertised and promoted by the church where we were members. That was an Assemblies of God church, which is a Pentecostal branch. They believe it is important for members to speak in tongues.

A standard practice in that church was the altar call. When the preacher call for sick people to come across the stage, that was an altar call. My church was a rather large downtown church, with the building somewhat Gothic-styled. It had towers at the front. The congregation was large enough to support two services on Sunday (morning and night), and two other regular services held at night during the week (Tuesday and Friday). At the end of every service, the preacher would call anyone who wanted Christ in their lives to come down and kneel at the altar steps. The altar steps at my church were covered with plush, bright red carpeting.

The altar call at the big tent revival meeting was like the one in our church, but many more people "came on down" there. I have watched televised Billy Graham crusades and his altar calls reminds me of that revival meeting I went to and that church I was a member of.

Billy Graham was deemed "nondenominational," so he preached in front of large numbers of people, at large venues - stadiums, permanent structures much bigger than big tents. His revival meetings required lots of seating, more than a large church could supply. In large events like that there have always been altar calls that people respond to.

Robert Tippett

As Episcopalians, we have a different version of an altar call at the end of each service. In a way, we are not that different from our Pentecostal brothers and sisters. Our altar call is to pass out the sacraments of bread and wine.

In the Assemblies of God church I was raised in, they only celebrated Communion a few times a year ... as I recall. They do not drink wine, so they passed out Welch's grape juice, in thimble-sized glasses. They gave us that along with part of a broken saltine cracker, rather than the "made-to-order" industrial wafers found in "catholic-style" churches.

During those times of Communion, everyone would fill the aisles, not the altar steps. Everyone took juice and cracker from Deacons holding trays, taken up by each person as he or she passed by to gather in an aisle. There was not an altar call made for that special occasion.

I never went down to the altar when those calls were made, although (at that young age) if they had offered fresh fried apple pies to everyone who came on down, I would have been there each week.

Therein lies the purpose of an altar call. You have to desire what is being offered ... not following the crowd, as if obligated.

One might wonder how the evolution of the churches first founded by the Apostles changed and diverted, becoming as diverse and different as they are today. Has it always been about symbolic gestures? Or was it originally about the symbolism of an inner change taking control of one's life?

You know that when Jesus passed out the first unleavened matzo for each of his disciples to eat; and then when Jesus passed around one of the ceremonial cups of wine that is at every Passover Seder meal for each of the disciples to drink, nothing happened to change anyone. The change occurred the Day of Pentecost (fifty days later). From then on, the symbolic ceremony of Communion has been as a REMINDER of having Christ with you … inside your heart, controlling your brain.

In the letter Paul wrote that we read today, he named his companions as coauthors, before sending it to the Thessalonians. Paul encouraged them, as Christians. He called them his "brothers and sisters." And, he stated it was their hope that the Thessalonian Christians would continue to be steadfastly committed, to withstand the pressures attempting to influence them NOT be Christian.

There were obviously pressures put upon them by their fellow Jews, as the greater majority of early Christians were Jewish (Hebrew-speaking peoples). Paul commended the faith that the people who made up the church of Thessaloniki had shown.

Paul wrote, "We always pray for you, asking that our God will make you worthy of his call and will fulfill by his power every good resolve and work of faith, so that the name of our Lord Jesus may be glorified." The people of that "gold star" church were called by God **to serve** him at his altar … **not to be served**.

And they responded. They answered the call. Thus, their faith grew abundantly and increased the love of "everyone of (them) for one another." Just as Paul, Silvanus, and Timothy wrote a letter of support and encouragement to their brothers and sisters, each member of the church of Thessaloniki also supported and encouraged one another.

That is answering the altar call to the fullest.

The early Christians needed support and encouragement because of the persecution they faced. Paul wrote the second letter to the Thessalonians, according to many scholars, around 52-54 AD. Christ, as we know, died and resurrected around 33 AD, so we are talking about 20 years later. At that time, the Roman Empire did not feel threatened by Christians, enough to persecute them for their religious beliefs. At least, not in Greece.

The history of the Bible, in both the Old and the New Testaments, focuses on the plan God had for preparing a specially groomed, hand-picked lineage of human beings. Those would be who evolved to be the ones called to His altar, to serve Him as his priests. The Holy Bible is not a history of all mankind. It is specific to a lineage stemming from Adam to the Apostles of Christ. We are part of the continuation of that lineage, thus a reflection of that history.

This means that the story we read today, written by Habakkuk, is focused on the failure of many of those chosen people who were called by God. They were expected to respond positively and faithfully to God's call to serve Him; but, they failed to do that. Therefore, they suffered because of that failure.

The story of Paul's letter is about those chosen people, ones who not only responded to the call to renew the faith their ancestors had lost, but also ones who responded by believing Jesus was their promised Messiah, their *Christos*. They were continuing the spread of the Gospel by calling upon Jews and Gentiles to "come on down" and serve God through the Christ who has been delivered.

The story of Jesus going into Jericho is one where he called Zacchaeus to the altar.

That story is of that same historical period as Paul, but the Luke account focuses on a time when some Jews were taking sides: either following Jesus to see his next big tent meeting (like his sermon on the mount, and like on the shore of the Sea of Galilee); or, those turning against Jesus (as he preached and debated on the steps of the Temple).

# After Pentecost Sermons: Proper 26, Year C

The detractors of Jesus were plotting the persecutions that would be continuing into Paul's ministry, even as Jesus was preparing those who would be called to serve God, through him.

In the Habakkuk reading, it ends by stating, "Look at the proud! Their spirit is not right in them, but the righteous live by their faith."

In other words, the ones who take pride in their faith do not have the right spirit. That would be found in the detractors of Jesus ... the Pharisees, the Sadducees and the Temple priests.

This can be explained as them misunderstanding the word "faith." It could be like them mistaking "faith" as meaning their religious denomination. That designation today, as Jewish, is confusing.

To some, it means a race, as a specific lineage that is different from Arabs, although similar in many ways. Still, to many Jews, being Jewish means being faithful to the practices and dogmas of a religion that is different from others, although possibly similar in some regards.

The Jewish religion, as a branch of faith, was and still is a set of rituals they learned (aided by parents and enhanced by regular attendance at synagogues) because they were born into that faith. They are taught to take pride in being Jewish, as the people chosen by God personally. To many, the word "faith" means being special, as specific dedication to a certain set of rules pertaining to how one relates to God.

We are of the Episcopalian "faith," which is different from, although similar to, the Roman Catholic "faith," the Methodist "faith," the Lutheran "faith," ... and yes ... even the Pentecostal "faiths," and the Jewish "faith."

When the LORD told Habakkuk to write down on a tablet, "the

righteous live by their faith," this is stating why the chosen people ... the children of Israel ... would be punished and sent into exile, losing everything.

Being special in the eyes of God means living by a faith that God is all-powerful and He will protect you from being persecuted for living by God's law ... as long as you live by faith and not simply do as you please, claiming to be a member of a "faith."

That is answering the call ... living by faith in God.

Now in the story of Jesus today, where he saw short Zacchaeus in the sycamore tree, trying to see Jesus. As the chief tax collector, Zacchaeus was chosen as the one in whose house Jesus would spend the day. We need to see this story more as a metaphor for each one of us here today.

Jesus has come into view, for each one of us to see. There is an appeal, an attraction ... there is a big tent and hot fried apple pies, so we all want to get close. If for nothing more than for the entertainment of a spectacular event, we want to be able to say,

"Jesus is coming to town! I saw him! I was there!"

We are each Zacchaeus, as we come up short. We do not measure up to the purity that Jesus represents. We are all sinners, but we want to be pure. We know we are sinners because we have put way too much time and energy into establishing material security, warm and comfortable lifestyles ... persecution free. We know others see our sins, but we ignore them, because we see others as sinners too. In fact, if it is okay for others to not be persecuted as sinners, then it is okay for us too.

We support and encourage one another by our acceptance of sin!

Suddenly, we hear the call. "YOU! Yeah, YOU SINNER, come on down! Jesus wants to stay within YOU. Jesus wants to save

After Pentecost Sermons: Proper 26, Year C

YOU because you are a sinner."

You want to make Jesus happy and you want to stop being a sinner, so you welcome Jesus in.

When Jesus is at your emotional center ... written upon your heart, just as we read a couple of weeks ago ... we begin to pray to the LORD.

We say, "Look, half my possessions, Lord, I will give to the poor; and, if I have defrauded anyone of anything, I will pay back four times as much."

In other words, when Jesus is written into our hearts ... when we welcome him in ... when we answer the call ... we forget all about our desire to have wealth and riches save us, realizing it is much more important to have God and Christ save us. We promise to give whatever the cost ... whatever the persecution may be ... because of the ultimate reward is so much better.

The call is not about your religious affiliation. It is about your living by faith in Christ, God, and the Holy Spirit. Living by faith means depending on God's help to make one worthy of his call and to use His power for every good resolve and work of faith.

The call does not only occur in big tents, large stadiums, cathedrals, or small churches like this one. The call comes 24-7, wherever you are. The call does not offer deep-fried pies or wine and wafers. The call demands you actually welcome faith as the means to serve others ... even willful self-sentencing to hard labor, if need be.

We must answer that call and support and encourage all others who do likewise.

Amen

Robert Tippett

----------

**Amendment:** In Roman Catholic churches, non-Catholics are denied the sacraments of Communion. This is because the Roman Catholic Church requires one be baptized by a Roman Catholic priest ... not some splinter-group leader that has never been baptized as a true Roman Catholic Christian. In Episcopalian churches, the priest will mention "anyone who has been baptized is welcome" to partake of the wafer and wine given at the altar rail. The "Catholic style" churches offer Communion every time they turn the lights on at the church and have a service. Other denominations offer Communion less frequently. It is worthwhile to realize the expansions and limitations placed on parishioners is because denominations of **true Christ**ianity have taken the truth and twisted it into untruths.

The original intent was <u>**only**</u> those who were <u>**baptized by the Holy Spirit**</u>, ... <u>**reborn as Jesus Christ**</u>, ... <u>**AS CHRISTIANS**</u> ... to be considered in possession of that collective title. The word implies all who were truly saved and given eternal life, with their soul promised heaven with God - sin free forever. That Saintly character then meant that **once** a year (on two nights of Seder rituals) **Christ**ians were able to eat the Passover *matzah* and drink from the Passover Seder cup of Redemption wine (cup of wine number three) separately ... exclusively from all others. All others were still Jews (or Israelites) or heathen Gentiles. The Christians then spent the rest of their free time preaching the Gospel to Jews and Gentiles, trying to get others to personally experience the same inner changes. Thus, an "altar" is the table upon which the Passover Seder meal is placed; and, it is for <u>**family**</u> to share (the family of all being Sons of God), while lounging on pillows. There is no need to call anyone down.

# TWENTY-FIFTH SUNDAY AFTER PENTECOST

## Proper 27

## YEAR C

**Relevant readings:**
Haggai 1:15-2:9
Psalm 145:1-5, 18-22
 *or* Psalm 98
  Job 19:23-27a
  Psalm 17:1-9
2 Thessalonians 2:1-5; 13-17
Luke 20:27-38

Robert Tippett

# Not a God of the dead, but of the living: for all who live unto him

In the reading today from the *Book of Haggai*, we heard God ask the post-exilic Jews, "Who is left among you that saw this house in its former glory?" We then heard the questions, "How does it look to you now? Is it not in your sight as nothing?"

In the reading today from Paul's second letter to the Thessalonians, we heard Paul warn, "Let no one deceive you in any way," especially those who come "declaring himself to be God."

In the Gospel reading from Luke today, we hear the concept of resurrection mocked. The Sadducees, the keepers of the Temple, tried to trick Jesus with a question about a widow who had been taken as wife by each of seven brothers. They wanted Jesus to tell them who would be the widow's heavenly husband. They did not believe in resurrection, although they had themselves been risen from the ashes of the Levites, as those reborn in the Second Temple of Jerusalem.

For them to present a scenario to Jesus about sterility and a lack of heirs as an example of no resurrection, could Jesus not have asked them, "Who is left among you that saw this house in its former glory? It was said to be 'Nothing,' are you not married to those who died, leaving no heirs?"

Have you ever heard the saying, "What goes around comes around"? We are the present coming around of what has gone around before us.

Paul wrote to the Thessalonians saying, "God chose you as the first fruits for salvation through sanctification by the Spirit and through belief in the truth." As Christians, we are the continued fruit of those first fruits. For Christianity to continue onward, we have the responsibility of bearing fruits too. Otherwise, we are barren ... like the widow in the Sadducees' imaginary scenario.

Because those first Christians were called the first fruits, the people of the Second Temple would then be considered "wild grapes" or **not** those of the marriage between God and his chosen people. God's chosen people are fertile, not barren. Paul said God chose Christians, after he had sent His Son to be His bridegroom in that marriage. God is the Father with Jesus the husband and the church the wife.

The scenario painted by the Sadducees was of a church that had initially served God, until God died in that church's view. It then married a Ba'al, then another, and another, until, finally, the church died when Jerusalem was overrun and the Temple of Solomon destroyed.

The Sadducees can then be seen as asking Jesus, in essence, who would be the rightful husband of the Jews upon the death of Judaism. Would it be 'big "G" God' or one of the other 'little "g" gods'?

Jesus answered that God is only the husband of a living church. God is not the husband of a dead one - meaning a collection of human beings not filled with God's Holy Spirit.

Therefore, Paul named the first Christians as the brides of God, in a new marriage that took place after the death of the old church. Since the old church had not yielded children that could sustain it as it was, it became married to churches of other varieties, serving different gods. Those who followed Jesus as their Messiah were the first fruits of a New Arrangement made in Heaven.

Because today's issues are so often centered around our laws, which (believe it or not) are morally based – from a Judeo-Christian foundation of law – it is easy to see how one could be deceived into believing new laws are for the welfare of those of whom Jesus would approve. That would have us believe Jesus thinks it is okay for Christians (those serving God in his name) to serve the poor of all faiths and beliefs (anyone), like a prostitute would serve any client coming through her door. We would think it was okay to serve those who openly admit their sins, but not to change; as if one were capable of receiving the Holy Spirit through legal forgiveness ... to receive the blessings of the State. Our societal laws make it seem that Jesus would think it was okay to recognize marriage as an **intentionally childless** union.

Because we now see politicians as our new high priests, with our temple being the institutions of Washington D.C., we should understand that we bow down before the Sadducees, just as did the Jews of Roman Judea. We must be able to see how they were politicians, more than spiritual advisers, as the keepers of the Temple.

With the fall of Jerusalem, the exile to Babylon was complete. King Nebuchadnezzar destroyed the Temple of Solomon and with that death so too died the Levites. The Levites had been given no allotment of land by Joshua, due to the prior sins of Levi and Simeon, sons of Jacob. God was to be their inheritance, so the Levites were given the opportunity to serve God as those who maintained the Tabernacle, and then the Temple Solomon built. The Sadducees were not of Levite descent. Instead, they were who took it upon themselves to rekindle that role. As a result, they became the ones who immediately held a higher status than the rest of the common Jewish people.

Not only did they prepare the sacrifices for the feasts and festivals and perform other ritualistic services, they acted as the politicians of those days. Jerusalem, after all, was a crown jewel city held by emperors. First, there were the Persians, who had freed them from their Babylonian captivity and financed the rebuilding of the temple, making it possible for the Sadducees to come to be. Then there were the Greeks, under Alexander the Great.

# After Pentecost Sermons: Proper 27, Year C

That was followed by the Seleucid Empire, and then the Romans came into power over Palestine and Judea. So, the Jews stayed, each time marrying new husbands.

The Temple of Jerusalem was then like Vatican City is today – a city-state with political and ambassadorial links to governors and kings, as a powerless entity that commands an army of faithful, who are best kept content and peaceful.

The Sadducees were like the Senate in our government. The Pharisees were like the House of Representatives in this country. President Barack Obama [and all his brothers in that position] is like King Herod, with each state's governor like Pilate. In the times of Jesus there was a corrupt form of government, much like today in our country. The Second Temple of Jerusalem was the resurrection of its former self, resurrecting its final state as a corrupt form of government, a model of the same that led to its downfall. After Jesus died, as he predicted, the Second Temple was destroyed and the Sadducees died with it; presumably going to Sheol, since they did not believe in resurrection.

This is the meaning of today's readings: DO NOT GO TO SHEOL!

GO TO HEAVEN INSTEAD!

Haggai tells us believers, "Take courage, all you people of the land; work, for I am with you." Because the LORD's "spirit abides among (us), do not fear."

Politicians rise to power, **not** because they are truthful and capable of working miracles, but because they lie and promote fear.

Repeatedly, we hear them say, "Elect me because the other candidate will make your life a living hell!" "Elect me because the other candidate is a sinner greater than I!" "Elect me because the government is a satanic beast that will consume you, and I promise to single-handedly slay it for you!"

Haggai told the returning Jews, "In this place God will give prosperity."

But who is electing God to run the country?

No one.

Paul wrote how there would come the day when one will come who "opposes and exalts himself above every so-called god or object of worship." One will come who says he is better than religious beliefs.

Paul continued that this one would be "declaring himself to be God," but he will the "lawless one, the one destined for destruction." That is a son of Satan, the one who tries to deceive us with words and letters, who tries to alarm us with fears, who tries to shake our minds away from spiritual links.

We place our faith in the hands of liars and cheats ….

And we get what we deserve, because of that lost faith.

We are afraid to change our way of living, just as the Jews of the post-exilic period were. They were not filled with the Holy Spirit, so they could not know for sure that their leaders were leading them to another fruitless death. God sent His son, Jesus, so we would be able to protect ourselves from the same fate, because the Holy Spirit alerts us … like tweets from God on our high-tech phones.

"Don't trust him. G"

"Ignore those lies. # OneGod"

"Stay calm and impeach everyone. The Boss"

# After Pentecost Sermons: Proper 27, Year C

We all want to stick our heads deep down into some nice, warm, comfortable sand, close our eyes, cover our ears, and chant, "Na na na na na na." We do not want to hear what we need to know.

The world is going to hell in a hand basket and we just laze about and do nothing.

Paul wrote about the return of Christ, saying, "That day will not come unless the rebellion comes first and the lawless one is revealed."

Haggai prophesied how God will "shake the heavens and the earth and the sea and the dry land, and shake all the nations."

If that happens in our lifetimes, will we be married to God in name only?

What will the fruits of our marriage to God be?

Will we be dead in spirit, so that God will not be our God?

Only you can answer those questions.

Amen

# TWENTY-SIXTH SUNDAY AFTER PENTECOST

## Proper 28

## YEAR C

**Relevant readings:**
Isaiah 65:17-25
Canticle 9
  Malachi 4:1-2a
  Psalm 98
2 Thessalonians 3:6-13
Luke 21:5-19

After Pentecost Sermons: Proper 28, Year C

# A man was born, he lived and died. The end ... of the temporary.

Here we are in the middle of November. Halloween has come and gone. Now, Thanksgiving is right around the corner. Next Sunday is the last week of the Pentecost season and the first Sunday in December begins the Advent season.

During Advent, we focus on the coming birth of Christ; however, on Christ the King Sunday – next week – we will read about Jesus on the cross, alongside two criminals. The death of Jesus, his end of his physical life, recycles the liturgical focus back to the beginning of that life, as we prepare for the birth of Jesus.

It is important now to begin seeing how the religious year cycles. The evolution of Christ reflects the revolution of life. It is reflective of how our lives revolve and evolve. Literally and figuratively, we are born, we live, and we die.

Charles Schulz drew a cartoon in Peanuts that I have remembered since I first read it, a long time ago. I laughed hard then.

It was four panels depicting Charlie Brown and Linus leaning on the rock wall, their positions not changing. They are philosophizing, reflecting on their young lives. In this story, Linus informed Charlie that he read a book. He then told Charlie about the book: and it went like this: "A man was born. He lived and died. The end."

The third panel was without comment, as a pause to soak up all that had been conveyed between Linus and Charlie Brown.

Then, in the last panel, Charlie Brown still with his chin in his hands and with his elbows leaning on top of the rock wall said, "Gee. It makes you wish you knew the man."

I laughed so hard as a ten-year old. I thought, "How could he say such a thing!?!?"

As I grew much older, I began to understand the esoteric meaning of that cartoon.

Jesus is that man. The book was one of the Gospels from the Holy Bible.

We read from a book that tells about him each week - his birth, his life, his death. We need to wish we knew him, ... just from the words of a book telling of a man none of us knew personally, in the flesh.

In the reading from Isaiah 65, we see how a lineage was coming to an end. That bloodline was supposed to be dedicated to the One God forever, never dying. However, it proved to be mortal.

It was born, lived and would soon die. That would have been the end, a sad ending; but, God told Isaiah that he would create a new line, without all the faults and failures of the first. It would be eternal.

Isaiah wrote lyrics that sing about what should have happened to the children of Israel, had they not failed God. Instead of them weeping and crying about their distresses - the symptoms of a terminal disease - they should have been rejoicing. They could have been delighting in God's protective graces having been spread out before them.

Instead they professed faith, but had none.

They faced death and were buried - scattered to the winds and the four corners of the earth.

That was the end of a God-selected group of people, the hand-picked humans of Abraham, Isaac, and Jacob. They lost eternal life by gambling that their pedigree granted them favor, regardless of their actions. That mistaken belief found them giving nothing back to God, as was promised in the Covenant.

So, they lost their life.

God was going to fix that flaw by sending his Son to renew a human lineage; and, God was going to make it clear just how great the reward is for having faith in the LORD, and maintaining that faith.

You can say that was going to be a reincarnation on earth, with the plan being for a resurrection to Heaven – after the new line was born, lives, and would die faithfully, allowing for resurrection.

Eternity would mark the end of their soul's time in the physical realm.

You see, the children of Israel and Judah, meaning the people who possessed those lands, died when they lost those lands. They were more concerned with thinking those plots of soil were worth more than an unseen Heaven. Because God gave them that land to use, they thought those lands could never be taken away.

They were wrong.

The contract stated, in LARGE LETTERS, "You must work to keep the land."

The people of Israel and Judah were misled - misled by their political and religious institutions. Kings, queens, priests, and prophets slowly began to tell them it was okay to bend the rules and live like the other peoples of the world.

They said it was okay to honor some of the foreign gods. They misplaced trust, putting faith in outsiders coming into their ranks, pretending to be like them. Foreigners rose to rule over them and they then appointed corrupt priests and prophets - ones not dedicated to only one god. They served Mammon. They served Ba'al.

The children of God were misled by snakes – serpents – just like Adam and Eve were misled by the serpent in the Garden of Eden. Adam and Eve had the benefit of being the son and daughter of God, so they were immortal. They had been given eternal life; but, they lost their eternal lives through sin and fell to earth. They became mortals.

They were born through creation, they lived, and then they died. The end.

The snake who influenced that expulsion from eternal life was called crafty. It says that in Genesis 3. He was "more crafty than any of the other wild animals."

The symbolism of craftiness is letting your head lead your body, instead of your heart leading your brain. I call this a condition of "Big Brain Syndrome." A fat head is too heavy for Heaven. So, if it falls to earth, then it cannot rise to Heaven. Its food shall be dust, because crafty people long for material objects, rather than spiritual rewards.

In the Gospel reading in Luke today, we find how a conversation between Jesus and his disciples has turned to the beauty and adornments of the Second Temple. Those things, those objects, those physical niceties were grabbing their attention and making them marvel over the earthly realm.

Jesus acted as the prophet he was, when he heard their adoration. He told the disciples (who had small brains) some of what the future holds.

After Pentecost Sermons: Proper 28, Year C

He told them that the temple would fall to the earth. It would suffer death and cease to be.

That was the Second Temple. The Temple of Solomon had been destroyed by the Babylonians of Nebuchadnezzar. It had been risen from dust, lived for centuries, then returned to the dust.

The disciples had been marveling at the second coming of the temple - the reincarnation of a great achievement by man. Jesus told his disciples that the building only appeared to have life, in the here and now; but, the here and now was an illusion that would not last forever. The Second Temple too would fall from its heavenly state.

Think about that for a moment.

The Temple was more brain than heart. It had been contrived by the minds of men.

Men who thought, "Let us go back to square one and pretend the failures of our ancestors never happened. We will recreate the state of Israel-Judah, as it was in Jerusalem, the way it was when the last breath of the Israelites left them."

Thus, the Second Temple was not honoring God - it honored those who had been given a chance to renew a path that led to death. The minds running the Temple were rejecting Jesus and his message. They would later turn on the Apostles.

Jesus forewarned his disciples, "Beware that you are not led astray."

The same warning could have been told to Adam and Eve. The same warning applies to us today ... and to our children tomorrow.

Jesus warned the disciples that there would come many people

– not just in their lifetimes, but in our lifetimes too – who would try to act as did the serpent and say, "I speak for Jesus! The end is coming, so you need to do as I say. Come, follow me!"

"Do not go after them," Jesus said.

The reason is the same reason Eve could have used to reject the serpent in the Garden of Eden: With God within your heart, God will tell you everything you need to know, so you have no reason to think someone else has God telling them, "Go! Tell the world to follow you!"

Why would one who is connected to God, directly (as was Eve) or indirectly (through Christ), need to follow someone else? With God in your heart, God will lead you.

I heard a term the other day ... not a nice term ... which is "sheeples."

It means people with herd mentality, who are ready, willing, and wanting to follow someone ... anyone ... who is bold enough to say, "Follow me!"

Being a "sheeple" does not mean you are brainless. It means finding good reason to follow, because following makes one less responsible for one's actions. If all goes wrong ... point the finger and say, "He, she, it said to do it."

Jesus said, "I will give you words and a wisdom."

This means he will tell you what to do from within your heart, not by sending some stranger to lie to you. Jesus will tell you what to say and he will tell you how to act upon those words. This is the Holy Spirit, which Christ advocates for you to receive, so you do not need to follow the lead of strangers.

If you need a good shepherd to prepare you to use your own

After Pentecost Sermons: Proper 28, Year C

Holy Spirit-driven abilities, Jesus will give you the wisdom to listen. But, you do not follow a good shepherd either.

That is because you alone control your destiny. No one but you can get you beyond this plane of existence, to eternal life.

Thus ... having the Holy Spirit within you means hard work. It is a 24/7 commitment – and I do not mean 24 days a month, seven months a year. I mean twenty-four hours a day, seven days a week. Full time ... with the best benefits possible, although those come with a very high deductible ... constant work.

Hard work scares a lot of people off.

It certainly scared off the children of Abraham, Isaac, and Jacob. They ended a sacred line. They became a dead branch, a stump.

Still ... a shoot grew from the root of Jesse, which led to that dead stump. A new line was started by Christ, which had the bloodline that went back to Adam and Eve. Jesus used the same genetics of the remnants of Israel - the DNA of a dead body ... beginning Christianity with Jews who possessed the same flawed potential of past failures. Thus, that lineage has been inherited by Christians.

The same tendency to look for the easy way, to look for excuses, to let others do our work, and to shun the deeds of faith is born in us. Paul wrote to the Thessolonians and told them to beware the lazy Christians. He said to look out for the ones living in idleness, who were unwilling to do the work of a true Christian.

Paul told them; and, as a living branch from that new tree, Paul waves before you today in full blossom, telling you too: "Do not be weary in doing what is right."

Jesus told the disciples that the Second Temple would die. He told them that around 32-33 AD. It died in 70 AD, or thirty-seven to thirty-eight years later. Today, it is still dead, although there has long been talk about reincarnating it.

If only the Muslims had not built the Dome of the Rock in its place. If only Christians had not built their own holy monument-temples ... many times over, since then.

How many people here today expect to be still living in thirty-seven or thirty-eight years? That would be the year 2040 or 2041.

In my case, if all goes well, I will be ninety-six or ninety-seven years old in thirty-seven to thirty-eight years.

The point of that question is, in the grand scheme of things, on the timeline of the history of the earthly realm, thirty-seven to thirty-eight years is no more than a drop in the ole time bucket. That means, for a mortal, the end IS ALWAYS NEAR.

The end means the end of our life in this world; and, when the world comes to an end for us individually, everything in our world ceases to matter.

Who can you follow that will take you to Heaven, so you can live forever with God?

The answer is you ... and only you.

You need to be led by your heart well before the time you pass on.

You want your personal biography to read: You were born. You lived and died in the physical realm. The end of misery was granted by God.

No one left on earth will know of your resurrection. Once entered into an eternal life, nothing else needs to be rewritten. You were reborn ... endlessly.

Now, all you have to do is watch out for snakes in the grass.

Amen

# LAST SUNDAY AFTER PENTECOST

# Christ the King Sunday

# YEAR C

**Relevant readings:**
Jeremiah 23:1-6
Canticle 16
  [Jeremiah 23:1-6]
  Psalm 46
Colossians 1:11-20
Luke 23:33-43

After Pentecost Sermons: Christ the King, Proper 29, Year C

# The place of The Skull and the mind of Christ ... one is death, while the other is rebirth

I mentioned last week that today, Christ the King Sunday, marks the end of a cycle. It not only ends the Ordinary season after Pentecost, but next Sunday marks the beginning of the Christmas season, Advent.

Advent is rooted in an Old French infinitive verb, "*advenir*," meaning, "to happen, to occur, to come." It speaks of anticipation of something promised, as a beginning, not an end.

Thus, today we have reached a symbolic death in the cyclic story of Christ, as told by the Lectionary schedule and the Church's seasonal focus. A figurative death is once again upon us. The record has reached its end; and, although we flip it over and play the next side, the song remains the same. The same song, next verse, as sung by other books and writers of Scripture than those we have read over the past year.

Today we read of Christ on the cross, before his death; and thus also before his resurrection and his ascension. For all of that cycle "to happen, to occur, to come to be," Jesus must first be born.

Thus, from death comes life. From a life ended comes resurrection; and then, from birth comes death. It is the continuing cycle of life on earth. It is the continued repeating of mortality.

As I said last week, we are born, we live and we die. However, the end is how it seems from a linear life's perspective. While it is true a song plays from beginning to end, and a book is read from introduction to conclusion, because the song can be played again and the book can be read again, there is not a straight line being drawn. There is, instead, a spiral.

We continue onward, cycled into a new level of existence, with a new birth and a new life. This is literally seen in biographies, where the dead come back to life. It is figuratively seen in a belief of heaven … or hell; but, more so in the philosophy of reincarnation. Same soul, next body.

In the scene set today at Golgotha, the place named The Skull, it becomes one of decision time for us. It is a reflection on what is about to be born next, what will happen next, what will occur next, what will come next to those who die.

It represents Advent Eve in that way.

Today's Gospel reading may seem quite clear. We see Jesus making the promise, "Today you will be with me in Paradise."

We hear those words and fondly think, "Jesus is speaking to me. I am going to Heaven."

But, it is not as clear as you may think.

All of us have a tendency to see us as Jesus' companion, whenever any of the stories of Jesus' life comes into our minds. As Christians, this is a natural way to think, but it can be a flawed way to see the value of Scripture.

We identify with the criminal hanging on the cross, presumably to Jesus' right-hand side (to our mind's eye left). He believes Jesus will go to his Father's kingdom, in another realm; and, he asks Jesus to remember him when he gets there. Jesus told him that he would join him there that day.

We see ourselves as disciples of Christ, as Christians, so invariably we believe Jesus will see us in Heaven too.

# After Pentecost Sermons: Christ the King, Proper 29, Year C

What we fail to realize is it has been fourteen hundred years of tweaking that has led us to believe getting to Heaven is that simple. We have been trained by our leaders to believe this. I may have given that impression in some things I have said before. Certainly, those before me have helped you believe you are saved because Jesus died on the cross for your sins.

From the Gospel reading today, we do not think any of the Roman soldiers, the criminal to Jesus' left-hand side, or any of the leaders who all mocked Jesus – telling him to save himself, if he was the King of the Jews – were going to see Jesus in Heaven.

At least, they would not be going there in that state of mind. So, while Jesus asked God to forgive them for not knowing they were sinning, that forgiveness was only going to give them a second chance. They would be allowed to find the right path later.

Jesus did not forgive the sins of the criminal about to die to his left side, as if that forgiveness would send everyone happily to Heaven when their time to die came. Otherwise, Jesus would have told the criminal to his left, "Yeah, you'll see me in Heaven too, in a short while; but, brother you'll have some thanking to do then."

Jesus didn't say that.

In the Lectionary schedule of readings, this is year C. Typically, there is an alternate Old Testament reading to pick from as our reading selection, although we usually go with the first option. Today, the reading from the *Book of Jeremiah* has no other option.

Our elders, the ones who prayed and discussed how the Lectionary should be laid out, they saw Jeremiah 23:1-6 as necessary to be read along with the Luke reading of Jesus on the cross at Golgotha. We need to understand why that is.

Robert Tippett

In the Jeremiah passage, we read God telling us, "I will raise up shepherds over [His people] who will shepherd them, and they will not fear any longer, or be dismayed, nor shall any be missing."

We have to see the plural number in "shepherds" in order to understand that Jesus would not be the only shepherd raised by God to attend to His flocks. This means I am a shepherd, and you are a flock of God's people. However, Jesus becomes the model for the good shepherd, for all shepherds who will attend to God's people.

When God told Jeremiah to write, "Woe to the shepherds who destroy and scatter the sheep of my pasture," we think that was only a reference to the ancient kingdoms of Israel, which had fallen. While they were part of this failure, the failure will always be possible should bad shepherds again lead the flocks improperly.

After Jeremiah wrote his books, Jesus came. This is interpreted to mean that, once again, bad shepherds were improperly leading the flocks of God, scattering them away from their true purpose as God's chosen people. As a result, God was not properly served. Same song, another verse.

To think that the creation of Christianity would always mean good shepherds attending properly to God's people is wishful thinking and fanciful imagination. From our perspective, looking back at the history of Christianity, we can see how many have been misled and scattered. The decline of Christianity, as a religion, is well upon us now ... and growing yearly ... monthly ... weekly.

This means the shepherds ... in the plural number ... are the churches of Christianity. From the churches come priests, pastors, preachers, and ministers, who are the shepherds of their respective churches, more than they (we, I) are shepherds to you

# After Pentecost Sermons: Christ the King, Proper 29, Year C

sheep. As much as you think you are my flock, you are the flock of the Episcopalian Church and I am only a replaceable part of that machinery.

If you let it be that way.

Jesus told his disciples that the future would bring, "Many who will say, 'I am Christ,' and that the end is near." Jesus warned the disciples, "Do not follow them."

Now, if we see Jesus warning his disciples about people who would actually have people follow them, rather than telling them about terrible people trying to get good people to follow them, when good people would spot a terrible person a mile away and stay clear of them, never to follow them, then we have to see the warning being, "Do not follow wolves in shepherd's clothing."

Bad shepherds pretend to be good shepherds. They come in all sizes, shapes, and colors. So, you have to hear Jesus warn, "Do not follow a Church that says it is Christian, when it does not attend to the people of God properly."

When Jesus said that a church was formed whenever two or more people gathered in his name, this can be seen as happening in one of three ways.

First, when two or more gather in the name of Christ, one is filled with the Holy Spirit and the others are wanting to be filled. So, following the good shepherd means to learn how to also be a good shepherd. This is the circumstances under which we meet today, in a building called a church, such that I represent the good shepherd and you represent the flock. All of us are here in the name of Christ … as Christians. I want all of you to be able to recite this sermon to those you come in contact with, in the future.

Second, when two or more gather in the name of Christ, they are (both or all) already filled with the Holy Spirit. This is represented in the letters sent by Paul and the other Apostles (those filled with the Holy Spirit) and to the churches they had founded. You have to see how those "churches" were not buildings or cities; but instead, they were other living members of our Lord Jesus Christ … Christians … who had also been filled with the Holy Spirit and were themselves filling their flocks. The gathering was to encourage and support, to ask questions and share the knowledge of the Holy Spirit, so that could be passed on as would good shepherds.

Finally, when two or more gather in the name of Christ, they have died and risen to Heaven. The Holy Spirit having been within them, through Christ as the advocate, so it has protected them from sin for their remaining days on earth AND in those remaining days they will have shepherded flocks of God's people properly. Those souls will have left behind churches of Christians who are continuing to attend to God's people, so the lineage thrives and grows, producing good fruits.

Jesus never indicated a church was a beautiful building, made of finely cut stones and adorned with the beauty purchased by the tithes of God's people. Jesus said a church like that would be thrown down, with no stone left in place. It would decay and collapse, just as had the Temple priests of the Israelites failed its people and led them to ruin.

When Jesus warned that "many will come after me saying, "I am he! Follow me!" He was telling of the corruptions that take hold of buildings and the people who own those buildings, because it is costly to own and run buildings. It is also costly to pay men (and now women) to stand above the people of God and tell them, "We come in the name of Christ to tell you to follow our creeds, dogmas, rules, procedures, and rituals. By doing so, you will be upheld as good Christians."

Jesus warned, "Do not follow them!" Unless these people bring the Holy Spirit to you, in your midst while filled with the Holy Spirit, so that "the kingdom of God has come near," for the sole purpose to have you open up your heart to receive the Holy Spirit within you, then you have been in the middle of snakes of wisdom. A church is a gathering for the purpose of passing on the Holy Spirit, which comes with infinite wisdom for each and every Christian to possess.

The model left by Jesus, for all good shepherds to become, was to teach the faithful why they should have faith. Jesus taught his disciples this; and, for as much as they wanted to be like Jesus and for as much as they said they believed all Jesus taught, the day Jesus died on that cross they all hid in fear and trembled.

They were not filled with the Holy Spirit simply by going to hear Jesus' sermons every Sabbath. They were not filled with the Holy Spirit simply by following Jesus, the model of a good shepherd.

Jeremiah wrote how the LORD told him, in the future there will come the times when good shepherds will make God's people so "they shall not fear any longer, or be dismayed, nor shall any be missing."

The Psalm of Zechariah sings, "The dawn from on high shall break upon us, to shine on those who dwell in darkness and the shadow of death."

Paul wrote to the Colossians, "He has rescued us from the power of darkness and transformed us into the kingdom of his beloved Son, in whom we have redemption, the forgiveness of sins."

Luke recalled Jesus saying to the sinner who admitted his acts deserved punishment, begging Christ to remember him after he enters his kingdom upon death, "Today you will be with me in Paradise."

The disciples were not filled with the Holy Spirit until after the resurrected Christ had taken the knowledge of those who followed him to a higher level. A follower cannot ascend to that higher level. Only one who has the courage to admit, "Without the Holy Spirit within me, I can only lead myself to sin; and, all others I follow only help lead me there."

A leader receives the Holy Spirit by wilfully stepping aside from him or herself and asking Jesus to remember that acceptance of punishment. By asking Jesus to resurrect oneself, to ascend within one's heart and take control over one's mind, so one can lead others to the same dawning, then one can ascend to the level of good shepherd. One's heart must be sincere and love God.

On this Christ the King Sunday, as we prepare for the coming of Christ in the physical realm once again, take this time to reflect on why you are here today.

Are you following someone who says, "I am Christ resurrected!" because they told you, "All you have to do is say you are Christian!" Can you see how that is what Jesus warned against? Can you step before others and explain Scripture, from possessing the mind of Christ, so others will be likewise inspired?

Or, will the baby Jesus be reborn within you later, to grow and develop within your body ... to become your head, to make you the Church of Jesus and to make you the shepherd God wants you to be, leading others to the same higher state?

God is the God of the living. Let Christ make you come alive and remove the fear that holds you back.

Amen

# After Pentecost Sermons: Christ the King, Proper 29, Year C

Robert Tippett

# After Pentecost Sermons: Christ the King, Proper 29, Year C

www.ingramcontent.com/pod-product-compliance
Lightning Source LLC
Chambersburg PA
CBHW071947110526
44592CB00012B/1022